ISBN: 9781313053518

Published by:
HardPress Publishing
8345 NW 66TH ST #2561
MIAMI FL 33166-2626

Email: info@hardpress.net
Web: http://www.hardpress.net

A HISTORY OF
THE ROYAL DUBLIN SOCIETY

THE OLD GATEWAY, LEINSTER HOUSE,
AS IT APPEARED IN 1885
(*From a photograph by Mr. A. McGeagan*)

A HISTORY OF
THE ROYAL DUBLIN
SOCIETY

BY

HENRY F. BERRY, I.S.O., LITT.D

BARRISTER-AT-LAW

" Hoc anno (1731) ad ornandam agriculturam Societas coaluit Dublini, quae hebdomatim suas adnotationes edidit, et prima est societatum quae ad agricolendi artem colendam coaluerunt."—ALBRECHT VON HALLER.

WITH ILLUSTRATIONS

LONGMANS, GREEN AND CO.
39 PATERNOSTER ROW, LONDON
FOURTH AVENUE & 30TH STREET, NEW YORK
BOMBAY, CALCUTTA, AND MADRAS
1915

Arthur Edward Baron Ardilaun

Born at St. Anne's, Clontarf, 1 November 1840
Died at St. Anne's, Clontarf, 20 January 1915

LORD ARDILAUN, at whose instance this book was written, did not live to see its completion, as he passed away a few days before its issue from the press. The considerations which led him to design the publication of a history of the Dublin Society are mentioned in the preface, and during the last year of his life, notwithstanding much weakness, the work was constantly in his thoughts, and its progress was watched by him with solicitude. His portrait will be found opposite p. 287, where it was placed at his desire instead of being made the frontispiece as the author had intended.

PREFACE

To the patriotism and munificence of Lord Ardilaun the publication of this History of the Royal Dublin Society is due. During his long connection with the Society he had gained an intimate knowledge of the leading part that for many generations it had taken in the development of the resources of Ireland; and he believed that it would be of service to his country that an account of the Society's operations and of the men who had directed them, should be compiled.

I have to thank Lord Ardilaun for much help and many valuable suggestions during the preparation of the work, and I regret that it did not appear before his resignation of the office of President, which he held for the lengthened period of sixteen years. The season of its publication, however, is not altogether inappropriate, as it synchronises with the centenary of the Society's possession and occupation of Leinster House.[1]

In publishing this History, Lord Ardilaun has carried out a suggestion made considerably more than a century ago by Arthur Young. Writing in 1780, that eminent agriculturist expressed the opinion that Ireland deserved great credit for having given birth to a society which had been the precursor of all similar

[1] On the 14th of December, 1814, the purchase of that mansion was completed, and on the 1st of June, 1815, the first meeting of the Society within its walls was held.

v

societies then existing in Europe[1] He added that a history of its transactions would be a work extremely useful to Ireland, as in every part of that country he had found traces of the Society's influence, exercised by means of instruction. The origin of the Society was attributed by Young to a single individual, Dr. Samuel Madden, whom he pronounced to be one of the most patriotic men that any country had produced.

The present members of the Society, as well as the general public, may have certain ideas as to the utility and importance of its work in the past, without any definite conception of the varied and comprehensive character of the very thorough methods adopted in the course of their labours by the long line of distinguished men who joined in carrying out the Society's objects. It is well that now, at the close of nearly two centuries, through the public spirit of Lord Ardilaun, the details can be systematised, and some account in historical shape be given of its endeavours, so that the innumerable obligations under which our country stands to generations of Irishmen who have worked for the common good under its auspices may be recognised.

The multitude of interests which from time to time occupied the attention of the Society is striking, and while many great undertakings were carried out, nothing appeared too small or insignificant for the

---

[1] Young meant that it was the precursor of all existing agricultural societies—not the very first of its class. The Scottish Society of Improvers in the Knowledge of Agriculture, which had similar objects in view, was founded in June 1723, lasting to 1745.

members to interest themselves in, provided it tended to any practical result for the benefit of the community. From agricultural machinery and the great fishing industry; from science and the fine arts down to rag-picking and rat-catching, nothing seemed to come amiss. All who came forward with plans or inventions, of even the humblest character, had a patient hearing, and if possible, a helping hand extended. How many a promising art student was stimulated to further effort, and afforded the means of completing his education! What numbers of impoverished country tenants were enabled to live more comfortably, and enjoy improved conditions through the Society's enlightened efforts! In Dublin alone, not to speak of country districts, thousands of artisans and skilled workmen have been indebted to its schools and teachers for their means of livelihood. It were needless to point out the improvement in the breed of cattle and horses effected by the Society's operations, or to recount the measures taken to promote the fisheries round our coasts.

In the long period during which the Dublin Society has laboured, many important changes in social and economic conditions have taken place, and a perusal of this volume will make it plain that for years it performed many functions which at length the Government of the country was compelled to discharge. The Art Schools, the Museum, Botanic Garden, and the Veterinary Department, which represent branches of work to which the Society's energies were devoted in the past, are all now placed under State control. The

Society itself, released from their direction, has found, and continues to find, fresh interests, on which its beneficent labours may be expended, under the guidance of men who, like their predecessors, at much self-sacrifice, unite in a common effort for the benefit of their fellow countrymen.

Mr. R. J. Moss, Registrar of the Society, and his very courteous staff have been most helpful during the progress of the work. It is plain that no one so effectively as Mr. Moss could have written the history of the Society during the last thirty-five years, and dealt with the scientific aspect of its work, on which, as well from his own high attainments as from the traditions he has inherited, he speaks with exceptional authority. Mr. Moss most kindly contributes Chapters XVIII and XIX, which form a valuable addition to the work. To Dr. F. Elrington Ball my obligations are very great, as he not only read the proofs, but placed his experience and extensive knowledge of Ireland in the eighteenth century at my disposal. To Mr. Walter G. Strickland, of the National Gallery, my best thanks are due for help in the chapter on the Drawing Schools, in which his *Dictionary of Irish Artists* is frequently cited. Sir Frederick W. Moore, Director of the Botanic Garden, took a kind interest in the chapter on his Department, and afforded much valuable information. Mr. T. W. Lyster obligingly read the portion of the work devoted to the Library, and his competent staff, true to their traditions, were ever ready to meet any demands on their technical knowledge. The Council of the Royal

Irish Academy was good enough to permit the portrait
of Dr. Richard Kirwan to be photographed for the
work, and thanks are due to the Very Rev. the Dean
of Christ Church for allowing the Prior monument
in the south-west porch of the Cathedral to be photographed. Thanks are also due to Count Plunkett,
Director of the National Museum, for lending the
block which illustrates the Statue Gallery, School of
Art. Mr. A. Redding, of the National Museum,
was entrusted with the task of photographing the
various portraits and views reproduced in the volume,
which he has admirably fulfilled; and Mr. A.
McGoogan's successful restoration of a view of the
old gateway of Leinster House must not pass un-
noticed. (*Frontispiece.*)

The original Minute Books of the Society now
remaining of record, which have been used in the
compilation of this volume, are as follows :—

        25 June 1731 — 1 Nov. 1733
        15 Nov. 1733 — 12 Nov. 1741
        19 Nov. 1741 — 10 July 1746
         3 May 1750 — 24 Nov. 1757
        20 Feb. 1752 — 24 Apr. 1755 (rough)
         9 Mar. 1758 — 13 Aug. 1761
         6 Mar. 1766 — 26 Nov. 1767
         3 Dec. 1767 — 6 July 1769
        13 July 1769 — 24 Jan. 1771
        31 Jan. 1771 — 9 Apr. 1772
        16 Apr. 1772 — 14 Oct. 1773
        21 Oct. 1773 — 29 June 1775

THE ROYAL DUBLIN SOCIETY

They do not appear to have been preserved after this date. From the 15th of March, 1764, the minutes were printed.

The *Dictionary of National Biography* has been largely used in the numerous biographical notices throughout the volume, and the splendid collection of pamphlets formed by the late Mr. Charles Haliday, now in the Royal Irish Academy, afforded valuable information on many questions in which the Dublin Society was from time to time interested.

Albrecht von Haller (1707–1777), whose allusion to the Society and its work appears in the quotation in the title-page, was a Swiss anatomist and physiologist, who obtained a European reputation. King George II conferred on him the chair of medicine in the University of Göttingen, and in 1743 the Royal Society elected him one of its Fellows.

H. F. BERRY.

Dublin,
15th December, 1914.

CONTENTS

LIST OF ILLUSTRATIONS

LIST OF ILLUSTRATIONS

A History of
The Royal Dublin Society

CHAPTER I

ORIGIN OF THE SOCIETY

ALTHOUGH the Royal Society of London was not founded until the year 1660, it is a well ascertained fact that long prior to that date a number of scientific men were wont to meet together in London for the discussion of subjects interesting to them. The Oxford Philosophical Society, which commenced its career in 1651—a continuation or offset of one that occasionally met in Gresham College, London, and numbered among its members Sir William Petty—largely influenced the beginning, and helped to mould the early form, of the Royal Society. The troubled state of the country prevented regular meetings of the philosophers at Gresham College; but they still held to their purpose, and Evelyn's design and plan for a Scientific College, propounded in 1659 in a letter to the Hon. Robert Boyle, is believed to have also had no small part in furthering the foundation of the Royal Society, when, on the Restoration, the affairs of the kingdom were once more placed on surer ground. Sir William Petty, in addition, formulated a scheme for a Scientific Academy, and,

A

as a result of these and other influences, the Royal Society sprang into being in November 1660.

In the same way, the Dublin Society was heralded by one or two associations formed in Dublin by learned men interested in scientific pursuits and experiments. Though at no time distinctly scientific, being founded for practical purposes, which only took in science so far as it applied to them, the Dublin Society was moulded and fostered by men influenced by those of a prior generation, who had formed clubs for philosophic pursuits. In 1684, the Dublin Philosophical Society was founded by William Molyneux, agreeably (as he says) to the design of the Royal Society of London. Professor S. P. Johnston,[1] says that "it might in justice be called the embryonic form of one of the most prominent of Irish institutions—the Royal Dublin Society." William Molyneux was son of Samuel Molyneux, by Margaret Dowdall, his wife, and brother of Sir Thomas Molyneux, bart. He was born in 1656, and died in 1698. William Molyneux was appointed in 1684 Surveyor of Works in Ireland, and in the next year he was sent by Government to survey important fortresses in the Low Countries. He was elected M.P. for the University of Dublin in 1692, and was distinguished as a philosopher and astronomer. His most celebrated work, the *Case of Ireland being bound by Acts of Parliament in England stated*, was published in 1698. Sir William Petty[2] was the first president of the Philosophical Society—Molyneux himself being constituted secretary. The society at first

[1] Note contributed to a lecture on Marsh's Library in Dr. G. T. Stokes' *Worthies of the Irish Church*.

[2] Famous for his survey of estates forfeited after the rebellion of 1641, known as the Down Survey. Thomas, first Earl of Kerry, married Petty's daughter, Anne, and they were ancestors of the Lansdowne family.

consisted of about twenty members, and meetings for
the discussion of mathematics, physics, literature,
history, and medical science were held in a coffee-house
on Cork Hill. Dr. St. George Ashe, afterwards
provost of Trinity College, Dublin and Bishop of
Derry, one of Swift's circle, contributed; and Dr.
Robert Huntingdon, then Provost,[1] invited the infant
Society to meet at his abode. Copies of the minutes[2]
and communications were transmitted to the Royal
Society; they were read at the meetings, and are still
to be found among its records. Meetings were subsequently held at the Crow's Nest,[3] Crow street, where were
established a museum, laboratory, and botanic garden.

In Sir John Gilbert's *History of Dublin* (vol. ii., p.
173) will be found a very full account of this society,
and in appendix ii. of the same volume is a list of the
papers read before it—"Transactions of the Dublin
Philosophical Society to 1686"—classified by the late Sir
William Wilde, with names of the contributors. Among
them, Dr. Narcissus Marsh, who held successively three
archbishoprics, wrote an essay on the doctrine of sounds;
Molyneux a paper on the theory and practice of viewing
pictures in miniature with a telescope; Dr. St. George
Ashe discoursed on the evidence of mathematical demonstration; Dr. Huntingdon wrote on obelisks and
pillars of Egypt, and other members reported as to
experiments on dogs, blood, &c. On the outbreak of
hostilities between King James and William of Orange,
the society appears to have broken up.

[1] Later Bishop of Raphoe. He was a great Orientalist, and,
during a ten years' residence in Palestine, acquired a large number
of Oriental documents, which are now in Oxford and Cambridge.
(See *Life*, &c., by Thomas Smith.)
[2] The original Minute Book is now in the British Museum. (Add.
MSS. 4811.)
[3] Recently occupied by the Cecilia Street Medical School of
the Catholic University.

In 1693 a reorganisation of it was brought about in Trinity College, which was in active operation up to 1698. "This evening (26 April) at 6, met at the Provost's lodgings, T.C.D., in order to a renewal of our Philosophical meeting, when Sir R. Cox read a geographical account of Derry," &c. (Marsh's MS. Diary).[1]

A third society was in existence about 1706, of which Samuel Molyneux, son of William Molyneux, was secretary, and it is frequently mentioned in the *Familiar Letters* of Locke and Molyneux. Of this society Berkeley was a member. Sir Thomas Molyneux, brother of the originator of the first society, was the only person who appears to have directly connected the Dublin Society with the earlier associations.

When, after the Revolution, the country had settled down to resume its former peace and quiet, the condition of agriculture was low in the extreme. The most primitive implements were in use, and the crudest possible ideas on husbandry prevailed. Tenure of holdings was most precarious, and this, combined with the poverty and ignorance of the farming classes, prevented any real progress. Landlords began to find that pasturage was their easiest mode of making money, and they showed a marked preference for a few substantial tenants over a number of smaller ones, who could only engage in light tillage. Seeing there was no employment for labourers, whole neighbourhoods were turned adrift, and begging became a settled occupation of numbers of the people. These are Mr. Lecky's views as to the state of agricultural Ireland at the time, and in his *Essay on Trade*, Arthur Dobbs was forced to suggest the erection of workhouses as a remedy

---

[1] Now in the library which he founded in Dublin.

for the widespread want and destitution prevalent at this juncture.   Robert, first Viscount Molesworth, who was a close personal friend of William Molyneux, and to whom Swift dedicated the fifth of the *Drapier's Letters*, was author of a very remarkable pamphlet— *Some Considerations for Promoting Agriculture and Employing the Poor* (1723)—which Mr. Lecky observes[1] " exposed with a skilful and unsparing hand the gross defects of Irish agricultural economy, and at the same time proposed a series of remedies, which, if they had been carried out, might have made Ireland a happy and prosperous country."   Among the Haliday collection of pamphlets in the Royal Irish Academy's Library are a number of essays and papers dealing with Irish trade, manufactures, and husbandry in the first half of the eighteenth century, which will well repay perusal by those making such subjects a special study.   They show that in the south of Ireland farms were being largely consolidated and lesser tenants were being turned out, while the north groaned under the burden of excessive rents, and everywhere discontent became rife.

At the time of the accession of King George the Second to the throne, there was much cultivated society in Dublin, and throughout Ireland there were many thoughtful men, anxious to improve the condition of their country, and to raise the status of the agricultural population, on which its prosperity so largely depended.   As a result of these conditions, a small band of patriotic reformers, actuated by the purest and noblest motives, felt that a time had arrived at which they might unite in an effort to promote and improve the system of husbandry, the manufactures,

---

[1] *Ireland in the Eighteenth Century*, i. 302.

and useful arts of the country.   To them was due the
foundation of the Dublin Society.

Though the Society soon began to assemble in a
committee room of the Parliament House, its first
meeting was held in the rooms of the Philosophical
Society in Trinity College on the 25th of June 1731,
and the following is a transcript of the minutes of
that date :—

Dublin, 25th June, 1731

Present

Judge Ward.	Dr. Stephens.
Sir Th. Molyneux.	Dr. Magnaten.
Th. Upton, Esq.	Dr. [John] Madden.
John Pratt, Esq.	Dr. Lehunte.
Rich. Warburton, Esq.	Mr. Walton.
Rev. Dr. Whitecomb.	Mr. Prior.
Arthur Dobs, Esq.	W. Maple.

Several gentlemen having agreed to meet in the
Philosophical Rooms in Trin. Col., Dub., in order to
promote Improvements of all kinds, and Dr. Stephens
being desired, took the Chair.

It was proposed and unanimously agreed unto,
to form a Society, by the name of the Dublin Society,
for improving Husbandry, Manufactures, and other
useful arts.

It was proposed and resolved, that all the present,
and all such who should become members of the
Society, shall subscribe their names to a Paper, containing their agreement to form a Society for the
purposes aforesaid.

Ordered that a Committee of all the members
present do meet next Thursd., in the Philosophical
Rooms in Trin. Col., Dub., to consider of a Plan
or Rules for the Government of the Society, any
three thereof to be a Quorum, and that notice be sent

to the members in Town, the day before the time for meeting. The Society adjourned to this day fortnight.

The names of those who thus stood round the cradle of the infant Society must ever be held in honour in this country, and, though all were men of note, the names of at least eight stand out prominently as having, from the start and for years after, laboured assiduously and unselfishly in promoting the ends it had in view. Primarily, they set themselves to educate those concerned in the first principles of successful farming, and in endeavouring to promote industries which might afford employment. As our story proceeds and unfolds itself, the warmest admiration must be felt for them as men who seemed so much in advance of their age, and who aimed at making Ireland not only self-supplying, but also a great exporting country.

Michael Ward, of Castle Ward, co. Down, M.P. for the county of Down 1715; Justice of the King's Bench 1727–1759. He was father of the first Viscount Bangor.

Sir Thomas Molyneux, brother of William Molyneux, was born in Dublin in 1661, and studied for the medical profession at Leyden. He was a friend of Robert Boyle and Sir William Petty, and in London became acquainted with Sir Isaac Newton, John Evelyn, and Dryden; he also met Locke. Molyneux was elected a Fellow of the Royal Society, and in 1702 became President of the Irish College of Physicians. In 1730 he was created a Baronet, and died in Dublin in 1733. A monument to his memory was erected in Armagh Cathedral. Molyneux printed *Notes on the Giant's Causeway*, which was the first work that maintained it to be a natural formation. He published the earliest account of the *Sea Mouse*, and in 1696, the first scientific report on the Irish Elk (*Cervus megaceros*) in a

" Discourse concerning the large horns frequently found underground in Ireland." He also wrote an essay on *Giants*, a letter on the *Lyre of Greeks and Romans*, and a discourse on *Danish Forts*. There is in Trinity College a portrait of Sir Thomas by Kneller.

The Rev. Dr. John Whitecombe was born in Cork, and became tutor to Lord George Sackville, son of the Duke of Dorset, to whom he was chaplain. He obtained a Fellowship in Trinity College, Dublin, in 1720, being subsequently appointed Bishop of Clonfert in 1735, Bishop of Down and Connor, and in 1752 Archbishop of Cashel. He died there in 1753, and is buried in the old cathedral.

Arthur Dobbs, born at Girvan, N.B. (where his parents took refuge during the Irish troubles), in 1689. He was Engineer in chief and Surveyor-general in Ireland, and M.P. for Carrickfergus in the Parliament of 1727–1760. His essay on the *Trade and Imports of Ireland*, published by A. Rhames, Dublin, 1729, was designed " to give a true state of the Kingdom that may set us thinking what may be done for the good and improvement of one's country, and to rectify mistakes many have fallen into, by reason of a prevailing opinion that the trade and prosperity of Ireland are detrimental to their [*i.e.* England's] wealth and commerce, and that we are their rivals in trade." He advocated an improved system of land tenure, considering it a grievance that the Irish tenant had no fixed property in his land, and that he was thereby deprived of any incentive to improvement. The essay contains much information as to the condition of Irish trade and of the Irish people at the time. This treatise was followed by *Thoughts on Government in General* in 1731, which is among the Haliday Pamphlets. Dobbs took a very active part in promoting the search for a North-West passage to India and China, and a point of land in Hudson's Bay was named Cape Dobbs. He published an *Account of the Countries adjoining Hudson's Bay*, 1748, and he was also instrumental in carrying through an Act of Parliament for enclosing waste land and planting trees. In 1754, Dobbs was appointed Governor of North Carolina, and he died at the seat of his government in 1765.

THOMAS PRIOR
(*Marble Bust by J. Van Nost*)

William Stephens, doctor in physic, was physician to the Royal Hospital, Dublin, where he resided, being also physician to Mercer's and Steevens' Hospitals. He was a member of a very old county Wexford family, that owned property in that county and in the county of Kilkenny. Dr. Stephens became lecturer in Chemistry in Trinity College in 1733, and was President of the College of Physicians in that year and again in 1742. He published *Botanical Elements for the use of the Botany School in the University of Dublin*, and died in 1760.

Francis Le Hunte, M.D., succeeded his brother Richard Le Hunte in the family estates in co. Wexford, and, on retiring from practice as a medical man, went to reside at Brennanstown, co. Dublin. His extensive charities, benevolence, and great affability rendered him justly beloved. He died December 1, 1750. Mozeen, an actor, in an "Invitation to Dr. Le Hunte" (*Miscellaneous Essays*), says his abode was the home of every virtue and delight. (See *History of Dublin*, F. E. Ball, i. 106, and Swanzy's *French and Nixon Families*, p. 27.)

Thomas Prior, born in 1682, at Rathdowney, Queen's co., was educated at Kilkenny School, where he had as school-fellow the illustrious George Berkeley, with whom he formed a lifelong friendship. After graduating in Trinity College in 1703, Prior began to promote all kinds of industrial work in Ireland. His *List of Irish Absentees* appeared in 1729, and was intended as a rebuke to the large number of his fellow-countrymen and women who, while drawing enormous revenues from their properties, systematically resided out of Ireland. In 1741 he printed a *Proposal as to the Price of Corn*. Lord Chesterfield, during the period of his viceroyalty, had many opportunities of meeting Prior, and formed a very high opinion of him. He acted as Secretary to the Society from 1731 to 1751. Thomas Prior closed a career of exceptional usefulness on the 21st of October 1751, and a monument to his memory was erected in Christ Church Cathedral, Dublin, by the Dublin Society (see p. 80). The Society is also in possession of a marble bust of him by Van Nost, executed in 1751 by its order.

William Maple, a distinguished chemist, and operator in chemistry to the University of Dublin, was keeper of the Parliament House, and it was through his influence that the newly formed Society was enabled to meet in one of the committee rooms, until suitable premises were found. In 1723 he had been selected to give evidence before the House of Commons as to the composition of the metal in Wood's half pence. In 1727 the Irish Parliament presented Maple with £200 for discovering a method of tanning leather by the root of the *Tormentilla erecta* or Septfoil, and in 1729 he published a pamphlet entitled *A Method of Tanning without Bark*. Maple acted as curator and registrar to the Dublin Society until his death, which took place in 1762, at an advanced age. In his will he speaks of his modest fortune as the result " of a painful life of labour," and he bequeathed the greater part of it to a niece, Frances Potter. There is a bust of Maple, by Cunningham, in Leinster House.

At a meeting held on the 1st of July 1731, it was agreed that the word "Sciences" should be added after "Arts" in the title of the Society. Soon after, Anthony Sheppard, jun., was appointed its first treasurer, a post which he held until his death in 1737. A sum of 30s. was to be paid on admission to membership, and 30s. was to be the amount of the annual subscription.

Among the earliest admissions a strong clerical element was noticeable, and the following five dignitaries of the Irish Church joined the Society in September 1731: (i) Theophilus Bolton, archbishop of Cashel, one of Swift's correspondents. He was a leader in politics, opposed to Primate Boulter, and favourable to the Irish as distinguished from the English interest. The Archbishop was an improver of land, by draining bogs which were large and useless, and turning them into pasture and tillage. He placed the city of Cashel under great obligation by instituting a water supply at his own expense. Great rejoicings took place at its

WILLIAM MAPLE

(Marble Bust by Patrick Cunningham)

inauguration, and the new canal was named the " River Bolton." (Pue's *Occurrences*, 16th December 1732.) (ii) Welbore Ellis, bishop of Meath, who had previously held the See of Kildare. (iii) Josiah Hort, bishop of Kilmore, who subsequently became Archbishop of Tuam. (iv) Edward Synge, bishop of Clonfert. (v) Robert Clayton, bishop of Killala, 1730, who published a number of works. His *Essay on Spirit*, 1751, and some later pamphlets, were so Arian in their tendencies, that an Ecclesiastical Commission was appointed to bring the Bishop to trial, but he died in 1758, before any proceedings were had under it. Clayton was appointed to the Bishopric of Clogher in 1745, and he and Mrs. Clayton are frequently mentioned in the *Correspondence* of Mrs. Delany, who describes the splendid entertainments at their house in Stephen's Green.

Aaron Rhames was appointed as first printer to the Society, and the earliest work dealt with was Jethro Tull's *Horse Hoeing Husbandry*, which was ordered to be printed, or rather reprinted. This appears to be a clear case of piracy, as the work had only just appeared in England. The Irish edition printed by Rhames is among the Haliday Pamphlets, Royal Irish Academy, and the title-page describes the work as on the new *Horse Houghing Husbandry*, "wherein is shown a method of introducing a sort of vineyard culture into corn fields, in order to increase their product and diminish expense by the use of instruments lately invented." This was the drill husbandry practised in Lombardy; machines drilled the seed in rows, and cleaved and hoed the intervals.

Jethro Tull, the author of the work, was born in Berkshire in 1674, graduated at Oxford, and was called to the Bar at Gray's Inn in 1699, as he had intended entering

on a political career.   He, however, began farming near
Wallingford, where he invented and perfected his "drill."
For some years Tull was compelled to travel for his health,
and on his return in 1714 he carried out many improvements noted while abroad, but his views and experiments met
with much opposition.   His famous book was an *Essay on the
Principles of Tillage and Vegetation*.   In 1733 and 1753,
French translations of it appeared, and Voltaire was said to
have been a disciple of Tull, practising husbandry at Ferney
on the new system.   Tull's invention was the contriving
of an engine which would plant more surely than could be
done by hand, and he is said to have invented the four-
wheeled post-chaise.   His death took place in 1741.

A treatise on " A new method of draining marshy
and boggy lands" was presented in writing by
Mr. Prior, which, on being read, was ordered to be
registered, and this treatise is copied in full in the
original minute book.   A paper on *Hampshire Methods
in the Culture of Hops*, by Captain Cobbe, and a disserta-
tion on *Dyeing* by Dr. William Stephens, were also
read, and are to be found in the minute book.

The meeting of the 28th of October 1731 was held
in the Lords' committee room at the Parliament House,
where many subsequent ones were conducted.   Dr.
Stephens brought forward an account of the design
and method of proceeding of the Society, of which
2000 copies were ordered to be printed, distributed
among the members, and also sent into the country.

As showing the anxious desire of the Society, even
in its early infancy, for full enquiry and enlightenment
on every point that might tend to improvement, which
has been so characteristic of it in its subsequent career,
there is a record of Lord Barrymore having been requested to direct his agent in Cheshire to send over a
bushel of each species of marl found in that county:
also of Mr. Prior handing in a set of queries on

madder [1] which were to be sent to Holland, with a view to eliciting information. Dutch methods seem to have been highly appreciated, and among the earliest volumes acquired by the Society as a nucleus for its library were works by Dutch writers on agriculture and husbandry.

On the 4th of December 1731, the first election of officers was held, when Lionel Cranfield Sackville, Duke of Dorset, lord lieutenant, was named as president of the Society; the Primate (Hugh Boulter), vice-president; Anthony Sheppard, treasurer; Dr. Stephens, secretary for home affairs; Thomas Prior, secretary for foreign affairs; William Maple, curator and registrar. Subsequently, on being waited on at the Castle by a deputation to thank him for the honour done the Society by his consenting to become President, the Duke of Dorset signed his name in that capacity in the subscription book. Hugh Boulter, primate, who was chosen vice-president, held the See of Armagh from 1724 to 1742. He was born in London, and soon after entering on public life, his great talents made him a conspicuous figure both in Church and State. He lies buried in Westminster Abbey, where there is a monument to his memory. At this election Dr. John Van Lewen was admitted a member, and he appears to have been the first member of the Society admitted by ballot. He was son of a Dutch physician, and practised as an accoucheur, dying in Molesworth street in 1736. Van Lewen was father of Letitia Van Lewen, Swift's favourite, who married the Rev. Matthew Pilkington.

[1] Madder was grown in large quantities in Flanders, on which account cloth, made in England, was still sent over there to be dyed. Until the introduction of the coal-tar colours, more than a century later, madder was the principal source of all red dyes. (See *Hist. Roy. Soc. Arts*, p. 15.)

CHAPTER II

CONSTITUTION AND PROGRESS OF THE SOCIETY

On the 18th of December 1731, twenty-six members being present, rules for forming the Society and directing the method of procedure were approved. They are as follows:

1. That the election of members, after 100 shall have subscribed, shall be by Ballot.

2. That a President, Vice-President, two Secretaries, a Treasurer, a Curator and Register be chosen out of their members.

3. That a Standing Committee, annually elected, of twenty-one members, be appointed to meet an hour before the members of the Society, to order all matters relating to the economy of the Society, five whereof shall make a quorum, and all members that come to have voices.

4. That all the officers of the Society shall be chosen by Ballot on the second Thursday in November, yearly, and as often as any vacancy shall happen.

5. That in case the President and Vice-President shall be both absent from any meeting, the members then present, being seven in number, may appoint one of their number to be chairman for that time, with the same power as the President or Vice-President would have had, were they present.

6. That the President, Vice-President, or Chairman shall regulate debates, state and put questions, call for

Reports and Accounts, and see to the execution of the Statutes.

7. That the business of the Secretaries, one for home affairs, and one for correspondence, shall be to note down in writing the orders and material passages of the meetings, take care of the Books and Papers of the Society, direct the Register in making entries in the Register and Journal Books, draw up all such letters as shall be ordered to be written in the name of the Society, and which shall be approved of at one of the meetings, and give notice of members and officers to be elected.

8. That the Treasurer shall receive all the Society's money, and pay sums under forty shillings by order of the Standing Committee, and all sums exceeding forty shillings by order of the Society. That all bills for charges of experiments shall be signed by the persons appointed to attend the making them, and that the accounts of the Treasurer shall be audited by the Standing Committee four times in a year, and once in a year by the Society.

9. When experiments shall be ordered to be made in Dublin at the charge of the Society, the Curator shall prepare the instruments and materials; and one or more members shall be appointed to be assistants of these experiments, who, together with the Curator, are to attend the making thereof, and shall in due time report the same in writing to the Society.

10. When experiments are to be made in the country, proper instructions shall be sent to correspondents for making those experiments with care and exactness.

11. A Register shall be kept of all experiments made by order of the Society, and communicated from their correspondents, and observations made of their

agreement or disagreement with experiments of the like nature made in other places.

12. That whatever Statute or Standing Order shall be proposed to be made or repealed, the making or repealing thereof shall be twice voted, and at two several meetings.

13. That the Society hold a correspondence with other Societies and private persons.

14. That all the works, journals, and transactions which shall for the future be published by other Societies and private persons, which shall contain any useful improvement or discovery in Nature or Art, be purchased, by the order of and at the charge of the Society.

15. That the Ordinary Meetings of the Society be held once a fortnight, at such time and place as the Society shall appoint, where none shall be present but the members, without the leave of the Society.

16. That a Committee of Arts shall sit once a fortnight in such weeks wherein the Society do not meet, to which Committee all members may come at pleasure, and may admit artists, tradesmen, and husband-men, to assist and inform the members, in such Arts and improvements as shall be thought useful, and fit to be encouraged and propagated in this kingdom.

17. That it be the business of the Committee of Arts, particularly to enquire into the state of Husbandry and the several mechanic Arts in this kingdom, to find out wherein they fall short of the Arts of other countries, to consider what foreign improvements may be introduced here, or new inventions set on foot, by what means and at what expense this may be done.

18. That models of the instruments of every Art be procured, more especially of such instruments which are made use of in other countries, and not

known here, and of such complicated engines, whose use and formation cannot easily be discovered by the figure thereof.

19. That every member of this Society, at his admission, be desired to choose some particular subject, either in Natural History, or in Husbandry, Agriculture, or Gardening, or some species of Manufacture, or other branch of improvement, and make it his business, by reading what had been printed on that subject, by conversing with them who made it their profession, or by making his own experiments, to make himself master thereof, and to report in writing, the best account they can get by experiment or enquiry relating thereunto.

20. To the end that all members may be fully informed of all particulars relating to any Art or Manufacture which shall be proposed to be improved, proper queries shall be drawn up, and transmitted to such persons and places, who shall be thought most likely to give the best account thereof, and that all answers to such questions, when well considered and approved of, be printed for the use of the public, in order that the skill, manner of work, and the instruments made use of in other countries, or in some parts of this kingdom only, may be transferred and set up in other places, where they are not known, or improved in such manner as they are capable of.

On the 20th of January, 1732, two additional rules were added :—

21. When any Officers are to be elected :—let there be got ready as many balls as there are members present, three whereof shall be of a different colour from the rest; put them all into a box or cup, and shake them. Let the box be put on some height, and every member take out one. They that take out the

B

three coloured balls are to agree in the nomination
of candidates for offices vacant or expiring. These
candidates are to be voted for by ballot, by the rest
of the present members, and if any should not have
two-thirds of the voices present, let there be a new
drawing for nominees, in order to choose new candidates to be balloted for, and so proceed until the
respective vacancy of Officers are filled.

22. That no Statute or Rule of this Society be
made or repealed from the first of May till the first
of November in any year.

The nineteenth of these Rules, namely, that as to
each member choosing some particular subject either
in husbandry or manufacture, and making himself
master of it, was of great importance, and was loyally
carried out, many Essays on various subjects being contributed to the proceedings.

The bill due to Rhames for printing now amounted
to £12, 10s. 3d. Richard Gunne of Capel street was
employed as stationer to the Society.

The next year opened with experiments as to
methods of cleansing corn, and clover grass seed, and
reference to a committee to draw up short instructions,
by way of question and answer, for the use of charity
schools. The Society also interested itself in distri-
buting copies of Slater's *Culture of Flax*, received from
the Linen Board, and in the growing of saffron.

At this time there existed great cider plantations
at Castle Hyde, at Mr. Crotty's and Mr. Hill's, near
Fermoy, and at Curryglass. Colonel Barry of Rath-
cormack, and the owner of Waterpark, co. Waterford,
cultivated apples extensively, while near Lismore were
many noted orchards. From its inception, the Dublin
Society interested itself in cider and its manufacture,

and succeeding pages will show how earnestly it strove to develop this branch of industry, as the climate and soil of the south of Ireland seemed most favourable for raising good cider apples.

Another step taken was to have a catalogue drawn up of all books of husbandry and mechanic arts, in English, French, Greek, and Latin; also to ascertain what books in foreign languages gave the best account of same, as practised in France, Flanders, Holland, Germany, Poland, and Italy. A very practical suggestion was also made and carried out, namely, that letters should be sent to correspondents in the country to engage them to form local societies in the principal towns and cities, for the promotion of husbandry and agriculture, which might establish communications with the Dublin Society. A set of Maps of Ireland, published by Grierson, was ordered to be purchased. There is a reference to these maps in Dean Swift's correspondence, in a letter of 25th December 1734, from the Rev. Thomas Sheridan to Swift.[1]

On the 3rd of February 1732, a letter from Mr. William Colles, of Kilkenny, was read, which informed the Society that close to that city was a quarry of excellent black marble, in which, together with some mills on the river, he had secured an interest. He had tried experiments, and, as a result, he had now ten saws moved by water power, working night and day, which sawed the marble truly. An engine ground the marble with sand, to fit it for polishing, and Mr. Colles added that he employed thirty hands in turning out chimney pieces, tables, mortars, tombstones, &c. He had also brought to perfection the boring of marble pipes, which served to convey water underground and from the tops of houses. The firm had executed an order

---

[1] *Correspondence*, ed. by F. E. Ball, v. 121.

for a set of these at Mr. Sterne Tighe's in Usher's quay, Dublin. Enterprise such as this, and the success that crowned Mr. Colles' efforts, were welcomed by the Society, and every encouragement was given to any persons who might be willing to extend the industry in Irish marble.

The following members were invited to formulate queries on the several subjects assigned to them :— The Bishop of Down (Dr. Francis Hutchinson), *Bogs ;* Rev. Dr. Kearney, *Manures ;* H. Boyd, *Coals ;* William Hoey, *Lead* and *Copper ;* Rev. Dr. Jackson, *Ploughing* and *Harrowing.* Dr. Hutchinson was a native of Derby, and on his election to the see of Down he settled in Lisburn. During his episcopate a clergyman was first appointed to minister to the inhabitants of Rathlin Island, numbering about 500, and a *Raghlin Church Catechism*, with Irish and English in parallel columns, was printed for their use. Why the Bishop should have been asked to take up the subject of Bogs is not clear, but as he had written on employment of the poor, and published a statement of the case of the Island of Rathlin, he may have had special knowledge. In passing, it may be remarked that two other bishops of the Irish Church dealt with the subject of bogs. Archbishop King wrote a discourse concerning the " Bogs and Loughs of Ireland," and Ware says that Theophilus Bolton, archbishop of Cashel, was an improver of land by draining large and useless bogs, and turning them into pasture and tillage.

Though the Society was only a short time in existence, the matter of its applying for a Royal Charter was taken up in February 1732, and a copy of the Royal Society's Charter was ordered to be procured as a precedent.

Dr. Stephens read before the Society an account of

the Roman inscriptions lately found in Graham's Dyke in the west of Scotland, a subject which does not appear to have come quite within the scope of the proceedings. A paper of more interest to Ireland was one dealing with Colonel Prittie's silver mines in the county of Tipperary, which had been leased to an English company. The account of them was copied into the minute book.

When the summer recess approached, Dr. Stephens was directed to summon the Society to meet at Anne's coffee house on any extraordinary occasion. Later in the year, Dr. Stephens presented the Society with a manuscript of Sir William Petty as to making woollen cloth, and an account of Bees [1] was read before it.

In the winter, a number of new ploughs, for which one John Nummys had a patent, were imported, and the members were invited to attend a special trial of them in the Phœnix Park.

On the 9th of November 1732 appears a systematic account of the ballot held for election of officers. The Standing Committee of twenty-one being present, three gilded balls and eighteen others were put into a dish, and, being placed on high, were drawn, the gilded ones by Alderman Kane, Captain Cobbe, and Mr. Dobbs, who, retiring into another room, after some time returned, and proposed the Lord-Lieutenant as president, the Primate as vice-president, Anthony Sheppard treasurer, Rev. Dr. Whetcombe, secretary for domestic affairs, Mr. Prior secretary for foreign affairs, and Mr. William Maple curator and registrar, all of whom were separately balloted for and elected.

The implements, models, cider and flax mills, the property of the Society, had by this time accumulated

[1] *Instructions for Managing Bees*, drawn up and published by order of the Dublin Society, is among the Haliday Pamphlets, 1733, cxi. 5.

to such an extent, that application was made to the Lords Justices for accommodation in one or two of the vaults under the Parliament House, where they might be viewed by agriculturists, &c. This is the earliest instance recorded, in Great Britain or Ireland, of the formation of an Agricultural Museum. The exhibition was opened on the 22nd of February 1733.

In the early part of the year 1733, a report on collieries at Ballycastle,[1] and on some minerals from the volcano in Kerry,[2] engaged the attention of the members. The question of Hop culture[3] also came before them, and a sum of £5 was voted to Mr. Hatfield for a journey to the Hop country in England, for the purpose of ascertaining the best mode of managing hops, with a view to his giving instructions on his return. As possibly a result of these inquiries, hops from Farnham were planted in 1739 in the Society's field. The encouragement of tillage was a subject of such anxious care to the Society, that the Secretary was directed to open communications with the Society formed in North Britain, to ascertain its views and mode of proceeding. Attention was also being directed to paper manufacture, earthen, iron, and glass ware, salt, hemp, and dyeing stuffs. The earliest notice of anything connecting the Society with the fishing industry occurs on the 1st of November

[1] Haliday Pamphlets, cxi. No. 3. *Ballycastle Collieries set in their proper light, with answers to several objections against the benefits that may arise to the Kingdom thereby.* (Geo. Faulkner, 1733.)

[2] Smith, in his *History of Kerry* (p. 220), in mentioning the castles of Lick and Dune, near Ballybunion, speaks of what was termed a *Volcano*, which burst out on the high cliffs between these castles, some fourteen years previously. He considered it an accidental burning of combustible matter on the external surface of the cliff, in the composition of which were pyrite, sulphur, and iron ore.

[3] There is a pamphlet entitled, *Instructions for Planting and Managing Hops*, issued by the Dublin Society, among the Haliday Collection (1733, cxi. No. 4).

1733, when a paper on the destruction of fisheries by trawling was read. It may be remarked here that in February 1738 the Bishop of Down presented the Society with a new Treatise on Fisheries.

In Pue's *Occurrences* of the 24th of February 1733, the Society made its first appearance in the public press, with a notice as to its intention of publishing from time to time instructions in Husbandry. As characteristic of the methods pursued, and showing the care and thought voluntarily bestowed on the affairs of the Society by its working members, it will be of interest to reproduce the article :—

> "The Dublin Society, intending to publish instructions in several branches of Husbandry, desire gentlemen and farmers in the country will be pleased to communicate to the Society any useful improvement they know or practice in any part of Husbandry, by letter directed to Anthony Sheppard, jun., Esq. in Dublin. And whereas it has been found upon frequent trials, that the new invented plow, lately brought from England, plows lay and stubble ground very well with half the number of cattle required for the common plow, when it is managed by a plowman who knows the right way of using it, but has sometimes not answered expectation from want of skill in the person who held it. This is to give notice that if gentlemen who have got the new plow, will send their plowmen to Dublin, and direct them to Mr. Thomas Prior, at Mr. Gunn's, bookseller in Caple st., care shall be taken to have them instructed *gratis*, in two or three days at most, the right way of using the said plow, by persons well skilled, who live near Dublin."

Following up this practice, a further article, (on this occasion), as to the culture of flax, appeared on the 10th of April in the same year.

> "The Dublin Society has ordered the following account of extraordinary produce of flax seed to be published, in

order to let people see what increase of profit they may expect, if they sow their flax seed thin, and manage their ground and flax in the proper manner. Philip Ward, living within two small miles of Belturbet, co. Cavan, sowed last May two bushels and half a peck of flax seed on one plantation acre, and had a return of 22 bushels clean good seed, and above 2 bushels light seed. He sowed it as corn is usually sown.

. . . .

" The Society is fully satisfied of the truth of this relation, and recommend those about to sow, to sow flax seed thin— about 2½ bushels to a plantation acre ; plow the land well ; harrow fine before sowing ; seed to be very clean ; destroy all weeds ; not to pull the flax until the seed turns brown, and stack it after.

. . . .

" The Society desire gentlemen in the country will be pleased to communicate to them (directing to Anthony Sheppard, jun., Esq.) what success or improvements they meet in this or any other part of Husbandry."

Rhames published in 1734 a list of the Members of the Society for 1733,[1] which is as follows. It shows the state of the membership at the end of the third year of its existence. Some of the members to whose names numbers have been affixed, will be found subsequently specially noticed.

Lionel, Duke of Dorset, L.L., *President*.
Hugh, Archbishop of Armagh, Primate, *Vice-President*.
Lord Viscount Allen.
Hon. John Allen.
Robert Allen, *Secretary to the Commissioners*.
Stephen Allen, M.D.
Rev. Mr. Allynet, F.T.C.D.
Benedict Arthur.
William Aston.

Lord Boyne.
Henry Boyle, Speaker H.C. (1).
Rt. Hon. Francis Burton.
Hon. Humphry Butler.
Hon. Thomas Butler.
John Baldwin.
James Barry.
Arundel Best.
Nathaniel Bland, LL.D.
David Bindon.
Francis Bindon (2).
Thomas Bolton, M.D.

[1] Haliday Pamphlets, 1734, cxvi. No. 15.

Edward Bond.
Hugh Boyde.
Rev. Dr. Bradford.
Henry Brook (3).
John Brown, Westport.
John Brown, Dublin.
James Bryan.
John Bourk.
Thomas Burgh (4).
James Brennan, M.D.
Richard Buckworth.
Joseph Bury.
William Bury.
Colonel James Butler, co. Tipperary.
Theophilus, Archbishop of Cashel.
Earl of Cavan.
John, Bishop of Clogher.
Lord Castledurrow.
Rt. Hon. Thomas Carter, *Master of the Rolls* [1731–1754].
Rt. Hon. Marmaduke Coghill.
Rt. Hon. William Conolly.
Rt. Hon. Sir Edward Crofton, Bart.
Hon. Thomas Coote.
Rev. Caleb Cartwright.
David Chaigneau.
John Coldbeck.
Samuel Card.
Nathaniel Clements.
Captain William Cobbe.
John Coddington.
James Coghill, LL.D.
Rev. Francis Corbet.
Thomas Corker.
Mr. Coughlan.
Rev. Dean Cottrel.
Sir Richard Cox, Bart. (5).
John Cramer.
Baldwin Crow.
Sir Maurice Crosby, Bart.
Michael Cuffe.
John, Archbishop of Dublin.
Francis, Bishop of Down and Connor.
Henry, Bishop of Dromore.
Robert Dallway.

Rev. Richard Daniel, Dean of Down.
John Damer.
Joseph Damer.
Ephraim Dawson.
Rev. Dr. Delany (6).
Edward Dering.
John Despard.
John Digby.
Arthur Dillon.
Arthur Dobbs.
Rev. Richard Dobbs.
William Dobbs.
Sir Compton Domvill, Bart.
Rev. Dean Anthony Dopping.
Rev. Robert Downs.
Robert, Bishop of Elphin.
Richard Edgworth.
Dr. John Elwood.
Eyre Evans.
Benjamin Everard.
Colonel John Eyre.
John Fitzgerald.
Alderman Humphry French (7).
John Folliot.
Sir William Fowns, Bart.
Rev. William French.
Arthur French.
Lord Viscount Gormanstown.
Rt. Hon. William Graham.
Luke Gardiner.
Rev. Dr. Claudius Gilbert.
Rev. Mr. Gibson, F.T.C.D.
Mr. Goodwin.
Sir Arthur Gore, Bart.
Arthur Gore of Mayo.
Arthur Gore of Tenelick.
William Gore.
Rev. John Graham.
Godfrey Green.
Thomas Green.
Earl of Halifax.
Hon. Henry Hamilton.
Charles Hamilton.
Alexander Hamilton.
William Handcock.
Wentworth Harman.
William Harrison.
Joseph Harrison.
William Hawkins.

Arthur Hill.
William Hoey.
George Holmes.
Toby Hall.
Rev. Mr. Hutchinson, Dean of Dromore.
Earl of Inchiquin.
Rev. Dr. Wm. Jackson.
Rev. Daniel Jackson.
Rev. John Jebb.
Earl of Kerry.
Charles, Bishop of Kildare.
Robert, Bishop of Killala.
Josiah, Bishop of Kilmore.
Lord Kingsland.
Sir Henry King, Bart.
Alderman Nathaniel Kane.
Rev. Dr. John Kearney.
Patrick Kelly.
William Kennedy.
Counsellor Ker.
Charles King.
Dennis King.
Rev. Mr. King, F.T.C.D.
Edward Knatchbull.
Thomas Knox.
Colonel S. L. Legonier.
Francis Lehunte, M.D.
Thomas Lehunte.
Rev. George Lesley.
Sir Richard Levinge, Bart.
Nicholas Loftus.
Francis Lucas.
Peter Ludlow.
Colley Lyons.
Thomas Lyndsay.
Arthur, Bishop of Meath.
Viscount Mount Cashell.
Viscount Molesworth.
Chief Baron Marlay [1730–1741, C.J.K.B. 1741–1751].
Alderman John Macarroll.
Alexander Macnaghten, M.D.
Rev. Dr. Madden.
Thomas Madden, M.D.
Edward Madden.
Robert Magill.
James McManus.
William Maple, *Register*.
Isaac Manley.

Robert Marshall.
William Maynard.
Captain John Maule.
George Mathew.
John Maxwell.
Alderman Edward Mead.
Robert Meredith.
Rev. Dean Meredith.
Thomas Medlicot.
Sir Richard Mead, Bart.
Rev. Edward Molloy.
Sir Daniel Molineaux, Bart.
William Monsell.
Charles Monk.
Charles Moore.
Stephen Moore.
Mark Anthony Morgan.
Viscount Nettervill.
James Lenox Napper.
Richard Nedham.
William Newenham.
Christopher Nicholson.
David Nixon.
Earl of Orrery (8).
Rev. J. Obins, F.T.C.D.
Henry O'Hara.
Colonel Robert Oliver.
Lord Percivall.
Rt. Hon. Benjamin Parry.
Lt.-General Pearce.
Sir Thomas Prendergast, Bart.
Rev. Stackpole Perry.
Robert Percival.
Rev. Dean Percival.
Ambrose Philips (9).
David Power.
John Pratt.
Colonel Henry Prittie.
Nar. Charles Proby.
Thomas Prior, *Secretary*.
Nicholas, Bishop of Raphoe.
Abel Ram.
Robert Rochfort.
John Rochfort.
Robert Roberts.
Christopher Rogers.
Robert Ross.
Henry Rose.
Colonel Richbell.
Hercules Rowley.

William Rowley.
H. L. Rowley.
George Rye.
Lord Southwell.
Hon. Hayes St. Leger.
Rev. Dr. St. George.
Robert Sandford.
Rev. Dr. Sheridan (10).
Anthony Sheppard, junr., *Treasurer.*
Henry Singleton, Prime Serjeant.
William Smith, Headborough, co. Waterford.
Alderman James Somervill.
William Sprigg.
Colonel Richard St. George.
John Stothard.
John Stratford.
Colonel Edward Stratford.
William Stephens, M.D., *Secretary.*
Walter Stephens.
Rev. Dr. Charles Stewart.
Rev. Dr. Archibald Stewart.
Alexander Stewart.
Christopher Swift.
Rt. Hon. Richard Tighe.
Rt. Hon. James Tynte.
Edward Taylor.
Rev. Dean Robert Taylor.

William Taylor.
Thomas Taylor.
Berkley Taylor.
Thomas Tennison.
Colonel Frederick Trench.
Frederick Trench, B.L.
Thomas Trotter, LL.D.
John Vandeleur.
George Vaughan.
John Vernon.
Christopher Usher.
Lord Windham, Lord Chancellor of Ireland [1726-1736].
Hon. Baron Wainwright.
Hon. Justice Ward.
James Wallace.
Jacob Walton.
Richard Warburton, Garryhinch.
Richard Warburton, Donnycarny.
Richard Westby.
Warner Westenra.
William Westby.
Rev. Dr. John Whetcombe.
James Whitshed.
Colonel Samuel Whitshed.
Godfrey Wills.
Richard Wingfield.
Benjamin Woodward.
Rev. Dr. John Wynne.

In all 267 members.

1. Henry Boyle, who was born in 1682, was M.P. for co. Cork. In 1733 he was made a Privy Councillor, and Chancellor of the Exchequer, and finally Speaker of the Irish House of Commons, which post Boyle resigned in 1756, when he was created Earl of Shannon. Lord Burlington and Cork (whose daughter was his second wife) entrusted to him the management of his estates in Ireland, the value of which became enhanced, and Boyle promoted extensive improvements in the district. He died in 1764.

2. Francis Bindon, of Cloony, co. Clare, portrait painter, a man of high social position. He painted several portraits of Dean Swift, the best known being one executed in 1735 for

Lord Howth, which is now at Howth Castle ; and another executed in 1738, for the Dean and Chapter of St. Patrick's, now at the Deanery. A bust portrait of the Dean, in the National Gallery, Dublin, has been ascribed to Bindon. He also painted Provost Baldwin, Primate Hugh Boulter, and Archbishop Cobbe. In addition, Bindon practised as an architect : his chief architectural works were mansions for Lord Milltown, Lord Bessborough, and Sir William Fownes. He died in 1765.

3. Henry Brooke, who is well known as the writer of the *Fool of Quality*, and the tragedy of *Gustavus Vasa*, had more substantial claims to membership of the Society. To aid in obtaining Parliamentary grants for Inland Navigation, he published the *Interests of Ireland*. In 1760 he became secretary to an association in Dublin for registering proposals of national utility. Brooke was the first conductor of the *Freeman's Journal*, which was established in 1763. He was born in 1703, and died in 1783.

4. Thomas Burgh (or Bourgh), overseer of Fortifications and Buildings 1700–1730. He published in 1724 *A Method to determine Areas*. Burgh was asked to prepare plans for the new Parliament House in Dublin, but Sir Edward Pearce, who succeeded him, appears in all official documents as its designer.

5. Sir Richard Cox, second baronet, succeeded his grandfather, Sir Richard Cox (lord chancellor), who died 3 May 1733. He established a linen manufactory at Dunmanway, and was writer of the letter that appeared in 1749, addressed to Thomas Prior, " showing from experience a sure method to establish the Linen Manufacture, and the beneficial effects it will immediately produce," the authorship of which has been attributed to his grandfather.

6. Patrick Delany, born at Athy about the year 1685, became a Fellow of Trinity College in 1709. When Dean Swift came to reside in Dublin, Delany became one of his most intimate friends, and they held the same views in politics. Swift said of him that he was " the most eminent

preacher we have." He was successively Rector of St. John's, Dublin, Chancellor of Christ Church, and Chancellor of St. Patrick's, finally being appointed in 1744 to the Deanery of Down. Delany published a vindication of Swift and his circle, in reply to Lord Orrery's insinuations, which is said to contain the only extant account of the great Dean by one who had been acquainted with him when his intellect was in its fullest vigour. Delany was author of *Revelation examined with candour*, a performance on which he was said to set a high value, and of a *Life of David, King of Israel,* and his *Reflections on Polygamy* excited much criticism. Delany married, as his second wife, Mary Granville, Mrs. Pendarves, whose well-known *Correspondence* gives such charming glimpses of their happy domestic life and surroundings at Delville, Glasnevin, and of society in Dublin between 1740 and 1770. The Dean of Down died at Bath in 1768, and lies buried at Glasnevin.

7. Humphry French, born in 1680, was M.P. for Dublin 1733–6, and Lord Mayor 1732–3, being well known in his day as the "good Lord Mayor." He reformed a number of abuses, and when candidate for the representation of the city, Dean Swift exerted his powerful influence on his behalf, always appearing to regard French with strong feelings of admiration. One of the Dean's poems—a paraphrase of the 19th Ode of the Fourth Book of Horace—addressed to Humphry French, concludes as follows :

> " This the sovereign man complete ;
> Hero : patriot : glorious : free :
> Rich and wise : and good and great :
> Generous Humphry, thou art he ! "

He died in October 1736. Swift fully intended to have written his biography, and in a letter to Geo. Faulkner, the printer, begged him to procure particulars of his life, more especially from Mr. Maple (curator and registrar of the Dublin Society), who, Swift added, was French's "most intimate friend, who knew him best, and could give the most just character of himself and his actions. I will, though I am oppressed with age and infirmities, stir up all the little spirit I can raise to give the public an account of that great patriot : and propose him as an example to all future magistrates, in order to recommend his virtues to this most miserable kingdom."

8. John Boyle, 5th Earl of Orrery, and 5th Earl of Cork, born 1707 ; a friend of Swift, Pope, and Johnson. His *Remarks on the Life and Writings of Jonathan Swift*, 1751, was the first attempt made at any account of the Dean, who left Orrery a portrait and some silver plate. Though they had been friends, the work showed malice, and it is thought that some contemptuous remarks of Swift were repeated to the Earl. He died in 1762.

9. Ambrose Philips, born in 1675, was a Fellow of Trinity College, Cambridge, and a member of Addison and Steele's circle. His poetical *Pastorals* and tragedy of *The Distressed Mother* are well known. On his friend, Hugh Boulter, becoming Primate of Ireland in 1724, he brought Philips over with him as secretary, and he was elected M.P. for Armagh. In 1733 he was appointed Judge of the Irish Court of Prerogative, and died in 1749.

10. Thomas Sheridan, born in 1687, was a schoolmaster, and a friend of Dean Swift from the time of his arrival in Dublin as Dean of St. Patrick's. At Quilca, co. Cavan, Sheridan's place, Swift planned the *Drapier's Letters*, and wrote portion of *Gulliver's Travels*. Sheridan was generally believed to be one of the greatest scholars in the kingdom, and he published editions of some of the works of Persius, Juvenal, and Sophocles. Sheridan died at Rathfarnham in 1738.

It is noteworthy that Dean Swift, who was so deeply interested in everything that concerned the prosperity and advancement of Ireland, did not become a member of the Society, though many of its prominent members were well known to him, some of them indeed being intimate personal friends. Dr. Elrington Ball, an

unrivalled authority where anything concerning Swift
is concerned, points out that the Dean held Anthony
Sheppard, jun., the treasurer, and his father, in contempt[1]; and from Swift's well-known habit of mind,
especially at a period when he had begun to fail, he
may possibly have contracted dislikes also to others
connected with the Society. Berkeley, too, who, as
will be seen, helped it later on by his writings and
encouragement, never formally joined its ranks.

The list includes the names of twelve members of
the episcopal bench, and thirty-four clergymen (including deans), some of whom were subsequently
elevated to the episcopate ; of sixteen peers and several
sons of peers, five members of the judicial bench, including the Lord Chancellor and the Master of the
Rolls. The Speaker of the House of Commons was
also a member, and the remaining names are those of
baronets, retired army officers, country gentlemen,
barristers, medical men, Fellows of Trinity College,
and men holding high positions in the world of commerce. Thus all that was best in Dublin society, and
in the Ireland of the day generally, united in a common
and patriotic effort to improve the status of their
country, and we shall soon see how marked an improvement the labours of the Society effected in many
different directions.

During the year 1734, the Society appears to have
brought itself in touch with Holland and with Dutch
methods. Mr. Robert Ross, of Rostrevor, a member,
was in Holland, when he was requested to purchase
Jacob Leupold's *Laws of Mechanics*, and the five
volumes of *Dutch Laws*, which he brought back with

---

[1] Swift's *Correspondence,* vol. vi. 6. In a letter to Thomas Sheridan,
9th April 1737, he says : "The old hunks Shepherd has buried his
only son, a young hunks come to age."

him.   These will be found in the catalogue of books belonging to the Society reproduced at pp. 170–2.   A Mr. Teddyman was employed to translate the Dutch mill book.   A number of madder sets were also ordered from Holland, and a model of a Dutch mill for fining flax was to be made.   With a view to encouraging the import of good grass and garden seeds, the Society offered to lend £150 on good security, this being the first occasion on which the system of loan and bounties, so characteristic of its later working, began to be tried.

A committee was appointed to draw up heads of a treatise on the present state of the coin in Ireland, and the inconvenience resulting to trade from the want of small coin.

Sir William Parsons sent up from Birr what he called a " terrier," an instrument for pulling up small trees by their roots ; promising that a scoop spade for throwing up with ease and expedition strong roots of wild parsnips and other weeds would follow.   Sir William had already favoured the Society with a plan and account of his biangular harrow.   Thus, we see that nearly two centuries ago, the noble house of Rosse had already given evidence of the inventive genius which has made the name of Parsons famous, and also had exhibited that anxiety for the success of Irish methods of husbandry and agriculture which has been evinced in a marked degree by successive generations.

George Berkeley, the illustrious Bishop of Cloyne, was an intimate friend of both Prior and Madden, and he sought to help them in their efforts to stimulate the industries of the country by the publication of his *Querist*, which appeared anonymously in the year 1735. The volume was edited by Dr. Madden, and Mr. Lecky remarks that very pregnant hints on industrial development are to be found in it, while it anticipates many of the conclusions of Adam Smith.

Under date of November 11, 1736, at the annual election of officers, the Rev. Gabriel Jacques Maturin, who had joined the Society in 1734, was elected secretary in the room of Dr. Stephens. He was born at Utrecht, son of Pierre, and grandson of Gabriel Maturin, a Huguenot, who fled to Holland, from the persecution of Louis XIV, and thence came to Dublin, where his son was educated. Maturin became Dean of Kildare in 1737, and on November 29, 1745, was installed Dean of St Patrick's in succession to Swift. Maturin died in the following year.

CHAPTER III

THE "WEEKLY OBSERVATIONS" AND GENERAL
    HISTORY OF THE SOCIETY. (1736–1750)

An important step was taken, on the 2nd of December
1736, when the Society decided on publishing weekly
in the Dublin *News Letter*, a paper on some useful subject, which soon became known as the Dublin Society's
"Weekly Observations." The Society arranged to take
500 copies at half a guinea per week. The papers were
communicated to other journals, as they appear in
Pue's *Occurrences* and in Faulkner's *Dublin Journal*.
On the 11th of December the following statement
appeared in the former :

"Whereas the Dublin Society do intend to begin
in January to publish their observations on Husbandry
and other useful arts, which are to be inserted by their
order in this paper weekly, that they may at the
cheapest rate fall into more hands, and that their instructions to Husbandmen and others may become
more useful by being more universal : By this method
the public will be furnished with the best pieces on
agriculture &c., at a trifling expense, and by getting
them in small portions, they will insensibly be led into
a knowledge which otherwise, by the expense, want of
time or proper books, they would be ignorant of.
Such gentlemen as live in the country and are not
already supplied with this paper, and who are willing
to encourage so useful a work, are desired to send

notice thereof by the beginning of January next, and they shall constantly be supplied with the same ; also with the best collection of news, both foreign and domestic."

The Society printed a further statement on the 8th of January 1737 :—" The gentlemen who by a voluntary association formed themselves into a Society pretty well known at present by the name of the Dublin Society, having already given the public some general account of the design that first brought them together, and which they ever since have unweariedly pursued : it will be sufficient for the purpose of this Paper, to inform the reader of the particular reasons which have now engaged them to give their instructions a new form, and to endeavour the farther improvement of husbandry and other useful arts by observations." It goes on to say " that separate Papers, where the several errors and deficiencies in our present management will be considered singly and therefore more distinctly, seem to tally exactly with our wants, and afford the likeliest prospect of success. To these advantages must be added those which will accrue from the easier distribution of them. Pamphlets fall into few hands, but these shorter essays will reach every reader in the kingdom. Gentlemen of fortune, conversant with books, cannot be at a loss for directions. They can peruse the discoveries of Science and make experiments. The poorer sort, husbandman and manufacturer, are the proper objects of instruction. The object of the Society is to direct the industry of common artists, to bring practical and useful knowledge from libraries and closets to public view. This they hope will be understood as an invitation to all who truly love their country, to communicate to the Society experiments or observations — any loose hints, and whatever else may contribute to the perfection of these papers."

There is a minute of the 20th of January 1737, to the effect that a copy of every paper printed by the Society is to be written in a book to be provided for that purpose. It may be as well here to group together the various papers which appeared under the auspices of the Society from this time down to April 1740, when, on the starting of Dr. Madden's premium system, they ceased to be issued.

One of the earliest numbers has a list of commodities imported yearly, which on an average in money value amounted to £507,270. This calculation was made in order to direct public attention to those articles which would be most likely to remunerate producers. The succeeding numbers were as follows:

15th Jan. 1737. An Essay on the natural advantages of Ireland and the non-use of them. Everything is imported, and, in no way trusting to our own growth, we are dependent on foreign countries. Half the wealth yearly drained out of this kingdom might, with proper management, be kept in our own hands.

5th Feb. An Essay advocating the promotion of spinning. Also one on the benefits to be derived from owners living on their estates, and promoting husbandry and manufactures.

12th Feb. Irish beef, hides, tallow, and butter will always be wanted in the southern parts of Europe, and will always find a market. Wool is another valuable commodity. More of the necessaries of life might be procured by our encouraging tillage.

19th Feb. A letter from a correspondent :—Facility of export, certainty of demand, and cheapness of materials give a preference to some manufactures, and consequently advantage to those countries which are most generally engaged in them.   Of this kind is linen, the staple manufacture of Ireland.   Wool is the genuine English staple.   Every lover of his country should be engaged to promote the linen trade.

26th Feb. Instructions as to linen, choice of soil for flax.

Subsequent letters dealt with the dressing and tilling of the ground, choice and quality of seed for flax, and as to its stacking. In April appeared letters on flooding in places bordering the sea or on rivers; high tides; trenching and embanking; and on flooding of low flat lands. In May, the raising of hops in bogs claimed attention; then came road-making, and the manufacture of cider. In October, appeared a letter on the importance of letting *land* to husbandmen, and *tenements* to manufacturers, showing that a landed manufacturer suffers as a bad farmer. In November, the subject of flax-dressing was returned to, and throughout January and February 1738, breaking, scutching, cleansing, fining, and hackling were dealt with, some of the machines used being figured. Next came malt and brewing, and on the 28th of October a series of articles on tillage was begun. They bore on the culture of rye grass and clover, on hay and seed, and one letter sought to remove certain prejudices against tillage. In January 1739, the linen manufacture was again brought forward. It was declared not to be flourishing in this country, and it was said that different measures would have to be pursued to keep it alive.

Richard Reilly, Cork hill, printer to the Society, announced an edition of the *Weekly Observations*,[1] at

[1] See *Dublin Society's Weekly Observations*, 1736-1737 : Dublin, 1763 (in the National Library).

2*s*. 3½*d*. ; also pictures of the machines recommended,
neatly engraved on copper.

In January 1737, Lord Trimlestown communicated
an account of his new three-coulter plough, which
ploughed the earth very finely.   He also sent up the
plough for trial, with his own ploughman, when it was
tried in the Phœnix park, and approved.   This practice.
of making trial in the Park of agricultural implements
and machinery connected with scientific husbandry and
inventions was subsequently frequently adopted.   Sometimes members interested went down to the country
to view trials, and there is a record of Mr. Prior
and Mr. Dobbs having gone to Leixlip in December
1738, to see at work a drain plough, which is fully
described.   They recommended that a similar plough
should be procured for the Society.

Mr. Arbuckle was thanked in October 1737,
for a poem, addressed to the Dublin Society.   He
was asked to print it, and the Society agreed to take
200 copies.   This recalls Abraham Cowley's Ode
to the Royal Society, on the granting of the Royal
Charter in 1662.   The letters of "Hibernicus"
(Francis Hutcheson), were edited in 1725, and the
edition was dedicated to Richard, Viscount Molesworth,
by James Arbuckle, a Scotchman who held a post in
the Quit Rent Office, Dublin.   His will was proved
in the Diocesan Court of Dublin in 1744.   A poem,
entitled *Snuff*, by Arbuckle, was published in 1719
in Edinburgh.

There is in the King's Inns Library, Dublin, a
copy of his verses addressed to the Dublin Society
with the following title page :—

A POEM

INSCRIBED TO THE DUBLIN SOCIETY

Hanc olim veteres vitam coluere Sabini ;
Hanc Remus, et frater. Si fortis Etruria crevit :
Scilicet et rerum facta est pulcherrima Roma.
                              VIRGIL.

By Mr. ARBUCKLE

DUBLIN.   Printed by R. REILLY for GEORGE EWING at the
Angel and Bible in Dame St.   MDCCXXXVII.

The verses are as follows :—

When Rome was rising into Pow'r and Fame,
And all the wondering World rever'd her Name,
Her generous sons, the Boast of Human Race,
Thought Pleasure criminal, and Ease Disgrace.
The highest joy a Roman Soul could move,
Was to defend their Country, or improve.

Equally pleas'd, in Intervals of War,
To hold the Plough, as grace the Victor Car,
They deemed their work with Conquest but begun,
And till'd the Provinces their Arms had won.
Rightly they estimated Things, and knew,
To cultivate was more than to subdue.

Thus Quinctius, with three victories yet warm,
Retreats in Triumph to his humble Farm.
And thus stern Cato, on his spade reclin'd,
Convers'd with Nature, and improv'd his mind.
For, in that age of uncorrupted Hearts,
The rural shades were Nurseries of Arts,
And bred, though now it scarce will gain Belief,
The Senator, the Patriot, and the Chief.
The Praise to these sublime Examples due,
Descends, at last, Hibernia's sons, to You,
Who, in an age of sickening Virtue, strive
The antient Arts and Spirit to revive ;
Those Arts by Nature's God inspired, in aid
Ev'n of the wond'rous Works Himself had made,
With impious Arms while other Nations claim
Empires not theirs, and purchase unjust Fame.

Or else compell'd by Force, with force oppose
The fell Invader, and the Hosts of Foes ;
Or anxious watch those fluctuating Things,
The Views and Passions of ambitious Kings.
And, as contending Pow'rs by Turns prevail,
Adjust the Balance, or incline the Scale ;
Be thine, Hibernia, thine the happier Toil,
To turn the Glebe, t' enrich the labour'd soil ;
To rouse with Art the vegetable Pow'rs,
And catch the virtues of the vernal Show'rs ;
With skilful Hands to help our Parent Earth
To give her comely offspring, Plenty, Birth,
And to the neighbouring Realms make thine become
What once was Egypt to imperial Rome.

Happy the Patriots, who with gencrous Zeal
Devote their Labours to the Public Weal.
To them th' industrious Hand shall yearly raise
Successive Harvests of immortal Praise.
Avaunt Ambition !　Let thy sons no more
Boast their vain Triumphs stamp'd on shining Ore.
Know thou, and all the World's great Troublers know,
That 'tis but Earth's vile dross subsides below.

From her fair Bosom those true Riches spring,
That Happiness, or Fame to mortals bring.
By these are nourish'd, and from these have Birth
The living Statues of the Gods, on Earth.
And Heav'n th' Inscription gives—and thus we read ;
" To bless Mankind is to be bless'd indeed."

Hail Industry ! Parent of Joy and Health,
Great source of Commerce, Splendour, Pow'r, and Wealth.
At thy approach, the Graces, newly born,
Revisit Earth, and Plenty fills her Horn ;
Through Virtues' Banks her stream fair Freedom pours ;
And gay Delight points to the smiling Hours.
Amidst them sparkling Mirth asserts a Place,
And all the beauteous Family of Peace.
Around in pairs, the blooming Virgins flock :
One brings the Flax, and one adjusts the Rock.
Heav'n guides the Spindle, as it downward tends ;
And on the Thread a Nation's fate depends.
Begin, ye Nymphs, your glorious Task begin,
The Happiness of Crowds unborn to spin.
To future Times so shall Hibernia tell,
In virtue how her daughters did excel.
How their soft Hands confess'd the wond'rous Pow'r
From rotten weeds to deck the Nuptial Bow'r ;
To grace the Warrior's Tent ; the Board of Kings ;
And add to Britain's Naval Thunder wings ;
Nay more, transmit to each succeeding age
The works of Boyle, and Milton's sacred Page.

Fir'd with the Prospect, the glad Realm prepares
To these pursuits to bend her future Cares,
But first she bids, like a repentant son,
Her old companions from her sight be gone ;
Once tempting Sirens, but whom now she knows
Sad authors of her Follies, and her Woes ;
A loit'ring Brood, that long disgrac'd her Door,
The ground encumber'd, and consum'd her store.
Fond Superstition, who perversely pays
Heav'n back its gifts, instead of manly Praise,
Leads on, but slowly leads, the lazy Train,
Averse to Toil, yet grasping still at gain.

There yawning Sloth into a corner steals,
With Poverty, her daughter, at her Heels.
Fantastic Pride, of high extraction, fain
Would be excus'd, and sues, but sues in vain.
The same the Doom of Luxury and Waste,
Who fly from Care, but to Destruction haste.
Envy and Discontent, and sudden Spleen
Move off the last, and close the wretched Scene.

Thus if th' endeavours of the good and wise
Can ought avail to make a Nation rise,
Soon shall Hibernia see her broken state,
Repair'd by Arts and Industry, grow great.

A little later, on an occasion when Dr. Francis
Hutchinson, bishop of Down, was in the chair, he is
noted as having recommended to the Society the "care
of the English tongue." It will be remembered that
soon after its foundation, the Royal Society appointed a
committee to consider the improvement of the English
tongue. The Bishop wrote an English Grammar, and
dwelt on the many advantages of a good language to
any nation. He may have had in mind a project like
Swift's for the improvement of the English tongue
(Prose Works, xi. 5). As shown by his work on
Ancient Historians, he also took a great interest in the
Irish language and history, and published a Church
Catechism in Irish. *An Excellent New Ballad* (at-
tributed to Swift), printed for T. Harkin, opposite
Crane lane, 1725–6, a copy of which is in Trinity
College Library, has the following allusion to his
work in these fields:

I'll tell you a story, a story most merry,
Of a B[ishop] from Ed[munds][1] but not Canterbery,
Who for his great parts, and the books he has written,
Outdoes all the B[ishops] ere sent us from Britain.

[1] In 1692 Hutchinson had been appointed perpetual curate of St.
James', Bury St. Edmunds.

When first he came over to bless this poor Nation,
And found us a people without education,
Full sore did it grieve him, and therefore did he,
Resolve to reform us, and that speedily.

And 'cause we can't read, nor yet understand,
The Language that's spoken in old England,
First taught a Catechize wrote in our own,
In an easy new method, before never known.

In February 1738, the Society had the satisfaction of learning that by the aid of its screw pump, Mr. Barclay, "the Quaker," had cleared of all water a ship stranded on the North Bull, by which means, the vessel, which would otherwise have been lost, was saved.

In October, Mr. Prior informed the members that Mr. Arthur Dobbs had discovered by experiment that the polygon stones of the Giant's Causeway, when put into a smith's forge, ran into glass, and that he had brought to town some stones on which Mr. Maple was to make further experiments, by mixing other ingredients with them.

Mr. Steel produced a model of a machine with horizontal sails, which turned with any wind, with application to a corn mill and also to a ship, to make it move against wind and tide. He was asked to buy a small Norway yawl, to make trial by means of his sails and paddles.

In October 1739, the Society took in hand its own better regulation. Several members had withdrawn, and neglected or refused to pay their annual subscriptions, whereby the Society suffered in income. The deficiency had become so great that the funds were unequal to making useful experiments, procuring the best implements, &c. It had become necessary to fix a set day for arrears, and those who did not discharge their liabilities by the 1st of March 1740 were to be considered as no longer members. Meantime, private notices were to be sent, and public ones published in the papers. After the 1st of March, a list composed only of members who had paid up to date was to be printed. A notice from the Society appeared in Pue's *Occurrences* of November 8, 1740, to the effect that the number of members was not to exceed 100 ; no person to be looked on as a member who did not attend on the following Thursday at the Parliament House, to pay arrears, if due. The first Thursday in the months of November, December, and March were to be the fixed days for election of members. In November came on the question of the better division of the business, and assigning to members the share in it that might be agreeable to each worker. Besides the standing committee of 21, it was decided that several committees were to be appointed, each for a particular purpose, and twenty or thirty members disposed to discharge the duties of the various committees were thought to be a sufficient number to serve on them. Four, consisting of seven members each, were suggested. 1, Correspondence—on which Lord Abercorn, the Bishop of Kildare, Dean Maturin, Mr. Ross, Mr. Prior, Dr. Weld, and Dr. Wynne were elected. 2, Experiments—Bishop of Clonfert, Sir Thomas Prendergast, Mr. Prior, Dean Maturin, Mr. Maple, Rev. Mr. Percival. 3, Publication—Bishop of Kilmore, Mr. Robert Ross, Mr. Prior, Dean Maturin, Archdeacon Theophilus Brocas, Dean Hutchinson, Dr. Weld. 4, Accounts—Dr. Wynne, Arthur Dobbs, Mr. Fox, Dean Dopping, Bishop of Kildare, Bishop of Clonfert, Mr. Cramer. The Rev. Dr. Isaac Weld (mentioned above), minister of a Baptist congregation in Eustace street,

who was recently elected, was son of the Rev. Nathaniel
Weld, a friend of Sir Isaac Newton, which accounts for
his son, grandson, and great-grandson being named
Isaac. He resided at Harold's Cross, Dublin, and
married Anne, daughter of Jonathan Darby, dying
in 1775.

A short time before Weld's election, Robert Jocelyn,
attorney-general, had become a member of the Society.
He was son of Thomas Jocelyn, and grandson of Sir
Robert Jocelyn, bart., of Hertfordshire. Jocelyn was
called to the Irish Bar in 1706, and became M.P. for
Granard in 1725. He was appointed Lord Chancellor
in 1739, soon being created Baron Newport, and
in 1755, Viscount Jocelyn. His lordship died in
London in 1756, aged 68. He had literary and
antiquarian tastes, and took the keenest interest in
everything Irish. Jocelyn's son and successor was
created Earl of Roden. Viscount Jocelyn, in 1747,
during his term of office as Lord Chancellor, was
elected president of the Physico-Historical Society, and
Smith, the historian of Kerry, mentions his noble
collection of manuscripts relating to Ireland. About
1741 he took a lease of Mount Merrion, near Dublin,
and, whenever possible, it was his delight to retire
thither, wandering over the property, and entertaining
his friends.[1]

Early in 1744, a society, which in certain of its
objects was somewhat akin to the Dublin Society, was
formed, and met for the first time, on the 14th of April
in that year, in the Lords' committee room of the
Parliament House. It was known as the Physico-
Historical Society, formed to promote enquiries into
the ancient and present state of the counties of Ireland.
The minute book, the last date in which is the 22nd

[1] *History of County Dublin*, F. E. Ball, ii. p. 86.

of March 1752, is preserved in the Royal Irish Academy. Lord Southwell was its first president, and the membership included James Ware, Thomas Prior, Walter Harris, The Bishops of Dromore, Cork, and Clonfert, Dr. John Rutty, Dr. John Lyon,[1] James Simon,[2] Lord Strangford, and Richard Pococke, most of whom were members of the Dublin Society. In 1747, the Lord Chancellor (Robert Jocelyn, lord Newport) was elected president, and in the following year Martin Folkes, president of the Royal Society, became a member. The first business was to collect materials for a History of the City and of the County of Dublin, and Walter Harris undertook the former. Dr. Samuel Madden offered £10 towards paying itinerant persons to travel and collect observations on the various counties. The Histories of Fermanagh and Monaghan were offered to Madden, and the Rev. Philip Skelton. Dr. Charles Smith undertook Waterford, and Dr. Rutty, Dublin county. James Simon's *Account of Irish Coins*, as also Smith's *Cork*, were published under the auspices of the Society; and in 1752, Smith was engaged on his *History of Kerry* for the same Society. On the 14th of February 1754, a note appears in the minutes of the Dublin Society that Smith's *Kerry* was to be read by a committee, with a view to its publication by the Society, under whose auspices the work subsequently appeared.

At the election of officers held on the 14th of November 1745, Philip Stanhope, earl of Chesterfield,

---

[1] He had charge of Swift in his last illness, and was a witness to the Dean's will. Lyon was librarian of Trinity College, Dublin, and compiled a catalogue of the MSS. He was also secretary to Swift's Hospital.

[2] For a short time, in 1748, he acted as secretary. Between 1751 and 1756 he appears to have been secretary to the Incorporated Society. James Simon was a wine merchant in Fleet street, and is well known as author of the valuable work on *Irish Coins*.

PHILIP, EARL OF CHESTERFIELD

(*From a Mezzotint by J. Brooks*)

was elected president. In Chesterfield the Society had a true and appreciative friend, who did all in his power to further its useful work, and who fully acknowledged the benefits conferred on Ireland by its beneficent and disinterested labours. He was born in 1694, and, from the time of his entry on public life, he was known as a brilliant politician, wit, and letter-writer. Although only a short time Lord Lieutenant of Ireland, to his good government may be attributed the fact that the country was peaceful during the rebellion in Scotland. He aided all efforts for promoting its prosperity, and undertook public works at a time when distress was prevalent. Early in 1746, the Society applied to the Government for a grant to help it in carrying out its various projects, when His Excellency wrote to the Duke of Newcastle in these terms:

"The Dublin Society is really a very useful establishment. It consists of many considerable people, and has been kept up hitherto by voluntary subscriptions. They give premiums for the improvement of lands, for plantations, for manufactures. They furnish many materials for those improvements in the poorer and less cultivated parts of this kingdom, and have certainly done a great deal of good. The bounty they apply for to His Majesty is five hundred pounds a year, which, in my humble opinion, would be properly bestowed." [1]

On the 3rd of April appears a minute to the effect that His Excellency had showed Mr. Prior a King's letter or warrant for £500 a year, during pleasure, for the benefit of the Society. It was not, however, until the 8th of May that the Letter was officially communicated. By it, which bore date the 26th of March 1746, the Society was placed on the Civil Establishment of Ireland, for that

[1] Chesterfield's *Letters*, ed. by John Bradshaw, 1892, ii. 795

annual sum, " to be disposed of by them in such manner and for the like uses and purposes as their own voluntary subscriptions are applied." Lord Chesterfield, in a letter written on the 6th of May 1747, to Mr. Prior,[1] pays the Society the following well-deserved compliment :— " They have done more good to Ireland, with regard to arts and industry, than all the laws that could have been formed ; for, unfortunately, there is a perverseness in our natures which prompts us to resist authority, though otherwise inclined enough to do the thing, if left to our choice. Invitation, example, and fashion, with some premiums attending them, are, I am convinced, the only methods of bringing people in Ireland to do what they ought do; and that is the plan of your Society."

The Lord Lieutenant's warrant was dated 4th April, 1746, and payment was to commence on the preceding Lady Day. Official fees cost the Society £19, 6s. 11½d.

In 1769, as a mark of gratitude to Lord Chesterfield, who had been influential in obtaining the Society's charter, and also the grant of £500 a year, to aid its designs, it was proposed to place his bust in white marble in the meeting room. Van Nost, the sculptor, was entrusted with the commission, and was paid 35 guineas for his work. The bust now stands in the reception room in Leinster House. Lord Chesterfield wrote a very handsome acknowledgment of the honour the Society had done him.

In June 1746, William Telfier of Glasgow produced a machine for measuring the true run of a ship at sea, and a committee recommended that it should be made trial of in the river along the North Wall, at high water on the 25th of June. 1760 yards were measured on the

---

[1] Chesterfield's *Letters*, ed. by John Bradshaw, 1892, ii. 817.

quay, and the Ballast Office boat made an expedition with the machine fixed to the rudder, the index being set at the last degree of the circle 50 degrees. At the end of a mile, the index had moved 16 degrees. The machine was contrived so that the index went round 50 degrees while the ship moved a league. The committee tested going with and against the tide; with the tide, the boat sailed a mile, while the index moved 15 degrees; against it, the index moved 18 degrees in a mile, so that there were more revolutions of the wheel in going against the tide, and fewer in going with it. A further trial of the machine was made in July, when the committee decided that, for want of trials at sea, they could form no judgment of its use when the weather was stormy. Telfier was advised to bring it to the Admiralty in England, where proper experiments could be made, and the Secretary was directed to draw up a certificate of the success of the trial here, Telfier's instrument appearing to answer better than the log-line. It might be supposed that a Glasgow man could have had similar trials on the Clyde; and it must be taken as a special tribute to the position now occupied by the Dublin Society that a Scotchman was anxious to bring out his invention under its auspices.

The volume containing the minutes between the 10th of July 1746 and the 3rd of May 1750 is unfortunately not now forthcoming.[1] As it, probably, contained a record of the negotiations which led up to the granting of the charter, the story of that important event in the history of the Society has necessarily to be omitted here. (See p. 75.)

The newspapers of the day have to be fallen back on for supplying a few details as to the ordinary work of the Society. The practice was once more adopted

[1] This volume has been missing for nearly a century.

of printing useful suggestions in the form of letters.
" How to make Bread without barm ; also for preserving a large stock of the barm," was the title of
one which appeared in 1746.

During the year 1749, occurs the first mention of
John Nost or Van Nost, who afterwards developed so
remarkable a genius for sculpture. To show his skill
in modelling, he presented to the Society a bust in
clay, from which he was asked to carve a bust in
Italian statuary marble. Van Nost, who had come from
London, where he was born, was then residing in
Jervis street, where he exhibited models in plaster.
He executed for the Friendly Brothers of St. Patrick
a statue of William, lord Blakeney, the defender of
Minorca, which once stood in Sackville street, but is no
longer among the public statues of Dublin. Van Nost
also executed the equestrian statue of King George II,
now in St. Stephen's Green. He died in 1780.

On 21st March 1749, the Society published the
following notice—" The Dublin Society takes this
opportunity to inform the public that they have engaged Mr. John Cam (a Quaker), well skilled in
English husbandry, and making ploughs and carts in
the best manner, to attend gentlemen and farmers in
the country, as an itinerant husbandman, to advise
them in the right way of ploughing and managing
their land for the growth of corn. He will carry with
him some ploughs of his own making, &c. Said Cam
will set out from Dublin on Monday 27th, and will go
to Navan, and so proceed to the rest of co. Meath,
and the counties of Kildare, Carlow, Kilkenny, &c.,
where he may meet growers of corn, and instruct
them in the right way of tillage, and thereby save
labour, expense, and time. . . . " A letter of recommendation will be given him from the Society to

gentlemen of the country, and they are desired to give him a fair opportunity of showing his skill."

The Society also printed recipes for sheep-rot, and recommended *The Country Gentleman and Shepherd's Sure Guide*, by William Ellis, Gaddesden, Hertfordshire, then being printed by George Faulkner.

From its start, the Society ever evinced a warm interest in the question of employment for the people, and on the 29th of July 1749 was printed on its behalf a list of commodities imported into Ireland, consisting of such kinds as might be raised or manufactured in the country, as rated at the Custom House, taken at an average for the three years 1744–46. It was designed to show how much might be done at home which would afford employment.

Another notice appeared on the 9th of December, which advocated a method of feeding calves with a mixture of hay water and a little milk, whereby four or five calves might be reared in one season with the milk of one cow only; and on the 8th of May 1750 the Society communicated to the public a letter on a method of transplanting rape.

CHAPTER IV

DR. MADDEN'S AND THE SOCIETY'S PREMIUM SYSTEMS. (1739-1790)

A GREAT stimulus and impetus were now about to be given to the working of the Society, through the public spirit and generosity of one of its leading spirits. Samuel Madden, D.D., son of John Madden, M.D., was born in Dublin in 1686. His mother, Mary Molyneux, was sister of William and Sir Thomas Molyneux. He succeeded to the family estates in Fermanagh in 1703, and resided at Manor Waterhouse in that county. Madden was ordained, and became rector of Galloon, and subsequently of Drummully, which was a family living; and in 1729 the well-known Philip Skelton became his curate, and tutor to Dr. Madden's children.

On the 12th of April 1733, Dr. Madden became a member of the Society. In 1730 he had propounded a scheme for the encouragement of learning by a system of premiums, contributing largely himself. This was adopted by the University, and the details are fully explained in a *Proposal for the General Encouragement of Learning in Dublin College*, 1731. His *Reflections and Resolutions proper for the Gentlemen of Ireland as to their conduct for the service of their country* was printed in Dublin in 1738. This work was reprinted in 1816 by Thomas Pleasants, but without the original preface, the existence of which was denied by the editor. The backward condition of the country

SAMUEL MADDEN, D.D.

(From a Mezzotint by Charles Spooner)

was ascribed to the extravagance and idleness of the people, and a recommendation was made that the farming population should be taught by instructors who should travel through the country. He advocated a system of premiums (earning for himself the sobriquet of " Premium " Madden), which he brought under the notice of the Dublin Society, and in 1739 printed a *Letter to the Dublin Society on the improving their Fund : and the Manufactures, Tillage, &c. in Ireland.*[1] Dr. Johnson, who is said to have helped him in his poem entitled " Boulter's Monument," declared that Madden's was a name that Ireland ought to honour. He also appears to have been on friendly terms with Swift, and he was a member of the Physico-Historical Society, under whose auspices he undertook, but did not finish, a history of the County of Fermanagh. Largely through Dr. Madden's influence, the Charter of the Dublin Society was granted. He died on the 31st of December 1765. The Royal Dublin Society is in possession of a white marble bust, by Van Nost, of one who did so much to foster and encourage its beginnings.

Madden, finding at the end of seven or eight years, that the funds of the Society were totally inadequate to the projects it had in view, and to carrying out the ends for which the Society had been formed, penned his momentous *Letter to the Dublin Society on the improving their Fund*, which was published anonymously in 1739. In it, he considered the necessity of the fund being augmented, and the best means for contributing to that end ; then, on this being accomplished, the nature of the methods to be adopted ; lastly, the special purposes to which the increased fund should be applied. Madden advocated the application to

[1] Haliday Pamphlets, 1739, cxliv. 3.

persons of fortune for contributions, and also the procuring of a charter of incorporation for the Society,
with statutes which would regulate its proceedings, on
the model of the Royal Society. He urged the encouragement of certain manufactures, the importing of
which caused the country very serious loss. Thus,
the loss on earthenware was £5000 yearly; hardware
and cutlery, £10,000; saltpetre and gunpowder,
£4000; threadbone lace, £8000; paper, £4000;
sugar, £6500; salt, £25,000; corn, in time of dearth,
£100,000. Madden further proposed that the Society
should "take and improve a reasonable number of
acres in different soils and places near Dublin, as an
experimental farm for all points of husbandry," and
he specially pointed out the advantages to be derived
from encouraging the fine arts. The *Letter* concluded
with an offer of £130 a year for two years—£30 to
be devoted to experiments in agriculture and gardening; £50 to the best annual invention in any of the
liberal or manual arts; £25 for the best picture, and
£25 for the best statue produced in Ireland. The
voting on these several premiums was to be by ballot,
by a majority of two-thirds of the members present.
He further undertook that the writer would continue
his subscription until other larger contributions could
be raised, and would pay it for life when £500 was
procured, "provided the Society apply his little fund
to the views they are directed to with their usual
activity and prudence." Copies of the minutes of the
next few months, dealing with the inauguration of the
Premium Fund, which soon amounted to £500 a year,
will explain the course pursued by the Society in administering it.

"1739, Dec. 13—Dr. Samuel Madden's generous
proposal to enlarge the plan and fund of the Society

was this day laid before the Board by Mr. Prior; ordered that the same be considered at the next Board. Dec. 20—The Secretaries reported, that Rev. Dr. Madden having settled £130 per annum during his life, and having obtained a subscription of near £500 per annum for the encouragement of sundry arts, experiments, and several manufactures not yet brought to perfection in this kingdom : Ordered that a Committee be appointed to consider what manufactures are fit or necessary to be encouraged with regard to the said funds : Resolved, that the persons present be of the said Committee, and that all members have voices. Feb. 14, 1740—Present, Bishop of Dromore, Bishop of Clonfert (in the chair), Arthur Dobbs, Dr. Weld, Colley Lyons, Archdeacon Brocas, Dean Copping, Mr. Prior. This day the Board agreed to publish an advertisement proposing premiums to be given to such persons who shall make improvements in any useful arts or manufacture, and mentioning Dr. Samuel Madden's proposal for encouraging new inventions in architecture, and painting, and statuary in this kingdom. Rev. Dr. Madden, having now reported that the subscriptions obtained by him for promoting arts and manufactures do amount to near £900 per annum, including his own, and as he is going to the country, he desires to leave the subscription roll with the Society : Ordered that Dr. Madden be desired to leave the said subscription roll with the Secretary, Mr. Prior, for the use of the Board. May 8, 1740—Ordered that the advertisement hereunto annexed be published in the newspapers :—" The Dublin Society, in order to promote such useful arts and manufactures as have not hitherto been introduced, or are not yet brought to perfection in this kingdom, give notice that they intend to encourage, by premiums, annual contributions, or other

methods, any persons who are well skilled in such arts
and manufactures, and will carry them on in the best
and most skilful manner. To carry on this design,
they desire that gentlemen and others who are conversant with husbandry, trade or manufactures, and
wish well to their country, will favour them with their
company and advice, that they may be better enabled
to judge what improvements are proper to be encouraged, what encouragements are convenient, and in
what manner they may be best applied for the benefit
of the public. A Committee for that purpose will
attend at the Parliament House every Thursday at one
o'clock." May 29, 1740—Ordered that an advertisement be printed proposing rewards to be given to
such persons who shall produce in Dublin next winter,
the best hops, flax-seed, flax, cider, earthenware, thread,
malt liquor, lace, in their several kinds, according as
they are set down in a paper agreed to. June 19th—
Ordered : that the advertisements to be printed, for
giving rewards, be revised and altered by Dean Maturin,
Mr. Ross, Mr. Prior, and when the same is prepared
that it be printed, taking notice therein of many other
articles which the Society design to give rewards for
the next year. Nov. 20 — Ordered : that Dean
Maturin, Mr. Ross, Mr. Prior, Dr. Weld, Dr. Wynne,
be a Committee to take into consideration the collecting of the subscriptions to Dr. Madden's scheme, and
the premiums that may be proper to be given this year,
and that they meet on Wednesday next at Mr. Prior's
house, at 3 o'clock. Ordered : that the several schemes
of such as expect encouragement, for their improvements or inventions, be laid before them."

At a meeting held on the 15th of January 1741,
claimants attended, and exhibited specimens of their
handiwork, which were the earliest the Society had to

decide on. They included Spanish leather made with birch bark, lamp-black, blue and white earthenware, spinning cotton, twilled stockings, Bologna crape, engines for scutching flax, and a new instrument for surveying land with expedition. The paintings included four in water-colours of the Giant's Causeway, by Susanna Drury (engraved in 1744), landscapes by Rosse, Tudor, and Kiverly, and a cattle piece, by Ashton. Among the sculptures were a chimneypiece, with boys; stud of horses in a frame; and Hercules slaying a lion (in clay). It was determined that none of the statuary or sculpture deserved a premium, but a prize of £25 was voted to Miss Drury for her views of the Causeway. None of the inventions were allowed premiums, some not being considered inventions at all, and the remainder not being of any importance.

In February, a premium was granted to Henry MacClery, of Waringstown, for flowered damask napkins made by him in a loom, and in May a sum of £50 was voted to him. A sum of £25 was given to Michael Beans for twilled ribbed stockings, which included £18 given him for a frame. Both these men entered into an engagement to carry on the manufacture for seven years, and to instruct weavers and stocking-weavers recommended by the Society.

In June 1741, the premium list stood as follows:

Henry MacClery, damask linen, £70. (He had produced a piece of damask with Lord Howth's arms, worked by a boy instructed by him.)

John Roche, Usher street, buttons, buckles, &c., £50.

Benj. Whitton, Carlow, scythes and shears, £20.

Alexander Atkinson, instruments for spinning, weaving, and cutting fustians, £16.

Mr. Gent, Kilkenny, fining flax, £25.

Charles Monaghan and Denis Davis, improving ploughs, £5.

Eliz. Roberts and Mary Thornbald, bone lace, £10.

Robert Baker, imitation Brussels lace, £10.

Premiums were ordered to be announced for wheat, barley, hops, (Irish growth), cider, breaking up ground, sowing land with wheat, sowing with barley, sowing with turnips, for manuring the greatest quantity of land with marl; with lime, with limestone, gravel and sand; the largest quantity of wheat off one acre; greatest number of fruit trees raised in nurseries; timber trees in ditto; and for planting the greatest quantity of timber in groves or hedge rows. Watson was to print in his Almanac the premiums to be offered for 1741–2.

Several members of the Society and a number of brewers attended at the market house, Thomas street, on the 21st of December, to adjudicate on hops, when twenty-two candidates presented themselves. The first premium was awarded to Humphrey Jones of Mullin-abro, co. Kilkenny; and the second to Edward Bolton, Brazil, co. Dublin. The next in order of merit were Anthony Atkinson, King's co.; Mr. Lee, Wexford; and Samuel Ealy, Ross, co. Wexford. Matthew Yelverton of Portland, co. Tipperary, won £10, for having sowed the greatest quantity of land with turnips. On the 19th of September 1741, £10 premium was won by Isaiah Yeates, Booterstown, co. Dublin, for the best barrel of wheat produced at the market house. To mark the importance attached to such competitions, the Lord Mayor was present, and three bakers, specially requested, attended and assisted in the examination of the wheat. 2200 barrels of it were sold on that day, and it was observed that all the corn at the market looked better and cleaner than it generally looked.   From this, it is evident that the methods employed by the Society in instruction &c., had begun to bear fruit.   It may be observed that notices as to Dr. Madden's premiums appeared distinct from those issued on behalf of the Society.

On the 5th of December 1741, a letter to a member of the Dublin Society on the manner of scoring and crimping cod and other large fish, as practised in Holland and England, appeared in Pue's *Occurrences*.

When Dr. Madden's premiums for inventions were adjudicated on in February 1742, Francis Place won £30 for an engine for beetling linen cloth ; and John Mooney, King's county, £20, for a surveying instrument.   In sculpture, Mr. Houghton was awarded £15 for his story of *Orpheus*, and Mr. Ranalow £10 for another piece.

A notice as to premiums for wheat, hops, breaking up of ground, cider, and planting trees, which were to be decided by competition, appeared in Pue's *Occurrences* of the 2nd of March 1742 ; claims, affidavits, &c., were to be sent to Robert Ross, Stafford street, treasurer ; Dean Maturin, Grafton street, or Thomas Prior, Bolton street, secretaries.   It was also announced that the Society would publish the names of subscribers to the premium fund, " so that the public might be particularly informed to whom they are obliged." A list of subscribers appeared, and the net produce of the fund for premiums amounted to £593, 15s. 6d.

On the 25th of March, the following premiums were distributed—for sowing the greatest quantity of land, Denis McMahon, Clonina, near Ennis ; for the best pound of thread for lace, the Misses Maclean, Markethill, co. Armagh, £6 ; Edward Kershaw, Dublin, got £10 for fustian ; and Richard Hogarth, Chamber street, Dublin, £5 for a Turkey carpet.

On the 17th of June, the premiums for timber trees in nurseries were announced, when it was ascertained that the following persons had planted—

John Magrath, Ross, co. Wexford	. 490,600	timber trees
Oliver Anketell, Anketell's grove	. 61,750	,,
Mrs. Mary Norton, Arbour hill	. 28,000	elms
Charles Shelly, Rathcoffey .	. 27,838	timber trees
Archibald Noble, co. Fermanagh	. 25,920	,,
Pole Cosby, Stradbally . .	. 13,835	,,
Mary Norton . . .	. 15,138	fruit trees

A letter appeared in Pue's *Occurrences* on the 14th of December as to the crop of wheat, for which Mr. Yelverton got a premium. On application of the secretaries, he supplied all details, and his crop was believed to have exceeded every other crop heard of in the kingdom,[1] being 618 stone 11½ lbs., the produce of one acre.

At the end of this year, 1742, the number of members of the Society stood at 98, exclusive of the Dukes of Devonshire and Dorset, honorary members, and on the 6th of January 1743, the number of 100 was reached.

The year 1743 opened with a very gratifying tribute to the work of the Society, and to the estimation in which its labours were held, even by a section of society which might not be expected to be in sympathy with its aims and objects. At a meeting of the Charitable Musical Society, held at the Bull's Head, Fishamble street, Alderman Walker and others were deputed to attend and inform the Dublin Society that

---

[1] Arthur Young (*Tour*, ii. 230), mentions this famous crop, which he says had been written of in all the books on Husbandry in Europe, but nobody believed in it. Young explains that Yelverton himself was deceived; for, having selected and marked out an acre in a thirty-acre field, his labourers, aware of his intention, secretly put into it many stocks from adjacent parts of the field.

that body had resolved to place the profit of their fund, with the profits of a play, at the disposal of the Society, for the encouragement of husbandry and agriculture. The Society accepted the trust with hearty thanks. In pursuance of the resolution of the Musical Society, it was announced that on the 22nd of February *Love makes a Man, or the Fop's Fortune* would be produced at the Theatre Royal, Aungier street.

During this year £50 were granted to Maurice Uniacke, Woodhouse, co. Waterford, for the greatest number of timber trees (152,640) planted. Thomas Bacon was appointed printer to the Society in the room of Reilly, deceased.

On the 21st of April 1743 were adjudicated Dr. Madden's premiums for sculpture, &c., when Mr. Houghton won £25 for his "St. Paul preaching at Athens." The other piece presented was a representation of the Deluge by John Matthews, Temple Bar. A prize of £10 was awarded to Mr. Van Beaver, World's End,[1] for his "Feast of Bacchus," and £10 to Mr. Joseph Tudor for a painting.

Great attention was paid to draining and reclaiming bog, and John Baggot, Nurney, co. Kildare, won £30 for the former process, and Joseph Fuller, Grangemore, co. Westmeath, £20 for the latter.

In 1744, George Thwaites and Wm. Brereton took first and second places respectively as brewers who made use of the largest quantity of Irish hops in the year 1743.

Dr. Madden's premiums for lace, &c., were granted as follows: Anne Casey, "Black Horse," Plunket street, £10 for bone lace; Elizabeth Roberts, Lazer's hill, £5. Anne Page, Castle street, £10 for best

[1] World's End lane was subsequently called Mabbot street, and from 1876 Montgomery street.

imitation Brussels lace; Mrs. Baker and Miss Raymond obtained second prize, £5. Catherine Plunket, "Horse Shoe," Thomas street, for best edging, £5; Mary Casey, £3; Catherine Ricks (or Riggs), "Crown and Glove," George's lane, £2; Esther Haycock, Ormond quay, £10 for best piece of embroidery; David Davis, Marlborough street, £10 for best piece of black velvet; John Daly, Crooked Staff,[1] £10 for dyeing black cloth; Thomas Dun, Chamber street, £10 for dyeing scarlet cloth. Messrs. Wilson, Sharp & co., were awarded £25 for making the greatest quantity of salt fit for curing fish. This firm made 450 tons at Belfast on the 5th of May 1744. A notice appeared in Pue's *Occurrences* that salt made at Glenarm had been inspected by the Bakers' and Coopers' Companies, and that it was found to be stronger and cleaner than French salt.

The next industry that occupied the attention of the Society was that of brewing, and on the 21st of March 1745, a party of members and experts met at the Custom House coffee-house, for ale tasting. A sum of £6 was awarded to Thos. Byrne, sign of "Brow of the Hill," Sycamore alley, for the best barrel of ale made of Irish malt—in this case it was of Wicklow barley; £4 to Laurence Casey. For ale brewed with English malt, Daniel O'Brien, New street, was granted £6; Thomas Gladwell got £4.

An offer of £5 each was made by Mr. John Damer, Shroneen, co. Tipperary, to two masters of ships who would bring from Newfoundland a barrel of cones of black spruce, with the branches and cones on; and £5 each to two masters who would bring from Norway two barrels of cones of red deal. These were to be at the disposal of the Dublin Society.

---

[1] Now Ardee street, in the Coombe.

Premiums now began to be offered for such articles of domestic consumption as blackberry, currant, elderberry, and gooseberry wine.

Dr. Madden by no means restricted his bounty in the manner indicated in his original plan, and he is found offering £20 for the best stallion imported in 1744, which was won by Thomas Place, Barrack street. The horse cost £57, 15s. £12 were awarded to Edward Sims for bulls and heifers.

In the various objects of the bounty of the Society, nothing that might tend to the welfare of the community appears to have been forgotten, and the housing question was even then acute. In May 1745, plans for building houses with two to eight rooms on a floor were examined, with the assistance of Mr. Castle, the eminent architect, when the prize was awarded to George Ensor, clerk in a surveyor's office.

Hats were the subject of further competition, and Thomas Champion, of Meath street, won £6 ; second place was given to Mr. Parvisol, Skinner's row, and third to Mr. Boyton. Even the killing of rats was not deemed beneath the notice of the Society, and Michael Nedley was awarded a prize for having killed 1300. On 30th May 1745, the city of Kilkenny was given £10 for having cleared itself of beggars by affording employment to the poor. About 100 of the poor were supplied with work, they being usefully employed in cleansing the streets. It is refreshing to read of a community which in the middle of the eighteenth century had such enlightened views on employment, and on keeping a town clean.

Nearly five pages of the minute book are occupied with particulars as to the premiums agreed on for the current year. They include prizes for sowing land, reclaiming, manuring, planting trees, grass, broad cloth, hops, saffron, madder, fustian, brewing ale, cider, worsted, salt, beaver hats, drawing. Dr. Madden's premiums include awards for damask, velvet, lace, silkwork, stallions, bulls, heifers, tapestry, fish, paintings, and sculpture.

Several children under fifteen years of age attended in March 1746 to compete for premiums in drawing, when Jane Tudor won £5 for her work in black and white, after Raphael and Titian. Soon after, first prize for best buff was awarded to Mr. Fombally,[1] and second to Mr. Gibal. It will be observed how frequently names of Huguenot traders and artisans in Dublin occur in the proceedings of the Society.

A new and strange subject next attracted the attention of the Society—namely the collection of rags in the city. It was computed that about 5000 lbs. weight of rags were gathered weekly in the city and county, to supply the paper mills near Dublin, which employed a large number of hands. The greatest quantity was sold to Thomas Slater, Templeogue mills, to Robert Randal of Newbridge, and to Michael McDaniel (or McDonnell) of Tallaght. In 1747, on the adjudication of premiums for the best writing and printing paper, the above named firms took rank in the order mentioned. In 1751, the competition for bounties for rag gathering was adjudicated on by certain papermakers, when there were 182 claimants, and rags to the amount of £2086 were purchased, on which the Society distributed a sum of £34, 15s. 6d. An announcement was made that the paper manufacturers were now sufficiently supplied with material, and that they purposed to improve further in the quality of paper made by them.

---

[1] A corruption of the name Fonvielle, that of a Huguenot family, from which Fumbally's lane, off New street, was named.

In 1748, in the adjudications on Tapestry, John Van Beaver, (for his historical piece, " Meleager and the Boar "), John Paulet, and Daniel Reyly took places.

During the years 1749 and 1750, premiums for planting trees were won by Colonel Hugh Maguire, Tempo, and Oliver Anketell, Anketell's Grove; for cider trees, Martin Kennedy, Oranmore, co. Galway, and Edward Dally, Brohall, King's co.; for draining bogs, Phillip Reilly, Derraugh, co. Longford : for making bog profitable, Rev. Thomas Hemsworth, Abbeyville, co. Tipperary ; for reclaiming coarse mountain land, John Smith, Violetstown, co. Westmeath, and William Mulhall, Ireland's Grove, Queen's co.; for using most oxen in ploughing, John Keating, Shanballyduff. For building the most complete mills for making white paper, &c., Joseph Sexton, Limerick, got £40 premium ; Michael McDonnell, Tallaght, £25 ; Daniel Blow, Belfast, £20; William Slater, Rathfarnham, £15; for green glassware, Rupert Barber, £20. £10 were granted to Messrs. Perry & Malone for specimens of printing with letters of their own making.

In January 1750, John Paterson, Pill lane, scale-maker, produced before the Society an artificial tree made of iron, furnished with fruit and branches, to hold candles, which was designed for a dessert table ; for his ingenuity in devising and carrying out this work the Society gave him a premium.

A sum of £6 was granted to Robert Horan, co. Limerick, for best cider, made from Kachagea apples, and £4 to Dr. Hearn, for cider made from golden pippins. John Sturdy, Capel st., described as a painter, obtained a prize of four guineas for enamelled watch-plates. Rupert Barber, who had erected at Lazer's

E

hill[1] a glasshouse for making vials and green glass-ware, laid some specimens before the Society, when he obtained a grant of £20 for his encouragement, such ware having hitherto been altogether imported from abroad.[2]

In 1751, the Madden premium of £10 for tapestry—a flower piece, a Neptune, and a Trophy—was awarded to Richard Paulet.

For most fish caught, cured, and made marketable, John Lyne, Ardgroom, co. Cork, and John Flynn, Dungarvan, obtained £15 and £10 respectively. At this time there is a note in the minute book that Dublin was supplied with fat mutton from Tipperary chiefly, the reason being that as so much land near the city was sowed with turnips, there was no room for grazing.

Richard Mathewson, of Ballsbridge mills, obtained two guineas as the first manufacturer in this kingdom of the blue paper called " sugar loaf."

£12 each were granted to Henry Wrixon, Glenfield, co. Cork, and Wills Crofts, Churchtown, co. Cork, for manuring most land with lime ; and Arthur Maxwell, Castlehill, co. Down, got a prize for manuring land with sea shells or sand.

On the Art side, William Thompson, who served under Mr. Bindon, painter, produced a Madonna, with twenty figures, from an Italian print, which was highly approved.

Dr. Madden's premium of £50 to the author who should write and print the best written book in the year 1750 was awarded to Rev. Samuel Pullein, for two pieces

---

[1] Now Townsend st. A hospital for pilgrims going to the shrine of St. James, the patron of lepers, or *lazars*, is said to have been founded here.

[2] Rupert Barber was a son of Swift's friend, Mrs. Barber; he was a portrait painter and author of a volume of poems, and is frequently mentioned by Mrs. Delany.

translated from the Latin of Vida—*Game of Chess*,[1] and *Silkworm*. This was adjudicated on by the Provost and Senior Fellows of Trinity College. A pamphlet by Pullein, *Hints for promotion of Silkworm Cultivation*, is among the Haliday collection, 1750, ccxxxiii. 9.

A sum of £12 was awarded to Joseph Miller, James' st., Dublin, for tanning hides with *tormentil*[2] roots, and some good boots made from the skins were produced. It was recommended to gentlemen residing in places where tormentil abounded, to encourage the poor people around to gather the roots, for which they would be paid by Miller and others at the rate of 3*s*. 6*d*. per cwt., cut, dry and clean.

For best imitation Brussels or Mechlin lace, £8 were voted to Mrs. Mihil, Peter street, "whose work exceeded any ever produced before." Mrs. Eliza de Glatigny produced a piece of lace made on catgut, equal to Mechlin, an art in which she gave instruction.

The premiums for paper were adjudicated on by booksellers specially requested to attend for the purpose, when Sexton of Limerick and Slator of Dublin, as on a previous occasion, gained them.

The premiums for collecting linen rags continued to be distributed, and in 1752 a sum of £10 was reported as having been expended in Limerick, and £10 in Belfast. Philip Troye won a prize for Tapestry, and Richard Paulet one for a figure of Falstaff, in the same material. Children were also being taught to

[1] *Scacchia ludus* written by Marcus Hieron. Vida, translated into English verse. This, and Vida's two books on *Silkworms*, translated into English verse, with the original Latin on the opposite page, and a few observations on Vida's *Precepts*, were advertised in the newspapers of the day. Vida, an excellent Latin poet, flourished in the time of Leo the Tenth.

[2] From *tormentum*, pain, as said to be useful in allaying the toothache. Order *Rosaceæ*, which is often included under *Potentilla*. It is common in heathy or waste places in Europe.

spin worsted the "long way of the staple," when 294 girl pupils attended, fifty women being employed as teachers.

The year 1753 was remarkable for a paucity of claimants in some of the branches in which premiums were offered. Osiers, willows, and apple trees failed to find competitors, while no claims were sent in for Dr. Madden's premiums for mares, and for £20 offered for importing a jackass from Spain or Portugal. Edward Walsh, Dolphin's Barn, Anthony Grayson, Mark's alley, and Francis Ozier, Dame street, were prizemen in flowered velvet and silks; and Henry Delamain, of the Strand, in earthenware. Nicholas Planchard, a French refugee, won two guineas for best dyed pressed black cloth. Matthew Querk, Kilkenny, took £10 for the best eight pairs of blankets, and £12 were awarded to Rev. George Ormsby, Bellvoir, co. Sligo, for draining bog. In 1754, the premium for sowing most land with acorns or other timber seeds was won by Lewis Roberts, Old Conna Hill (now represented by Captain J. Lewis Riall, a vice-president, no less active in promoting the interests of the Royal Dublin Society, and the objects for which it was founded), and by William Tighe; those for osiers and willows by Henry Waring, Waringsford, co. Down, who planted 73,820; and by David Oldis, Bally-lanagan, co. Tipperary, who planted 53,169. The prizes for best cider were awarded to Lancelot Crosbie, co. Kerry, and Samuel Raymond, Ballylongford, co. Kerry. Premiums were offered for planting most timber trees in woods or clumps, when Lord Kenmare came first with 70,500 planted at Killarney and Kil-beheny; the Rev. R. N. Gifford, Woodstock, co. Galway, obtained a premium for 857 apple trees.

The list of premiums for the year 1766 occupies

26 pages in manuscript in the minute book, and it is thought well to reproduce it as showing the immense number of objects that came under the Society's care, and the varied interests represented. (Appendix No. II.)

At this time, £50 were offered for a Natural History of any County, and a prize was to be awarded to any practical farmer who would write a Farmer's Monthly Calendar. Dr. Rutty's *Natural History of County Dublin* obtained the £50 premium.

A memorial was presented to the Society by Nicholas William Brady,[1] gold and silver thread manufacturer, setting forth that in 1757 he had been brought over from London by Robert Calderwood, since deceased, after whose death the manufacture came to a stand-still, and his workmen were in distress. Brady had himself certain machinery, and he begged the Society to help in establishing him in trade, but the request was refused. Another memorial came from Edmond Blood, bell founder, who asserted that he was the only qualified one in the kingdom. He had cast bells weighing from 6 to 70 lbs., and so had been the means of preventing their being imported.

James Hamilton's new and easy method for sea fishing near the shore, which had been exhibited and worked at the Rotunda Gardens, was much commended, and a sum of £40 was granted to him for making a machine.

In July 1772, 4000 copies of *Sleater's Newspaper*, with lists of the Society's premiums, were purchased for distribution throughout the kingdom.

The deep-sea fisheries again claimed attention, and a sum of £40 was awarded to Patrick Gumley, master of the "John" of Skerries, who, with seven sailors,

---

[1] Grandfather of Sir Maziere Brady, bart., lord chancellor of Ireland.

tried fishing off the north-west coast. The voyage lasted from 30th April to 3rd July 1773, during which period 1392 ling and 82 cod were caught. Similar prizes were given to other Skerries men, who appear often to have been pioneers in developing the untried fishing ground of the north-west coast. During the years 1776 and 1777, premiums for curing fish on this coast were awarded. In 1774, a resolution was passed to defend all fishermen prosecuted with vexatious law suits, for watching and drawing their seins (or nets) ashore, provided complaints were properly laid before the Society. In July 1781, a sum of £200 was rateably divided among a large number of claimants, for consuming, in the cure of fish on the north-west coast, home-made imported salt, at 10s. per ton, on the amount of salt. At the same time, Gardiner Boggs and Andrew Moore, received premiums for 694 and 100 barrels of herrings respectively, taken on the north-west coast, and exported to foreign parts. Next year, Boggs was able to show that the larger number (860) for which he had claimed had been actually sold in the island of Antigua, when allowance for the whole was made him. Moore having later on proved that the 178 barrels for which he had originally claimed were actually sold in Jamaica, he having received sales account from Bell and La Touche, his factors there, full allowance was also made to him. Fifteen guineas were also paid to Thomas Gregg, being a premium on 210 barrels of herrings, which had been taken on the north-west coast, and cured with bay or other foreign salt. These had been exported to the island of St. Kitts, in the ship *Elinor*, which was captured by an American privateer, and Gregg concluded that the cargo was disposed of in foreign parts. In 1782, £50 were paid to Messrs. Chambers, Hope, and Glen, of

Londonderry, for having similarly exported herrings which were sold in the island of Jamaica.

The work of the Society in the north-west of Ireland closely resembled that of the present day carried out by the Congested Districts Board. In 1783, £100 were advanced to Alexander Young, inspector of fisheries in the Killybegs district, towards erecting perches and affixing buoys in Ballyweel Harbour, and for building quays at which to land the fish. It was suggested that Lord Conyngham's bequest should be utilised for this purpose. In the previous year, £100 had been bequeathed by him to the Society, which it was determined should be appropriated to the extension of the Killybegs fishery. Under the direction of the Right Hon. William Conyngham, a committee was appointed to take into consideration the present state of the Fisheries and Fishery Laws of Ireland. In 1784, premiums were offered for the destruction of seals on the north-west coast, at the rate of 2s. for each, when a sum of £39, 4s. was divided between Messrs. John Barrett and co., James Scanlon and co., and Messrs. Davit and O'Cannon, for 392 seals destroyed. In 1799, Dr. Lanigan, the Society's librarian, was employed in making such translations from the French of works on Fisheries as might be directed by General Vallancey and Dr. R. Kirwan.

In May 1774, there is a note as to the existence of an old by-law, which provided that anyone possessing £500 a year in landed property or £10,000 personal estate, should be precluded from receiving money premiums: their claims were to be recognised by means of medals.

At this period, the Society was devoting much attention to small and poor renters of land, and offering small prizes with a view to encouraging them in their efforts. No less than 42 pages of the minute book for July and August are occupied with lists of such renters in the various counties, when a sum of £960 was distributed among them. Arthur Young says that this design was meritorious, but that abuses and deceptions were numerous.

Captain Francis Blake of Galway informed the Society that he had discovered that sea wrack or weed might be made into good kelp, without drying and saving. A great quantity was thrown up on the shore at Galway, which he burnt while wet, a process that enhanced the value and reduced the price. He prayed aid towards erecting a furnace, but the Society was unable to help him, as the Linen Board was the authority to which application should have been made.

The premium of £200 for establishing a new brewery in the province of Ulster in 1780 was granted to Edward and Nicholas Peers, Lisburn, who brewed 115 barrels of ale.

In 1781, premiums to the amount of £250 were awarded to Robert Brooke, the Hon. Baron Hamilton, and others, for cotton, velvets, velveteens, fustians, &c.; and William Allen, of Coleraine, was granted £60 for having tanned hides on Dr. MacBride's method (see p. 144). Allen's memorial contained full information as to his experiments.

Premiums were offered in 1782 for white cottons, Marseilles quilting, and corded dimity, when Messrs. J. G. Kennedy and William Nicholson, skilled in such manufactures, assisted the Society in determining them. Samuel Lapham, William Summers, William Browne, and Messrs. Joy, McCabe, and McCraken were awarded prizes. A gold medal was voted to Richard Reynell, Reynella, co. Westmeath, for having planted a very large number of cedars of Lebanon, Newfoundland

spruce fir and two-thorned acacia. A foreign firm,
(Beaune and co. of Brussels, who manufactured superfine cloth at Amersfort, in Utrecht), made overtures
to the Society, sending over samples and proposing,
if encouraged, to come over to Ireland and exercise
their art for the benefit of the kingdom. Nothing
appears to have been done in the matter. David
Bosquet, probably a Huguenot, laid before the Society
samples of sheet lead and copper rolled by him at his
mills on the Dodder, and the Society agreed that he
was worthy of every encouragement.

A premium was granted in 1785 to Messrs. Chamney
and co., for bringing to Dublin, by the Grand Canal,
a boat loaded with twenty tons of potatoes for sale
they being of the growth of the year 1784.

In 1786, premiums for planting trees were awarded,
among others, to Francis Madden, for 240,000 ; George
Cottingham, for 121,000; and to Robert Power, for
102,000. A very large number of premiums, in sums
varying from £1 to £18, were awarded to claimants
who had planted beans within four miles of Dublin.
To show the increase in acreage and trees, the following
particulars are given in one of the Society's publications.
In 1784, plantations on only 90 acres were claimed
for, when the premiums amounted to £468. In 1788,
the acreage had risen to 9664, and the amount of
money distributed was £4876. Between the years 1766
and 1806, premiums for planting amounted to £18,460,
and (exclusive of 60 nurseries) the number of trees
planted, for which premiums were granted, was
55,137,000. A sum of £6000 was also paid for
such trees as poplars, quicks, sallows, willows, and
Scotch firs.

In February 1787, the Society took a new departure in instructing the Committee of Agriculture to

consider the propriety of offering premiums for planting and enclosing old Danish forts, mounds, raths, motes, and churchyards. It was recommended; and 1s. per perch, running measure, was the rate fixed on. Twenty shillings per acre were to be awarded for every acre planted with 2000 forest trees, and £100 were to be expended in this class. When claims were adjudicated on, those of Messrs. Richard Warburton, Andrew Walsh, John Augustus Ievers, and William Spaight were allowed. They had each enclosed between twenty and thirty perches of old forts, and Mr. Warburton had planted his enclosure with forest trees. In 1790, sums varying from £2 to £19 were awarded to sixteen persons in the counties of Antrim, Cavan, Carlow, Clare, Galway, Kilkenny, Meath, Tyrone, Wexford, and Wicklow, for enclosing and planting, &c. Lord Dillon headed the list with three acres planted, and 131 perches enclosed.

A premium of £44, 12s. 6d. was awarded to Messrs. Richard Williams & co., of Dublin, being at the rate of ten per cent. on the value of plate glass (£446, 4s. 5d.) manufactured and sold by them, which was superior to similar glass imported. A sum of £55, 7s. 6d. was rateably divided between the same firm and Thomas Chebsey & co. for flint glass manufactured and sold by them. William Penrose won £50 for glass made in Waterford; and John Smilie and co. and Benjamin Edwards a similar sum for glass made in Belfast.

CHAPTER V

THE SOCIETY'S CHARTER, AND ITS FURTHER PROGRESS. (1750-1767)

So far back as the year 1739, Dr. Madden had advocated the procuring of a Royal Charter by the Society; the matter was not, however, taken up in earnest until 1748, when, on the 15th of September, we find Lord Chesterfield,[1] who was always a firm friend, writing to him in terms that indicated his fear lest incorporation might possibly be injurious to its best interests. "The Dublin Society," he said, "has hitherto gone on extremely well, and done infinite good; why? Because that, not being a permanent incorporated Society, and having no employments to dispose of, and depending only for their existence on their own good behaviour, it was not a theatre for jobbers to show their skill upon; but, when once established by Charter, the very advantages which are expected from, and which, I believe, will attend that Charter, I fear may prove fatal. It may then become an object of party, and parliamentary views (for you know how low they stoop); in which case it will become subservient to the worst, instead of the best designs. Remember the Linen Board, where the paltry dividend of a little flax seed was become the seed of jobs, which indeed produced one hundredfold. However, I submit my fears to your hopes; and will do all that I can to promote that Charter, which you, who, I am sure, have con-

[1] *Letters*, ed. John Bradshaw, 1892, ii. 887.

sidered it in every light, seem so desirous of." In a subsequent letter,[1] Chesterfield informed Madden that he saw reason to promote the scheme, adding that the draft of the Charter shown to him seemed " to have all the provisions in it that human prudence can make against human iniquity." On the 2nd of April 1750, the Charter[2] incorporating " the Dublin Society for promoting Husbandry and other useful Arts in Ireland " was granted ; and on the 3rd of May, in the Parliament House, the first election of members under the new constitution was held.

LIST OF MEMBERS NAMED IN THE CHARTER[3]

William, Earl of Harrington, Lord Lieutenant, *President.*
William, Duke of Devonshire.
Lionel Cranfield, Duke of Dorset.
Philip Dormer, Earl of Chesterfield.
George, Archbishop of Armagh, Primate, *Vice-President.*
Robert, Lord Newport, Lord Chancellor of Ireland.
Charles, Archbishop of Dublin, *Vice-President.*
James, Earl of Kildare, *Vice-President.*
John, Earl of Grandison, *Vice-President.*
Wills, Viscount Hillsborough.
Humphrey, Viscount Lanesborough, *Vice-President.*
Robert, Bishop of Clogher.
Charles, Lord Tullamore.
Richard, Lord Mornington.

Henry Boyle, Chancellor of the Exchequer.
Sir Arthur Gore, *Vice-President.*
Sir Thomas Taylor, *Vice-President.*
Hercules Langford Rowley.
John Maxwell.
Thomas Butler.
Thomas Tennison.
Robert Downes, *Treasurer.*
Thomas Prior, *Secretary.*
Arthur Jones Nevill.
John Putland.
Thomas Waite.
Alexander McAuley.
William Maple, *Registrar.*
Samuel Hutchinson, Dean of Dromore.
Richard Pococke, Archdeacon of Dublin (1).
John Kearney, D.D.
John Wynne, D.D., *Secretary.*

[1] *Letters*, ii. 897.
[2] On the 21st of January 1836, Mr. William Watson, Temple street, sent to the Society the original warrant of King George II, to the then Lord Lieutenant of Ireland, for granting the Charter, which he had lately found among some of his family papers. It is now in the National Library.
[3] Haliday Pamphlets, ccxxix. 2.

Members elected since the date of the Charter, most of whom were members of the late voluntary Society.

William, Earl of Blessington.
Charles, Lord Boyle.
William Bristow.
Thomas Adderly.
Oliver Anketell.
Henry Brownrigg.
John Bury.
William Bury.
John Blumfield.
Arthur, Archbishop of Cashel.
John, Bishop of Clonfert.
Jemmett, Bishop of Cork.
Rt. Hon. William Conolly.
Sir Samuel Cooke, Bart.
Sir Richard Cox, Bart.
Robert Callaghan.
Colombine Lee Carré.
Shapland Carew.
Michael Chamberlain.
Richard Castles (2).
Rev. Charles Coote.
William, Bishop of Derry.
Capt. Theophilus Desbrisay (3).
William Henry Dawson.
Arthur Dobbs.
Anthony Dopping.
William Deane.
Michael Dally.
John Dawson.
Alderman James Dunn.
George Evans.
William Forward.
Dr. John Ferral.
Lord Gormanstown.
Joseph Gascoygne.
John Grogan.
Barth. William Gilbert.
Charles Hamilton.
Rev. Sir Philip Hoby, Bart.
Ralph Howard.
Rev. Daniel Jackson.
Colonel Nicholas Loftus.
Robert Longfield.
Rev. Dr. George Leslie.

James Digges La Touche (4).
Richard Levinge.
Dr. Thomas Lloyd.
Viscount Massereene.
Bishop of Meath.
Hon. Baron Mountney.
Sir Capel Molyneux, Bart.
Sir Charles Moore, Bart.
Charles Monck.
Henry Monck.
John Macarrell.
James McManus.
Hervey Morres.
Aland Mason.
Marc Anthony Morgan.
Dr. Barthw. Mosse (5).
John Magill.
Edward Nicholson.
David Nixon.
Edward Noy.
Earl of Orrery.
Rev. Dr. Obins.
Colonel Joshua Paul.
Rev. Keene Percival.
Lord Rawdon.
Brigr.-General Edward Richbell.
John Rochfort.
Robert Roberts.
Lewis Roberts.
Robert Ross.
Viscount Strangford.
Colonel Robert Sandford.
James Smith.
Enoch Sterne.
James Stopford.
John Stratford.
William Stewart, of Killymoon.
Richard Supple.
William Tighe.
Rev. Holt Truell.
George Vaughan.
John Wade.
Rev. John Wynne, junr.

Several of these members have been already noticed, and many of them are so well known as to require no remark in this narrative. A few, however, deserve especial mention, as having been regular attendants at the meetings of the Society, and as working on various committees.

(1) Richard Pococke (who was at this time Archdeacon of Dublin) was a native of Hampshire. He was chaplain to Lord Chesterfield, and Bishop of Ossory 1756 to 1765, when he was translated to Meath, a see which he held for a very short time, dying almost immediately after his translation. Pococke was a great traveller, and published an account of his *Travels in the East.* His *Tour in Ireland* in 1752 was edited by the late Rev. Professor G. T. Stokes. He collected fossils, stones, minerals, &c., and bequeathed his collection, as well as one of coins and medals, to the British Museum. Pococke was a Fellow of the Royal Society.

(2) Richard Castles, or Castle [1] (as he himself wished to be called), whose real name was de Richardi, as appears by his will, was a native of Saxony, and an architect by profession, who settled in Ireland under the patronage of Sir Gustavus Hume, bart., and was the first to introduce here the Palladian style. He is said to have arrived in the country about 1727, and his principal works include the Printing House and Dining Hall, Trinity College; Leinster House, Kildare street, and Tyrone House, Marlborough street, all dating between 1734 and 1745, as well as several other mansions in Dublin. He designed Powerscourt House, co. Wicklow; Ballyhaise, co. Cavan (one of the most remarkable of his works); Hazlewood, and Summerhill, "which in his own day was considered his masterpiece." In conjunction with Bindon, Castle erected Lord Aldborough's mansion at Belan, co. Kildare, and Russborough, co. Wicklow, for Lord Milltown. He published

---

[1] "Richard Castle, Architect," by T. U. Sadlier, *Journal R. S. A. I.,* xli. 241.

an *Essay towards supplying the City of Dublin with Water*. Castle died at Carton in 1751, and is buried at Maynooth.

(3) Theophile Desbrisay, " Captain of Halberdiers of Ireland," b. 1693, married Madelaine, daughter of Colonel Jacques Daubussarques, a Huguenot resident of Portarlington. Desbrisay, who was agent for Huguenot regiments, had a military office in Cork hill, and in 1746 resided in Frapper lane.[1]   He, who died in 1772, and his wife, were buried in the French Nonconformist cemetery in Stephen's Green.

(4) James Digges La Touche (son of David Digges La Touche, banker, of Dublin), sided with Charles Lucas, when that patriot started his campaign against the Board of Aldermen.   They became opponents, however, when La Touche and he both decided to contest the representation of Dublin in 1745, and Lucas afterwards accused him of trying to injure certain branches of Irish trade.   La Touche published *Papers concerning the late Disputes between the Commons and Aldermen of Dublin*, 1746 ; and *Collections of Cases, &c., and Proceedings in Parliament relating to Insolvent Debtors, Customs and Excises, Admiralty Courts, and the valuable liberties of the citizens*, 1757.

(5) Bartholomew Mosse was born at Maryborough in 1712.   In the year 1745 he founded a Hospital for lying-in women in George's lane, which was the first of its kind in the British Islands.   The foundation stone of the Rotunda Lying-in Hospital, designed by Castle, was laid in 1751, and that institution, conducted by Dr. Mosse, was opened in 1757.   Mosse died in 1759.   A memoir of him will be found in the *Dublin Journal of Medical Science*, vol. ii.

A little later, a seal for the use of the Society was ordered to be prepared, the design to be Minerva with a cornucopia ; motto, *Nostri plena laboris*.[2]   On the 8th

[1] Now Beresford street (N. King street).
[2] Virgil's *Æneid*, 1. 460.

of November 1750, the annual election of officers took place, when William, Earl of Harrington, lord lieutenant, became president; George, Archbishop of Armagh; Charles, Archbishop of Dublin; James, Earl of Kildare; John, Earl of Grandison; Humphrey, Viscount Lanesborough; Sir Arthur Gore; and Sir Thomas Taylor — vice-presidents; Robert Downes, treasurer; Dr. John Wynne and Thomas Prior, secretaries; William Maple, registrar; and William Hawker, clerk. The most remarkable name in this list is that of Primate George Stone, who had been Vice-President for some years previously, As pointed out by Mr. Litton Falkiner,[1] the office at this period was much more political than ecclesiastical, and Stone's appointment was due to his known aptitude for the management of affairs. He was an able statesman and parliamentarian, and as such his connection with the Dublin Society was of great importance to its interests.

On the 21st October 1751, the Society sustained a severe loss in the death of Thomas Prior, who for twenty years had laboured incessantly in its behalf, and who had acted as Secretary from its commencement. The newspapers stated that he died after a tedious and severe illness, and on the 25th of October, "the corpse of that great and good man" was deposited in the church of Rathdowney, Queen's county. Faulkner's *Dublin Journal* contained a most appreciative notice of his useful and beneficent life and labours. At the meeting held on the 31st of October, the Bishop of Meath (Henry Maule), moved that a monument be raised to the memory of Mr. Prior, and subscriptions were to be invited. The commission was

---

[1] *Essays Relating to Ireland* (Archbishop Stone), ed. E. Dowden, 1909.

PRIOR MONUMENT, CHRIST CHURCH, DUBLIN

(*J. Van Nost*)

entrusted to Van Nost, but it was not until the 15th
of January 1756, that the monument neared completion, and the Dean and Chapter of Christ Church
Cathedral, in which it was proposed to erect it, were
asked to assign it a suitable position. It was put up in
the nave, where it remained for more than a century.
In 1870, on the restoration of the Cathedral by Mr.
Henry Roe, the monument was removed to the crypt.
The Council of the Royal Dublin Society, deeming it
undesirable that a memorial of so much interest should
remain in obscurity, sought permission to have it restored to the body of the church. This was granted,
and in 1890 the expenditure of a sum of £60 was
authorised by the Society for its restoration, and removal
to the south porch, where the monument is still placed.
The Society's minute book shows that Van Nost was
paid 150 guineas for the monument, and 30 guineas
for its erection. Berkeley, who penned the elegant
inscription [1] on the monument, styled his friend
"Societatis Dubliniensis, auctor, institutor, curator."
On a scroll in the hand of one of the figures are
the following words—"This monument was erected
to Thomas Prior, Esq., at the charge of several
persons, who contributed to honour the memory of
that worthy patriot, to whom his veracity, actions and
unwearied endeavours in the service of his country
have raised a monument more lasting than marble."
The following is the inscription to Prior's memory in
Rathdowney Church :— [2]

Sacred to the memory of Thomas Prior, Esq.,
who spent a long life in unwearied endeavours to

[1] *Inscriptions, &c., Christ Church Cathedral*, Rev. John Finlayson,
1878.
[2] "Preservation Memorials of the Dead," *Journal*, 1911, vol. viii.,
No. 4, p. 425.

promote the welfare of his NATIVE COUNTRY. Every manufacture, every branch of Husbandry will declare this truth. Every useful Institution will lament its Friend and Benefactor. He died alas! too soon for IRELAND. October the 21st, 1751, aged 70.

In June 1752, the Society was called on to take into consideration a Bill exhibited against it by Charles, archbishop of Dublin, and Richard Levinge, surviving executors of the will of Sir Richard Levinge, bart., deceased, which had been filed in Chancery on the 1st of April. Sir Richard had bequeathed to them £2000 on trust to lay it out at interest, and pay the accruing profits for a period of twenty-one years to the treasurer for the time being of the Dublin Society, to be disposed of yearly in premiums, as the Society should think proper, for the encouragement of husbandry in Ireland. At the expiration of that term, or if the Dublin Society should, for three years together, cease to act, or discontinue its proceedings, then the principal sum was to go to the younger children of testator's nephew. He appointed the Archbishop of Dublin, Richard Levinge, and Thomas Prior, executors. The testator died in 1747, and from that date, until his own death in 1751, Prior managed everything. It was ordered, under a decree of the Lord Chancellor of the 4th of July 1758, that the £2000 should be paid into the hands of Thomas Stopford, one of the Masters in Chancery, to be by him laid out at interest, to the uses in the will of Sir Richard Levinge. On the 8th of July 1756, the money had been mortgaged to the Viscountess Allen. The testator, Sir R. Levinge, 2nd baronet, was son of Sir Richard, 1st baronet, and he married Isabella, daughter of Sir Arthur Rawdon, bart.

Among those who had joined the Society within

the previous three or four years were Dr. Isaac Mann and George Faulkner.   The former, who was born in Norwich in 1710, came over to Ireland as tutor to the son of Robert Jocelyn, afterwards Lord Newport and Lord Chancellor, to whom he was chaplain.   Mann was incumbent of St. Matthew's, Ringsend, and Archdeacon of Dublin, and in 1772 he was appointed Bishop of Cork.

Faulkner, born in Dublin in 1699, who became a printer and publisher of note, was satirised by Foote, as " Peter Paragraph."   He was Swift's printer, and on one occasion underwent imprisonment in Newgate for publishing a pamphlet by Bishop Hort.   He was vain and fussy, and delighted in offering splendid entertainments to talented authors and men of rank. During his vice-royalty, Lord Chesterfield became on intimate terms with Faulkner, professing high esteem for the printer, whose work was in every way creditable to the character of the Dublin printing of the day. Faulkner died in 1775.   A bust of Dean Swift, which he had intended should be placed in a niche in front of his house in Essex street, was presented by his nephew and successor in the business to St. Patrick's Cathedral, where it is placed near Swift's monument.   For many interesting particulars with regard to Faulkner and his circle, the reader is referred to Gilbert's *History of Dublin*, vol. ii. p. 30.

Certain rules, which were approved in November 1756, were laid down for the better government of the Dublin Society.   Among them was one to the effect that no instrument or printed book, its property, was to be lent to anyone without order.   From the 1st of November in that year, the annual subscription was to be two guineas, and each person was to pay an admission fee of two guineas ; twenty guineas to be the com-

position for life membership.   In the ballot, two nega-
tives in seven were to exclude, and so on in proportion.

A curious entry occurs about this time, namely,
that a crown would be paid at the Prerogative Office
for each separate intimation of a legacy being left to
the Society.   It was not, however, until the year 1772
that a legacy was bequeathed (see p. 149).

In April 1759, Thomas Butler, of Balmoola, co.
Wicklow, miner and smelter, produced *Lapis calaminaris* [1] discovered and raised by him at Rosses, co. Sligo,
and also some brass wrought by him : on the affidavits
produced in support of his claim, the Society voted
him £15.   Some mention is made of the Society's
Osiery in Wexford, but no further particulars appear.

The *Interest of Ireland*, a volume written by Henry
Brooke, was proposed as deserving the premium offered
for the best work on Agriculture.   It was ordered to
be read, and was recommended.

In November 1760, John Putland, treasurer, the
Rev. Dr. Wynne, secretary, and William Maple, registrar, were asked to accept gold medals, " in grateful
acknowledgment of the advantages the Society had
received from their kind and assiduous attention to
its useful purposes."

A sum of £100 was lent to Anthony Crouset, of
Cork, on security, for the cultivation of white mulberry
trees, and for carrying on the manufacture of raw silk.

When King George the Second, the sovereign
under whom the Society had been originally founded,
and who had granted the charter, died in October
1760, and King George the Third ascended the
throne, the Society presented to His Majesty an
address which will be found copied into the minute
book.   Anthony Foster (1), Dr. Constantine Barbor

---

[1] Calamine stone is an ore of the metal zinc.

(2), Simon Luttrell of Luttrellstown (3), Sir Robert Deane, bart. (4), and the Bishop of Waterford (Dr. Richard Chevenix, Lord Chesterfield's friend) had now become members. The two last-named were constant in their attendance, and frequently presided at the meetings.

1. Anthony Foster, chief baron, from whom the magnificent avenue opening off Stillorgan road, Dublin, is named, built the mansion known as Merville, which stands in the angle formed by the main road and the avenue. The Chief Baron was a friend of Mrs. Delany, and formed one of the brilliant circle in which she moved. "He was one of the first persons of position in Ireland to interest himself in a practical manner in the improvement of agriculture and the development of Irish industries."[1]   Arthur Young visited him at Collon, co. Louth, where his operations " as a prince of improvers " exceeded anything Young could have imagined. He helped in amending the laws as to the linen manufacture. Foster had been M.P. for Dunleer, and afterwards for the county of Louth, and was father of the last Speaker of the Irish House of Commons.

2. Dr. Constantine Barbor, sch. Trin. Coll. Dub. 1732, was King's Professor of Materia Medica and Pharmacy in 1749, and in 1754 President of the College of Physicians, an office to which he was again elected in 1764 and 1769. He also became physician to the Blue Coat Hospital, in succession to Dr. Richard Weld, on the death of the latter in 1755. Barbor died in 1783. In a poem descriptive of the Medical Faculty in Dublin published by John Gilborne, M.D., in 1755, the following lines are devoted to him :—

" Wise Barbor can prolong the days of youth,
By maxims founded on undoubted Truth :
With pharmaceutic art he plainly shows
How to prepare, preserve, compound and chuse
Drugs and materials medical, that will
All indications curative fulfil."

---

[1] *History of Co. Dublin*, F. E. Ball, ii. 78.

3. Simon Luttrell was created Baron Irnham and Earl of Carhampton, and became father-in-law of Henry, Duke of Cumberland, George the Third's brother. He was M.P. for various English constituencies, and on one occasion he was returned to Parliament with no less than three of his sons. At one time he resided a great deal at Luttrellstown, which was visited, during his tour in Ireland in 1776, by Arthur Young, who enters fully into the system of cultivation pursued by Lord Carhampton.[1]

4. Sir Robert Deane, bart., a privy councillor, was father of the first Lord Muskerry. He had a charming seat at Dromore, near Mallow, co. Cork, and owned considerable property. He subsequently became a Vice-President of the Society.

There is a note that on the 29th of January 1761 John Tickell was balloted for, but not chosen, which appears to be the first instance in the history of the Society of a candidate being rejected. He was son of Thomas Tickell of Glasnevin.

The minute books between the 13th of August 1761 and the 6th of March 1766 are not forthcoming, but the gap is partially supplied by the printed volumes of *Proceedings*, which commence on the 15th of March 1764. These, while evidently transcripts of the original minute books, do not, for a considerable time, give the names of members attending the meetings. The newspapers of the period help to supply further particulars.

In the year 1761, the first parliamentary grant was made to the Dublin Society by the Irish House of Commons, and amounted to the sum of £12,000. It was given " to promote and encourage agriculture, arts, and manufactures." In 1763, 1765, and 1769, £10,000 were granted, and each year there was a most careful

---

[1] *History of Co. Dublin*, F. E. Ball, iv. 17-19.

calculation and allotment of the amounts to be set apart for particular branches of the Society's work.

A sum of £500 was allocated in 1765, for distribution in sums of £5 each, to discharged soldiers and sailors, who had served the King outside Great Britain and Ireland, and who took farms of 5 acres to 20 acres in extent, on leases for lives, in Munster, Leinster, and Connaught.   Candidates for these premiums should have been for one entire year settled on the farms.

CHAPTER VI

HOMES OF THE SOCIETY

As will have been seen, the earliest meetings of the Society were held in the Philosophical Society's rooms in Trinity College, and in the Parliament House, while one meeting is noted as having been held on the 19th of April 1739, at the Society's "ground," and a few subsequent meetings, up to the 8th of June, took place in its "House." These premises in Mecklenburgh street, which were taken for the purposes of a Botanic Garden, were abandoned by 1740 (see p. 186). Though a table, chairs, cloth, &c. appear to have been ordered for fitting up the rooms, the Society in a short time resumed its meetings in the Parliament House. Finding this increasingly inconvenient, especially in view of the numerous properties and accessories which were beginning to accumulate, a committee was appointed to look for suitable premises, and in December 1756, a report was made that such had been found in Shaw's court, off Dame street, now partly included in the site of the Commercial Buildings. The necessary legal arrangements having been concluded, the Society met for the last time in the Parliament House on the 3rd of February 1757, and the first meeting in its new home was held on the 10th of February, the Earl of Lanesborough, vice-president, occupying the chair, and twelve members being present. Part of the business transacted at this meeting had reference to a method communicated by Mr. Bermingham, of Ros-

SOCIETY'S ESCRITOIRE, 1753

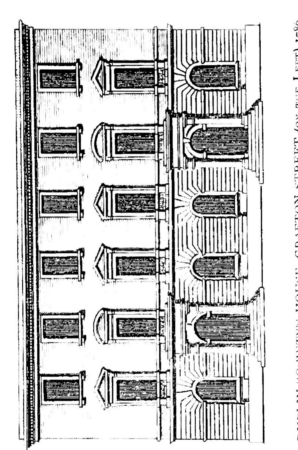

DUBLIN SOCIETY'S HOUSE, GRAFTON STREET (ON THE LEFT) 1786

common, for preventing labourers from imposing on their employers, into which method a committee was appointed to enquire. Special oilcloth and stair-carpeting were ordered for the new house, and a map of Ireland was to be hung in the Board-room. The Society was already in possession of an escritoire, as a minute of the 15th of February 1753, ordered that one to be used for keeping books and papers should be purchased; and the words "This belongs to the Dublin Society" were to be inlaid in large letters in front. This venerable piece of furniture, which must have disappeared a great number of years ago, was recovered some time since, being purchased by the Society for a sum of £11 from a Liffey street dealer; and it is now placed in the Council room. The date "1753" appears after the words ordered to be inlaid. For the first time, on the 25th of January 1759, the minutes of the previous meeting were signed by the chairman, Humphrey, 1st Earl of Lanesborough, a zealous supporter of the Society, and one of the most regular attendants at its meetings.

By the year 1761, the Society's house in Shaw's court was found to be inconvenient, and, as the tenure by which it was held was unsatisfactory, it was resolved to look for more suitable premises or for building ground. Sir William Yorke's house in William street was favourably reported on, but the Bishop of Derry stepped in and purchased it before the Society could take steps in the matter. Sir Capel Molyneux's mansion in Peter street, Lord Antrim's house in Dawson street, and ground on which the old Theatre in Aungier street stood, were inspected. Finally, a plot of ground on the west side of Grafton street, adjoining the house of the Navigation Board, was decided on as suitable, and on the 23rd of January 1766, Mr.

Myers[1] was ordered to prepare plans and estimates. A consideration of £1600 was paid, and the rent was £32, 5s. During October and November 1767, the meetings were held in the great room over the gateway in Trinity College, and later, in the Parliament House. On the 3rd of December 1767, the Society met for the first time in its new premises.

The *Gentleman's Magazine* for 1786 (vol. Jan.–June, p. 217) contains the following notice of the place :—

"This [is a] view (see opposite page) of a house erected in Dublin for the use of the Dublin Society and the Company for carrying on the Inland Navigation from our city to the river Shannon, commonly called the Grand Canal Company. . . . This edifice stands upon the ground formerly occupied by the late Earl of Mornington in Grafton street, opposite the house of the Provost of Trinity College. The building [on the left] is that which appertains to the Dublin Society, whose room upon the second floor from the street is about 40 feet long, and 20 wide, and near 20 feet high ; fitted up all round with three sets of mahogany glasses rising one above the other ; a handsome gilt and ornamented chair for the presiding member ;[2] decorated with an elegant fretted stucco ceiling, and accommodated with two fireplaces, with chimneypieces of Irish marble. On each side of these fireplaces is a large white marble bust of one of the original promoters[3] of the Society, which was instituted for the encouragement of agriculture and useful arts, and whereof the President and Vice-President of the London Society for Encouragement of Arts are standing honorary members. Over the

---

[1] Christopher Myers was architect of Trinity College Chapel, and a man eminent in his profession. He was father of Lieut.-Col. Myers, a distinguished officer, who was created a baronet, and died at Myersville, now Wynberg, in 1789.

[2] This chair, which is still in use, was designed by James Mannin, master of the school for ornamental drawing, and carved in 1767, by Richard Cranfield. (*Dict. Irish Artists*, W. G. Strickland, i. 219.)

[3] These were Prior and Madden. The busts were executed in 1751 by John Van Nost.

PRESIDENT'S CHAIR, 1767

meeting room is a library and repository for mechanical models, save those relative to husbandry, which are deposited in another place belonging to the Society.

"The rest of the building consists of the necessary offices and the apartments of the Assistant Secretary. Behind the house are the Society's drawing schools, where children of indigent persons are educated in the arts of drawing, in architecture, ornament, and the human figure.

"The other building [on the right] appertained to the Canal Company, but now belongs to the newly established Royal Irish Society [The Royal Irish Academy], and is similar in design to the Dublin Society's House; but the meeting room is not finished with equal elegance, although of the same dimensions."

£2200 were paid in the first instance to Myers, and a sum of £375, 16s. 2d. additional was voted for the new academies for drawing. Another room (for casts from the antique and busts), to adjoin the schools and to be over a stable which was to be built in the rear (the gateway and passage leading to which still exist), was to be provided. On the site of the house itself have since been erected the houses now known as Nos. 112 and 113 Grafton street. In the early part of 1781, a warehouse in Poolbeg street, with its appurtenances, which belonged to the Trustees of the Linen Manufacture, was lent to the Society (on condition of the ground rent being paid), as a temporary repository for implements of husbandry brought from England, for which a sum of £273, 17s. 2d. was paid, it being the intention of the Society to supply them to the public. The Linen Trustees' interest in the premises was subsequently vested in the Dublin Society by the Act 21 and 22 Geo. III, c. 35, and in connection with this, the Right Hon. John Foster reported that he had engaged (as he had been requested), Thomas Dawson, an English farmer, to come over, at a salary

of £70 a year, to instruct such as might desire to improve the mode of agriculture in the kingdom.   Public
notices were printed in *Faulkner's Journal* and *Saunders's
News-Letter*, that persons anxious for instruction should
apply to the Assistant Secretary of the Society, who
would arrange the times for Dawson's attendance—12s.
per week to be paid for each week of his engagement,
together with his expenses.

It became necessary to extend the Poolbeg street
concerns, and a favourable opportunity presented itself
when Mr. Edward Laurence, in consideration of a
sum of £800, sold his interest in some ground and
houses adjoining, for which rent was paid to Mr.
William Morris.   In 1786, a further extension became
desirable, and a portion of ground opening into
Hawkins street, with another portion opening into
Poolbeg street, which had buildings erected on it, was
taken from Mr. Thomas Acton.   A fine of £885 was
paid, and a small terminable rent incurred, while a
sum of £2700 was expended on the new buildings and
the works which were being carried out there.   Soon it
was found that the work of the Factory would be
furthered by the addition of a house and piece of
ground on the north side of Poolbeg street in possession of Mr. William Chapman, of which the Society
decided to take a lease, paying £250 for his interest.
In January 1788, the new premises being in a forward
state, Mr. Peter de Gree was directed to execute an
emblematical painting for the Society's meeting room
in Hawkins street, which, when finished, was highly
approved.   This painting is in monochrome, and still
hangs on the Society's walls in Leinster House.

It now appeared that the purpose for which the
Factory in Poolbeg street and Hawkins street was
originally intended had been answered by the exten-

sive sale of implements of husbandry, so the Society resolved to give up the Factory business, and the buildings erected for it were to be devoted to the following purposes :—As a repository for every implement of husbandry, and for the reception of the Society's books on husbandry, natural history, and mechanics ; also for specimens of minerals, fossils, &c. Next, as a place for receiving such implements of husbandry and machines as any craftsman might send for sale, which were to be sold for the owners by the superintendent. Mr. John Brien, registrar and collector, was to reside on the premises, to regulate delivery of goods ; to keep the books, &c., and to see that the apartments were in order, for which he was to have a salary of £30 a year, with allowances. A room was fitted up for a model maker, who was to repair and keep in order the models, and who was also to make new ones when directed. In 1784, the premises in Poolbeg street had been insured for £2000, and the Grafton street house, furniture, &c., together with the drawing schools in the rear, for £2500.

It now became the practice, instead of bestowing money premiums, to deliver implements of husbandry from the Factory in Poolbeg street to prize winners, in value up to the amount awarded them. When the repository became ready for the reception of implements, a form of advertisement for the newspapers was drawn up. The institution was intended not only to facilitate sales of useful machines, but also to give ingenious workmen an opportunity of making themselves known, and to bring into competition the various productions of agricultural artisans in the kingdom. In 1795, Sir John Sinclair, on behalf of the Board of Agriculture, London, offered to have anyone deputed by the Dublin Society instructed *gratis*

by the celebrated Mr. Elkington in the art of draining
land. The committee did not, however, then send
anyone, in view of the likelihood of Elkingtcn's
coming here himself, which he afterwards did.

In March 1796, the Society notified its intention of
giving up the Grafton street premises, and advertisements for proposals for their purchase were to be inserted in the daily papers. The offer of James Blacker,
Parliament street, and Ambrose Moore, Dame street,
to purchase them for £3000 fine and payment of the
ground rent was accepted. From the 11th of August
in that year the Society met at the repository, Hawkins
street, whither also the drawing schools were moved.
The two chimneypieces which stood in the meeting
room in Grafton street were taken down and put up
in the new premises. They were not found among
the débris after the fire at the Theatre Royal, which
at a later period occupied the Hawkins street site.

In 1800, at an extraordinary meeting of the Society,
the Wide Street Commissioners were requested to
complete the purchase of all the ground and houses
on the east side of Hawkins street, and in Poolbeg
street, lately valued, as the Society proposed to become
tenants of these, together with the premises in their
possession held under the Bishop of Raphoe. It was
proposed to assign the leases to the Commissioners,
the Society taking one lease of the whole in perpetuity,
at a rent of £391, 7s. 6d. The Society also requested
a valuation of ground on the south side of their
holdings at the rear of Townsend street. All this was
effected, and the Society had then at its command,
for carrying out its objects, extensive premises in a
very central part of the city, while still further accommodation was found in the Fleet Market (Hawkins
street), where in 1802 premises were purchased. From

a report of the Committee of Economy, dated 11th of August 1803, it appeared that works unfinished in Hawkins Street would cost £571, 1s. 5d. In the class of works not begun, but estimated for to Parliament, the drawing school estimate amounted to £1667, and that for the gallery to £1145, 10s.

The Building Committee advertised in 1813 for tenders for the erection of a library, board-room, &c., and for a proper entrance at the south front of the Hawkins street house. The master of the architectural school prepared a ground plan and elevation, and £2000 were reserved for these works, while in the next year another sum of £2000 was reserved for the same purpose. At the same time, a sum of over £1100 was voted for completing the exhibition room. Soon, however, the Kildare street premises came into the market, and were purchased by the Society, which met in Hawkins street for the last time on the 25th of May 1815.

The theatre and connected buildings fronting Poolbeg street were at this time held under a renewable lease from Margaret Hawkins, representative of William Hawkins, at a rent of ten guineas a year, and the remainder of the premises under a renewable lease made to the Society by the Wide Street Commissioners, at a rent of £600 a year, which was then vested in Trinity College. The Society for the Suppression of Mendicity had occupied portion of the premises for a time, for the purposes of that institution, paying £300 a year rent, and mendicants were accommodated there. In 1819, the Guild of Merchants agreed to purchase the laboratory lot for £900, but afterwards declined to carry out its agreement. It was decided that the proceeds of any sale of the Hawkins street premises should be devoted to completing the buildings and necessary accommodation in Kildare street, but, as will be seen, nothing was derived from their disposal. In August 1820, Henry Harris, lessee of the Theatre Royal, made a proposal. Considering the expense he would be put to in converting the place into a theatre, he found that he could not afford to pay any purchase money, but was willing to take an assignment at a rent of £610 a year, to which the premises were subject. This offer was accepted, and the Society freed itself from further liability with regard to a place that was ill contrived, and which, from damp, was not suited for the purposes of the Society, which expended a vast sum in trying to make the premises meet all requirements. On the disposal of the place to Harris, a bill was filed in Chancery on the 18th of August 1820, by the Society of Irish Artists against the Dublin Society and Henry Harris, for an injunction, restraining them, as the exhibition room was in use for exhibiting their works. The plaintiffs in the suit were Thomas C. Thompson, Charles Robinson, T. J. Mulvany, William B. Taylor, Joseph Peacock, John Banim, and William Mossop, but it does not appear to have come to anything.

Some account of the Hawkins street premises at the time of their being given up has been preserved,[1] from which it appears that the front and sides of the completed buildings of the Society included a quadrangular area, 97 feet in length. The façade to Hawkins street was of hewn granite, with a centre and two wings, each of two stories, with Doric pilasters, without bases, and the centre ended in an attic story above the entablature. The door was of the Doric order, and in a niche above was a figure of Minerva, with a cornucopia; on the shield at her feet was an

---

[1] Whitelaw and Walsh's *History of Dublin*, ii. 957.

DUBLIN SOCIETY HOUSE

DUBLIN SOCIETY'S HOUSE, HAWKINS STREET (WEST FRONT), 1801

Irish harp, with the motto, *Nostri plena laboris.*[1] In the interior was a broad room, 39 by 25 feet, lofty, well-lighted, and richly ornamented, with a square lantern. There were two spacious apartments for the Leskean museum and the gallery for Irish specimens. Then a noble and well-proportioned gallery, 90 by 30 feet, well lighted by three elegant lanterns, round which were disposed the Society's busts and statues, the group of Laocoon ending the vista. Off this were the drawing schools. The library occupied three rooms. The exhibition room was lofty and spacious, the light being so disposed from the roof as to display the paintings to the best effect, and, next to the Louvre, it was considered the finest of its kind in Europe. In the rear of the quadrangular court were the chemical laboratory and the lecture-room, around which was a gallery with seating accommodation for eight hundred people.

It had been suggested that a new front might be erected on the south side of the building, to correspond with Trinity College, as the origin of a fine square, into which eight streets would lead, and in the centre of which might be erected the Wellington trophy.[2] The Society's house would then not only have been near the most central but also the most ornamental part of the metropolis. It was said that a sum of over £60,000 had been expended on the Hawkins street buildings, and the account concludes

---

[1] When the Theatre Royal was burned, almost the only part left standing was the stone façade, which had been erected by the Dublin Society. The figure of Minerva (or Hibernia), by E. Smyth, which occupied a niche over the entrance, was removed, and placed on the old gateway of Leinster House. It is now in the colonnade, outside the door of the theatre.

[2] There was some idea of erecting the trophy in commemoration of Wellington's victories in the open space where the Crampton memorial now stands.

G

as follows :—" This large edifice is now abandoned, its collections removed to an inconvenient distance, and crowded into ill-adapted rooms. The Society, having expended vast sums to render one house unfit for any other purpose, have purchased another which no money will render suitable—a splendid edifice well calculated for the mansion house of the Lord Mayor, but ill-adapted indeed for the residence of science and philosophy."

LEINSTER HOUSE

In ancient times portion of Kildare street and Kildare place, together with part of St. Stephen's Green, formed what was known as the Mensons' or Mynchens' fields, which were the property of the Nunnery of St. Mary del Hogges, founded for elderly nuns of the better classes, known as Mynchens.[1] The district, at the beginning of the eighteenth century, was called the Molesworth fields, having been acquired by that family, to which belonged Robert, John, and Richard, first, second, and third Viscounts Molesworth; the first distinguished by his writings in defence of liberty, the second as a successful ambassador, and the third as a warrior who served in all the campaigns in Flanders. An Act of Parliament, passed in 1725, enabled the Molesworth family to make leases of certain portions unbuilt on, including the site of Kildare House—the present Leinster House.

Soon after succeeding to the title in 1744, James FitzGerald, twentieth Earl of Kildare, decided on erecting a town house on this part of the Molesworth fields, which he had purchased from the third Lord Molesworth for £1000. He commissioned Richard

---

[1] *Minch*, a nun. The nunnery at Littlemore is still called the Minchery.

Castle, the eminent architect, to furnish plans, and the foundation stone of Lord Kildare's new mansion was laid in 1745, inscribed as follows :—

DOMUM
CUJUS HIC LAPIS FUNDAMEN
IN AGRO MOLESWORTHIANA
EXTRUI CURAVIT
JACOBUS
COMES KILDARIAE VICESIMUS
ANNO DOMINI MDCCXXXXV
HINC DISCAS,
QUICUNQUE TEMPORUM INFORTUNIO
IN RUINAS TAM MAGNIFICAE DOMUS
INCIDERIS,
QUANTUS ILLE FUIT, QUI EXTRUXIT
QUAMQUE CADUCA SINT OMNIA
CUM TALIA TALIUM VIRORUM
MONUMENTA
CASIBUS SUPERESSE NON VALEANT

RICHARDO CASTELLO, ARCH.[1]

The site of his new house was supposed to lie far from the fashionable quarter of Dublin, but to one who suggested this to him, Kildare replied that the fashion would follow in whatever direction he led. Time amply justified his prophecy, as within a few years the immediate neighbourhood began to be extensively built over. Lord Kildare married, in 1746, Lady Emily Lennox, sister of the then Duke of Richmond, a celebrated beauty, by whom he had seven-

[1] The house, of which this stone is the foundation, James, twentieth Earl of Kildare, caused to be erected in the Molesworth field, in the year of our Lord 1745. Hence learn, when in some unhappy time you chance on the ruins of so magnificent a house, how great was he who erected it, and how perishable are all things, when such monuments of such men cannot survive adversity. Richard Castle, architect.

teen children, of whom the fifth son was Lord Edward FitzGerald, the noble-hearted and ill-fated enthusiast who sacrificed his life for his patriotic principles. Lord Kildare was a resident nobleman, and spent his time between Dublin, where he took his full share in the House of Lords' debates and work, and his country seat of Carton, which he greatly improved and enlarged. He took an independent tone in opposing Ministers on the Money Bill in 1753, and acquired great popularity on the occasion by his public-spirited conduct. In 1761, Kildare obtained a step in the peerage by being created Marquis of Kildare, and in 1766 he became Duke of Leinster, by which name what was originally called Kildare House has since been known. The Duke died in 1773, at the comparatively early age of fifty-one, and lies buried in Christ Church Cathedral.

A narrow lane connected St. Stephen's Green with the present Nassau street; this was called Coote street, a name which was changed to Kildare street on Kildare House being erected, when the lane was also widened. The house was approached through a grand gateway of rustic masonry, leading to a spacious court.

Though the account of Leinster House, written by James Malton in 1794, has been given at length by Gilbert in his *History of Dublin* (iii. 282), and by Mr. T. U. Sadleir, in his article on the mansion, in the *Records of the Georgian Society* (iv. 57), to which this chapter owes much, it seems quite impossible to omit it here, so comprehensive and descriptive is the account, although it be not written in classic English :—

" Leinster House, the town residence of His Grace the Duke of Leinster, is the most stately private edifice in the city. Pleasantly situated at the south-east extremity of the town, commanding prospects few

CONVERSATION ROOM, LEINSTER HOUSE

places can exhibit, and possessing advantages few city
fabrics can obtain by extent of ground both in front
and rear; in front, laid out in a spacious courtyard;
the ground in the rear made a beautiful lawn, with a
handsome shrubbery on each side screening the adjacent houses from view; enjoying in the tumult of a
noisy metropolis all the retirement of the country.   A
dwarf wall which divides the lawn from the street
extends almost the entire side of a handsome square,
called Merrion square.   The form of the building is a
rectangle, 140 feet long by 70 feet deep, with a circular bow in the middle of the north end, rising two
stories.   Adjoining the west front, which is the
principal, are short Doric colonnades communicating
to the offices, making on the whole an extent of 210
feet, the width of the courtyard.   The court is sur-
rounded by a high stone wall ornamented with rusticated piers, which, after proceeding parallel with the
ends of the building as far as a gateway on the western
side and another opposite it, the court being uniform,
it takes a circular sweep from one gate to the other, but
broken in the middle by a large and handsome gateway
directly fronting the house, communicating to the
street, and exhibits there a plain but not inelegant
rusticated front.   The house, or rather the gateway
of the courtyard, is in Kildare street—so named from
one of the titles of His Grace, who is Marquis of
Kildare—and is the termination of a broad, genteel
street called Molesworth street.   The garden front
has not much architectural embellishment: it is plain
but pleasing, with a broad area before it the whole
length of the front, in order to obtain light to offices
in an under story, but which received none to the
west, to the courtyard.   From the middle of the
front, on a level with the ground floor, a handsome

double flight of steps extends across the area to the lawn. The greater part of the building is of native stone (quarried at Ardbraccan, in the county of Meath), but the west front, and all the ornamental parts throughout, are of Portland. South of the building are commodious offices and stables. The inside of this mansion in every respect corresponds with the grandeur of its external appearance. The hall is lofty, rising two stories, ornamented with three-quarter columns of the Doric Order, and an enriched entablature; the ceiling is adorned with stucco ornaments on coloured grounds; and the whole is embellished with many rich and tasty ornaments. To the right of the hall are the family apartments; the whole convenient, beautifully ornamented, and elegantly furnished. Overlooking the lawn is the great dining parlour,[1] and adjoining it, at the north end, is an elegant long room,[2] the whole depth of the house, 24 feet wide, called the supper room, adorned with sixteen fluted Ionic columns supporting a rich ceiling. Over the supper room is the picture gallery,[3] of the same dimensions, containing many fine paintings by the first masters, with other ornaments chosen and displayed with great elegance. The ceiling is arched and highly enriched, and painted with designs by Mr. Wyatt. The most distinguished pictures are — a Student drawing from a bust, by Rembrandt;[4] "The Rape of Europa," by Claude Lorraine; the "Triumph of Amphitrite," by Luca Giordano; two capital pictures by Rubens, and two wives by Van Dyck; dogs killing a stag; a fine picture of St. Catherine; a landscape, by Barret; with many others.

---

[1] Now the council-room.   [2] Now the conversation-room.
[3] For a number of years used as the Society's library. Now the reception-room.
[4] This is a mistake: the picture is not one of Rembrandt's.

COUNCIL ROOM, LEINSTER HOUSE

"In the bow, in the middle of one side, is a fine
marble statue; an Adonis, executed by Poncet [now
in the National Gallery of Ireland]; a fine bust of
Niobe, and of Apollo, placed one on each side. In
the windows of the bow are some specimens of
modern stained glass by Jervis [Thomas Jarvis].

"Several of the apartments on this floor are enriched with superb gildings, and elegantly furnished
with white damask. From the windows of the attic
story to the east are most delightful prospects over
the Bay of Dublin, which, for three miles, is divided
by that great work, the South Wall, with a beautiful
lighthouse at the termination. The sea, for a considerable extent bounds the horizon, and every vessel
coming in and going out of the bay must pass in distinct view. To the left is seen the beautiful pro-
montory of Howth, the charming low grounds of
Marino, and Sheds of Clontarf; to the right the
pleasing village and seats of the Black Rock, the remote grounds and hills of Dalkey, and the Sugar
Loaves, backed by the extensive mountains of Wicklow
which most picturesquely close the view. The finishing of the picture gallery, and making several improvements at the north end of the house, were reserved to
display the taste of the present possessor, William
Robert, Duke of Leinster, whose excellent judgment
therein is eminently conspicuous, as well as in many
other instances, at His Grace's country residence, at
Carton, near Dublin; and all evince his patriotism
and refined enjoyment of a domestic life."

It has been stated that Leinster House served as
a model for the White House at Washington, the
official residence of the President of the United States.[1]

[1] It was designed by James Hoban, an Irish architect, who
settled at Charleston, U.S.A. See *Century Magazine*, 1884, p. 803.

One of the finest features in the interior is the hall, which is unusually lofty and well proportioned, and forms a stately entrance to what was the largest and most magnificent of the town houses of our Irish nobility. The ceiling is beautifully decorated, and the first floor is reached from an inner hall by a flight of white stone stairs which branch into two divisions from a landing. The mantelpieces in the dining-room and drawing-rooms were removed to Carton. Those that remain are beautiful, the mantelpiece and the grate in the small hall leading to the lawn entrance being considered specially worthy of notice. The registrar's office, formerly the study, has a splendid mantelpiece, and is a well proportioned, highly orna-mented apartment.

It was concerning the acquisition of this palace, that, on the 14th of November 1814, a committee of the Royal Dublin Society sat to deliberate. It consisted of the Right Hon. John Claudius Beresford, Jeremiah D'Olier, P. Digges La Touche, John L. Foster, Henry Arabin, Nicholas P. Leader, John Pomeroy, and Richard Verschoyle; who found that the premises would be disposed of for £10,000, and a yearly rent of £600, or they would be sold rent free for £20,000. It was thought at this time that part of the ground might advantageously be let for building, and that the Society would obtain a good price for the concerns in Hawkins street. The former suggestion was never carried out, and in the latter expectation the Society was grievously disappointed. An agreement was entered into with Augustus Frederick, fourth Duke of Leinster, for the sale of his interest for £10,000, with £600 yearly rent, which was ratified by the Society on the 14th of December 1814, it having previously been submitted to the Government. On the 19th of January 1815, it

appeared that £5000 had been paid to the Duke, and possession had been delivered to Mr. Wilson on behalf of the Society. The premises and ground on which stood that part of Kildare street and Leinster street that led from Leinster House to the house of Mr. Hamilton Rowan in Leinster street, were held under a fee farm lease from the Molesworth family, subject to £150 a year. Some of the ground which had been built on was held under leases from the Duke, which produced £64 a year above the head rent, and it was thought advantageous to purchase this profit rent from his Grace for a sum of £1000.

A select committee, of which Francis Johnston, Alderman Thorp, and Mr. Gandon were members, was appointed to decide on necessary alterations in the house, and Mr. Baker, master of the architectural school, was engaged to superintend repairs and alterations. The premises were insured up to £20,000. The committee recommended that the picture gallery should be used as the library, and that six rooms on the first floor should be assigned to the department of natural history. On the ground floor, the ball-room was to be the bust-room; the dining-room the board-room; and other rooms were assigned for newspapers, the secretary's office, as well as committee and house-keeper's rooms. It was finally arranged, however, that on the ground floor, No. 1 in a certain plan was to be the board-room; 2, conversation-room; 3, ante-room; 4, secretary's office and committee room; 5, housekeeper's room; 6 and 7, model rooms. On the first floor, the gallery was to be the library, and rooms nos. 2 to 7, museums. Up to £600 was to be spent on the house and concerns, and enquiries were set on foot as to the best mode of erecting a laboratory and theatre, with apparatus rooms

for the professors.   A gallery for busts, with school
and modelling rooms adjacent, and a gallery for exhibition of pictures, were also necessary.   It was suggested that the out-building called the kitchen might
be converted into a laboratory and theatre, and that the
other buildings might be placed adjacent, with entrances
from the house, and outside entrances for the public
by the colonnade.   The lawn in the rear was unoccupied,
and Lord Fitzwilliam leased it to the Society at £300
a year.   The Merrion square boundary of the lawn
was a sunk fence, and in 1834–5, £200 were expended
in lowering the parapet wall and erecting an iron
railing, which protected the fence from being a re-
ceptacle for nuisances.

The last meeting of the Society in Hawkins street
was held on the 25th of May 1815, though the committees still continued to meet there; and it met for
the first time in Leinster House on the 1st of June
1815, Lord Frankfort de Montmorency in the chair,
and a large number of members attending.   A marble
bust of himself was offered to the Right Hon. J. C.
Beresford, lord mayor, for his successful exertions in
the removal of the Society from Hawkins street to
Kildare street, but his lordship declined the honour.

A sum of £4000 was to be set apart to complete
the necessary accommodation in Leinster House, and
a further sum of £2000 was voted.

Having now a proper site on which to erect it,
and in consideration of King George the Second having
granted to the Society its charter, the Corporation, in
November 1815, was requested to consent to the
removal of the statue of that monarch from St.
Stephen's Green to Kildare street, but the Commissioners of the Green declined to acquiesce in the
proposal.

THE RECEPTION ROOM, LEINSTER HOUSE

Up to the 30th of May 1816, the following amounts were expended on the house and new buildings:

Repairs	.	.	.	£2536	16	7
Furniture	.	.	.	524	6	0
New buildings	.	.	3040	8	4
Superintendent	.	.	104	13	0
				£6206	3	11

In 1819, a resolution was passed that all sums received on the admission of members were to be invested in Government stock, so as to create a fund for fining down the rent due to the Duke of Leinster, which was finally extinguished long before the premises became Crown property. In July 1835, £1200 were allocated out of this admission fee fund towards the construction of an exhibition room. Representations were made to the Chancellor of the Exchequer as to the success of the exhibition of manufactures held on the Society's premises during the last two years, and the want of proper accommodation both in reference to the convenience of the public, and the satisfactory placing of exhibits. It was hoped that the Government might grant a similar sum, an expectation which does not appear to have been realised.

CHAPTER VII

THE DRAWING SCHOOLS

THE precise period at which the original drawing school of the Society was opened is not now known, as the volume of minutes in which it would have been recorded is not forthcoming, but it may probably be assigned to the years 1742–46.

Mr. Prior laid before Lord Chesterfield, in 1746, a report on the Society's work in the field of fine arts, and submitted a plan for an academy.

On the 12th of March 1748, the Society communicated to the press a statement, that on the competition for the Madden premium of £15 for the best drawing by boys or girls under sixteen years of age, eighteen candidates attended, who produced drawings, which were hung, numbered, round two large rooms in the Parliament House. The boys were directed to sit round two tables, on which were placed busts, which they were directed to draw before the Society; this task they readily performed in an hour's time. Most of the drawings were excellent, and the candidates placed in the first rank got two guineas, and those in the second one guinea. On the 5th of November, a similar plan was adopted, when the newspapers reported that "as this day's entertainment had all the appearance of a foreign academy for drawing, it is hoped it will lay the foundation of establishing such an academy among ourselves."

Eight boys who obtained premiums for drawing in 1747 were pupils of Mr. Robert West's academy, in George's lane. In 1749, it was announced that the Madden premiums for drawing were secured principally by his pupils. The Society had already arranged for his instructing a certain number under its auspices, eventually taking over the school itself. West, who was born in Waterford, had studied under Boucher and Vanloo on the continent. On the 27th of May, on adjudication of the Madden premiums, twenty-eight boys presented themselves and produced specimens. They had been employed for two months in drawing from the round copies of bustoes, group figures, as well as subjects from the life, "a lusty naked man" being placed on the middle of a large table, when the boys were placed on seats all round so as to draw the figure in different attitudes. £16 were distributed in sums varying from 2s. 6d. to one guinea. "They improve every day in their skill, and it is hoped that several good geniuses for drawing will in time appear, much to the credit of this little academy, who perform so well beyond all expectations." On the adjudication in February 1750, thirty candidates appeared, when the boys were directed to draw "the face of a remarkable man, Hugh Roberts, which most of them did off-hand very well."

From the year 1750, a good deal of attention was paid to the drawing school, as it will have been seen that the Society was determined to cultivate this art among the young people of the city to the utmost of its power. In May of that year, there is a note that Van Nost, the sculptor, had taken as apprentice Patrick Cunningham, who received his earliest instruction under the auspices of the Society, for which he subsequently executed several commissions. Such is the first notice of this Irish sculptor who attained to considerable eminence in his art. Before November 1750, the Society had provided an academy for drawing in Shaw's court, which laid the foundation of a School of Art that reflected much honour on it, and which produced so many artists who attained distinction in sculpture, portrait and landscape painting.

In 1752, the following distinguished artists are found adjudicating on the competitions, in which they showed much interest—Bindon, Lee, Drury, and Van Nost. On this occasion James Forester took first place, and in the following year, John Dixon was first, when Patrick Cunningham was also among the competitors. Pue's *Occurrences* of the 7th of August 1753 remarked that the art of drawing had within a few years (by the encouragement of the Dublin Society) made great progress in the city, "so that we may hope to see most of the great men who have been ornaments of their country immortalised in the works of our young artists." Pue's *Occurrences*, on the 26th of January 1754, called attention to its work in this direction, and speaks of "that patriot body, the Dublin Society, whose labours were attended with even more than the wished-for success, which is every day apparent in their academy for drawing founded in Shaw's court, Dame street, under the direction and care of that ingenious gentleman and useful member of society, Mr. West." Again, in February, attention was called to a great variety of handsome drawings which were produced to the Dublin Society by boys under sixteen, among which was a beautiful head of the Duchess of Cleveland in crayons. They also produced several modellings in clay, one of which was a bust of George, Prince of Wales, by Mr. Van Nost's sister; and a whole-length figure from life, in plaster of Paris, of

Master Cox, son to the Archbisbop of Cashel, by one of Mr. Van Nost's apprentices; "from which it is evident how great a progress the Polite Arts are making in this Kingdom, to the immortal honour of that patriot body, the Dublin Society, who have been their chief encouragers."

Agreements were concluded with persons who consented to act as models for the boys, and the Madden premium for 1754 (£15) was bestowed on Patrick Cunningham for a group in white marble, of boys playing with a basket of flowers. Cranfield, of Cope street, won the Madden prize of 1755, for two *basso relievos*—a *Sleeping Beauty* and a small landscape with beasts. In 1756, Mr. Mannin agreed, for £25 a year, to teach the art of drawing foliage, &c., for two years, to two boys who were to be recommended by the Society.

When the Society entered on their new premises in Shaw's court (p. 88), in 1757, four rooms were assigned to Mr. West, and one room to Mr. Mannin (a Frenchman), the drawing masters, and the stable at the back was fitted up in October 1758, so that the boys might use it as a drawing academy. It was also used for keeping the collection of plaster busts and casts which was being formed by the Society. Lord Duncannon, who was abroad, had interested himself in procuring some of them that were required. A sum, not to exceed £20, was to be allowed for a living model, who was to sit twice a week for a year. At this period, Robert West had charge of the figure drawing. Thomas Ivory, who was responsible for the design of the Blue Coat Hospital, Dublin,[1] taught architectural

---

[1] His designs for it were of exceptional excellence, both from an artistic and technical point of view, but it was found too costly to carry them fully out. They are now in the British Museum. Another

drawing : and the pupils were instructed in ornament by James Mannin. The *Recollections* of John O'Keefe, the dramatist, who studied in the school, contains a vivid picture of the drawing academy. He says that it was frequently visited by members of the Society, the Lord Lieutenant, and some of the nobility. In his day, the students' text-book was the *Preceptor*, by Robert Dodsley, published in 1748.

Joseph Fenn, described as Professor in Nantes University, brought before the Society in 1764 a plan of instruction for the schools, which was approved by it four years later. It will be found embodied in his work entitled *Instructions given in the Drawing School established by the Dublin Society* . . . 1768. Mr. W. G. Strickland, in his *Dictionary of Irish Artists*, ii. 583, gives an interesting account of the Fenn episode, and remarks that his ambitious and varied programme seems never to have been carried out, or even attempted.

Joseph Wilton, sculptor, of Charing Cross, London, wrote in June 1757, that several cases of busts, &c., which had cost £219, 15s., had been packed and put on board vessels for transit to the Society. John Crawley, one of Van Nost's apprentices, and a Madden prizeman, petitioned to be sent abroad, and £80 were agreed to be paid by instalments to Dr. Pococke, the bishop of Ossory, with a view to Crawley's receiving instruction on the continent. In May 1761, Matthew William Peters, another pupil, asked for £30, to be expended on his being sent to Italy, for his improvement in the art of painting.

fine work of Ivory, was Newcomen House, opposite the Upper Castle gate, now used as offices by the Corporation of Dublin. Ivory had been master of the architectural drawing school from 1759, and died in 1786.

Peters returned to Dublin in 1766.   Patrick Cunningham was paid for moulding and casting figures of
a *Roman Slave*, a *Venus*, and a *Dolphin*, and in 1760,
ten guineas for a statue of King George.   To enable
him to carry on business as a statuary, £20 were
granted to him, on bond.   The following advertisement appeared in Faulkner's *Journal*, at the time of
his setting up business in July 1758: "Patrick Cunningham, apprentice to Van Nost, by agreement with
the Dublin Society, opens a yard and shop for statuary
in William street.   As he is the first native that has
been bred to that business, he humbly hopes for the
favour of the public."   The year after, he was granted
£30 by the Society to purchase at Van Nost's auction
such moulds and models as might be useful in his
business.

Late in 1767, or very early in 1768, the Society
having moved to their new premises in Grafton street,
the drawing schools were accommodated in the back
of the house, the gateway and entrance to which still
remain (see p. 91).   Here they were situated until
1796, when the Society moved to Poolbeg street.

In the early part of the year 1767, the question of
the continuance of the school for figure drawing was
raised, and, on a full discussion of the matter, the
opinion of the following artists was invited—Messrs.
Bertrand, Carver, Collins, Ennis, Fisher, Hunter,
Reiley and Sheehan, as also Richard Cranfield, carver,
Simon Vierpyle,[1] carver in statuary, James Madden,
seal cutter, Nathaniel Murray, engraver, and James

[1] Vierpyle was probably of Dutch origin.   He was brought over
from Italy by Lord Charlemont for work at his mansion of Marino,
Clontarf, specially for the Casino there.   He copied in *terra cotta*
a large number of busts of Roman Emperors, &c., at the Capitol and
in the Vatican, which in 1868 were presented by the last Earl of
Charlemont to the Royal Irish Academy.

H

Wilder, landscape painter. At a very large meeting held on the 5th of March, the motion as to its being suppressed was negatived. £5 were voted in payment for the following books ordered for the use of the scholars attending Mr. Thomas Ivory's classes in the architectural school—Gibb's *Architecture;* Loudon's *Art of Building;* Hopper's *Architecture;* Halfpenny's *Builder's Assistant;* Price's *British Carpenter; Jesuits' Perspective.*

On the 7th of May, the Madden premiums were awarded as follows—10 guineas to George Mullins for the best original landscape in oils; 5 guineas to James Mannin for the next best; and 10 guineas to Mary Hunter, for the best original full-length portrait in oils, life size. A silver medal was granted to the Rev. Mr. Campbell, author of a pamphlet entitled *Essay on Perfecting the Fine Arts in Great Britain and Ireland,* which was inscribed to the Dublin Society. In March 1769, Van Nost represented that a poor country boy named William Graham, aged sixteen years, who was his apprentice, displayed great genius in sculpture and the fine arts, when £10 were granted for his maintenance and clothing. In 1770, Graham exhibited a bas-relief in marble, but nothing is known of his subsequent career.

In November 1780, the Duke of Leinster laid before the Society a certificate signed by the following artists, namely: Hugh D. Hamilton, Richard Cranfield, William Ashford, Charles Robertson, and Walter Robertson, adjudging silver medals to the undernamed boys, whose works were of great merit:—landscape—1, William Hartwell; 2, John Mannin; 3, John Lacam; ornament—1, Chr. Connor; 2, William Dartis; 3, William Gumley. Premiums for figure drawing were awarded to—1, Peter Hoey; 2, Henry Stoker (from the round); 3, Matthew Hunter (from the flat); ornament drawing—William Hartwell; landscape—Robert Connor; ornament—John McCready. Drawing in architecture—Robert Connor, plans and elevations; Hoban, stairs, roof, &c.; William Guinness, practical geometry. With regard to these and many other pupils mentioned in this chapter, it must not be supposed that all became artists, as a large number of them, on leaving the schools, entered on business careers or became artisans. Colonel Burton, Mr. Caldwell, Alexander Montgomery, Captain Burgh, the Bishop of Killaloe, Mr. Braughall, Morgan Crofton, Messrs. Ford, Wallis, Trant, Ladaveze, and Major Waring were appointed members of a committee to superintend the Society's drawing schools for one year.

In 1781, Frederick Prussia Plowman, who had been educated in the Society's drawing schools, laid before it several copies of paintings executed by him under the inspection of Sir Joshua Reynolds, which were highly approved. The Society subscribed two guineas for a cast of the statue of *Hercules*, to be executed by James Hoskins, Westminster, for the use of the schools.

In November 1782, the silver medals in the art schools were awarded as follows:—Matthew Hunter, portraits from nature; John Mulvany, drawings from the round; John O'Keely, drawings from the flat; Martin Shee and John Mulvany were specially recommended for landscape drawings. John Babington was declared entitled to a medal for ornament drawing; Henry Seguin won that for plans and elevations. In 1783, Martin Shee won the medal for portrait painting. In November 1786, the progress of the drawing schools appears to have given much satisfaction to the superintending committee. Several drawings from life, executed by Martin Shee, portrait painter, who resided in Dame street, and who had received his art education in the schools, under Robert L. West, were laid before the Society, when a silver palette, with suitable inscription, was presented to him, in testimony of its approbation. Shee, afterwards Sir Martin Archer Shee, and President of the Royal Academy, was born in Dublin. In 1788, he went to London, where he had a number of sitters drawn from the best classes, and, being a man of considerable culture, he had access to the most cultivated society in the capital. Shee published some poems, and to his work as painter and poet, Byron alludes in *English Bards and Scotch Reviewers*—

> " And here let Shee and Genius find a place
> Whose pen and pencil yield an equal grace."

Shee's *Life* was written by his son.

A figure taken from a book entitled *The Sorrows of Werter*, finished in the new stipple engraving, executed by Henry Seguin, who had received his art education in the Society's school, was laid before it, and greatly commended. In May 1785, this artist requested that the Society should subscribe to a work in preparation, entitled *The School of Fencing*, which was to contain fifty folio copperplates, the engravings to be executed by him. To encourage so promising an artist, and to excite emulation in the schools, his request was acceded to, but the work does not seem to have been published. Soon after, a sum of £7, 3*s.* was paid to Michael Angelo Pergolesi for publications of ornamental designs in the Etruscan and grotesque style, for the use of the schools.

The architectural school sustained a great loss in December 1786 by the death of Thomas Ivory, who had for so many years successfully conducted it. Henry Aaron Baker was appointed to succeed him.

As it is of interest to learn the titles of text-books in use at this time, it may be noted that the following were ordered to be purchased for the architectural drawing school, viz. Gibb's *Rules of Architecture*, Sir William Chambers' *Treatise on Architecture*, Palladio's *Works*, Richardson's *Ceilings* and *Chimney-Pieces*. Two marble figures, a *Venus de Medici* and a *Dancing Faun*, were presented by Joseph Henry, Esqr. At this time, the Society was in possession of the following statues and busts—*The Listener*, *Boxers*, *Venus aux belles fesses*, *Alexander's Head*, *Apollo of Belvedere*, *Antinous*, *Flora*, *Laocoon's Head*, *River God's Head*, *Commodus*, and *Ariadne*, which were removed to a more commodious apartment to give students a better opportunity of copying them.

When Mr. de Gree[1] died in 1789, Mr. Beranger exhibited several of his drawings, which in Mr. West's opinion were likely to be of great use in the schools, and they were purchased for five guineas. In November 1790, David La Touche, Esqr., presented an excellent cast of the Laocoon, from the original work at Rome, which was placed in the repository, Hawkins street. In 1791, William Ashford's collection of statues, models, casts, &c. was sold to the Society for £91.

The Society having in the year 1796 removed to premises in Poolbeg street, the drawing schools were established there, and schools for the living figure having been prepared, the Dublin artists were invited to choose a committee, to act as directors, each to take charge of the *Living* academy for four weeks. The

[1] Peter de Gree, a native of Antwerp, who came to Dublin about 1781, and painted pictures for Mr. La Touche.

following were chosen—Hunter, Ashford, Chinnery, Cuming, Robinson, Waldron, O'Neil, Smyth, and West. In 1800, Henry Brocas became master of the ornament school in the room of William Waldron.

On the 1st of May 1800, it was arranged that the figure school was to be continued on its then footing, but that the other two schools were to be consolidated, under the name of the engraving and ornament drawing school, under one master, and that Messrs. Waldron and Baker were to be pensioned. The committee of fine arts, in consequence of a letter from Mr. Chinnery, secretary to the Society of Artists, recommended that, instead of premiums, the sum intended for them should be expended in purchasing the works of Irish artists that possessed merit, which might remain in their exhibition room, as the property of the Society, for the benefit and emulation of young students. One hundred guineas were to be allotted for the purpose. In accordance with this recommendation, *Attention*, by George Chinnery, a landscape by Wm. Ashford,[1] and a *Portrait of a Student*, by Wm. Cuming, were purchased at the Exhibition of Irish Artists, held in the Parliament House in July 1801. The committee regretted being unable to buy Ashford's fine picture of a *Land Storm*, at ninety guineas. It was resolved that, on the recommendation of governors of the respective institutions, the boys of the Blue Coat Hospital and the Hibernian Marine School[2] were to be instructed in the schools.

---

[1] Ashford was born in Birmingham in 1746. He came to Ireland in 1764, and practised landscape painting. Ashford was patronised by Lord Fitzwilliam, and made many paintings and drawings of Mount Merrion, five of which are now in the Fitzwilliam Museum, Cambridge.

[2] For children of decayed seamen ; at that time located on Sir John Rogerson's quay.

MEDAL AWARDED TO GEORGE PETRIE IN THE ART SCHOOL

MEDAL OF THE FARMING SOCIETY

George Petrie took a first-class premium for a group of figures in the year 1805, and a couple of years after this, while still a student, he asked that a landscape painted by him should be hung in the Society's exhibition room.   The former is the first mention in the minutes of this distinguished artist, archæologist, and man of letters.   George, son of James Petrie, artist, was born in Dublin in 1789. He painted landscapes in Kerry, Wicklow, and other parts of Ireland, and illustrated Cromwell's *Excursions in Ireland*.   In addition to his artistic talent, Petrie was a cultivated man of letters, learned in Irish antiquities and ecclesiastical architecture, and a musician.   From 1833 to 1846, he was employed on the Ordnance Survey of Ireland.   His *Essay on the History and Antiquities of Tara Hill* gained him the gold medal of the Royal Irish Academy, which also bestowed a similar distinction on him for his *Essay on the Origin and Uses of the Round Towers of Ireland*, which was published in 1845 as the *Ecclesiastical Architecture of Ireland*.   Petrie's *Ancient Music of Ireland* appeared in 1855.   This talented man died in 1866, and a very charming and appreciative memoir of him was written by his friend, Dr. William Stokes, which contains a list of works illustrated by Petrie.

The *Beggar Woman and Child*, by George Gratton, who was educated in the schools, was purchased in 1807, for 100 guineas, in recognition of the artist's distinguished merit, and to enable him to go to London. He was to have the picture framed, and had permission to have it exhibited in London.   This picture now hangs on the wall near the door of the conversation-room, at the foot of the staircase in Leinster House.

Martin Cregan obtained a medal for drawing from

the round ;[1] and, to enable him to go to London, fifty guineas were paid to Robert L. West[2] for a portrait of the Right Hon. John Foster, a vice-president. A little prior to this, Andrew R. Twigg, a late student of the Society's schools, presented a full-length portrait of General Vallancey, for which the General sat to him. It was offered "as a first fruits of his academic studies, in the hope that it may be deemed worthy of a place in the new board-room." Fifty guineas were voted to Twigg, that he might journey to London to study the works of eminent artists.

On June 20, 1805, a letter was read from Caleb Whitefoord, chairman of a committee of subscribers (who were members of the Society for the Encouragement of Arts, Manufactures, and Commerce, London), to a fund being raised for James Barry, artist, "who has enriched this island by his productions; and whose works would have done honour to the most polished and enlightened ages of antiquity." Barry was represented as having had long and painful struggles with adversity and privation, while his independence of character concealed the fact. The members of the Dublin Society were invited to subscribe towards providing an honourable ease for the remainder of his days, and an annuity of £120 per annum was secured to him. Barry was born

[1] Martin Cregan, born in 1788, practised painting both in Dublin and London. He was a foundation member of the Royal Hibernian Academy, and for years its President. Cregan died in 1870. The National Gallery, Dublin, possesses a copy made by him of Reynolds' "Master Crewe."

[2] Son of Francis R. West. On his father's death in 1809, he succeeded him as master of the school, a post which he held until 1845. In that year he was granted a pension by the Treasury, and he died in 1849. His memorial stated that he had thirty-five years' service, and that his grandfather, father, and himself had served the Society during a period of ninety-five years. R. L. West painted portraits and historical subjects, and in 1808 exhibited in the Royal Academy a subject from Gray's *Elegy*.

in Cork in 1741, and studied in the Dublin school under West. He first attracted notice in 1763, when he came to Dublin, by his " Conversion by St. Patrick of the King of Cashel," which procured him the patronage of Edmund Burke, who introduced him to Reynolds ; and in 1764 he went to London. Barry also painted " Adam and Eve " (now in the collection of the Royal Society of Arts) ; " Cymbeline " (in the collection of the Royal Dublin Society) ; " Jupiter and Juno," and " Lear and Cordelia." Between the years 1777 and 1782, Barry decorated with a series of paintings, illustrative of human culture, the great room of the Society of Arts, for which he received 250 guineas and a gold medal.[1] He had a quarrelsome temper, and was unhappy in his dealings with those around him. Barry died in 1806, and lies buried in the crypt of St. Paul's Cathedral.

The plans for drawing schools, which were to be erected in the new premises in Poolbeg street at a cost of £1871, had been approved in April 1806, and the building was to be proceeded with without delay.

In May 1808, on behalf of Faithful Christopher Pack, a number of artists signed a statement to the effect that the art of painting as practised by Titian and the Bassanos[2] had been lost for 200 years, and that Sir Joshua Reynolds, Pack's master, after numberless experiments, had failed to discover it. Pack now claimed to have done so, and he copied a Venetian picture said to be by Titian. The artists believed the

---

[1] See an account of these pictures, by Barry, published in 1783. In the *History of the Royal Society of Arts*, by Sir H. T. Wood, 1913, pp. 70–9, will be found a very full account of them.

[2] Tiziano Vecelli, commonly called Titian—the greatest painter of the Venetian school. The North Italian family of Da Ponte, known as the Bassani, from Bassano, the city in which they lived, were among the famous painters of the sixteenth century.

method to be the same as that practised by the Venetian school, and as Pack was now old and feeble, they thought that "by having command of his invaluable art, the Irish school will more than vie with those of other nations." It will be of interest to add the names of the artists who signed this statement. They were —Hugh Hamilton, Wm. Ashford, John Comerford, Robert L. West, William Cuming, Jonathan Fisher, Henry Graham, Samuel Burton, Charles Robertson, William Woodburn, Andrew R. Twigg, Graves Chamney Archer, George Meade, James Petrie, George Petrie, Samuel Woodhouse, John C. Hone, William Chalmers.[1]

A large number of pages of the printed *Proceedings* of the year 1809 are occupied with a report and recommendations of the committee of fine arts (of which James Gandon was a member) on the drawing schools. As the resolutions and recommendations are of interest and importance in view of the future development of the schools, it may be well to summarise them briefly :—

1. It was necessary to have able masters and good models, as a number of young artisans and manufacturers attend. The Society is tolerably rich in casts from the antique, and at small expense the ornament and architectural schools may be supplied. 2. The number of scholars is considerable and increasing. 3. Boys are irregular in attendance, and remiss in application, displaying a want of energy. 4. The number on the foundation in each school should be limited to forty. 5. They should be allowed on the foundation for three years only. 6. Regular lists

[1] Mr. Strickland remarks that notwithstanding the encomiums of the artists, the Dublin Society did not appear to have been much impressed with Pack's discoveries. (*Dict. Irish Artists.*)

and accounts should be kept.   7. The premium system to be remodelled.   8. Money premiums to be given up.   Instead, books on geometry, &c., and portfolios, with the stamp of the Society and inscription, to be substituted.   9. Artists of repute might be appointed professors or visitors.   10. Good drawings for sale are wanted.   11. Catalogue of paintings and drawings to be made out.   12. Really good pictures by ancient masters to be purchased ; £200 to be spent on furnishing the ornament and architectural schools with good drawings and engravings.   13. In future, all models to be provided at the Society's expense.   14. The Committee to use the funds most advantageously for the benefit of the schools.   15. The masters' salaries to be increased.   16. The new figure master to be the best possible, and advertised for in England, if necessary.   17. As the figure school is for the higher branches of art, none to be admitted to it without a probationary drawing.   18. This school must be raised to importance, and made capable of attaining the highest walks.   19. A living figure to be ready to sit nearly all the year round.   20. Lectures on the theory and practice of painting, and the anatomy of bone and muscle, to come later.   21. A school of engraving to be constituted later.   22. Instructions in modelling and sculpture to be given. 23. A school for females to be a subject for future consideration.   24. Boys under 13 not to be admitted to the architectural school. 25. Pupils in the architectural school to be instructed in the principles of practical geometry, and how to draw by scale.   266. A higher school of architecture might be instituted, wherein perspective might be fully taught, and private pupils admitted on payment.   27. The same might be made to apply to the other two schools.   28. A room for the continual exhibition of pictures, &c., for sale, to be provided. It was added that £700 a year might be approved of for salaries and expenses. English candidates for the post of master of the figure school were to be permitted to draw from the figure of *Antinous* in the Royal Academy.

In December 1809, George Gratton's works, *Race of Hippomenes and Atalanta*, and *Antinous* were purchased by the Society for 100 guineas. In 1811, Solomon Williams, portrait painter, was allowed the use of the drawing school for the purpose of painting a picture on a very large scale.[1]

With a view to establishing a school for modelling and sculpture, Edward Smyth, sculptor, was employed on a probationary term of six months, and later he was appointed master of the school, at a salary of 50 guineas a year. He, however, died before the end of 1812, when his son, John Smyth, took up the work, and in November 1813, he was placed, as to salary, on a footing with the other masters.

In 1813, £100 were spent in completing the pedestals in the statue gallery, the walls were coloured, and the long gallery was finished. The Society of Artists was allowed the use of the school-room three days in the week, from 7 to 9 o'clock A.M., for the study of the human figure. On the 9th of February 1815, the roof of the drawing school was found to have been injured by the late great storm.

Certain resolutions were drawn up in November 1813, for reference to the Committee of Fine Arts for report. The masters' salaries were to be advanced, and a number of professional artists (which included the names of Comerford, Gandon, Gratton, Kirk,

---

[1] During this year, Williams exhibited portraits of the Duke of Cumberland and Dr. Troy ; also an altarpiece, "Taking down from the Cross." It was probably for the painting of the last-named work that he obtained permission to use the school.

Mossop, Mulvany, and Williams), with the four drawing masters, were to be invited to assist in selecting
works of art and old paintings for the gallery. Proper
apartments were to be provided for the life school.
A gallery of marbles and casts, drawings and etchings,
was to be formed, and a fund was to be appropriated
yearly for the acquisition of " Old Masters." Government was to be requested on public days to guard
the main entrance, and commissioned officers were
to be admitted to the landscape and perspective
schools, with a view to qualifying as civil and military
engineers.

The committee reported against most of the resolutions, as having been drawn up without accurate
knowledge, while many of them had been acted on as
rules for years. The resolutions implied that the
schools were intended solely for forming artists and
painters, whereas they were for those employed in arts,
science, and manufactures. The regulations which had
been already drawn up were arrived at, the committee
said, on mature advice and deliberation with artists, the
Royal Academy, and the British Institution. The 9th
resolution would abrogate the gratuitous instruction,
which already occupied most serious attention ; many
youths of promise might be kept away, and it would
create invidious distinctions.

In 1815, the Hibernian Society of Artists and
other Dublin artists, presented a memorial to the
Society, and on the report of the committee appointed to consider it, a general committee from among
the artists was nominated to manage the annual
exhibition.

The use of the exhibition room in Hawkins street
was granted in 1815–16–17–19, for united exhibitions
of artists' works.

The committee included Kirk (1), Mossop (2), and George Petrie.

1. Thomas Kirk was born at Newry in 1777. He early settled in Dublin, and worked chiefly on busts and relief on mantelpieces. Kirk executed the colossal statue of Nelson for the column in Sackville street, and a statue of King George the Fourth for the Linen Hall, which now stands on the staircase landing in Leinster House. Many of his busts adorn the College of Surgeons, Leinster House, and the library of Trinity College.

2. William Mossop, whose real name was Browne, assumed that of his mother's second husband. He was born in 1751, dying in Jan. 1805. Mossop acquired a great reputation as a medallist, and engraved some of the finest medals and coins of the pre-Union period. A list of his works (which includes a medal of the Dublin Society, 1800), will be found in Gilbert's *History of Dublin*, vol. ii., appendix vii. His son, William Stephen Mossop, also achieved distinction in this art, and a list of his medals will be found in appendix viii. of the same volume.

In the year 1818 Bartholomew Watkins [1] took first premium in the landscape school.

During the years 1813–1819 (inclusive), it was found that 314 boys had received instruction in the figure school, which, founded in 1759, had then existed for sixty years. It was a means of improvement for engravers in wood and copper, for herald painters, engravers in cameo and intaglio, die sinkers, and sculptors.

Five hundred and five pupils were admitted to the school of ornament during the same period of seven years; and the course of instruction pursued in it was of incalculable benefit to sculptors in stone, wood, metal, to glass workers, chasers, silversmiths, calico printers, pattern-drawers, paper-stainers, embroiderers,

[1] Uncle of B. Colles Watkins, the artist. Starting as an artist, Bartholomew Watkins became later a picture cleaner and dealer.

jewellers, fancy workers, damask, carpet, and silk weavers, stucco men, cabinetmakers, upholsterers, and carpenters. The training of boys and girls in the arts connected with industry was a chief object of the Society, which took a leading part in promoting technical education.

In the architectural school, from 30 to 35 pupils attended each year. During the time of Mr. Henry A. Baker, who had served as master for a period of thirty-three years, there was not a working tradesman or mechanic in the building line in Dublin and the chief towns in Ireland, who, during his apprenticeship, had not received instruction in it. Even the rapid improvement noticeable in shop fronts and the ornamental parts of private houses during the period were attributed to the skill acquired by artisans educated in the school.

From 1813 to 1819, pupils to the number of 139 were admitted to the modelling school, which had already produced Behnes,[1] the sculptor, of London.

From June 1817 to November 1819, 3982 persons visited the casts from the Elgin Marbles, which had been purchased in 1816 for £210.

Mr. Thomas Pleasants, a warm friend of the Society, who died on the 1st of March 1818, bequeathed to the Society a number of valuable paintings (see p. 236).

In February 1823, a plan was devised for altering the stable and coachhouses at Leinster House, which, at a cost of £1500, would have given a new bust gallery and drawing schools. In addition, £500 would have been necessary so as to adapt the new premises

[1] William Behnes, sculptor, was a member of a Hanoverian family that settled in Dublin for a time; he distinguished himself in the schools here, and, between 1820 and 1840, his reputation stood very high. He executed busts of celebrities, among them, Lyndhurst, Clarkson, and Macready, and his statuette of Lady Godiva was much admired.

for the reception of the students. The plan, however, was not adopted.

In 1823, some specimens of sculpture by John Hogan, Cork, "a very young artist," were purchased for £25, as an encouragement; they included legs, arms, &c., which are now in the National Museum. In 1829, a gold medal was voted to Hogan for his *Dead Christ*, then being exhibited in the Royal Irish Institution, College street. Hogan was born in Tallow in 1800, but his family soon settling in Cork, he worked at an anatomy school in that city. In 1824 he went to Rome, where he remained until 1849, and his *Drunken Faun*, executed there, was admired by Thorwaldsen. Among his most celebrated statues are those of Bishop Brinkley at Cloyne; of Daniel O'Connell and Thomas Drummond, in the City Hall, Dublin, and of Thomas Osborne Davis, in Mount Jerome Cemetery. Hogan died in 1858.

In May 1823, a sum of £1000, together with the amount of the legacy bequeathed to the Society by Major-General White,[1] was voted, to be expended in erecting drawing schools and a gallery for casts from the antique.

A year later, Mr. Henry Hamilton, who was then in Rome, procured and presented to the schools a mould from the Apollo Belvedere.

About this time, two pupils of the modelling school —Constantine Panormo and John Gallagher—began to distinguish themselves, and to exhibit signs of exceptional talent. At the end of 1823, it was arranged that they were to be sent to London as pupils to Mr. Behnes, for two years, at £60 a year each. He wrote to the Society "on behalf of these two young

---

[1] By his will, proved in the Prerogative Court in 1822, Major-General Sir Henry White, K.C.B., bequeathed £500 to the Society.

STATUE GALLERY, SCHOOL OF ART, 1866

geniuses of Dublin," whose group of *St. Michael and the Fallen Angel*, and a bust from life, respectively, had been awarded silver medals.   In July 1825, Behnes announced that Panormo had been awarded a large silver medal by the Sociey of Arts, for his model of the *Fallen Giant*.   Soon after, it was resolved to give both pupils a third year under Behnes, for the purpose of acquiring the art of carving in marble, preparatory to their being sent to Rome for a final course of study.   In 1827, two original group designs by Panormo and Gallagher [1] were sent over to the Society, as well as two marble busts from the antique—their first essays in the art of sculpture. Both students were sent to Rome for two years, at a charge of £100 a year each while there, and £60 travelling expenses.   Their early works in clay and marble are still preserved by the Society.   The new buildings were completed in March 1827, and the committee of fine arts was authorised to move the schools into them.

In April 1829, James Christopher Timbrell, a pupil, presented a print, entitled *The Scotch Fisher*, being his first lithographic production.   On one occasion, when presenting the gold medals at the Royal Academy, Sir Martin Archer Shee complimented Henry Timbrell, sculptor, a former.pupil, and brother of J.C. Timbrell, far beyond any of the other competitors, for his sculpture.

A menagerie was opened in Great Brunswick street, in April 1830, when the most competent pupils were sent to it, to make models or drawings from the life of the celebrated lion, "Wallace."   At the close of this year, the exhibition of pupils' drawings was visited by Their Excellencies, the Duke and

---

[1] One of these is a group of *Adam and Eve over Abel's Body*—the other, *Theseus Slaying a Centaur*.

Duchess of Northumberland, who also spent some time in one of the schools, which was then in full work. In 1832, a similar visit was paid by the Marquis of Anglesey and the Ladies Paget.

On the 9th of June 1836, was announced the death of Henry Aaron Baker, who for a period of forty-nine years had guided the architectural school.

In the silver trade, the modelling school was found especially useful. A splendid piece of plate was executed by Tear, who had been brought up in the schools, for Lord Combermere, when commander of the forces (to the order of Messrs. Law). This was taken to London for exhibition. Another piece of plate, executed by Percy, also of the schools, (to the order of West & Son), was a gift to Lord Manners, lord chancellor, from the Bar.

The following is a list of some noted artists and sculptors who received their education in the Society's schools, up to the year 1836, taken from the report of the select committee on the Royal Dublin Society made in that year.

Historical and Portrait Painters

Henry Tresham, R.A. (1).	Robt. L. West.
Matthew Wm. Peters, R.A.	George Gratton.
James Barry, R.A.	Charles C. Ingham.
Jacob Ennis.	Thomas Foster.
Sir M. A. Shee, P.R.A.	

Portrait Painters

Hugh D. Hamilton (2).	Thomas C. Thompson.
Somerville Pope (afterwards Pope-Stevens).	Andrew R. Twigg.
William Cuming.	Richard Rothwell.

Landscape Painters

William Ashford.	George Barret, R.A. (3).
Thomas Roberts.	Henry Brooke.
T. Sautelle Roberts.	Robert Carver.
Thomas Pope-Stevens.	John Killaly (civil engineer).

Figure and Landscape Painters

Thos. James Mulvany (4).   Wm. B. Sarsfield Taylor.
John George Mulvany.   John Moreau.

Marine Painter

Joseph F. Ellis.

Miniature Painters

John Comerford.   Edward Jones.
Thomas Robinson.   Buck (? Frederick).
Wm. J. Cooke.   Andrew Dunn.

Sculptors

John Hickey.   Constantine Panormo.
Edward Smyth.   John Gallagher.
John Smyth.   Thomas Kirk.
William Behnes.

Many names eminent in Irish art are not included in this list, and it is doubtful if some of those mentioned were educated in the schools. Several of them have already been noticed in these pages, and, in addition, the following are worthy of some mention.

1. Henry Tresham, one of our most eminent Irish painters, who was born in Dublin in 1749, received his art education in the Dublin schools under Ennis and Robert West. He accompanied his patron, Lord Cawdor, to Rome, and remained on the continent for fourteen years. His work was modelled on the Roman school, and he chiefly painted subjects from scriptural, English, and Roman history. Tresham died in 1814.

2. Hugh Douglas Hamilton was born in Dublin in 1739, and studied in the schools under Robert West and James Mannin. He excelled in crayon drawing. His portrait of the Right Hon. John Foster, last Speaker of the Irish House of Commons, is in possession of the Corporation of Dublin, and that of "Dean Kirwan preaching" is now in England. Hamilton died in Dublin in

1808. (For a very full account of him and his works, both in oils and crayons, see an article by Mr. W. G. Strickland in the annual volume of the Walpole Society, 1812–1813.)

3. George Barret, who was born in Dublin in 1728, and died in 1784, studied here under West. He painted many landscapes for Lord Powerscourt, and the Dukes of Buccleuch and Portland possess many examples of his work. The Society's collection includes some specimens.

4. Thomas James Mulvany and his brother, John George Mulvany, were among the first fourteen Academicians elected to the Royal Hibernian Academy on its foundation in 1823. George F. Mulvany, son of the first named, was the first Director of the National Gallery of Ireland.

On the 31st of May 1838, John Papworth of Dublin, A.R.H.A., was appointed master of the school of architecture, and Henry Brocas, master of the school of landscape and ornament. In 1840, Constantine Panormo succeeded John Smyth as master of the school of modelling. He was son of Edward Smyth, former master, and is well known as having executed the figures on the General Post Office, Dublin.

Earl de Grey, lord lieutenant, presided at the distribution of prizes to the pupils in the drawing school in December 1842, on which occasion Mr. Isaac Weld, honorary secretary, delivered a long speech, in which he detailed the history of the Society, dealing especially with the drawing and modelling schools, and noticing the many distinguished artists and sculptors who had received their early training in them. These meetings became annual, and one of the secretaries or vice-presidents generally discoursed on the schools. Their orations are marked by eloquence and scholarship, some of them dealing with ancient art, and others with the continental schools ; they contain a vast fund of information, and the series of addresses, as contained in the *Proceedings*, is well worth perusal. In 1843, when Earl de Grey again presided, Mr. Lundy E. Foot spoke learnedly and eloquently on the low state of the fine arts in Ireland 150 years previously, illustrating his remarks ; and he then proceeded to establish the Society's claim to have been the nursing mother of a great deal of the Irish talent since employed in their cultivation. On another occasion, Mr. Henry McManus delivered an address on the origin and utility of schools of design.

The Royal Irish Art Union presented to the Society the original cast of *The Youth at the Stream*, by J. H. Foley, a former student, a work that had acquired for him a considerable reputation at the national competition held in 1844 in Westminster Hall.

John Henry Foley was born in Dublin in 1818, and at the age of thirteen entered the Society's drawing schools, gaining first prizes in them. He went to London in 1834, becoming a student of the Royal Academy, and in 1839 exhibited *The Death of Abel* and *Innocence*, sculptures which at once attracted attention. Foley executed the statue of Hampden, now in the entrance corridor of the House of Commons. His great equestrian statues of Lord Canning, Lord Hardinge, and Sir James Outram are much admired, and the figures of Burke and Goldsmith, which stand outside Trinity College, Dublin, show that Foley's was a master hand. He also executed the statue of Father Mathew now in Cork, Lord Gough's equestrian statue in the Phœnix Park, Dublin, and those of Grattan, Faraday, and Reynolds. Foley bequeathed his models to the Royal Dublin Society. He died in 1874.

In 1849 the Government determined to establish a school of design. A representative of the Board of

Trade attended in May of that year, and on his reporting that the schools were suitable, it was resolved that the new gallery, once the drawing schools, should be appropriated to the purposes of the Government, as the school of design was to be in connection with the Society. The drawing schools were to be the basis for this school, which was specially intended for artisans, and was to be open five evenings in the week, under the superintendence of a head master, to be appointed by the Board of Trade. The masters were to be appointed by the fine arts committee, in which was vested the general government of the school. The drawing and modelling schools were to be consolidated into one department as "The Government School of Design in connection with the Royal Dublin Society." It was opened on the 1st of October 1849, Mr. Henry McManus being appointed head master, with the masters of the four schools as assistants. Three hundred and six pupils attended at the opening.

In June 1852, Panormo died, and J. R. Kirk, A.R.H.A., succeeded him as master of the modelling school.

In February 1860, Messrs. Charles E. Bagot and Charles Leech, executors of Captain George Archibald Taylor, of Mespil parade, Dublin, submitted a plan for endowment of prizes for the encouragement of art students in Ireland, in conformity with the terms of his will. The Master in Chancery sanctioned the Society taking charge of the trust, believing it to be eminently suitable for the purpose, and Captain Taylor's executors were thanked for selecting the Society as the medium for carrying the trusts into execution. In connection with this, an annual Exhibition of pupils' works sent in for competition was inaugurated, the judges being Catterson Smith, re-

presenting the Royal Hibernian Academy, Sir George
Hodson the National Gallery, and R. J. Macrory the
Society. Thirteen works were sent in, when William
McEvoy was awarded £7 for the best landscape in
oils; Annie C. White a similar sum for the best architectural drawing—*Interior of St. Paul's;* Mary Alment
and Henry Crowley obtaining lesser prizes for their
landscapes. The administration of this trust still
remains in the hands of the Society, and in recent
years many artists of repute were, in their student
days, winners of Taylor art scholarships or prizes.

From 1749 to 1849, when fees were first paid, all
students were admitted free to the schools. From
1854, when the grant was withdrawn, and the functions of the Board of Trade devolved on the Science
and Art Department, all schools of art were to be
self-supporting.

The Society's control over the schools ceased in
1878, when, with other sections under its superintendence, they were placed under the Science and Art
Department.

CHAPTER VIII

EXPERIMENTS IN AGRICULTURE, AND GENERAL PROCEEDINGS OF THE SOCIETY. (1764-1780)

NOTWITHSTANDING the premium system, and the efforts of the Dublin Society through its members in various parts of the country, agriculture and husbandry in Ireland were in a declining condition about the middle of the eighteenth century. Faulkner's *Dublin Journal* of the 17th of October 1752, spoke of the great neglect of tillage, and complained that our best lands were being devoted to the grazing and feeding of stock, for the supply of our enemies and rivals in trade, whilst the poor inhabitants were obliged to go abroad for work. It was remarkable that in times of scarcity, "the sourest and most fusty corn and flour were imported from Europe, and even from our American colonies." On the 18th of June 1754, the same *Journal* apologised for leaving out many advertisements, so that the list of premiums to be awarded in the ensuing year might be printed, averring that, as the generosity, care, and diligence of the Dublin Society contributed more to the welfare of the nation than all other Societies whatever, the people at large would derive more benefit from such a course being taken. Two columns very closely printed, containing lists of premiums, follow.

The Society, taking all circumstances into consideration, decided on appointing a man skilled in agriculture to carry out experiments, and instruct others in the art of husbandry. The name of John Wynn Baker appears for the first time in the *Proceedings* in the year 1764. He did a great deal for the Society on its agricultural side, and obtained no small reputation for the thoroughness with which he performed his duties, being frequently mentioned in complimentary terms during his tenure of office. Baker was an Englishman and a member of the Agricultural Society of the Hundred of Salford, Lancashire. The missing minute book would no doubt give a full explanation of his initial position, but when first mentioned he had leave to resign as an honorary member; he was, however, requested to attend the meetings when convenient; and a sum of £100 was voted for his expenses in the cultivation of cabbages, turnips, &c., and for his remuneration. In his *Experiments in Agriculture*, 1765 (Haliday Pamphlets), Baker says that in 1762 he addressed an anonymous pamphlet—*Hints on Husbandry*—to the Dublin Society. "Encouraged by people who knew me to be the author, I, in 1763, took my present farm (Loughlinstown, near Celbridge). In 1764, I printed a short epitome of my plan. The Dublin Society, always attentive to what appears to be to the advantage of the public, adopted it, and gave me encouragement." Next year he was reported to have made experiments in agriculture with great skill and accuracy, and to have discharged the trust reposed in him to the satisfaction of the Society. He was then voted £200, and 500 copies of his special report were printed.

Soon after, Baker conceived a plan for educating youths in husbandry, which, to a small extent, was afterwards carried out. They were to be apprenticed to farmers of repute in various counties ; but at first, Baker was to take upon him the instruction of five boys, for whom £12 a year for their food and clothing were to be paid. Two of them were to be instructed in the manufacture of agricultural implements. Baker's pupils were to be selected from inmates of the Foundling Hospital,[1] and 1500 copies of his scheme were printed. Yet another year elapsed, when it was resolved that his experiments were to be extended, and, with this object in view, a further grant of £200 was made to him. The implements of husbandry manufactured by him at Loughlinstown (which was afterwards renamed Wynnsfield), where the school of agriculture was situated, were sold, and he was allowed a premium on the amount. At the end of 1768 the value of implements disposed of during the year amounted to £501, 5s. At this period, agricultural implements were few, and of a most inferior kind, mainly consisting of the plough, harrow, flail, sickle, reaping hook, and scythes : "the quarter of a century immediately following 1760, is memorable in our agricultural annals for the introduction of various important improvements." Many subsequent grants of £100 were made to Baker for his encouragement, and in payment of necessary expenses. In December 1769, at a very crowded meeting of the Society, a sum of £300 was proposed as a fixed yearly salary for carrying out his experiments, and for affording instruction and advice to persons applying to him ; he was also to have 10 per cent. on sales of implements, the

[1] The first stone of this building was laid in 1704. It stood at the west end of James' st., on a site granted by the city (now occupied by South Dublin Union Workhouse), and was originally intended for aged and infirm poor. Under Act of Parliament, it became in 1730 a Foundling Hospital and Workhouse, where children were taught trades.

total amount of this source of profit not to exceed
£200 in any year.

Baker was author of *Hints for Improvement of
Agriculture by Experiments*, which was much approved,
and the Society specially requested him to experiment
on the culture of rape as food for cattle, &c. He
also compiled an abridgment of Arthur Young's two
works, *Six Months Tour through the Northern Counties
of England*, and *Six Months Tour through the Southern
Counties of England*, 3000 copies of which were ordered
to be printed at an expense not exceeding £70. Baker
wrote a treatise entitled *Practical Agriculture epitomised
and adapted to the Tenantry of Ireland, with considerations on the Dublin Society's list of Premiums for
Husbandry.*[1] In 1771, £300 were given him to establish a regular factory for implements, to build offices,
&c. Next year, as the beneficial nature of his work
became more apparent, Baker was asked to make a
tour through the provinces, with a view to his finding
out what improvements might be made in agricultural systems, and reporting. Baker died on the 22nd
of August 1775, and it does not appear that the Society
appointed any successor to carry on the special work
in which he was engaged. From his will, which was
proved by his daughter, Sarah Baker, on the 4th of September 1775, he seems to have had another farm, in the
county of Meath. Possibly, this account of Baker's
work and connection with the Society has been given at
too great length, but it seems fitting that prominence
should be afforded to the enlightened policy of the
Society; and the story of John Wynn Baker shows in

---

[1] Among the Haliday Pamphlets (1765, cccxxiii. 3) will be found
this work, and also his *Experiments, Plan for Instructing Youth in
Husbandry, Description of Instruments of Husbandry*, and *Considerations on the Exportation of Corn.*

a remarkable manner what care and discrimination were evinced in carrying out its plans for the encouragement of more scientific methods in agriculture.

Arthur Young (*Tour*, i. 20) speaks of visiting Baker's farm, and it is only right to say that he considered, with all Baker's exertions, he had not answered the expectations formed about him. Young says that he needed capital for getting the farm into order, and that he ought not to have been employed in making experiments. What the Society really wanted was a farm cultivated as experience in England and elsewhere had shown that it should be. As an example for Irish farmers, the land should have been in a mountainous tract, with some bog and tolerable soil. Arthur Young, frequently mentioned in this chapter, was born at Bradford in 1741, and is one of the highest authorities on the social and agricultural condition of Ireland in the latter part of the eighteenth century. He managed Lord Kingsborough's estates in Cork for some time, and the famous *Tour in Ireland*, published in 1780, reviews the general condition of the country, dealing with farming, wages, rent, public works, &c. Young died in 1820.

In the sister country of England, though agriculture was not included in the original scheme of the Society of Arts (founded in 1754), for some fifty years from the year 1758, it occupied probably the first place in the premium lists of that Society. Indeed, that institution became the most important agricultural society in the kingdom.

On the 6th of March 1766, the Dublin Society confirmed the amendment of the by-laws, which had been agreed to at a general meeting in November 1765. They were 45 in number, and included provision for the election of officers; prescribed duties of presidents, vice-presidents or chairman, treasurer, secretaries, registrar ; laid down rules as to the drawing masters, the order of proceedings of the Society, election of members, and granting of premiums and rewards.

A report on loans was subsequently made, when it appeared that various persons were indebted to the Society in the sum of £2060, 8s. 9d., and that bad debts amounted to £344. The committee came to the conclusion that loans of money should not in future be granted.

William Sleater, printer and publisher of the *Public Gazetteer*, proposed to print all the Society's publications, including lists of premiums, for £10 a year, provided the Society would not make use of any other newspaper. The offer was accepted, and Faulkner of the *Journal* and Dyton of the *Gazette* were notified not to insert in future any of the Society's publications without further directions.

The labours and methods of the Society must have made a deep impression on men of note in exalted stations, for in December 1766, Baron Mountney,[1] when going as judge of assize in the ensuing circuits, offered to bring with him copies of the premium list, for distribution through the country. In April 1768, Redmond Morres, K.C.,[2] who had been appointed to sit as judge in the last circuit, informed the Society that he had, pursuant to their request, viewed the manufacture of bone lace at Castlebar, where he found it carried on with great spirit and industry.

[1] Richard Mountney, baron of the Exchequer, a distinguished scholar. He married in 1759 the Dowager Countess of Mount Alexander.

[2] M.P. for Thomastown, and for Dublin (1773-1776); father of the first Viscount Frankfort de Montmorency. He was a vice-president of the Society.

Among those who had recently joined the ranks of the Society were Dr. Thomas Leland (1), Gorges Edmond Howard (2), and Hely Hutchinson (3). Rev. C. Chais, minister of the Walloon Church at the Hague, Mr. Vavesseur, secretary to the Royal Society for Agriculture at Rouen, and the Lady Arabella Denny (4) had been elected honorary members.

1. Thomas Leland, D.D., born in Dublin in 1722, was a pupil of Dr. Sheridan. He became a Fellow of Trinity College, Dublin, in 1746, in which for twenty years he filled the professorship of oratory. Leland has been spoken of as "the eloquent divine of whom Parr and Johnson speak with enthusiasm, and who carried on a controversy with the redoubtable Warburton."[1] He was author of editions and translations of *Demosthenes*, of a *Life of Philip of Macedon*, and of a well-known *History of Ireland*. His sermon "Love of our Country" is in the Haliday collection (1782, ccccxlv. 5). Leland died in Dublin in August 1785.

2. Gorges Edmond Howard, a poet, and dramatic, legal, and political writer, was also educated by Sheridan. He was an attorney by profession, and his *History of the Irish Exchequer* did for Ireland what Madox's *History of the Exchequer* did for England. Howard also wrote on Chancery, and on the Revenue and Trade of Ireland. His miscellaneous works were published in three volumes in Dublin in 1782. He appears to have been registrar to the commissioners for making a proper street and approach to the Castle about 1760. Howard died in 1786.

3. The Right Hon. John Hely Hutchinson was at one time prime serjeant at law, and subsequently became provost of Trinity College and Secretary of State. He was also M.P. for the city of Cork. Hely Hutchinson never obtained Fellowship, but was admitted Provost under letters patent of King George III. He was a master of oratory, and his success at the Bar was remarkable, while

[1] *Trinity College, Dublin*, by W. Macneile Dixon.

he enjoyed a considerable reputation as a statesman. He erected at Palmerston the fine mansion which is now incorporated in the buildings of the Stewart Institute. Hutchinson's wife was created Baroness Donoughmore, with remainder to their eldest son, who was afterwards created an Earl. Hutchinson's appointment to the provostship created bitter hostility, and he was attacked in *Pranceriana*,[1] a series of scurrilous letters and verses. Hutchinson was tyrannical in his methods, and was frequently in dispute with other members of the College, who resented his highhanded proceedings. He successfully managed the College estates, and built the Examination Hall, one of the finest to be found in any College. The Provost died in 1794.

4. The Lady Arabella Denny[2] was born in 1707, the second daughter of Thomas Fitzmaurice, 1st Earl of Kerry, by Anne, only daughter of Sir William Petty. At the age of twenty she married Arthur Denny, M.P. for Kerry, and was left a widow in 1742, from which time she devoted herself to works of benevolence and charity, making Dublin and its neighbourhood her residence. Though limited in means, Lady Arabella took charge of infants in workhouses, of sick nurses, &c., and looked after many institutions. She devoted much time and energy to checking the abuses of the Foundling Hospital; but the Magdalen Asylum in Leeson street, which was opened in 1767 in a house belonging to Sir William Cooper, was the object of her unceasing and special care. Lady Arabella helped the Dublin Society in every way in her power, and was often mentioned in the minutes. She lived for years at Peafield cliff, now known as Lisaniskea, Blackrock, and died there on the 18th of March 1792. Her name is frequently mentioned in the *Life of Lady Huntingdon* and in Mrs. Delany's *Correspondence*.

In March 1768, Richard Woodward, dean of Clogher, was specially thanked for his public-spirited

[1] "Prancero" was a nickname bestowed on the Provost, in allusion to a riding school which he projected in Trinity College, Dublin.
[2] *Account of the Magdalen Chapel, Dublin, its Foundress, &c.*, by A. Peter, 1907,

and ingenious pamphlet, *An Argument in Support of the Right of the Poor in the Kingdom of Ireland to a Rational Provision*, and at the same time 2000 copies of the *Scheme for establishing County Poorhouses in Ireland*, published in 1766, were ordered to be reprinted.

Dr. David MacBride [1] had been bringing to perfection a new mode of tanning, much easier and cheaper than the old system. There are many notices in the minute books of Dr. MacBride's method, for which the Society voted him a silver medal, and he was elected an honorary member. Subsequently, great satisfaction was expressed at a Mr. Laban's success in carrying it out. MacBride's *New Method of Tanning* is in the Haliday collection (1769, cccxlvi. 8).

In June 1768, a sum of £250 was voted for the erection of a Pharmacopœia Pauperum, for dispensing medicine to the poor of Ireland, according to a plan of John Wade, chemist.

The Society arranged that the money voted by Parliament was to be assigned in the following proportions to the various industries:

Silk	£3800	Gold and silver thread, &c.	£50
Wool	2500	Stamping linens, &c.	300
Leather	100	Mixed goods	300
Iron and Steel	570	Oil of vitriol	100
Copper and brass	100	Saltpetre	100
Paper	150	Phar. Pauperum	250
Glass	200		
Earthenware	150		

In 1769, a prize was offered for the best plan of a county gaol, to cost from £1000 to £3000, in which

[1] Born at Ballymoney, co. Antrim, 1726; died in Dublin, 1778; a distinguished physician, who published many important medical works.

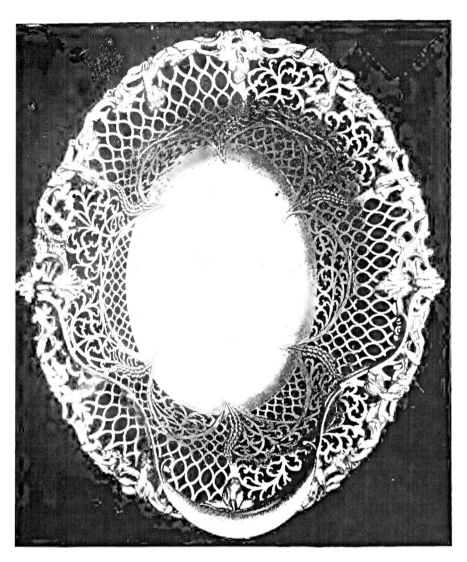

SILVER CAKE BASKET, AWARDED AS A PREMIUM, 1772

were to be suitable apartments for the gaoler and his family. The building was to be one for the detention of criminals and debtors of both sexes, and was to contain two condemned cells; it was to include a house of correction, and a yard in which prisoners might take the air.

A sum of £100 was granted to the Rev. Benjamin Domvile,[1] to be laid out in the purchase of a new mill, and implements for making thread, to enable Mrs. Eliz. Madden (widow of the Rev. John Madden), to extend the manufacture of thread which she had established at Dungiven, co. Derry. It was thought that encouragement extended to her would lessen the importation of foreign thread, which amounted to a considerable quantity each year.

Gold medals were presented to Wentworth Thewles, and to Robert French, of Monivea, for reclaiming bog;[2] to John Darley for ditching; and to the Rev. Charles Coote, dean of Kilmacduagh, for land sown with turnips in drills—for feeding cattle in the Queen's county; and a silver medal was awarded to John Longfield, of Longueville, for extensive plantation. A piece of plate, in the form of a pierced silver cake-basket, of Dublin manufacture (hall mark 1772, John Locker), was presented by the Society to Lancelot Sandes for reclaiming bog in the Queen's county in 1769. He was awarded a premium of £25, and the basket, with suitable inscription, was perhaps given in lieu of the money. In the year 1912 there was a risk of this being sold outside

[1] Rev. Benjamin Barrington, dean of Armagh, inherited the estate of his uncle, Sir Compton Domvile, at Loughlinstown, co. Dublin, on the latter's decease in 1768, when he assumed the name of Domvile and retired from the deanery. Ball's *Hist. Co. Dublin*, i. 93.

[2] Mr. French sent an account of his reclamation of bog in a letter to the Society which is printed in full in Arthur Young's *Journal*, i. 369.

Ireland, and the Council of the Royal Dublin Society contributed £30 towards its purchase for the National museum. (Report of Mr. Dudley Westropp, *Museum Bulletin*, Sept. 1912, p. 8.)

On the 1st of March 1770, certain by-laws as to subscriptions and arrears were passed. The Society's collector laid before it an account of the subscriptions, which in March 1769 amounted to £228, 12s. 9d.

In 1772, Colonel William Burton presented to the Society a chart of the Shannon from the sea to Limerick, executed by John Cowan. It was proposed that £25 should be given to Cowan, when he should have succeeded in taking a survey and chart of the river above Killaloe, towards its source, so far as the Society might think him deserving of it.

In May 1772, the Dublin Society took quite a new departure, when it was suggested that a select standing committee should be appointed to enquire into the ancient state of the arts, literature, and other antiquities of this kingdom ; and to examine the several unpublished manuscript tracts in possession of the Society, and all other tracts on those subjects, of which the committee could obtain perusal. The committee included the president, vice-presidents, secretary, treasurer ; Lord Charlemont, Lord Moira, the Bishop of Derry, the Speaker, Dean Woodward, Dr. Ireland, Major Vallancey, the Marquis of Kildare, and Lord Dartrey. Dr. Ireland and Major Vallancey were appointed secretaries. The Society authorised the Chevalier Thomas O'Gorman to apply to the college of the Lombards in Paris, and to other learned bodies, for copies of any ancient manuscripts, records, &c., illustrative of the history and antiquities of Ireland. At the time, Charles O'Neill was principal, and Lawrence Kelly prefect, of the Irish community of the college. At a meeting held there on the 11th of March 1773, under the presidency of Arthur Richard Dillon, archbishop of Narbonne, to which all Irish gentlemen resident in Paris were invited, a select committee was appointed, which resulted in the establishment of a branch in Paris. The Book of Leacan, which was believed to have been lost during a season of turbulence, while in possession of Dublin University, or to have been brought away by an Irish clergyman, who had prevailed on the librarian to lend it to him, and who was suddenly obliged to fly to France, was stated to be the only important manuscript in their possession, and the college undertook that a copy of it should be made. Sir John Gilbert, in his *History of Dublin* (iii. 235), states that, in September 1787, the Book of Leacan was sent through the Abbé Kearney, of Paris, to the Royal Irish Academy, of which institution it still " forms one of the chief literary treasures," and for which it was edited in facsimile by Dr. Atkinson. It was also hoped to open correspondence with colleges, religious houses, and libraries throughout France. In his *History of Dublin*, Gilbert states that this antiquarian committee of the Dublin Society generally met in Trinity College library, and that they assembled for the last time on the 24th of February 1774. It does not appear to have accomplished anything of practical value during its short existence.

The first mention of Major (afterwards General) Charles Vallancey, of the French family de la Vallence, who was born in England about the year 1721, has been made above. He must have become a member of the Society between 1761 and 1764, during the period when the minute books are missing, as there is no mention of his admission in those now extant. He was in the corps of Royal Engineers, and first came to Ireland in 1761, to assist in a military survey, from which time he adopted this country as his home. The history, philology, and antiquities of the country greatly interested him. The General published *Collectanea de Rebus Hibernicis* between 1770 and 1784; *Essay on the Irish Language*, 1772; *Grammar* (Irish), 1773; *Vindication of the Ancient Kingdom of Ireland*, 1786; *Ancient History of Ireland proved from Sanscrit books*, 1797. He was elected a Fellow of the Royal Society in 1784. It must be admitted that, in the light of modern research, most of the theories promulgated by Vallancey are baseless, and, though a man of learning, he allowed himself to be led to many false conclusions, and often wrote in a silly and extravagant strain. As far back as 1761, a new piece of artillery invented by Vallancey, which it was thought would be of great service in field and garrison, was tried in the Phœnix Park. A newspaper of the day, in commenting on the trial, remarked "that the Military are already obliged to this gentleman for his *Essay on Fortification*, and the public for his treatise on the *Inland Navigation of the Ancients and Moderns*." During the rebellion, he furnished the Government with plans for the defence of Dublin.

Vallancey will always be remembered by the series of Barony Maps which he copied in 1790–1, in Paris, for the British Government. The originals had been compiled from the Down Survey barony maps between 1660 and 1678, and were in course of transit, in 1710, from Dublin, to Sir Wm. Petty's son and heir in London, when the vessel in which they were being brought was seized by a French privateer cruising in the Channel. The maps were immediately carried to Paris, and deposited in the Bibliothèque du Roi, where they have ever since remained. Vallancey's copies are in the Public Record Office of Ireland. In

GENERAL CHARLES VALLANCEY

(*From an oil painting by Solomon Williams*)

February 1812, when very old and feeble, Vallancey resigned his custody of the Society's nummarium, and presented to it any coins or medals which were his own property, when a cordial vote of thanks was passed to him for his successful endeavours at all times to promote its interests. In the course of his fifty years' connection with the Society, he must have devoted an immense amount of time and attention to its affairs. Mr. Isaac Weld, secretary, in giving evidence before the Select Committee of 1836, said that General Vallancey "was always on the spot, and was a sort of dictator in the Society." He was a member of most of the committees, working indefatigably on each, and no new movement appears to have originated, as to which his advice was not sought and his co-operation invited. General Vallancey died on the 8th of August 1812. There is a portrait of him by Chinnery, in the Royal Irish Academy, and another by Solomon Williams in Leinster House.

In 1772, the Society had the pleasant experience of receiving a legacy under a will. Henry Jesse, of Jessefield, county Tipperary, bequeathed to it £300 for the "encouragement of agriculture." Mr. Jesse's will, dated 1769, was proved on the 3rd of May 1770, by John Scott, barrister, the executor.

During the ensuing year, a select committee of commerce was appointed, which issued a circular addressed to the gentlemen and clergy of Ireland, with 26 queries for reply. The committee subsequently made a special report on the tanning trade.

About this time, the amount of arrears due in subscriptions was becoming very serious, and on the 13th of June 1782, on the motion of the Earl of Aldborough, it was resolved that a circular letter be sent to members in arrear, stating that in consequence of the great

deficiency in the funds, the Society would be unable
to continue the premium system. They were to be
informed that on payment of 20 guineas all further
claims would be discharged, and they were to be considered as life members. In case of non-payment,
their names were to be inserted in the Dublin and
London papers, when they would no longer be considered members of the Society. In April 1792, the
collector was directed to inform every member in
arrear, of certain clauses in an Act of Parliament
passed in the last session (32 George III, ch. 14, secs.
5 and 6), with a request to discharge the arrears. By
this Act, arrears might be sued for by civil bill, provided that if they did not exceed sixteen guineas, and
one-fourth were discharged by a certain day, such
payment should be deemed in full satisfaction. Should
any defaulter pay twenty guineas, he might be
deemed a life member. Any money so paid was
to be applied towards the purchase of a cabinet of
mineralogy, of models for the drawing schools, and for
the establishment of a Botanic Garden. In November
1793, Mr. Henry Tisdall, attorney, having taken all
necessary steps towards getting in arrears, but without
success, was directed to prepare a case for counsel, to
advise that further steps should be taken, pursuant to
the Act of Parliament. Having obtained Mr. Caldbeck's opinion, he was authorised to commence pro-
secutions against defaulters. Mr. Caldbeck, who was
a member, returned his fee, begging that "his services
might be accepted as a small mark of that gratitude
which every Irishman owed to the Society." By July
1795, a bill of £493 had been incurred to Mr. Tisdall
for the recovery of arrears. They amounted, on the
1st of November 1794, to £3957, 7s. 3d.

For some time, the attendance of members at the

meetings had been very small, on some occasions only two being present.   Frequent complaints were also made of the vice-presidents being constantly absent, important business, which could only be transacted when one of them was in the chair, having to be held over, and the meetings proving abortive.   From the time that the Society proceeded to take active steps as to arrears of subscriptions, a period of decline seemed to set in.   Ballots had to be postponed, and, in addition, applications for membership fell off considerably, while many members retired from the Society. A great improvement in every respect began to manifest itself from the year 1800 onwards, when the attendance became more satisfactory, and applications for admission to the Society more numerous.

On the 9th of December 1773, Mr. Agmondisham Vesey moved that, as a mark of the Society's sense of Mr. Secretary Blaquiere's great attachment to its endeavours, a gold medal, with suitable inscription, should be presented to him.   On the vote, this motion was rejected —the necessary two-thirds majority not having been obtained.   On the 27th of January 1774, Mr. Blaquiere was elected an honorary member, and in 1780, on payment of twenty guineas, he became a life member.

John Blaquiere, born in 1732, was son of a French emigrant who settled in London.   He acted as secretary of legation in France under Lord Harcourt, 1771–2, and when Harcourt became lord lieutenant of Ireland in the latter year, Blaquiere went with him as chief secretary.   From time to time, he represented in the Irish Parliament, Old Leighlin, Carlingford, Charleville, and Newtownards.   He was created a baronet in 1784, and Baron De Blaquiere in 1800.   Many of the principal improvements in Dublin in his time were carried out under his fostering care, and he may be said to have enjoyed a larger share of popular regard than generally falls to the lot of chief secretaries. Among other things, Blaquiere was in favour of a tax on absentee landlords. He died at Bray in 1812.

On the 12th of June 1777, Messrs. Taylor and Skinner asked the Society to grant them 200 guineas towards publishing a large map which was to be constructed by connecting the several roads appearing in the work [1] published by them, into a continuous map, on a scale of three miles to an inch. After some consideration, their request was acceded to. Messrs. Robert Pool and John C. Cash, who had both been educated in the Society's drawing schools, laid before it their plans of public buildings in Dublin, when it was decided that they had great merit, and deserved patronage. They subsequently sent in a memorial praying for assistance in their projected work, *Eblana Depicta*, afterwards published as " Views of the most remarkable buildings in Dublin," 1780.

For some years, Mr. Morgan Crofton had been frequently employed on committees, and appears to have been much engaged in the Society's work. Mr. Abraham Wilkinson [2] was another member whose name is constantly met with in the *Proceedings*, and who was also very active in carrying out the Society's objects. The vice-presidents, too, especially Mr. John Leigh and Mr. Sydenham Singleton, were most regular in their attendance.

At the close of the year 1779, it was found that arrears to the amount of £4615, 19s. 6d., were due by the members up to the previous year. A by-law was passed in November 1780 that the collector was to

[1] *Maps of the Roads of Ireland Surveyed,* 1777.
[2] Of Bushy Park, co. Dublin. His daughter and heiress, Maria Wilkinson, married Sir Robert Shaw, 1st bart.

attend in the room on those ballot days on which any sum of money was to be voted, or on which an election of officers was to take place, so that it might be certified who were incapacitated from voting by reason of their being in arrear.   Any such persons were to leave the room, or pay the amount due.

The Society at this time was engaged in forwarding the interests of the cotton manufacture.   A sum of £35 was paid to Robert Brooke, which had been expended by him in bringing over artisans from England for carrying it on ; which sum, with £53, 6s. granted to him on the 7th of September for bringing over thirteen persons, was for twenty persons out of thirty-nine voted for.   Subsequent payments were made for the full number.   The Hon. Baron Hamilton also presented a memorial, stating that he had established a cotton manufacture at Balbriggan, and asking aid for bringing over six persons from England, skilled in this branch of industry, which was agreed to.

CHAPTER IX

THE SCHOOLS OF CHEMISTRY AND MINERALOGY
(1786–1836)

A SCOTCHMAN named Donald Stewart was in 1786 employed by the committee of agriculture in making searches for fossils and minerals, along the banks of the Grand Canal and in the county of Wicklow, for which he was paid a guinea a week while at work.[1] After a time, he reported in writing on his searches, the reports being referred to a special committee, in whose opinion his observations on surveys of the counties of Wicklow and Wexford were valuable. In March 1787, Stewart was directed to go to the northern parts of the kingdom, for the purpose of sending to Dublin a sufficient quantity of Fuller's earth from pits which he had discovered, so that its qualities might be tested by Dublin manufacturers. He sent up above 3 cwt., which was divided between Messrs. Rickey, Parker, and Rankin, woollen manufacturers. In March 1788, he again reported on the counties of Wicklow, Wexford, and Waterford, and he was directed to make a tour through the county of Clare, under the orders of Sir Lucius O'Brien, bart.

In 1789, the committee of agriculture reported that the different clays raised from a pit on the estate of His Excellency the Marquis of Buckingham, in the county of Clare, might be of great use, but it was

---

[1] A report on mines and minerals in the county of Dublin will be found in the Statistical Survey of that county (1800).

necessary that larger quantities should be sent up for investigation. This clay had been discovered by Donald Stewart. In 1791, Stewart announced that he had found in the county of Waterford a very valuable clay fit for glasshouse pots.

When making a tour through the county Longford in 1794, he found several valuable quarries of flags, slates, and fine variegated marble, on the estates of Lord Oxmantown and Mr. Shuldham, near Ballymahon. During this year, Stewart was directed to make a descriptive catalogue of the minerals, fossils, clays, &c., discovered by him, and deposited with the Society, and to label the collection. In 1799, he proceeded to Banbridge to search for coal, and he had to experiment for mines on the estates of Morley Saunders and F. W. Greene in the county of Wicklow. On one occasion, he laid before the Society samples of marble raised from the quarries of the Marquis of Hertford, in the county of Antrim, which was said to be of excellent quality and to bear a fine polish. He was also paid for quarrying and drawing away specimens of various pillars and marbles from the Giant's Causeway, &c., to Port Ballentrae, for the Society. In November 1797, Stewart was directed to go to the island of Rathlin, to examine if it yielded any stratum of *Terrass*, General Vallancey having informed the Society that some of that substance, equal to any imported from Holland, had been found there. Soon after, Mr. Joseph Allen informed the Society that he had found immense quantities of *Terrass* and *Terra Pozzuolana*[1] at Larne. When Stewart had completed a good deal of his work, Dr. Percival was invited to advise as to the arrangement

---

[1] *Terrass* and *Pozzuolana* are soft ferruginous tufas, that possess the property of consolidating when mixed with a portion of lime, and employed as cement.

The Leskean cabinet consisted in all of 7331 specimens, and was pronounced one of the most perfect monuments of mineralogical ability extant. William Higgins was appointed professor of chemistry and mineralogy to the Dublin Society in June 1795, when the cabinet was placed under his care. It was deposited in a spacious apartment, open to students, and special rules regulating admission were printed. The chemical laboratory was established, and Higgins was instructed to make experiments.

In 1815, on the report of Giesecke, professor of mineralogy, and Thomas Weaver, an authority on the same science, German manuscripts and drawings, concerning mineralogy, geology, and mining, the property of the late Dr. Mitchell, were purchased for £100. They had originally been collected with a view to the formation of a mining board, long a project of Dr. Richard Kirwan.

During the next year it was considered important to establish communication between the Society's museum and the Imperial museum, Vienna, and Giesecke was directed to send Baron Schreiber, the director, in accordance with his expressed desire, specimens of the meteoric stone which fell in Tipperary (see p. 228), and to thank him for specimens of some that fell in Moravia and Bohemia. In 1829, the committee of chemistry recommended that the Leskean cabinet should be restored and completed in all its parts, and a more suitable apartment provided for it, where the whole cabinet might be open for inspection by the public.

In April 1794, it had been found necessary to provide fitting rooms on the north side of the Poolbeg street premises for the due arrangement of this valuable collection, together with accommodation for the drawing schools, and £800 were expended on the additional buildings. When Dr. Kirwan had completed his examination and arrangement of the museum, a medal of Irish gold, with a suitable inscription, was presented to him. In 1802, he was asked to sit to Hugh D. Hamilton for his portrait, which was to be hung in the museum, in acknowledgment of "his eminent services and indefatigable labours in chemistry, mineralogy, &c." Fourteen years after, 120 guineas were paid to Miss Harriet Hamilton for finishing the portrait commenced by her father, who only completed the painting of the head. This portrait now hangs in the reception room in Leinster House. The Royal Irish Academy is in possession of another and much better portrait. Richard Kirwan, chemist and natural philosopher, was born in 1733, son of Martin Kirwan of Cregg, co. Galway. He was a Fellow of the Royal Society, and corresponded with all the *savants* of Europe. His *Elements of Mineralogy* was the first systematic treatise on the subject published in the kingdom, and his papers on *Chemical Affinity* obtained for him the Copley Medal of the Royal Society. Kirwan became a Doctor of Laws of Dublin University in 1794, and was elected President of the Royal Irish Academy in 1799, a post which he held until his death, which took place on the 1st of January 1812. He was buried in St. George's, Temple street. The Society purchased for £10 Kirwan's "burning glass," which is still in its possession. The glass is illustrated on the opposite page.

Between 1795 and 1800, a sum of almost £2500 was expended on different buildings and works at the repository, and when in the latter year the museum was opened, many persons sent donations of shells, specimens preserved in spirits, beetles, &c. The Royal Irish

DR. R. KIRWAN'S "BURNING GLASS"

Academy presented a collection of volcanic specimens and hard woods, to be annexed to the Leskean cabinet. In 1809, it was reported that a complete and scientific survey of mineral productions was necessary, and Richard Griffith, jun., was recommended as eminently qualified for the undertaking. £300 were allocated in 1816, to complete the systematic part of the collection, so as to include specimens of all known species of simple minerals. The collection was then deficient by 129 species and substances. Major Birch, R.A., in 1817, presented to the museum many articles, among them Roman remains and marbles from Cateja, Andalusia; from Malta, two long swords used by the Knights, and part of the coat of mail of the Grand Master Wignacourt, 1615; from Egypt, a sarcophagus and phallus, and idols from the Great Pyramid; from Agrigentum, porcelain vases; also an antique Irish vessel from a bog in the county Roscommon, and a number of minerals. Mr. Gregory, of Coole, sent specimens of marble found in a quarry on his estate.

For some time the Society had been in a transition stage. The old order was more or less passing, and a new set of circumstances and new conditions were being developed. With the advent of the Farming Society, as to which more will be said in another chapter, the Dublin Society abandoned the premium system, which had so much, and for so long a period, occupied its attention. It was felt that the time had come when the formation of schools of science, in which qualified professors might lecture, were, under altered conditions in the country, and in accordance with the example and precedent set in such matters in England and Scotland, more likely to further the purposes for which the Society had originally been founded. Accordingly, on the establishment of the

Botanic Garden, Dr. Wade had been appointed pro-fessor and lecturer.   A sum of £50 and a gold medal were offered for answering at a public examination in Botany, and in the subject of vegetables connected with the feeding of cattle ; and subsidiary prizes at an examination as to hay, grasses, &c.   These prizes were to be confined exclusively to farmers, their sons, ap-prentices, and working men.   At the same time it was resolved to establish a veterinary school in the Hawkins street premises, for the purpose of helping to preserve the health of cattle, by the study of the diseases peculiar to them.   In this department, Mr. Peall and Mr. Watts, both Englishmen, were appointed respectively professor and lecturer, and assistant and practitioner. A forge, dissecting-room, and museum were provided. Boxes for invalid horses were also erected, to be used for clinical lectures and cures by operation.   In addition to horses, cattle, sheep, pigs, &c., poultry were after a time to be included.   Pending the erection of suitable buildings, Mr. Peall was allowed to engage temporary premises for his operations.   He died in 1825, and the veterinary department was then given up.

In the year 1800, a committee was appointed to report on the plan of the London Institution for diffusing knowledge, which reported that the Dublin Society had taken the lead of it and all other like institutions in Europe in everything except philo-sophical lectures.   Accordingly, a suitable room was furnished in the new repository, and James Lynch, of Capel street, optician, was appointed professor and lecturer in hydraulics, mechanics, experimental philo-sophy, &c.   He delivered three public courses of twenty-five to thirty lectures each, in the year, and was paid twenty-five guineas for each course.   The committee furnished a general syllabus of the subjects on which he lectured. The museum was open, and Mr. William Higgins, who had been appointed professor and lecturer in mineralogy, conducted his lectures in that department.

Between May 1800 and March 1804, the Society expended no less a sum than £17,841 on buildings at the repository. In 1800, the committee of chemistry and mineralogy offered a premium of £200 for the best geological and mineralogical survey of the county of Dublin.

The Society was of opinion that it might be advantageous to bring over from England distinguished lecturers, and in 1810, the Royal Society was asked to allow Professor Humphry Davy to deliver a course of lectures on electro-chemical subjects, which he did; 500 guineas were paid to him, and 337 persons attended his first lecture. Next year, he gave another set of lectures on chemical philosophy, and repeated the course in geological science that he had read before the Royal Institution. Professor Davy was also asked to superintend the construction of a voltaic battery of large plates. At the conclusion of the lectures, the committee of chemistry reported that the total amount received for admission tickets was £1101, 15s. 1d., all expenses amounting to £327, 15s. 1d., which left a credit balance of £773, 6s. 11d. Out of this, a sum of £750 was sent to Davy, with thanks for having " materially increased the spirit of philosophical research in Ireland." In a reply, dated the 9th of December 1811, Davy said that he was proud of the Society's opinion that his lectures would be useful to the Irish public ; and added that as long as he lived, he would remember with gratitude the attention, candour, and indulgence of his audience.

L

In 1812, it was decided to appoint a professor of chemistry, and a professor of mineralogy and geology; the latter to have a salary of £300 a year. Mr. Jameson, professor of mineralogy in the University of Edinburgh, was appointed to the post. Greater care was now to be taken in the arrangement of the museum, and the professor, it was thought, would find himself in a more favourable position for making geological surveys and reports. A time-table for lectures was also permanently fixed.

A mining engineer, competent to examine mines and open collieries, was also to be appointed. He was to have a knowledge of levelling and surveying, and to be prepared to visit England and Scotland, to bring over models of improved machinery. Richard Griffith, jun., was appointed to that position in May 1812, at a salary of £300 a year for three months spent in actual survey under the Society, and three months in preparing reports, maps, sections, &c., and in delivering a course of lectures. £500 was allocated for mining purposes, which would leave £200 for contingent expenses. It was arranged that he was to put himself in touch with proprietors of mines and their agents in Ireland, so as to lay the foundation of a minute mineralogical survey. He was also to make himself master of the position of the several coalfields and beds of coal, as well as to describe machinery, and the plan of working mines, and to suggest improvements. He was expected to furnish accurate maps, specifying objects of mineralogical interest in the country, and explanatory sections of stratification, and was also to deliver public courses of lectures on the geology of Ireland, and the application of machinery to mines. As a result of his appointment, Griffith was first invited to

SIR CHARLES L. GIESECKE

(From an oil painting by Sir Henry Raeburn)

the Queen's county and to Kilkenny: Mr. Gorges of Kilbrew, and Mr. West of Clontarf, also asked him to view their properties, but on Kilbrew he reported unfavourably. He reported on the coal districts of Kilkenny, Queen's county and Carlow, and stated that he was making a geological map of Ireland. In 1814, Griffith visited Newcastle-on-Tyne, "a centre of admirable management in coal-mining, machinery, &c."; here his attention was much attracted by a newly constructed steam carriage, in use for drawing loaded waggons along railways to the exclusion of horses! He thought that most important results would flow from it.

After a short time, the professorship of mineralogy was declared vacant, and four candidates were selected —Robert Bakewell, an author and lecturer in London, Charles Lewis Giesecke, Dr. James Miller, a Scotchman, and Thomas Weaver, who, having been a pupil of Werner at a mining school in Freiberg, Saxony, had conducted mining operations at Cronebane, Glendalough, and Luganure. Giesecke was elected by a majority of 46 over Weaver, and on the 27th of January 1814, "he was introduced by the vice-president in the chair to the Dublin Society."

Karl Ludwig Metzler, who afterwards assumed the name of Giesecke, was born in 1761, in Augsburg, and is believed to have been educated at Göttingen, under Blumenbach, though it is doubtful whether there be not confusion in this particular between him and one of his brothers. The youth and early manhood of this extraordinary man were spent amid scenes and occupations far removed from those of his maturer years. He had a passion for the stage, especially for music and the opera, and for a time he was an actor, bringing out at Vienna a translation of *Hamlet*, a character in which he himself appeared. In 1786, Giesecke is found editing an actor's newspaper in Regensberg, and from 1791 to 1799, he wrote a number of librettos and operas. He was a friend of Schiller, Klopstock, and Goethe, with whom he corresponded, and it is not improbable that he was the original of *Wilhelm Meister*. He was also associated with Mozart, and there is no doubt he had a large share in writing the libretto of the *Magic Flute ;* indeed, in a work on German opera, it is recorded that he stated himself as responsible for the whole of it, except the parts of Papageno and Papagena, which may be attributed to Schikaneder, a musician and manager of operatic companies, who was also associated with Mozart. During the middle and at the close of the eighteenth century, Freemasonry flourished in Vienna, where Mozart arrived in 1781, and both he and Giesecke were members of the order. Mozart composed a great deal of Masonic music, but by far his most important composition in this line was the opera of the *Magic Flute*, which was written in 1791. It is understood to contain sympathetic allusions to Freemasonry, and, under cover of a representation of Egyptian mysteries, to have been intended as a glorification of the order in Austria.

Giesecke began in 1794 the serious study of mineralogy, a science towards which he had always had a particular inclination. He subsequently travelled a good deal, and for a time entered the Austrian service, finally settling in Copenhagen, where he conducted a school of mineralogy and became a dealer in minerals. In 1806, the King of Denmark sent him to Greenland to study mineralogy and to make charts, &c. In that country Giesecke underwent great privations, and, returning in 1813, he found his way to Edinburgh. Particulars of his discoveries with regard to the old Norwegian colonists who some 900 years previously had settled on the east coast of Greenland, were afterwards published in the *Transactions* of the Royal Irish Academy, vol. xiv.; and one of his charts of the west coast of Greenland was in the museum of the Royal Dublin Society. Before leaving Greenland, Giesecke shipped for Copenhagen a quantity of valuable minerals, which were captured by a French privateer. Being recaptured by an English frigate, the collection was brought to Leith, where it was purchased by Mr. Allan, a banker of Edinburgh. Giesecke went thither in pursuit of his collection, and became a warm friend of Allan, who introduced him to Sir George Mackenzie, whose friendship he also gained. Soon after, Giesecke became a candidate for the professorship of mineralogy in the Dublin Society, to which, as we have seen, he was appointed.

The school became famous, and Mr. Isaac Weld, one of the secretaries, in 1831, spoke of its head as " one whose superlative attainments in the science were acknowledged from one end of Europe to the other." The collection of minerals in the museum numbered 30,000 specimens, including *gieseckite*.[1] At the time of his appointment, Giesecke was unable to lecture in English, but undertook to devote himself to its study, which he did with such success that in a short time he spoke the language with ease. He was soon able to report the arrangement of the Leskean museum, and of his own Greenland collection, which he presented to the Society. On 22nd May 1817, a gold medal, with inscription, was presented to Sir Charles Giesecke, at a meeting of the Society, when the

---

[1] Gieseckite is a hydrous silicate of aluminium and potassium of the mica group, named after Giesecke, who brought it from Greenland.

chairman made a complimentary speech. The medal cost £17, 9s. 9½d., and was executed by William Mossop, jun. Giesecke was absent from this country on special leave, from July 1817 to the end of the summer of 1819, when the cause of his prolonged absence was fully explained in a report of the committee of mineralogy. Having been originally employed by the Danish government in Greenland, he was compelled to go over to Copenhagen to close the business relations in reference to his commission to that country. Serious illness overtook him, and his life was despaired of. On recovery, he had to visit his native Augsburg, to settle private affairs before taking up his permanent residence in Ireland. After that, he journeyed to Vienna, to present specimens obtained in Greenland for the Austrian government. Giesecke further explained in his report that he had been working at his *Lectures on the Natural History of Greenland*, which he hoped might reflect credit on the Society whose professor he had become.

In August 1825, Giesecke undertook a mineralogical tour in Galway, Mayo, and the island of Achill, and, in 1826, through Donegal. One hundred and fifty guineas were voted to him for the latter tour, and his reports on both are printed in the *Proceedings*. In 1828, he went through Derry, Antrim, Tyrone, and Down, and in the *Proceedings*, vol. lxvii. app. i., will be found a report on the scientific results of this journey. Sir Charles Giesecke, K.D. (as he was generally called from 1816, when he was made a knight of the Danish order of the Dannebrog), died very suddenly on the 5th of March 1833. The museum was closed for a fortnight as a mark of respect to his memory. The Society, at the meeting subsequent to his death, expressed its high sense of his long-tried talents as a

MEDAL AWARDED TO MR. LEWIS ROBERTS, 1765

MEDAL PRESENTED TO Sir C. L. GIESECKE, 1817

(*William S. Mossop*)

scientific professor, and of his amiable manners and character as a gentleman. Sir Charles Giesecke was very popular in Dublin, and a tablet to his memory, which stands on the staircase wall of St. George's Church, states that "he was beloved as a friend and sought as a companion by all who knew him." His portrait by Sir Henry Raeburn—the gift in 1817 of his friend, Sir George Mackenzie, bart., to the Society —hangs in the reception room, Leinster House. There are two small autograph albums of Giesecke's in the National Museum, Dublin, which began to be filled by his friends (many of them eminent scientific men) in 1781, and their contributions extend to about the year 1829. The first volume is inscribed "Fautoribus amicisque sacrum." They contain original sentiments and verses, with quotations in Latin, French, German, English, and even Hebrew; sketches in pencil and water-colours, and silhouette portraits. One volume was presented to the museum by the Misses Hutton, whose father was Giesecke's executor, and the other came from the collection of the late Mr. Thomas H. Longfield. Very full particulars of Giesecke's career will be found in an article in the *Dublin University Magazine*, 1834; in *Mozart's Operas*, by Edward J. Dent (1913); in an article by Professor K. J. V. Steenstrup, on Giesecke's mineralogical journal kept in Greenland, together with a biographical notice of Giesecke, which appeared in the *Meddelelsen om Grönland*, Copenhagen, 1910; and in a paper on "Mozart and some of his Masonic Friends," by H. Bradley, in the *Ars Quatuor Coronatorum*, vol. xxvi. 241.

Dr. Scouler, professor of natural history in the University of Glasgow, succeeded him as professor of mineralogy here. Other candidates for the post included Dr. Whitley Stokes, lecturer in natural history, Trinity College, Dublin, and G. B. Somerly, of London.

To return to the labours of the mining engineer. In 1814, he reported on the Leinster coalfields, which he had found to number eight beds. The Grand Canal Company and the owners of the beds had recently made over two hundred trials for coal, at a cost of thousands of pounds, in districts where, on a mere inspection of the map and sections, it was clear that no coal could be found. Griffith next laid before the Society his geological and mining survey of Connaught, and then directed his attention to the Ulster coal district, where, between Emyvale in Monaghan and Pettigo in Fermanagh he made a minute survey, but found only thin beds of coal. In 1827, he was engaged on a general geological survey of Ireland, with a view to the publication of a memoir and map of each county, following the Ordnance Survey. He examined from Slieve Gallen in Derry, south to Enniskillen and Clogher, where were found some thin beds of coal; and he also reported on the metallic mines of Leinster. He hoped soon to report on Munster, and had found Audley, near Crookhaven, and Ross Island, Killarney, among the most promising places in the British Empire. Soon after, Griffith informed the Society that there was no part of Ireland, in the geological examination of which he had not made considerable progress. " The chief public object of my life is to complete an accurate map, geological and descriptive, of Ireland." Griffith resigned his post on being appointed a Commissioner of valuation of lands in Ireland, but stated that he intended to continue his researches towards the completion of the geological map.

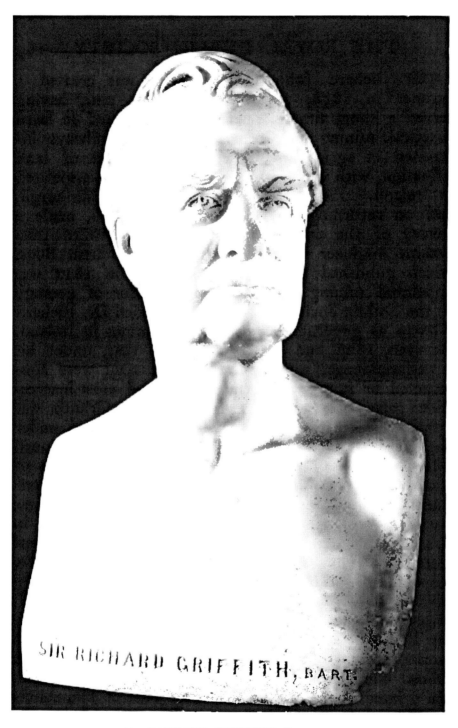

SIR RICHARD GRIFFITH, BART.
(*Marble Bust by Sir Thomas Farrell*)

Sir Richard John Griffith, who was created a baronet in 1858, was born in 1784, and, having served a short time in the army, commenced to learn practical mining in Cornwall. He was always interested in agriculture, and in the subject of land valuation, with which his name will ever be associated in Ireland. He studied for some time in Edinburgh, and on returning to this country in 1808, made a survey of the coalfields of Leinster. Griffith then became engineer to the Commission on Irish Bogs, which published valuable reports, and in 1812 was appointed mining engineer and professor of geology to the Dublin Society. He also succeeded Dr. Richard Kirwan as government inspector of mines in Ireland. Between 1822 and 1830, it is said that, under his superintendence, some 250 miles of road were constructed or improved in the wildest and most inaccessible parts of the country. In 1827, Griffith was appointed Commissioner of Valuation in Ireland, under the Act 7th George IV, a post which he held until 1868. From 1850 to 1864, he acted as chairman of the Board of Public Works. So great was the confidence reposed in this remarkable man, that there was hardly a work of public importance undertaken in this country, from about 1830 until his retirement into private life, on which he was not asked to give his opinion. His *magnum opus*—the Geological Map of Ireland—which took its final form in 1855, will always remain a monument of his industry and ability. Sir Richard Griffith published a number of scientific works, and all the reports made by him during his official connection with the Society will be found in the printed *Proceedings*. A marble bust of him stands in the reception-room in Leinster House.

CHAPTER X

THE LIBRARY; AND THE STATISTICAL SURVEYS OF COUNTIES

ONE of the rules for the government of the Society, approved in December 1731, laid down that all the works, journals, and transactions which should be published by other Societies and by private persons, and which might contain any useful improvement or discovery in nature or art, were to be purchased. Thus, at the earliest possible period, was the formation of a Library provided for, and this rule governed the purchase of books for more than a century.

The earliest catalogue of the library was very technically drawn up about 1735–6. The books included in it were in English, French, Greek, German, Low Dutch, Latin, and Spanish, and treat of Agriculture, Arithmetic, Bridges, Civil Law, Flax, Farm Buildings, Hemp, Husbandry, Hydraulics, Hydrotechnics, Machinery, Metallurgy, Mills, Police, Rural Economy, Statistics, and Silk Worms. (Preface to catalogue, suppl. 1850, by Edward R. P. Colles, librarian.) The library, then comprising thirty-seven volumes, increased during the ensuing sixty years to 2105, and the following are the titles of the books as they appeared in the original catalogue :

Folios.

Theatrum Machinarum Generale, by Leopold [Leupold], in High Dutch. Leipzig, 1724.

Theatrum Machinarum Hydraulicarum, by do., in High Dutch. 1724.

Theatrum Machinarum Hydraulicarum, by do. in do. Tome first. Tome second. 1724.

Theatrum Pontificiale, by do. in do. 1726.

Theatrum Staticum, pars prima, by do. in do. 1726.

Theatrum Arithmetico Geometricum, by do. in do. 1726.

Theatrum Machinarium, by do. 1725.

Traité de la Police de France, par Mr. De la Mare. Amsterdam, 1729. Tome premier. Tome second.

The Dutch Placaats or Laws, in five volumes :
Volume 1st, by Cau, to the year 1658.
Vol. 2nd, by Cau, to the year 1664.
Vol. 3rd, by Simon Van Leeuwen, to the year 1683.
Vol. 4th, by Jacobus Sibellus, to the year 1700.
Vol. 5th, by Paulus Scheltus, to the year 1720.
Tables or titles of all the Placaats.

Georgius Agricola de Re Metallica. Basileæ, 1657.

Theatrum Machinarum Universale, or the Great Dutch Mill Book, with Cutts, by Van Zyland Schenk. Amster. 1734.

The Great Dutch Mill Book, part 1st, 1734 ; part 2nd, 1736, by Natrus, Polly, Vuuren, and Punt.

Quartos.

Machines et inventions approuvées par L'Academy Royale des Sciences. 1735, à Paris. Tome premier. Tome second. Tome troisième. Tome quatrième. Tome cinquième. Tome sixième.

Oeconomie Générale de la Campagne, ou nouvelle Maison Rustich. Par Louis Liger, à Paris. 1708. Tome premier. Tome second.

Govierno Politico de Agricultura, por Lope de Deca. En Madrid, 1618.

Rei Agrariæ auctores legesque Variæ, per Goesium. Amstelodami, 1674.

Tusser's Husbandry.

Octavos.

Geoponicorum sive de Re Rustica. Libri Viginti. Basso collectore, Græce et Latine. Cantabrigiae, 1704.

Varronis Opera omnia cum Notis. Dordrecht, 1619.
Jethro Tull's Horse Hoeing Husbandry. Dublin, 1733.
The Practice of Farming and Husbandry, by W. Ellis.
    Dublin, 1735.
Tull's Horse Hoeing Husbandry. The first part. Dublin,
    1731.
Slator's Instructions for Cultivating and Raising Flax and
    Hemp. Dublin, 1724.
Instructions for Planting white Mulberryes for Silk Worms.
    Paris, 1665.

When the library was being formed, Dr. Tennison,
bishop of Ossory, presented a number of books.

In 1755, the Society purchased, for a sum of £500,
the collection of manuscripts made by Walter Harris,
the editor of Ware, who died in Henry street, Dublin,
in July 1761 ; and an obituary notice, in mentioning the
purchase, added, that " from it some excellent history
may be compiled." Archbishop King had cherished
the idea of writing a Church History of Ireland, and
his *Collectanea* were added to and used by Harris.
They were also made much use of by Archdall, in
compiling his *Monasticon*. The collection consists of
seventeen volumes folio. Eleven of them contain
deeds, patents, letters (Irish History, 1170–1690).
The twelfth deals with convents, monasteries, and Irish
ecclesiastical affairs. Another volume contains translations from Stearne's collection, among them extracts
from the *Annals of Innisfallen*. The contents of the
remaining volumes are of a miscellaneous character.
In August 1761, Lord Clanbrassil applied by letter to
Dr. Mann, requesting that Harris' collection of manuscripts should be sent to Dr. Warner [1] in England. The

---

[1] Ferdinando Warner, LL.D., rector of St. Michael's, Queenhithe,
a man of great ability and wide learning. He wrote a *History of
Ireland*, of which the first volume only—to 1171—was published.
While gathering materials for an ecclesiastical history, he came to

application was refused, on the ground that sending the documents beyond sea would be inconsistent with the trust reposed in the Society by the House of Commons, which had enabled it to purchase them. These manuscripts were transferred to the National Library of Ireland, when the Society's library was taken over by the Government.

In March 1780, £36, 14s. 1½d. were paid for fifty-five volumes of the *Encyclopédie*, and Albert Von Haller's *Bibliotheca Botanica* (1771), purchased for the library at Dr. MacBride's auction. From about the year 1780, the library received a good deal of attention. A number of valuable books were purchased, both on the continent and at home, and several members, qualified by their literary tastes and attainments, helped by their experience and advice in forming a remarkable collection of works. In May, 1781, a sum of £238, 11s. 6d. was paid to Payne, of Pall Mall, for the purchase of books acquired at the sale of the late Mr. Beauclerk's collection in London. An additional sum was required for the completion of the set of the *Flora Danica*,[1] and of the *Encyclopédie*. A little later, Mr. Conyngham, who has previously been mentioned as taking a deep interest in the library, when in Portugal, was requested to purchase some scarce volumes to the amount of £200. Four guineas were paid for two volumes of *Iconology, or a Collection of Emblematical Figures*, "a scarce and valuable work," published in London.

Dublin, where he consulted manuscripts in Trinity College, Marsh's Library, and the Record Tower, Dublin Castle. *Warner's History of the Rebellion, and Civil War in Ireland*, which appeared in 1767, is a very accurate work.

[1] This magnificent work—*Icones Plantarum Floræ Danicæ*, by George Christian Oeder, and others—was issued from time to time between 1761 and 1883.

In 1784, Mr. Conyngham laid before the Society a catalogue of several books in Dutch and other foreign languages, which he had purchased abroad for the Society, they being scarce and valuable. The secretary was authorised to employ Mr. Gabriel Beranger, in translating the titles and indexes.

Beranger, whose family were French Huguenots, was born at Rotterdam in 1729. Coming to Dublin in 1750, he sold prints and kept an artists' warehouse in South Great George's street. He died at his residence in St. Stephen's Green in 1817, aged eighty-eight years, and was buried in the French cemetery, Peter street. Beranger's special patrons were Colonel Burton Conyngham and General Vallancey, who obtained for him the post of ledger clerk in the Exchequer Office. Beranger made a number of sketches of antiquities for Vallancey's *Collectanea*, and a series of these sketches now in the Royal Irish Academy shows the appearance of many buildings that no longer exist. He will always hold a high place in the history of Irish art, "as his accurate and beautiful work preserves with admirable fidelity the distinctive features of many Irish architectural remains." Sir William Wilde wrote a memoir of Beranger,[1] with a full account of his labours in the cause of Irish art, literature, and antiquities, between the years 1760 and 1780. A large number of sketches, elevations, landscapes, written descriptions of ruins, and manuscript accounts of his various tours from 1773 to 1780 came into Sir William's possession, from which material he was able to compile his very interesting memoir.

In 1787, Colonel Hamilton was paid a sum of fifty guineas for translating the indexes of thirty-two volumes of the *Transactions* of the Haarlem and Flush-

---

[1] *Journal R.S.A.I.*, vols. xi., xii., and xiv.

ing societies; and later, the Rev. Denis Taaffe[1] translated several tracts from Dutch and German authors, and made a catalogue of Dutch and German books belonging to the Society. R. E. Mercier compiled, in 1797, a catalogue of the library, and in 1806, the catalogue was ordered to be printed.

In 1795, General Vallancey recommended the appointment of the Rev. Dr. John Lanigan, whom he had known in Italy, for employment in the library, a recommendation that was endorsed by Lord Donoughmore. He became librarian in 1808, and during his tenure of that office he performed his duties with marked efficiency. Dr. Lanigan translated a number of works for the Society, and corrected the proof sheets of the *Statistical Surveys*. This remarkable man was born in Cashel in 1758, and being intended for the priesthood, he was sent at an early age to the Irish College, Rome. He was subsequently appointed professor of Hebrew and Divinity at Pavia, returning to Ireland in 1794. During the previous year had appeared the first part of his *Institutiones Biblicæ*, which caused him to be looked on as a Jansenist, and Dr. Lanigan found it difficult to procure an ecclesiastical appointment in this country. He was, however, made professor of Sacred Scripture and Hebrew in Maynooth College, a post which he speedily resigned on being asked to subscribe a special formula. It was at this time that Dr. Lanigan's valuable services were placed at the disposal of the Society. He began to suffer from brain disease in 1813, and in 1815 resigned the librarianship, retaining for a time his

---

[1] Born in the county Louth in 1743. He was author of a *History of Ireland*, and wrote several pamphlets on Ireland and the Roman Catholic Church. Rev. Denis Taaffe was one of the founders of the Gaelic Society in 1808, and he died in Dublin in 1813.

position as corrector of the press. He died at Finglas in 1828. Dr. Lanigan's *Ecclesiastical History of Ireland* is a well-known work. On his retirement, Dr. Samuel Litton, Dr. Ryan, Mr. Newenham, Mr. Berwick, Dr. Johnson, and Mr. Cramer became candidates for the vacant post, when Dr. Litton was elected by 154 votes in a house of 237 members. Between 1817 and 1824, the new librarian compiled a catalogue of the library.

In 1811, a committee, consisting of the seven vice-presidents, the two secretaries, Henry Hamilton, Isaac Weld, John Boardman, Edward Houghton, Samuel Guinness, Henry Adair, and the Rev. J. C. Seymour, was appointed to inspect the books, and consider the library regulations. It was arranged that from the 25th of March to the 29th of September the library was to be open from 8 A.M. to 5 P.M. and from 6 P.M. to sunset; for the remainder of the year, from 9 A.M. to sunset. (In 1836, it was ordered to be open from 11 A.M. until 5 P.M.) A special catalogue of such works as might be lent to members was to be prepared, and the Society's professors were to be permitted to borrow books, and bring them to the lecture rooms during lectures. An assistant to the librarian was necessary. The power of selection of books was to rest with the library committee, which was to be elected annually by ballot. The library room was considered totally inadequate, and, soon after, the architect was directed to furnish plans for a new library. The committee reported that its members were engaged in cataloguing the coins and medals. Two hundred pounds per annum was afterwards fixed as the librarian's salary, for six hours a day, in managing and cataloguing the library, and superintending the Society's publications. Mr. McDonnell was appointed assistant librarian at a salary of £100 a year. By November 1812, the new sub-librarian, under Dr. Lanigan's superintendence, had compiled a general alphabetical catalogue of all the books. The nummarium, which was under the direction of the librarian, was found to contain 23 gold coins, 14 gilt; 427 silver, 88 Roman, 2 Cufic; copper coins (Roman), 274; Moorish, 4; ditto, various, 253; of mixed metal, 124: 1 brass ring: 19 Egyptian coins: medals (lead), 24. The collection was directed to be deposited in the library, and the librarian was to arrange the coins and medals, supplying a catalogue.

It was arranged in March 1812 that there was to be a select standing committee in charge of the library and nummarium, when the Hon. George Knox, Rev. Henry Moore, Henry Adair, Robert B. Bryan, Richard Fox, Henry Arabin, Archibald St. George, Isaac M. D'Olier, Hugh Hamill, Isaac Weld, Nicholas P. Leader, Wm. Farren, and Thomas Wallace were nominated to serve on it.

Marsh's Library being considered as situated in a remote and inconvenient place, it was referred to the library committee to look into the Act which established it, and to confer with the trustees of that library as to the best means of making it accessible. Nothing further, however, appears to have been done, though in the year 1814, when the Society contemplated building a library, they thought the trustees might approve of obtaining an Act of Parliament, authorising the removal of their collection, in which case the Society would have granted them ground for a suitable building.

Mr. Thomas Pleasants presented to the Society books valued at £191, 9s.,—including *Hakluyt's Voyages* (5 vols.), £34, 2s. 6d. (only 75 printed); Fabian's *Chronicles;* Monstrelet's *Chronicles*—translated by T. Johnes (12 vols.), £9, 8s. 6d.; Burney's

M

History of Music (4 vols.), £9, 2*s.*; *Locke's Works,* (10 vols.), £9, 2*s.*; Playfair's *System of Chronology,* £2, 16*s.* 10*d.*; W. Roy's *Antiquities of Scotland* (Military Antiquities of the Romans in Britain), £5, 13*s.* 9*d.* In consideration of this and other valuable gifts to the Society, and of his having expended £10,000 in the erection of a stove tenter house,[1] as also £6000 for a hospital for sick poor in the liberties of Dublin, Mr. Pleasants was elected an honorary member.

A sum of £500 per annum was reported as available in 1816 for the purchase of books, newspapers, and periodicals. On the 11th of December 1817, a catalogue of the library was ready for delivery, and fifty guineas were voted to Dr. Litton on its completion. In 1820, Dr. Litton was paid the compliment of being elected an honorary member, and on the occasion of his taking his seat as such he was specially addressed by the vice-president from the chair.

Frederick Cradock, whose father had been librarian at Marsh's Library, was elected librarian in the room of Dr. Litton, on the latter's appointment in 1826 to the professorship of Botany. In that year the collection consisted of 8300 volumes, and £60 were paid to the sub-librarian for an index to sixty-one volumes of the printed *Proceedings.* Another catalogue (raisonné) was completed in 1829, in four folio volumes, for which a sum of £100 was paid to the librarian. On the death of Cradock in 1833, John Patton was elected librarian, two of the other candidates for the post being John Anster[2] and Robert Travers. In 1855,

---

[1] See p. 206 *n.*

[2] Anster was born in Charleville in 1793. He became Regius Professor of Civil Law in Dublin University, early published some poems, and was the first to render Goethe's *Faust* into English verse. His version of portion of the poem appeared in *Blackwood* in 1820. The first part was completed in 1835, and the entire by 1864. Anster

on the resignation of Patton, Edward R. P. Colles became librarian. He was succeeded in 1876, by William Archer, F.R.S., who from 1877 to 1895, was librarian of the National Library. On Mr. Archer's retirement in the latter year, Mr. Thomas W. Lyster, M.A., the present librarian, was appointed.

A most important addition was made to the Library in the year 1863, by Dr. Jasper Joly's gift to it of some 23,000 volumes, together with an extensive collection of Irish and Scotch song music. The deed of gift, which was subject to certain conditions, was dated 8th April 1863, and, in acknowledgment of his splendid donation, Dr. Joly was elected an honorary member of the Society. His portrait, by Catterson Smith, hangs in the library, Leinster House. The chief interest in the Joly collection lies in the large number of volumes which deal with Irish history and topography. A considerable portion is taken up with the story and campaign of Napoleon, while numerous works illustrate the history of the French Revolution, and French literature and works on the age of Louis the Fourteenth are well represented. Among the rare and curious volumes in the Joly collection are the following—*Orationes* of St. Brigid of Sweden (which is probably unique); *Lyra seu Anacephalæosis Hibernica*, by Thomas Carve, a Tipperary man, chaplain to the Irish troops in the Thirty Years' War. His works are very scarce, and only three copies of the first edition of the *Lyra* are known, one being the volume in this collection. The *Itinerarium* of Carve (1640–6), giving an account of the Thirty Years' War, is also there ; *Analecta Sacra*

was a frequent contributor to the *Dublin University Magazine*. This man of wide culture, wit, and high social qualities, as well as a true poet, died in 1867.

of David Rothe, Roman Catholic Bishop of Ossory, ed.
1617–19; a complete copy (rarely met with) of the
Acta Sanctorum of John Colgan (Louvain, 1645–7).
The Joly collection also contains a number of illustrated works—*Nuremberg Chronicle*, 1493; *Herwologia
Anglica*, Lond. 1620, the first book of English portraits; *Iconographie des contemporains*, Paris, 1832;
three *Voyages* of Captain Cook; and a set of plates
illustrating the coronations of Napoleon and King
George IV.[1]

In this collection are to be found, in addition,
about twenty volumes of manuscripts nearly all relating to Irish affairs. Among them will be found
a transcript of Keating's History of Ireland, made
in 1722 by Eugene O'Rahilly; a copy of the Down
Survey of the county of Tipperary; materials for a
statistical survey of Tipperary, 1833 (the volume
of this series for Tipperary was not printed; see
pp. 183–4); records of the French consulate in Alexandria (a fragment, 1687–1694), found in Alexandria
when the British captured the city in 1807; *Life of
Sir Richard Cox* by Walter Harris; Report of the
Commissioners on Bogs, and reports of surveyors employed by the Royal Dublin Society in making their
survey of bogs, bound in twelve volumes. One large
volume contains a number of unpublished plans and
sections. Translations from Buchoz's *Dictionnaire
Vétérinaire*, made by the Rev. Dr. Lanigan; *Instructions for Shepherds*, a translation made by Dr. Lanigan
in 1800–1; and four volumes on mineralogy by Sir
Charles Giesecke."

The Thorpe collection of Irish Historical Tracts,

---

[1] For these particulars I am indebted to *The National Library of
Ireland*, by Guthrie Vine (Library Association Record, 1902).
[2] From Report of the Librarian, National Library, 1900.

which was purchased in October 1840, is also to be found in the library. Thomas Thorpe, born in 1791, was a bookseller in Piccadilly, and later at 13 Henrietta street, Covent Garden, from 1839 to his death in 1851. Thorpe was celebrated for his extensive dealings in old books and manuscripts, and his carefully compiled catalogues were highly esteemed. The collection of tracts comprises ten volumes small quarto, 1629–1758; and two volumes, folio, 1641–1737. Each volume contains a printed list of contents, and a list will be found in the supplemental catalogue of the Society's library, published in 1850, pp. 45–65.

The Society was possessed of 218 volumes of old pamphlets, extending in date from 1634 to 1843, a detailed list of which appeared in the library catalogue, 1731–1859, p. 153. In it is also printed an alphabetical index to the first 80 volumes.

In 1838, Miss Tew, of Kingstown, delivered to the Society the library of her late brother, Rev. William Tew, of Ballysax, consisting of 180 volumes of divinity and classics, which he had bequeathed to it.

The report of the Commission of 1836 first definitely laid down that, as the library was supported by funds voted by Government, it ought to be open to all persons properly introduced. As in the case of the British Museum Library, the institution was to be looked on as the National Library. In 1849, more than 8000 readers attended. In 1878, about 27,000 were returned as using it, while in 1899, the number had reached a total of more than 155,000. The present National Library of Ireland is generally considered one of the finest, as it certainly is one of the most frequented, in the world. The average attendance is over 700 daily. £500 a year were allowed for expenses of the old library between 1816 and 1849; in 1862, it cost £930.

Under the agreement of March the 5th 1877, made between the Government and the Society, when its collection of books became the nucleus of the National Library of Ireland, the librarian of the British Museum was to be invited to give his opinion as to any books which it might not be necessary to transfer. Any such volumes were to remain in possession of the Society, and these became the nucleus of the very important library which the Royal Dublin Society has formed during the last thirty-five years. It now numbers between 40,000 and 50,000 volumes. Members of the Society elected prior to the 1st of January 1878 have the privilege of borrowing books from the National Library.

In 1881 the Society became possessed of a large number of volumes, almost altogether on theological and controversial subjects, bequeathed by the Rev. Aiken Irvine, of Coleraine. In 1889, it was enriched by what is known as the "Tighe Bequest," being 222 volumes of classics, especially of rare editions of Horace, from the collection of the late Robert Tighe, esq., of Fitzwilliam square. In March 1905, Miss Anne Winter bequeathed to the library the books belonging to her brother, Mr. John Winter, consisting of a number of volumes of general literature.

STATISTICAL SURVEYS OF COUNTIES

In the year 1801, the Society undertook the compilation of Statistical Surveys of the various counties of Ireland, arranging that each contributor should receive £80 for his work, and these surveys continued to appear up to 1832, when, at the time of Isaac

Weld's *Roscommon* being published, eight counties still remained to be dealt with. The first set included Hely Dutton's *Observations on Mr. Archer's Statistical Survey of Dublin.* "The volumes give a general view of each county, and form comprehensive guidebooks to the whole."[1] Weld's *Roscommon*, which gives an account of the social and archæological curiosities of the county, and Tighe's *Kilkenny* are considered the best of the series.

By July, 1829, the following had appeared :—

Queen's.	*Donegal.*
Sir C. Coote.	Same.
King's.	*Meath.*
Same.	R. Thompson.
Wicklow.	*Derry.*
R. Fraser.	Rev. G. W. Sampson.
Monaghan.	*Galway.*
Sir C. Coote.	H. Dutton.
Dublin.	*Tyrone.*
J. Archer and H. Dutton.	J. McEvoy.
Leitrim.	*Armagh.*
J. McParlan.	Sir C. Coote.
Down and *Ardglass.*	*Wexford.*
Rev. J. Dubourdieu.	R. Fraser.
Cavan.	*Kildare.*
Sir C. Coote.	J. J. Rawson.
Mayo.	*Clare.*
J. McParlan.	H. Dutton.
Kilkenny.	*Cork.*
W. Tighe.	Rev. H. Townsend.
Sligo.	*Antrim.*
J. McParlan.	Rev. J. Dubourdieu.

The counties for which surveys were not published were Carlow, Fermanagh, Kerry, Limerick, Longford, Louth, Roscommon, Tipperary, Waterford, and West-

[1] *Worthies of the Irish Church* (Stokes), p. 341.

meath.   Of these, Roscommon was completed by December 1831.   In the National Library is a volume of manuscript materials for the survey of the county of Tipperary, compiled about 1833, which had been entrusted to W. S. Mason.

Many of these volumes were defective, and would have required considerable amendment, but only those for the counties of Dublin and Cork were publicly attacked, the former, on the ground of its being a mere skeleton, and not a real survey of the county; the latter on the ground of religious intolerance. Lieutenant Joseph Archer's account of Dublin is stated to be an agricultural survey, but in the year after the publication of the volume, Hely Dutton's *Observations*, framed on similar lines, appeared.   It forms a second volume for the county of Dublin, and affords much fuller details.   In a short address to the reader, the Dublin Society hoped that the example afforded by the compiler would create emulation, and that others might be found who would make similar remarks on the surveys of other counties.

The Rev. H. Townsend's account of the county of Cork was also challenged, and in the Haliday collection (1811, dcccclxxxix. 3, 4, 5) is a *Letter to the Dublin Society from the most Rev. Dr. Coppinger, Bishop of Cloyne; occasioned by observations and mis-statements by Townsend*.   There is also a copy of the same letter, with supplement, &c., which was answered by *Observations on Dr. Coppinger's Letter to the Dublin Society*, by the Rev. Horace Townsend.   Dr. Coppinger accused him of representing the Roman Catholic clergy as bigoted and opposed to improvement, keeping their flocks in ignorance, and "preying on the vitals of the poor."   If not expressed in actual words, it was certainly implied, he asserted, in passages concerning schools at Mitchelstown, Clonakilty and Glanworth. Mr. Townsend replied that he had stated facts which, as facts, Dr. Coppinger did not deny, and to the " overweening authority assumed by the Church of Rome " he attributed the occurrences referred to by him. The conductors of the Mitchelstown charities disclaimed all knowledge of what was indicated in their case by Dr. Coppinger, and Townsend sought to controvert the Bishop's charges in the other instances.

CHAPTER XI

THE BOTANIC GARDEN

A RECORD of the earliest effort in connection with what afterwards became so celebrated all the world over, and which still retains its proud pre-eminence— the Society's Botanic Garden—appears in a minute of September 1732, which referred to a committee " to look out a piece of ground, about an acre, proper for a nursery." It was not until October 1733, that a plot of ground near Sir John Eccles' house was viewed. Another, on the Strand going to Ballybough Bridge, which belonged to a Rev. Mr. Hopkins, was subsequently taken. This was to be held rent free for three years, and at the end of that term, £6 per acre were to be paid for it; the place seems to have been known as the Society's Garden at Summer Hill. The members showed deep interest in the experiment, one of them—Mr. Ross—sending from Rostrevor, on a certain occasion, 500 poles for hops which were to be grown in the garden.

In March 1737, four acres near Martin's lane (later Mecklenburgh street, afterwards Tyrone and now Waterford street) and Marlborough street were taken, to be used for experiments. Soon after, a house was found near at hand, which was used for keeping implements and laying up flax. In 1738, an inventory of cider fruit trees on the ground was furnished. By April 1740, however, the gardeners are

found to have been dismissed, and the garden house given up. The soil having been found unsuitable for the Society's purposes, the field itself was subsequently disposed of.

It was not until fifty years later that the project was again taken up, when, under the Act 30 George III, c. 28, which granted £5000 to the Dublin Society, it was provided that £300 of that sum were to be employed towards the provision and maintenance of a Botanic Garden. A similar amount was specifically voted for the same purpose in each Act in favour of the Society down to 33 George III. On the 22nd of July 1790, the Society took into consideration the best method of applying the £300 appropriated in the last session of Parliament for a Botanic Garden, but it was not until almost a year later that Doctors Robert Percival, Walter Wade, and Edward Hill were invited to attend a conference, when, as a result of their deliberations with the Society, it was resolved that the University of Dublin and the College of Physicians should be communicated with, requesting their co-operation and advice. Both bodies were anxious to assist, and appointed representatives to meet in conference those elected by the Society, who were Sir William Gleadowe Newcomen, Andrew Caldwell, and Patrick Bride. Various sites near Dublin were examined, and in 1795, premises at Glasnevin, held by Major Thomas Tickell under a *toties quoties* lease from the Dean and Chapter of Christ Church,[1] were finally selected. The site consisted of sixteen acres, then in the occupation of John Kiernan, under a lease of which five and a half years were unexpired, at a yearly rent of £130.

---

[1] Archbishop Laurence O'Toole in 1178 granted Glasnevin to the Church of the Holy Trinity, Dublin, which had one of its granges there.

Tickell required £200 per annum on the determination
of Kiernan's lease, his interest in which the latter
agreed to sell for £800, giving instant possession. In
1804, Major Tickell assigned to the Society all his
interest in the ground for a sum of £1800. Not
alone the beauty of the site, but the historical interest
of the neighbourhood, must have told in favour of
its selection. Delville, the home of Delany, the friend
of Swift and Stella, was close by, and Parnell the
poet resided in Glasnevin.

The name of Tickell at once recalls that of Addison, and the connection of the two is generally supposed
to have made the site of the Botanic Garden classic
ground, as the former had a residence there which it
was believed had been frequently visited by Addison.
Mr. Herbert Wood, assistant keeper of the records,
in a charming and instructive paper, *Addison's Connection
with Ireland*,[1] shows how erroneous is this supposition,
for, though the house in which the curator of the
Botanic Garden now resides was once inhabited by
Thomas Tickell, he did not occupy it for some years
after the death of Addison, which occurred in 1719.
A shady path in the garden has long been named
" Addison's Walk," but it may have been so called by
Tickell in memory of his friend, who never himself
paced the walk.   Dr. Elrington Ball[2] places the matter
beyond dispute. He shows that Tickell had been under
secretary to Addison while he was Secretary of State,
and as such must have been known to Lord Carteret,
who appointed him Under Secretary in Ireland.   In a
letter to Bishop Nicholson, Bishop Downes mentions
" that Tickell landed in Ireland on 1st June (1724), and
refers to his being entirely unacquainted with that

---

[1] *Journal R.S.A.I.*, xxxiv. 133.
[2] *Correspondence of Swift*, iii. 198 *n.*

ADDISON'S WALK, BOTANIC GARDEN

country." [1]   The letter which Dr. Ball annotates is one from Swift to Tickell, dated 11th July 1723, in which he speaks of him as a "last comer and lodger." They had just become acquainted, and Tickell had a high claim to the Dean's regard as the friend and biographer of Addison.

Thomas Tickell was born in 1686 in Cumberland, and in 1710 was elected Fellow of Queen's College, Oxford. From the time of his arrival in Ireland in 1724, he made it his permanent residence, and, in 1726, married Clotilda, daughter of Sir Maurice Eustace, of Harristown. He died in 1740, and some of his descendants were resident in Dublin up to a recent period. Major Thomas Tickell, who sold his interest in the ground in Glasnevin to the Dublin Society, was Tickell's grandson. Tickell held a high place among the minor poets, and contributed to the *Spectator*. Dr. Johnson, in the *Lives of the British Poets*, says of his *Elegy on the Death of Addison*, that "no more sublime or elegant funeral poem is to be found in the whole compass of English literature." In it occur the oft-quoted lines :—

> "There taught us how to live, and (oh ! too high
> The price for knowledge) taught us how to die."

The ground at Glasnevin was ready by April 1796, when a committee was appointed to manage the place. Dr. Walter Wade, author of *Flora Dublinensis*, was invited to undertake the arrangement of the new plants, and to act as professor and lecturer in botany, so far as such might tend to promote agriculture, arts, and manufactures. Later, Wade lectured on botany in connection with diet, medicine, agriculture, and rural

---

[1] Nicholson's *Letters*, ii. 574.

economy; also on meadow, pasture, and artificial grasses. Nurserymen and others began to present valuable and curious plants, and donations came from England, including one sent by the professor of botany at Bath, which included roots of all British mints. John Underwood, a Scotchman, who came over under the patronage of Mr. Foster (Lord Oriel), was appointed head-gardener, and a furnished apartment was provided for him. In November 1798, £371 were paid to Messrs. Lee and Kennedy, of London, for valuable plants. The expense attending the Society's new undertaking was considerable, for in the period between February 1796 and March 1797, a sum of £1779 was expended in various ways. In 1799, £500 were voted for a greenhouse, for the preservation of a number of plants, and during the year 1800 the treasurer was further drawn on to the amount of £2500. The head-gardener was sent to England to purchase plants, which cost the Society £550, and, in addition, various small sums were disbursed from time to time for works, wages, &c., which reached another £500. By the committee's report, made in December 1800, it appeared that Mr. Parke, who superintended the buildings at the Garden, and at the new repository in Hawkins street, had received £7100, and had made payments to the amount of £7076, 14s. 10d. His remuneration as superintendent amounted to £700. Between the years 1800 and 1804, a sum of £9476, 7s. 4d. was expended on Glasnevin alone, as appears by the accounts. In 1798 and 1799, Parliament voted £1300 for the Garden, and in 1800, £1500 were voted for its support, and for payment of the professor of Botany.

By the month of May 1800, the Garden was in so forward a state, that proper persons to attend on visitors

and those anxious to examine the plants were appointed ;
separate catalogues of each class of garden were prepared, and a conservatory and stove were ordered.   A
Flora Rustica Hibernica was projected, and the professor of Botany was directed to forward to the drawing schools specimens of plants useful or injurious to
husbandry, with a view to the pupils copying them for
illustration of his work.   John White, under-gardener,
was sent in 1803 on a botanical enquiry through
Carlingford and the Mourne Mountains.

In 1801–2, catalogues of the hothouse plants, and
of the arboretum and herbarium, compiled by Underwood, were published, which showed that the collections,
even then, were very rich.   The hothouses and conservatories, designed by E. Parke, stood on the site now
occupied by the walk leading from the present entrance
gate to the octagon house.

The Society thought it advisable to have a lease
directly from the Dean and Chapter of Christ Church,
without an intervening one, and £1250 were paid to
the representative of the Rev. Travers Hume, assignee
of George Putland, for the interest in the chapter
lease to that family.   In 1807, £265 were paid to
Mr. Duffin, of the Linen hall, for a mill[1] and concerns adjoining the Society's ground, which it was
thought advisable to acquire ; and a plot of ground
belonging to the Grand Canal Company was leased
at £25 a year.   The Dean and Chapter of Christ
Church assigned Duffin's term, and renewed a lease
in which the Society agreed to leave him the mill,
house and garden, situate between the public road
to Glasnevin and the waste gate of the mill dam, for
thirteen years, at a yearly rent of £50.   In 1812, they

[1] The watermill in Glasnevin was granted in 1539 to the treasurer
of the Cathedral of the Holy Trinity.

took a renewal of the lease of the mill site and garden, retaining the plot of ground on the north of the mill race, which they held jointly with the mill site. The wall of the premises was thrown down, and rebuilt on range with the Society's wall; by which the road was widened eight or nine feet. The mill and house being in a ruinous state, the latter was removed, but the mill was repaired, as it was thought it might be useful for trials and experiments in dressing hemp and making cement for masonry. In any case, it was felt that the Society must necessarily have full command over the river Tolka, which bounds the Garden on the north. Later on, dangerous accidents were said to have occurred from insecure and improper passages to the islands in the river Tolka, and the matter was re-ferred to a committee. In 1817, special attention was directed to the ruinous and disgraceful state of the mill at Glasnevin, which cost the Society in purchase, fines, and rent, £1184, 11s. 11d. A flush weir was made at an expense of £13, and the mill and two acres adjoining were let to Mr. John Hill, of Eden quay, at £70 a year, he to expend £500. This tenant was afterwards proceeded against for wilful waste and non-payment of rent. Breaches were made in the wall, and in May 1823, a great flood caused breaches in the garden bank and weir. Obstructing matter had afterwards to be removed from the bed of the river when the water was low, and a wall to protect the bank was erected. In 1805, the gates of the Glasnevin turnpike were removed to the bridge over the river, as their then position was a hindrance to many attending the Garden.

The Rev. Thomas Hincks, in 1810, presented a *Flora* of the county Cork, and sent up rare plants for the hothouse. Soon after, an experiment was tried in apprenticing young lads of seventeen—six were given a trial in 1812—who were to receive 9s. weekly, and at the end of twelve months a sum of five guineas, provided that they obtained a proper certificate from the head-gardener, who acted as their master. He was to receive £5 for each apprentice, and the profits from sale of the catalogue, as his remuneration for instructing them. The school for young gardeners is still maintained. It may be observed that, in the year 1783, premiums had been offered by the Society to nurserymen for taking apprentices who were to be instructed in the art of grafting, rearing, and planting trees, when Robert Power, of Galway, was granted £20 for two apprentices taken by him.

Mr. Thomas Pleasants, whose liberality has been noted in connection with his bequests of pictures, &c., to the Society, in 1815 presented £600 for the Botanic Garden, and the amount was applied in erecting a suitable entrance and porter's lodge, which were much needed, and which would serve as a lasting memorial of his munificence. Subsequent expenses brought the total sum expended by him up to £700. About this time, the committee of botany made a calculation of averages, and came to the conclusion that the expense to be incurred in the improvement and support of the Garden should not exceed £1500 a year.

In 1817–1818, the range of hothouses was moved to a new site, being that of the present large palm-house.

The Norfolk Island pine now began to display symptoms of a sickly condition, its health and beauty became much impaired, and its recovery seemed doubtful. The injury was found to have arisen from the building—the octagon house—which was ordered to be erected round it, not having been put up in time, when a severe frost attacked the plant, which was unfortunately killed. The head-gardener was blamed for not having taken steps to protect it, and was about being dismissed, but the Society, taking a more lenient view, only censured and fined him. In July 1825 was announced the death of Dr. Wade, first professor of Botany, who from 1817 had taken up the duties of professor of Agriculture. Dr. Samuel Litton succeeded him, and on his death, in 1846, Dr. Harvey, the botanist and traveller, was appointed professor. Whitelaw and Walsh's *History of Dublin*, published in 1818 (ii. p. 1283), contains a very full description of the Garden and its contents at that time.

By 1830, the houses were becoming decayed, and it was found that what was known as the cattle garden was useless, while the Irish garden was unnecessary, the plants in it being in the general arrangement. The professor of Botany made a report, in which he stated that just the same arrangement existed then as had obtained in the year 1800. One portion was a *Hortus Hibernicus*, which contained the native plants of Ireland; the other portion was an illustration of the natural arrangement of Jussieu. In the first division—No. 1, the systematic, was rich in trees and shrubs. 2, The cattle garden was laid out according to the views of Linnæus, and was useful for agricultural experiments. 3, The hay garden, according to the plan of the Duke of Bedford's *hortus gramineus*, was laid out in plots of 9 ft. by 4 ft., with grasses used in Irish agriculture. 4, The esculent garden. 5, The dyer's garden. 6, Saxatile plants. 7, Creepers and climbers. 8, Bog and water plants. 9, Marine (only what grew naturally on shores). 10, Variegations of plants. There was also a *hortus medicus*. The hothouses and conservatories were reported on as being very imperfect, and there was a great lack of walled enclosures, privet hedges &c. Too little attention was said to be paid to florists' plants, and the fruit-bearing trees needed protection. An extension of the arboretum was considered necessary, and greater attention to the principle of pruning was recommended. A proper nursery and botanical museum, with library attached, were much required. The recommendations of the professor were carried out.

In the year 1833, the head and under gardeners, who had served since the establishment of the Garden, had become unequal to the duties of their respective posts, from age and infirmity. The former died in August of that year. On a ballot for the post of head-gardener, Mr. Ninian Niven, of the Chief Secretary's gardens, Phœnix park, and Mr. David Moore, of the College Botanic Garden, were candidates, and the former was elected. After his appointment, Niven went over by invitation to Arley Hall, Staffordshire, when the Earl of Mountnorris gave him 600 species of plants for the garden. He also visited Wentworth Fitzwilliam, Chatsworth, and the Botanic Garden, Sheffield, from each of which the Dublin Garden was liberally supplied. For the year ending 1st January 1835, the number of visitors to the Garden was 7110, and for that ending 1st January 1836, 11,477; which showed a very considerable increase. Mr. Niven initiated extensive alterations and improvements; the hothouses were repaired and stocked, the plan of the garden changed, and the various departments brought up to date. On resigning his post in 1838, Mr. Niven informed the Society that during his tenure of office fresh advances had been made in the rearrangement of the hardy herbaceous plants (according to Linnæus); about one half of the classes up to *Polyandria* had been gone over and added to; and he alluded to the fact of his having published a *Visitor's Companion to the Botanic Garden.* A new species of *Verbena*, from South America, had been raised from seed collected by Mr. John Tweedie of Buenos Ayres. The stock of what proved to be a very lovely plant raised in it (save one plant) was disposed of for 50 guineas, for the benefit of the Garden.

On the 8th of November 1838, Mr. David Moore, who afterwards became a Ph.Doc., was elected curator in the room of Mr. N. Niven. The title of his post was afterwards changed to that of Director. In 1878, in recognition of his scientific eminence, Dr. Moore was elected an honorary member of the Royal Dublin Society. Dr. Moore, a most distinguished botanist, laboured assiduously in the interests of the charge committed to him, and, on his death in 1879, left the Garden in a high state of efficiency. His son, Sir Frederick W. Moore, the present head of the department (who was knighted in 1911), succeeded him. Under Dr. Moore's régime, all the old houses, except the octagon, were removed, and the fine range of wrought-iron conservatories was built in 1843, at a cost of over £5000, of which sum £4000 were contributed by Government, the balance being paid by the Royal Dublin Society. Part of this balance was raised by private subscription among the members, and part was taken from the Society's reserve fund. The designs of these houses were furnished by Mr. Ferguson, master of architectural drawing in the School of Art, and by Mr. Frederick Darley. The first palmhouse, completed in 1862, was from a design of Mr. James H. Owen, architect of the Board of Works. This, being injured by the gales of 1833, was removed, and a splendid new one was erected in the next year. The

VIEW IN THE BOTANIC GARDEN

Orchid house was built in 1854, and the Victoria house, for the accommodation of the *Victoria regia* water-lily, was erected in 1855 by the Royal Dublin Society.

On the 6th of August 1849, Queen Victoria and the Prince Consort visited the Botanic Garden. (See p. 279.)

A considerable amount of friction occurred between the Government and the Society in 1861, on the question of opening the Garden on Sundays, a step which the Society resisted, and the grant of £6000 for the year was made conditional on the policy of the Government being carried out. In the end the Society had to give way, and on the Sundays, from the 18th of August to the end of September, 78,000 persons visited the place. The attendance for the year amounted to 133,780, and, notwithstanding the numbers, the Council of the Society paid a high tribute to the orderly and decorous behaviour of the visitors. The grounds then comprised about 43 acres, and their upkeep cost £1340.

The Society's connection with the Garden ceased in 1878, when it was placed under the control of the Science and Art Department.

Since that period, it has been largely added to, nine acres having been taken in on the north side for an arboretum, and seven acres for nursery ground, on the south side, nearer the city. As regards specialities, the garden has a world-wide reputation for possessing the most complete collection of *species* of orchids in existence. It is also well known for its collection of hardy herbaceous plants and *Cycadaceæ*, material for study being constantly supplied from its collections to the continent of Europe and to America.

The herbarium and museum have been transferred to the National Museum, Kildare Street.

CHAPTER XII

THE HIBERNIAN SILK AND WOOLLEN WAREHOUSES

THE guild or corporation of Weavers in Dublin (in conjunction with others interested in the silk trade), presented a petition to Parliament, in 1753, stating that, as a result of the extensive importation of foreign silks, the trade was declining, and the silk weavers were being ruined.   With a view to the revival of the trade, Parliament voted money to the Dublin Society, which decided on establishing a silk warehouse in which the parliamentary funds were to be expended in giving premiums on silks made in Ireland, the great object being to have everything of the kind that could be made in Ireland manufactured there.   The warehouse was to be strictly a retail one, and the Society in 1766 passed a special resolution that no part of the sum of £3200 allotted should be given for a wholesale trade in it.   In 1764, Alderman Benjamin Geale, Messrs. Robert Jaffray, Travers Hartley, Thomas Hickey, and Edmund Reilly were appointed by the Society to act with a committee of the Weavers' company, and their deliberations resulted in a house being taken in Parliament street for the sale of silk, on the amounts of which manufacturers were paid a percentage.   It was formally opened in February 1765, when a large number of ladies attended the ceremony, and made purchases.   In 1767, the master, wardens, and seventy-three brethren of the Weavers' company, as well as the Shearmen and Dyers of the city, presented addresses of thanks to the Society for their attention to the trade, and erection of a silk warehouse. The dyers were specially grateful for the translation of *The Art of Dyeing Wool and Woollen Stuffs*, made by M. Helott, member of the Royal Academy of Sciences, which was done at the expense of the Society.

The value of stock in the Warehouse in 1769 was £13,897, 18s. 7d. The Society was of opinion that the silk manufacture might be greatly stimulated if patronesses were placed at the head of it, and fifteen ladies were chosen yearly. Lady Townsend became president, and among the earliest names as patronesses appeared those of the Duchess of Leinster, Lady Louisa Conolly, Lady Drogheda, Lady Shannon, Lady Clanwilliam, and Lady Arabella Denny.

Lord Arran, Thomas Le Hunte, Redmond Morres, Dean Brocas,[1] and Dean Barrington [2] were directors of the warehouse on behalf of the Society. Sir John Gilbert says that popular toasts among the weavers were—" The Silk Manufacture of Ireland, and prosperity to the Irish Silk Warehouse " and " The Duchess of Leinster, and the Patronesses of the Irish Silk Warehouse ; may their patriotic example induce the ladies of Ireland to wear their own manufactures." For some time prior to 1780, a return of the sales and of the value of goods in the silk warehouse for each week was printed in the *Proceedings*. In December 1782, the value of goods in the warehouse amounted to £12,986, 18s. 10d. Unemployment among the silk weavers was so rife in Dublin and its liberties, that in 1784 they petitioned the Society for

---

[1] Theophilus Brocas, Dean of Killala, then resident in Dublin.
[2] See p. 145.

aid, owing to their distress; but, from the state of its funds, it was found impossible to do more than was being done.

Parliament had passed an Act during the session of 1780, which placed the regulation of the wages of journeymen silk weavers in Dublin, and a certain distance round it, in the hands of the Society, which was also empowered to settle the prices of work. The silk manufacture continued under the superintendence of the Society until it was found that the trade had not increased, and that the money spent on the warehouse might be more satisfactorily employed. Parliament enacted that from the 25th March 1786, none of the Society's funds were to be applied to or expended in support of any house for selling by wholesale or retail any silk manufacture whatsoever. At this period 11,000 persons were engaged in the trade in Dublin.

When the Society's connection with the warehouse ceased, the manufacturers took the burden of it on themselves, at an expense of about £400 a year; but by 1795, the trade was in a most declining state, which was attributed to change of fashion and preference for cottons. The manufacturers thought the direct patronage of the Society would be invaluable, and would afford employment, and the committee appointed to investigate the matter reported that it appeared to be essential to the preservation of the manufacture that the Society should resume the responsibility for working it. Some steps must have been taken of which there is no note in the minute book, as a committee is found negotiating between the masters and journeymen silk weavers. A book of orders for the regulation of the silk manufacture, agreed to by the Society on the 3rd of March 1796, appeared, and public notice was to be given of the agreement. In 1808 (at which period there were about 1500 silk weavers in the city), the masters and working silk manufacturers of Dublin, considering that it had been empowered to regulate wages, presented a memorial to the Society. They prayed that, as employment for males had been decreasing, females should be excluded; save in the case of a wife or daughter, who might help in the loom. The broad-silk weavers and master silk manufacturers sent in a contrary petition, and the Society, as their unanimous opinion, ruled that females should not be excluded from any branch of the silk manufacture.

The operative silk winders of Dublin claimed an advance in their wages in 1813, as to which the committee of trade and manufactures were asked to examine and report. The committee expressed the opinion that the Society was always most anxious to help those who sought its aid—" who, without it, might be driven to the mischievous and dangerous expedient of stubborn combination "; and impressed on the workers the necessity of keeping wages within reasonable bounds, so as to avoid the danger of foreign competition and injury to trade. A scale of wages was annexed to the report. For some time, manufacturers of fine silk had experienced inconvenience from delay in getting silks wound. In 1818, complaints were again being made, and a committee was appointed to examine the Acts of Parliament regulating the silk manufacture in Dublin, and report whether alterations were necessary. The silk winders had sent in a memorial stating that the masters had refused to comply with the Society's order fixing the rate of wages, and the committee recommended that the Act 19 and 20 George III should be amended by inserting " mistresses " in the penal clause of the first section, and that the Act should be extended to the regulation of the wages of journeywomen as well as of journeymen. A deputation on the subject was to attend the Chief Secretary. This Act expired in the year 1831, and the Society considered it inexpedient to interfere with respect to the rate of any new wages Parliament might establish.

A committee was appointed in 1816, to enquire into the state of the title to the silk warehouse in Parliament street, when it was found that the Society had no interest in it. A lease in trust, which was deposited with the Society, had been taken by Joseph Webster and Richard Brett. When by Act of Parliament, in 1786, the Society's patronage over the silk weavers came to an end, the lease, with declaration of trust (as to the house) from Webster and Brett to the corporation of Weavers, had been delivered to them.

What has been written has reference only to the silk manufacture in connection with the Dublin Society; but, in addition, it may be well to make a few remarks on the general aspect of the question, showing how it presented itself to outsiders. The silk trade in Ireland had been protected by paying a less duty on organised silk than the London merchants paid, but that ceased in 1821, when the duties were equalised. The silk was sent to the warehouse directly by the weavers, and all transactions were for ready cash, but the expense the Society was put to was greatly in excess of the revenue for encouraging arts, manufactures, &c. It was intended to take the weavers out of the hands of mercers and drapers, and let the silk manufacture come to market without any intervening profit. The mercer and draper were thus deprived of a good deal of their trade, which in reality taxed them severely. What they sold then must necessarily have been at a higher rate, and it was not easy to understand why master manufacturers had to be taxed to encourage a manufacture. When goods are dearer the consumption is less, so that consumption on credit was lessened, that the ready-money purchaser might get his goods at a cheaper rate. Many thinking persons saw that if the manner in which the Dublin Society acted in this matter of the silk warehouse was justified, then all the trade should be diverted thither, in which case no place would be left for mercers or drapers. Great jealousies became rife in the trade, and Arthur Young expressed the view that if a manufacture were of such sickly growth as to need all this nursing, it was not worth consideration. What in reality was brought about, was a great increase in the importation and consumption of foreign silks, a result the very opposite of what the Society had intended. One serious disadvantage operated against the mercers which compelled them to defend their own interests. When they were supplied with a good selling pattern, and entrusted it to be made, as soon as the manufacturer executed (say) ten pieces for them, he made probably thirty for himself, which he retailed to the warehouse at a less rate than he charged wholesale to the mercers. When the directors made a rule that no mercers were to be permitted to buy goods in the warehouse for retail, the latter were compelled to import foreign silks. The mercers should have been allowed to purchase for ready-money, at a reduction, in the warehouse, and the retail trade in shops should have been put on an equal footing with it; premiums should have been withdrawn, and the House opened for manufacturers who might not be able to dispose of their pieces by wholesale.[1]

[1] *Considerations on the Silk Trade in Ireland*, addressed to the Dublin Society; Haliday Pamphlets, 1778, ccccii. 2.

In November 1772, a resolution as to the necessity for the establishment of a warehouse in Dublin for the sale of woollen goods for home consumption was come to, and the vice-presidents, with Messrs. Ford, Vallancey, Andrews, and Lodge Morres were named directors. The warehouse, placed by Parliament under the management of the Society, was opened in Castle street in 1773, and at the end of the year 1780, the value of goods in it was stated to be £10,674, 4s. 1d., and in 1782, £13,311, 17s. 3d. To encourage woollen and worsted manufacture in the west of Ireland, £60 were voted to Arthur Greene, of Ennis, clothier, dyer, and presser, as an aid towards erecting proper apparatus for dyeing and finishing. A bounty of £60 was also voted to David Clark, late of Manchester, for having established in this kingdom the making of carding machines and spinning-jennies for cotton. Lady Arabella Denny laid before the Society specimens of twenty-four different kinds of woollen and worsted manufactures, such as were best adapted to the Portuguese market, with particulars which might lead to the introduction of those branches of manufacture. In 1784, on the consideration of the appropriation of £400 voted for the woollen warehouse, and as to any necessary alterations in the mode of conducting it, a memorial was received from the manufacturers who sold their goods through it, praying the Society to continue the mode of sale as before. A pamphlet, entitled *Remarks on a Pamphlet printed in the year* 1779, *containing Thoughts on the Inexpediency of continuing the Irish Woollen Warehouse as a Retail Shop*,[1] with some other papers of a like nature, was presented. An amend-

---

[1] For the pamphlet as to *Inexpediency*, see Haliday Pamphlets, 1779, ccccxi. 10. It contains powerful arguments against the system, and is well worth perusal.

ment was moved that the words "as a wholesale warehouse only" be inserted, but on the further representation of some clothiers, who thought that any alteration would materially injure the woollen manufacture of Ireland, the amendment was negatived.   In August 1784, another memorial was presented by the same manufacturers, who, being ready to end all controversies, stated themselves willing to relinquish retail sales for a term of two years.   The Society agreed to this proposition, and instructed the directors to adopt such regulations as would make it a wholesale warehouse only.   In June 1786, the Society resolved to open it again as a retail warehouse.

Robert Kemp, of Cork, clothier, stated that he had established several spinning-jennies, and had imported a carding machine at great expense.   He had also gone into some of the clothing counties of England, to make himself acquainted with the mode of business carried on there, and brought over, at a large salary, a person fully qualified to conduct the machinery.   Having incurred various expenses up to £400, he asked for aid.   Certificates of woollen drapers in Cork, in furtherance of his claims, having been read, and the matter enquired into by a committee, a sum of £100 was granted to Kemp.

During inclement seasons, the working poor in the liberties of Dublin, who were bred to the woollen manufacture, suffered great privations and destitution when, by reason of the wet, they could not have their wool, wraps, and cloths dried.   In 1809, they memorialised the Society to take steps to provide means for having this done.   Another petition on behalf of the same class of the poor was presented by the Lord Mayor and a number of eminent citizens, praying the Society to represent to Parliament the necessity for a grant to build a stove tenter house in the Liberties, which it was estimated would cost about £3500, when Mr. Thomas Pleasants, whose liberality was unbounded, offered a sum of £10,000 for the erection of the tenter house.[1]

The arguments urged against the woollen warehouse seem materially the same as those used in opposition to the silk warehouse, but in this case it was thought that a radical mistake had been made from the time of the introduction of the woollen manufacture into the kingdom, in establishing it in the capital city. Industry and frugality among the artisan class do not prevail to any extent in a large city, where its members estimate the value of their labours by the excessive prices that have to be paid for necessaries. Time, too, was more wasted, and much of it spent in amusement. Moreover, the system of apprenticeship necessary in the city was not suitable in the case of this industry in the country, and only augmented the dearness of labour. Great expense also attended the obtaining and preparing the raw material. The industry was essentially one for small communities scattered through the country, as in England, and the working people connected with it should be judiciously distributed, as the conditions of their labour would then be entirely favourable, and the

[1] In the process of the woollen manufacture, certain stages were reached at which the materials had to be sized and dried, which was accomplished by suspending them on *tenters* (hooks for stretching cloth on a frame), in the open air. The Irish climate was too uncertain for this being regularly or satisfactorily carried out, and during rainy seasons work had frequently to be given up for lengthened periods, which entailed on the weaving population a great deal of suffering and privation. In 1815, Pleasants, finding that no help was being afforded either by the government or the municipality, though much had been written and said on the subject, and sympathising, as he did, with the weavers in their trials, erected at his own expense, on an open space in Brown street, at the back of Weavers' square, a large tenter house, fitted with proper stoves, furnaces, and appliances, in which work could be carried on at all seasons. The building was said to have cost £12,964.

community at large would benefit. These are general principles; but with regard to the particular instance of the Dublin Society having established a retail warehouse, that body had in reality created a monopoly in the heart of a commercial city, with a result that in the end *a larger quantity of goods was imported.* As interest is ever the ruling principle in commerce, the drapers, finding this shop open for retail, whither all the ready-money went, and that the credit part of the business fell to them, increased their imports. In all European countries in which the woollen trade was carried on, the retail business was conducted by shop-keepers only, as necessary middlemen. The manufacturer sold his cloth, and was done with it; but the draper had a character for goods to maintain, and as the system inaugurated by the Dublin Society helped to ruin him, he, in self-defence, took the action that he found beneficial to his interests, which was quite opposed to the policy of the Society. Hence, after a precarious existence, the woollen warehouse was finally abandoned.

In connection with the work of the Society in the silk and woollen warehouses, it may be of interest to note what was being done in the matter of worsted in some parts of the country. In 1787, Sir John Parnell, bart., laid before it an account of the progress made in establishing a school in Maryborough for spinning worsted warps, when he was thanked for his exertions in promoting the woollen manufacture and market in the Queen's county. Twenty-five wheels were directed to be provided at the Society's expense for such girls in Maryborough as should appear to deserve rewards. It was resolved to open a second school there, to be conducted under a mistress, as the first. In 1790, a spinning school was opened in Cork. With a view to improving the art of worsted weaving, premiums were offered for machines called *Billies*, of not less than thirty spindles, which prepared the cardings of wool into slabs ready for spinning on the jenny; with further premiums for skeins, &c., worked on such.   One hundred pounds were to be applied in premiums on the value of scribbling cards, or of cards to be affixed on cotton-carding machines.

The principal hosiers of Dublin having represented that their trade would probably benefit by encouragement being extended to the construction of gig frames, and teaching working hosiers the mode of using them, six guineas were paid to a person who instructed two master framesmiths in the method of making gig frames of the most approved construction.

In vol. lii. of the *Proceedings* of the Society, app. B (1816), is a sketch of the origin and progress of the merino factory, Kilkenny, by Thomas Nowlan.   A report was made on this factory, in 1819, from which it appeared that its superfine cloth of native wool had obtained the chief premium of the Farming Society.

CHAPTER XIII

FINANCES OF THE SOCIETY, MEMBERSHIP, AND BY-LAWS. (1761-1836)

FINANCES

SOME grants of public money in aid of the Society have already been noticed, but it was not until the year 1761 that regular parliamentary grants were made. In that year a sum of £12,000 was voted (1 Geo. III, c. 1)—£2000 to enable the Society to continue the premiums in agriculture and manufactures, and £10,000 for distribution among petitioners for premiums. Under 3 Geo. III, c. 1, £2000 were voted for agriculture, and £8000 for manufactures, and similar amounts under 5 Geo. III. By 7 Geo. III, £3000 were given for agriculture and for completion of the Grafton street house, and £7000 for manufactures. From 1772, the regular sum voted in any year was £10,000, and this continued to 1783. From that period to 1792, £5000 were granted, increased in that year to £5500. In the year 1800, the last of the Irish Parliament, the Society's grant amounted to £15,000. In June, 1784, a requisition was received from the Commissioners of Imprest Accounts, under the Act 24 Geo. III, passed for the due accounting of all money granted for public works, and for ordering a regular account of moneys, entrusted to (among

o

others) the Dublin Society, requiring the Society to furnish such particulars. It appeared to the committee appointed to consider the requisition that the Society was not obliged to submit any accounts prior to the 1st of June 1784, and that it would be sufficient to lodge a statement of debts due and of funds unexpended.

In March 1789, a special committee was appointed to report on the state of the Society's funds, and how far they might be adequate to discharge premiums. It reported that on account of the large payments made within recent years, by reason of the increased number of claimants, and the great expenses incurred in the enlargement of the repository for implements in Hawkins street, the Society could only afford to offer £4500 for encouragement of planting and agriculture, and £1500 for manufactures and fine arts. In June, the outstanding orders liable to be demanded at any time were found to amount to nearly £4000, which would have to remain undischarged until the parliamentary bounty of last session was paid over by the Treasury. The expenditure on account of agriculture and planting exceeded the appropriated fund by more than £1700.

On the 30th of January 1800, the following proposal, in substance, was agreed to, for submission to Parliament, which was to stand as part of the Society's petition to it in that session :—Anxious to carry their great plan for the benefit of the country into execution, and hoping for a liberal bounty from Parliament, the Society propose to surround the Botanic Garden with a wall; to erect sheds where farmers may have ocular demonstrations; to rebuild the drawing schools; to erect at the repository a gallery for exhibition of works of Irish artists; and, above all, to establish a public Veterinary school, with sheds, &c., for diseased cattle, wherein methods of cure may be tried. The Society resolved that books on this art in foreign languages should be translated into English, and condensed and arranged under special heads for reference ; General Vallancey, Dr. Richard Kirwan, and Arthur McGwire were to form a committee for the purpose.

The Imperial Parliament, in 1801, made the Society a yearly grant of £5500 ; and in a petition to Parliament a sum of £27,141 was prayed for—£15,898 to complete the buildings, and £3000 to finish the statistical surveys of counties, partly completed. A sum of £3772 was stated to be due to tradesmen on account of buildings ; £2610 were required to finish the repository in Hawkins street, and £1667 to rebuild the drawing schools, now in a ruinous state. The petition went on to show that the Society had been encouraged by the liberality of the Irish Parliament in its last session, to enlarge their plans for the encouragement of agriculture and manufactures. It expressed the entire confidence of the Society in the liberality of the Imperial Parliament, and its desire to carry into effect the national improvements adopted by the late Parliament of Ireland. An immediate grant of £11,277, as absolutely necessary, was prayed.

In 1803, £5500 were granted for support of the Society, and £4500 for additional buildings. In May of that year it was resolved, owing to the want of funds, that no money was to be henceforth expended except in fulfilling engagements, and no new work was to be undertaken without a special report from the committee of economy. The statistical surveys were also to be discontinued. In August the economy committee made a report, which showed the then financial responsibilities of the Society to be as follows:

ANNUAL EXPENSES

	£	s.	d.
General Establishment, permanent . . .	1582	9	10
Premiums, agricultural, permanent . . .	1362	0	0
Premiums, agricultural, temporary . . .	452	4	4
Miscellaneous, permanent	667	0	0
Fine Arts, permanent	431	19	0
Fine Arts, temporary	20	0	0
Philosophy, permanent	191	8	6
Veterinary, permanent	155	0	0
Veterinary, temporary	132	17	9
Mineralogy and Chemistry, permanent . . .	643	14	6
Botany, permanent	1700	6	9
Apiarist (none now employed)	88	14	6
	7427	15	2
Debts now due, and that will become due this year	10,683	16	0
Works unfinished in Hawkins Street . .	571	1	5

Works not begun, but estimated for to Parliament—

	£	s.	d.
Hawkins Street Drawing School	1667	0	0
Gallery	1145	10	0
Veterinary Buildings . . .	4048	0	0

	£	s.	d.
	6860	10	0
Botanic Garden, surrounding wall	2984	13	0
Printing, &c., Statistical Surveys, @ £80 . .	1280	0	0
Due to Commissioners of Wide Streets, payable March 1805	1526	6	3

The committee made a second report which stated that there were no adequate means to discharge the demands within the year, and that strict economy would be necessary. A schedule was added, which showed the means to be applied to payments that were to be made in 1803 and 1804, according to which, if the Society found itself able to agree with the committee in postponements and restraints, there would remain only a sum of £1288, 6s. 4d. due at Christmas 1804. The distressed state of the funds had arisen from absolute necessity and unexpected events. In

1804 Parliament, as before, gave the Society £5500 for establishment charges, and £4500 for new buildings. By the end of the year arrears of subscriptions had been reduced to a sum of £2828.

The report of the committee of accounts, presented in May 1816, is selected as showing particulars which demonstrate the financial position of the Society after its acquisition of Leinster House.

		£	s.	d.
I.	Debts and engagements, including Establishment expenses, for the year ending March 1817 (showing what are now payable), amounted to	4614	12	4
II.	Debts due by the Society, incurred by undertakings previous to March 1816, and not applied to expenditure of the year ending March 1817	4366	1	6
III.	Unavoidable estimated expenses of year ending 25th March 1817	8076	16	8
IV.	Debts due, and requiring payment, included in estimated expenditure for year to 25th March 1817	248	10	10

Against this, £119, 2s. 3d. stood in bank; and there were also the Hawkins street premises, which were valued at £10,000; and the yearly subscriptions of members. (Full accounts for the year ending March 1817 will be found in *Proceedings*, vol. lii. p. 217.) In August 1831, when the estimates for the ensuing year were being prepared, it was found that the grant to the Society was to be reduced to £5500. The Imperial Parliament had granted £10,000 a year for twenty years from the date of the Union; then it was made £7000, and now it was again being reduced. In the *Proceedings* for 1831, p. 290, is a report on this matter. In *Proceedings*, vol. lxvii., appendix v., will be found a petition to the House of Commons on the threatened reduction.

In 1832–3, the Society's estimate for its needs was

£7016, 7s. 5d., which was reduced by the Government
to £5303, 9s. 11d., viz. :

	£	s.	d.
Botanic Department	1076	12	0
Chemistry and Mineralogy	509	2	0
Natural Philosophy, and Museum	269	2	0
Drawing Schools, &c.	481	16	0
Library	710	0	0
Establishment	537	12	0
Miscellaneous	1719	5	11
	5303	9	11

The free balance unexpended, amounting to £2714,
was to be applied in reduction of the rent of Leinster
House.

MEMBERSHIP AND BY-LAWS

In June 1801, by-law No. 37, relating to the
admission and subscription of members, was amended
by expunging "five" and inserting "ten" in the
amount of the admission fine. An addition was made
that every annual subscriber was to sign a bond in
£50 for payment of his subscription. It was further
altered in November by inserting "three" instead of
"two" in the amount of annual subscriptions for members elected after the 1st of November 1801; so that in
future members were to pay ten guineas on admission,
and two guineas yearly subscription. From 1802, the
vice-presidents were to be considered members of every
committee. In 1811 another amendment was made,
by which it was provided that every new member was
to pay a sum of thirty guineas on admission, and there
were to be no more yearly subscribers. The whole
sum was to be paid by the day fixed for ballot, and the
admission of anyone not paying was to be void. Every
candidate, whether honorary or ordinary, was to be

publicly proposed, and no election was to be valid unless thirty members were present. The election, as well as the proposal of honorary members, was to be regulated in the same manner as in the case of ordinary members. On the 5th of March 1812, a by-law was confirmed, that annual members should be deemed life members on a further payment of fifteen guineas, and on such payment they were to be discharged of all arrears. In November 1812 it was resolved to add a new by-law to those already in force, namely: That no order for payment or appropriation of money was to be made without a previous reference on the subject-matter thereof to the committee of economy, and their report being obtained.

Later, it appeared that the seventieth by-law was founded on a misapprehension of the true interpretation of a clause in the charter, which was to be interpreted that the Society had power at any general meeting to confirm such by-laws as had been proposed and agreed to at any previous stated general meeting.

On the 25th of May 1815, the 42nd, 43rd, and 46th by-laws were amended by the word "thirty" being expunged, and the word "fifty" substituted; so that for the future intending members had to pay a sum of fifty guineas, and no annual subscription had to be met by them. This was found not to work, and in 1821, the fee of thirty guineas was again resumed. On the 28th of November 1816, several new by-laws were confirmed (*Proceedings*, vol. liii. p. 46). Among the principal, one of the by-laws arranged that each of the six committees was to consist of not more than fifteen members. No one was to be a member of more than two of the five first committees on the list (which excluded that of Economy). The committees were to be elected by ballot yearly, and each committee was to keep a rough book of its proceedings, which were afterwards to be entered in a fair book to be laid before the Society.

The 14th by-law was also amended by the substitution of the word "fifteen" for "eighteen," which caused the committee of fine arts to consist of fifteen members, exclusive of the vice-presidents and secretaries.

From 1825, balloting for admission of members was arranged to be carried out by means of white and black beans, which were to be dropped into a box placed beside the President. A special committee appointed to consider the matter in 1830, recommended that yearly subscribers, who were to pay five guineas on admission and three guineas yearly in advance, should be elected.

In 1832, it was resolved that the by-laws were to be classed under heads. There were to be eight standing committees, viz. :—1, Botany; 2, Chemistry and Mineralogy; 3, Natural Philosophy; 4, Museum, and Natural History; 5, Fine Arts; 6, Library; 7, Economy; 8, House—which were to consist of nine members each, besides the seven vice-presidents and the two secretaries. Twenty guineas were now to be paid on admission, and not thirty. A new class of annual subscribers, to be called "Associate Annual Subscribers" (who would not be corporate members or have any power of voting), was to be elected, on the recommendation in writing of five members, one of whom was to be a vice-president. They were to have access to the library, the lectures, exhibitions, botanic garden, museum, galleries, lawn, &c., and were to pay three guineas a year, in advance.

CHAPTER XIV

GENERAL HISTORY OF THE SOCIETY
(1781-1815)

HAVING now had separately under review, in the last
five or six chapters, the various departments into which
the Society's activities had branched out, namely, the
drawing schools, the botanic garden, the schools of
agriculture and chemistry, and the library, it becomes
necessary to take a survey of its general work during
the later portion of the eighteenth and the earlier part
of the nineteenth centuries.   As if to show how
widespread was the Society's influence, the period to
be considered opens with a communication from the
West India Islands.   A letter, dated Barbadoes, 14th
July 1781, was received from Joshua Steele, an honorary member, announcing that several gentlemen in
that island had formed themselves into a Society for
discovering the useful qualities of native productions,
animal, vegetable, and fossil.   Mr. Steele had been
chosen president, and the Barbadoes Society offered
help, begging to be admitted to correspondence with
the Dublin Society.   The request was granted, and
it was agreed that the president of the foreign Society
for the time being was to be considered an honorary
member.   During successive years, reports were received from Mr. Steele, which contained acounts of
its proceedings, and described the different natural
productions of the island.

On the 15th of May 1783, Abraham Wilkinson was elected Secretary in the room of Michael Dally, deceased.

Two years later Sir William Gleadowe Newcomen [1] was elected treasurer of the Society in the room of Mr. Thomas St. George, deceased. At this period, the meetings appear to have been very badly attended, sometimes only five or six members being present, and a vice-president rarely occupying the chair.

The Society had before it on many occasions the case of John Grahl, a native of Saxony, who claimed some recognition of a process by which cut glass was gilt, so as to resemble burnished gold; and at length, in 1785, he was granted 35 guineas. Mr. Grahl was noted as having communicated to the committee all the secrets he possessed in this art. Richard Hand was granted 15 guineas, but declined to furnish the recipe for making copal varnish, a necessary ingredient in his mode of gilding; which, however, he subsequently disclosed.

The net sum of £2425, out of moneys granted by Parliament during the session of 1785, was appropriated as follows:—

Irish Woollen Warehouse	£400
Irish Silk Warehouse	£400
Encouragement of Silk Manufacture	£400
Finishing Woollen Goods	£200
Importation of Oak Bark	£600
Encouragement of the Dyeing Business	£175
Drawing Schools	£250

Lord Charlemont having laid before the Society an account of a piece of mechanism whereby, it was

---

[1] Newcomen's bank, originally in Mary's Abbey, was removed in 1781 to a new edifice in Castle street, planned by Thomas Ivory. It is now used as offices by the corporation.

alleged, perpetual motion might be discovered, the secretary was directed to lay it before the Royal Irish Academy, with a request for its opinion. The Academy did not think the principle new, nor did it look on the machine as being likely to be useful in mechanics.

Mr. Richard Vincent, secretary, died in 1788, and Captain Thomas Burgh was elected in his room. In June 1792, Burgh was elected a vice-president in the room of John Wallis, resigned.

Within eight years prior to this date, Abbé Raynal (1), Brussels, John Howard, Abbé Commerell, and the Rev. Dr. Daniel Augustus Beaufort (2) had been elected honorary members.

1. Guillaume François Raynal, born in 1713, was for some time a Jesuit, but, having been excluded from the Order, he devoted himself to literature and society. His *Philosophical and Political History of European Settlements in the Two Indies*, published in Amsterdam in 1770, was written in collaboration with several others, and the work was translated into some European languages. It was full of "philosophic declamation" (as Voltaire said), which, perhaps, accounted for its popularity with a certain section of the public. Horace Walpole declared that it "told one everything in the world." Hatred and contempt for religion, and passion for justice and freedom, were the keynotes of this remarkable book, which many ascribed to Diderot. It was ordered to be publicly burned, and the author arrested ; but he escaped, and was subsequently allowed to return to Paris. Raynal died in 1796. See *Diderot and the Encyclopædists* (John Morley, ii. 222). Among the Haliday Pamphlets (1782, ccccxxxiii. 3) is a *Letter to Abbé Raynal, Author of the Work on the Revolution in North America*, by Thomas Paine.

2. Daniel A. Beaufort, son of a French refugee minister, was born at East Barnet in 1739. He held the rectory of

Navan from 1765 to 1818. Beaufort took an active part
in the foundation of the Royal Irish Academy, and his map
of Ireland, 1792, with a memoir of the civil and ecclesiastical state of the country, was a valuable contribution to
geography.

In 1794, a sum of twenty guineas was paid to
Richard Hand for the Society's "Arms" in stained
glass, for the centre of the window purchased from
him in 1793 for a sum of 120 guineas. The Society
never had a grant of arms, and this must have been
the device of Minerva (later called *Hibernia*) with a
cornucopia, adopted by the Society.

A sum of £400 was divided in 1795 among a
number of persons for having enclosed not less than
ten acres with sufficient fences, and planting with forest
trees not less than 2000 plants to each acre. The
prizemen included Lord Belmore, Lord Mountjoy,
Lord Riverston, Major Le Hunte, Richard Aldworth,
and Walter Kavanagh. Premiums were also distributed for preserving bees through the winters of 1793
and 1794.

In May 1796, new medals were ordered to be
struck for the Society, and the pupils in the drawing
schools were asked to send in designs, the reverse to
have several devices, each appropriated to some one
object for which that body granted premiums. Among
the works of William Mossop, senior, appears the
medal of the Dublin Society, 1800, "given as a
premium for the various national objects encouraged
by the Society."

The office of registrar was abolished in the year
1798, and the emoluments applied to the payment of
persons to superintend the collections of scientific
books at the Botanic Garden and the Repository.
The late registrar and collector had given the Society

trouble.   The solicitor was also a source of annoyance, and a threat as to legal proceedings against him had to be made.

In August 1799, £40 were paid to George Fitzgerald for a sinecal circumferenter,[1] for land surveying.   The instrument was referred to the Royal Irish Academy for examination, and Dr. Elrington and Dr. Brinkley were of opinion that ingenuity had been shown in its construction, and that it would answer its purpose more satisfactorily than the instrument in use.

About the same time the Rev. Andrew Callage presented specimens " of a curious fossil called *asbestos*," which he obtained from Corsica.   A bust of the late Right Hon. William Conyngham was procured from Edward Smyth, statuary, and soon afterwards, Sir John Sinclair, president of the English Board of Agriculture, sent to the Society a statistical account of Kilronan parish, co. Roscommon, written by Mr. Conyngham, which he had presented to the Board in 1773.   This gentleman had been William Burton, son of the Right Hon. Francis Burton, of Buncraggy, co. Clare, M.P., and Mary, daughter of Henry Conyngham, M.P.   He assumed the name of Conyngham on succeeding to the family estates on the death of his uncle, Henry, Earl Conyngham.   Mr. Conyngham was M.P. successively for Ennis and Killybegs, teller of the exchequer in Ireland and a privy councillor, and he died, unmarried, 31st May 1796.   He took an unwearied interest in the objects of the Society, and is frequently mentioned in the minutes, more especially in connection with the library and fine arts departments.   Conyngham travelled much on the continent, and on such occasions he took the opportunity of

---

[1] An instrument used by surveyors for taking angles.   A sinecal circumferenter was one that read the sines of the angles.

purchasing scarce and valuable books and works of art for the Society's collections.

For almost half a century Farming Societies had been established in various parts of the country, all more or less in correspondence with the Dublin Society, and looking up to it for help and guidance. In the year 1755, a resolution as to their formation had been passed, and societies were founded in the counties of Antrim, Kildare, and Louth, as well as in other places. In 1784, an advertisement was ordered to be inserted in the *Dublin Journal* and *Evening Post*, that the Dublin Society desired the farming societies in the various counties to convey such information on the subject of agriculture as might be considered useful. Later are mentioned societies in Mayo, Roscommon, and Fermanagh, and in 1799 one was established in the county Clare, for agriculture, manufactures, fisheries, and for breeding cattle. Early in 1800 was started, by the Marquis of Sligo and the Right Hon. John Foster, a General Farming Society, which elected the vice-presidents of the Dublin Society and the members of its committee of agriculture as honorary members. This new body agreed to be called the Farming Society, " under the patronage of the Dublin Society," and its committee of fifteen members had permission to meet in the repository in Hawkins street until accommodation was provided elsewhere. It received a State grant of £5000 per annum, and concerned itself almost entirely with the practical side of agriculture to the exclusion of the theoretical, which so much occupied the attention of the Dublin Society. The Farming Society sought to improve the breed of cattle, and cattle shows were held under its auspices. In imitation of the Dublin Society's old plan, it revived the practice of sending an itinerant instructor to country districts, and in connection with it was a factory for the sale of implements of husbandry. This society was brought out more or less under General Vallancey's auspices, and from the time of its formation the Dublin Society ceased to give encouragement to agriculture in the way that it had formerly done, and the prize system was more or less abandoned. The Farming Society lasted not quite thirty years, disappearing in 1828, when the Dublin Society resumed its labours in that branch. In the *Proceedings*, vol. xxxvi., will be found a prospectus of premiums offered by the new society, the secretary of which was Charles Mills. Under it, a show of neat cattle and sheep was held at Ballinasloe in October 1800, and one at Smithfield, Dublin, in November of the same year. Reports on these shows appear in *Proceedings*, vol. xxxvii. On the 7th of May 1801, £200 were paid to this new body by the Dublin Society.

In 1818, the Committee of Botany recommended to the Society the recently founded Horticultural Society, and in 1822, a Farming Society for North Kerry was founded at Listowel, which requested aid from the Dublin Society.

The Rev. Wm. Hickey, Bannow Glebe, Taghmon, sent to the Society, in February 1823, an account of an agricultural school which, in conjunction with Mr. Boyse, he had established in his own parish. The latter gave forty acres for experiments, and £700 were laid out in starting the school. It accommodated nineteen youths, and two masters instructed them in the theory and practice of husbandry. Chemistry, botany, and mechanics were also taught, and it was hoped they might yet have a greenhouse and botanic garden. In 1824, Mr. Hickey and Mr. Boyse were presented with the Society's gold medal, in acknowledgment of their successful labours, and the former was granted a pension from the Royal Literary Fund. Hickey had early been impressed by the poor condition of Irish farms, and began to study improved methods for such of them as consisted of a few acres. In 1817, he published *The State of the Poor in Ireland.* His first work on farming—*Hints to Small Farmers*—was published under the pseudonym of " Martin Doyle," under which name he continued to print a large number of pamphlets on cattle, planting, gardening, roads, &c. He also conducted the *Irish Farmer's and Gardener's Magazine.*

In May 1801, Philip, Earl of Hardwicke, was elected President in the room of the Marquis Cornwallis, resigned. A new seal was ordered from Mr. Mossop, who also received a commission for a figure of " Hibernia," to be affixed to a wand carried by the Society's hall-porter. A large steel-press seal, with the figure of "Hibernia" (the Society's " arms ") executed by John Milton, was sent from London, for which he was paid £31, 10s.

Two special communications on the culture of potatoes from the shoots, received from R. Griffith and George Grierson, were highly commended, and their plans recommended for general adoption. The Rev. Dr. Maunsell was voted a medal in Irish gold for his services to the same art of potato culture.[1]

During the previous eight or nine years, Dr. Walter Wade ; Sir John Sinclair, bart., president of the Board of Agriculture, London ; Mr. Secretary Pelham ; and Benjamin, Count von Rumford, of Bavaria ; the Duke of Argyle, president of the Highland Society, and William McDonald, its secretary ; the Duke of Norfolk, president of the London Society of Arts, and Charles

[1] See his *Essay,* Haliday Pamphlets, 1802, mcccxxxiii. 6.

Taylor, its secretary, had been elected honorary members. Count von Rumford was voted a gold medal, with suitable inscription, for his attention to the Society during his late residence in Ireland.

Sir Benjamin Thompson (Count von Rumford) was born in Massachusetts in 1753. He attended Harvard University lectures, and became a schoolmaster at Rumford (subsequently called Concord) in New Hampshire. He married a lady of independent fortune, and soon sailed for England, where he arrived in 1775. Being of a scientific turn, he experimented in gunpowder, and in 1779 he was elected a Fellow of the Royal Society. He went to Bavaria, where the Duke Maximilian became his patron, and in 1795 he was created Count von Rumford of Bavaria. King George the Third also knighted him. In 1796 Count Rumford came to Ireland with Lord Pelham, where he introduced many improvements into workhouses and hospitals. He was particularly interested in the cooking of food, the proper warming of houses, and in domestic economy generally. The Dublin Society and its working had great attractions for the Count, who spent a good deal of time in Poolbeg street, and " Count Rumford's kitchens " are mentioned in the minutes. He was so much pleased with the lecture theatre, and the prospect of instruction opened up by it, that on returning to London he projected the Royal Institution, Albemarle street, an additional proof that the Dublin Society may be considered as the prototype of numerous societies for the diffusion of knowledge. Count Rumford's collected works appeared in 1796 as *Essays, Political, Economical, and Philosophical.* He died in 1814.

In 1802, Thomas Lysaght, junior, was appointed solicitor to the Society in Mr. Tisdall's place, and a list of members present at each meeting began to be printed, this not having been done since the series of printed *Proceedings* was commenced.

In the same year the Right Hon. John Foster was asked to sit for his portrait by Hamilton, which was to be hung in the board-room in acknowledgment of his exertions in the study of agriculture, botany, mineralogy, and the veterinary art. Foster was born in 1740, and early devoted himself to a political career. He was member of Parliament for Dunleer in 1768, became Chancellor of the Exchequer in 1785, being elected Speaker of the House of Commons in August 1785. Bitterly opposed to the Union, he exerted his utmost endeavours to prevent that measure being carried, and declined to surrender the mace of the House, saying that " until the body that entrusted it to his keeping demanded it, he would preserve it for them." It is still held by his descendants in the Massereene family. After the Union, Foster represented Louth in the Imperial Parliament, and accepted the post of Chancellor of the Exchequer for Ireland. In 1821, he was created Baron Oriel, and died on the 23rd of August 1828, aged eighty-seven. Foster was indefatigable in his labours on behalf of the Dublin Society, of which he was a vice-president for many years. He was most diligent in his attendance on committees, and took an especial interest in the department of mineralogy and botany, and in the foundation of a school for the cultivation of the veterinary art. The Society was in possession of a portrait of Foster which hung in the board-room, but in 1813 it was ordered to be replaced by one painted by Sir William Beechey.

Early in 1803 Abraham Wilkinson, secretary, died, and the Rev. Dr. Thomas Smyth was elected to the vacant post.

A letter from the Rev. Thomas Hincks[1] was re-

---

[1] Thomas Dix Hincks, born in Dublin in 1767, was a Presbyterian divine, ordained in 1790 for Cork, where he conducted a school. He projected the Royal Cork Institution, of which he became an officer, and in which he lectured on Chemistry and Natural Philosophy. Hincks also edited the *Munster Agricultural Magazine*.

ceived, which stated that an attempt had been made
to establish in Cork lectures in natural philosophy,
chemistry, and mineralogy.   He had procured from
London many specimens of foreign minerals, and
requested assistance in his endeavours.   The Society
allowed him to have some duplicate fossils, and he was
to have copies of the *Transactions*, with lists of Irish
minerals.

In the same year Adam Seybert, secretary to the
American Philosophical Society, Philadelphia, requested
that it might be allowed to correspond with the
Dublin Society, which was approved, with exchange
of publications.

Premiums were given, in 1803, to John Tem-
pleton, Belfast, and Dr. Scott, Marlborough street, for
discovering plants—natives of Ireland—not previously
described by any botanist.   Premiums were also awarded
for discovery of a new species of rose in the counties of
Down and Kerry.

In 1807, Captain Theodore Wilson was appointed
housekeeper; and Sir Thomas G. Newcomen, treasurer,
in the room of Sir William G. Newcomen, deceased.
On 14th January 1808, at a meeting at which 235
members were present, a report of the committee of
economy (David La Touche, v.p., chairman, General
Vallancey, Arthur McGwire, the Rev. Dr. Smyth,
Edward Houghton, Lundy Foot and Jeremiah D'Olier),
was considered, when new rules, &c., were made, bearing
on the offices of assistant secretary, registrar and collector, assistant librarian and housekeeper.   The office of
assistant secretary was separated from that of registrar,
and £300 a year was fixed on as the salary attaching
to it.   The registrar and collector was in future to act
as accountant.   The Rev. Dr. Lyster having just
died, Bucknall McCarthy, B.L., was appointed to the

vacant post of assistant secretary; Thomas Lysaght, registrar and collector; and Dr. John Lanigan, assistant librarian and translator, at a salary of £150 a year.

In February 1810, so as to give additional solemnity to the formal introduction of members, it was resolved that on a new member taking his place, the name in writing was to be delivered to the chairman, who would desire him to be presented to the chair by a member. The chairman would then announce the new member, who was to be seated at his right hand. Count de Salis was the first member who was formally introduced and took his seat in this way. On 7th March 1811, John Comerford, Dame street, miniature painter, who had been proposed as an ordinary member, and taken down, to be proposed as an honorary member, was rejected as such. He had been proposed by Lord Frankfort, vice-president.

At the end of vol. xlvii. of the printed *Proceedings* will be found an analysis, by Professor William Higgins, of the meteoric stone which fell on the property of Maurice Crosbie Moore, of Mooresfort, co. Tipperary, in August 1810.

The *Proceedings* of the Society having become voluminous, and it being difficult to refer to particulars, Mr. Wilson was directed to compile a general index to the first fifty volumes, which was completed in July 1814. Seven hundred and fifty copies were printed, and Mr. Wilson was paid one hundred guineas for his labours.

About 1812, and for some time previously, Mr. Jeremiah D'Olier was a constant attendant, and frequently occupied the chair. The Rev. Dr. Beaufort, Dr. Harty, Richard Griffith, Dr. Wade, Sir Robert Langrishe, Major Sirr, Alderman Exshaw, Dr. T. H. Orpen, and Messrs. Samuel Guinness, Austin Cooper,

Humphrey Minchin, P. Le Hunte, and Luke White were also remarkable for the number of meetings which they attended, and for their close attention to the business of the Society.

In November 1812, Robert Shaw was elected a vice-president in the room of General Vallancey, and in December 1812, William Hogan, junior, York street, "a student of Trinity College," was elected a member of the Society, this being the only instance, up to this period, of the admission of anyone so described. At the same time, Peter Brophy, who was proposed by John Boardman and seconded by the Rev. Dr. Handcock, was rejected.

Professor Von Feinagle was permitted, in February 1813, to deliver before the Society two lectures explaining his system, and its applicability to all branches of education and science. Gregor Von Feinagle, born in Baden in 1785, became a public lecturer in a new system of mnemonics and methodics, for which he was much ridiculed on the continent, both in the press and on the stage. He came to this country in 1811, and soon after superintended a school in Mountjoy square, Dublin, which was conducted on his principles. The *New Art of Memory*, edited by J. Millard, appeared in 1812. Von Feinagle died in 1819 in Dublin, and there is a bust of him in the reception-room, Leinster House.

Richard Lovell Edgeworth (father of Maria Edgeworth), who appears to have been a mechanical genius, conducted in 1815, in the yard of Leinster House, public experiments as to an invention of his with regard to wheeled carriages.[1] The committee to which the matter was referred was of opinion that the apparatus invented by Edgeworth was adequate to

[1] *Memoirs*, vol. ii.

the purpose intended, and that the affixing of springs to carriages, which was part of his scheme, greatly facilitated their draft. He was elected an honorary member of the Society on the 29th of June 1815. As early as the years 1767 and 1769 R. L. Edgeworth had obtained medals of the Royal Society of Arts for inventions.[1]

During the first quarter of the nineteenth century, a number of remarkable names appear among those admitted to honorary membership of the Society, while some of the newly admitted ordinary members were conspicuous in various ways. In may be appropriate to close this chapter with some mention of them. Citizen Goldberg, The Hague, minister of Political Economy to the Batavian Republic; Citizen Coquebert de Moubray, commissary of the French Embassy; Prince Barintrinsky, chamberlain to the Emperor of Russia; Humphry Davy; Thomas William Coke,[1] (Holkham Hall, Norfolk); the Earl of Sheffield; the Archdukes John and Lewis, of Austria; the Right Hon. Nicholas Vansittart, Chancellor of the Exchequer; the Grand Duke Michael of Russia; Sir Benjamin Bloomfield (2); Sir Michael Seymour, bart., K.C.B.; The Princes Nicholas and Paul Esterhazy, Count Joseph Esterhazy, Prince Victor Metternich, and Chevalier de Floretti were elected as "foreigners of high scientific attainments, and for repeated acts of attention to the Society"; the Right Hon. George Canning was also elected.

Among those who became members of the Society during the same period were the Lord Chief Justice of Ireland (afterwards Lord Downes) (3), the Rev. Charles Elrington, F.T.C.D. (4), Sir William Betham (5), Lord Kilmaine, who was a regular attendant, and frequently

---

[1] *History of the Society*, 247, &c.

occupied the chair, the Earl of Charlemont, the Earl of Pembroke, James Gandon (6) a member of committees, and a very regular attendant, Lord Cloncurry (7), Mr. Benjamin Lee Guinness (8), and Dr. John Anster.

1. "Coke of Norfolk," the son of Robert Wenman, was born in 1752; on succeeding to the estates of his maternal uncle, Thomas, Earl of Leicester, he assumed the name of Coke. He was elected member of Parliament for Norfolk in 1776, a seat which he held almost continuously up to 1833. Coke was created Earl of Leicester in 1837. When he became owner of the estates they were unenclosed, and the system of cultivation on them was wretched. On taking up farming, he collected round him a number of practical men, who advised with him, and within the years 1778–1787, the land had so much improved that he might be said to have converted West Norfolk into a wheat-growing country. He became a noted breeder of stock, and is believed to have raised his rental from a little over £2000 to £20,000 a year. Over £100,000 were laid out in farmhouses and buildings. Coke's portrait, by Gainsborough, in his broad-brimmed hat, shooting jacket and long boots, in which costume he is said to have presented an address to King George the Third, is well known. Lord Leicester died in 1842.

2. Sir Benjamin Bloomfield was born in 1768, and, entering the army, became a lieutenant-general and A.D.C. to King George the Fourth, whose private secretary he was for some time up to the year 1822, when he was sent as minister plenipotentiary to Stockholm. In 1825 Bloomfield was created Baron Bloomfield. In 1884 Georgina, Lady Bloomfield, published a memoir of Lord Bloomfield, her husband's father, who had died in 1846. He was owner of estates near Newport, co. Tipperary.

3. William Downes was born at Donnybrook, near Dublin, in 1752. He became member of Parliament for Donegal, and in 1792 was appointed a Justice of the King's

Bench, being promoted to the Chief Justiceship eleven years later. He was created Baron Downes in 1822, and died in 1826. There is a very fine portrait of Lord Downes by Hugh D. Hamilton ; and one painted in his robes as Chief Justice, by Martin Cregan, has been engraved and published.

4. The Rev. Charles R. Elrington, regius professor of Divinity in the University of Dublin, was born in Dublin in 1787, and was a son of Thomas Elrington, bishop of Ferns. He was successively rector of St. Mark's, Dublin, chancellor of Ferns, and rector of Armagh. Elrington effected great improvements in the Divinity School, managed the Church Education Society, and helped the Board of National Education. In 1847 he commenced his edition of the collected works of Archbishop Ussher in seventeen volumes ; the two last, which he did not live to finish, were completed by Dr. Reeves, afterwards Bishop of Down. Dr. Elrington printed many theological works and pamphlets on education.

5. Sir William Betham, born at Stradbrooke in Suffolk in 1779, came to Dublin in 1805, and, having been for a time Deputy Ulster and Deputy Keeper of Records in the Record Tower, Dublin Castle, he became Ulster King of Arms in 1820. Betham compiled a number of indexes and repertories, and, in 1830, appeared his *Dignities, Feudal and Parliamentary*, and in 1834, *Origin and History of the Constitution of England, and of the Early Parliaments of Ireland*. He was secretary of the Royal Irish Academy, and that body purchased a large collection of Irish manuscripts which he had acquired.

6. James Gandon, architect, was born in London in 1743, his grandfather having been a Huguenot refugee. Gandon came to Dublin in 1781 to superintend the construction of new docks, and he planned the Custom House, which was finished in 1791. He designed the east portico and circular screen wall of the Parliament House, as well as the west screen and the portico in Foster place. His works also included the Four Courts, and the King's Inns build-

ings, Henrietta street, and he was responsible for designs for many private residences. James Gandon died in 1823, and a memoir of him from the pen of Thomas J. Mulvany appeared in 1846.

7. Valentine Browne Lawless, second Baron Cloncurry, was born in 1773, and when quite young became imbued with Nationalist principles. He entered on the field of politics with enthusiasm, and was sworn as a United Irishman in 1795. His *Thoughts on the Projected Union* appeared in 1797, and several pamphlets on the same subject from his pen subsequently appeared. Lawless was arrested on suspicion in London in 1798, but was discharged on bail. He was again arrested in 1799, and committed to the Tower, appearing to have been an active agent in the United Irish conspiracy. When released in 1801, he travelled for a time on the continent, and, returning to his native country four years later, he settled on his property at Lyons, co. Kildare, taking a deep interest in agriculture and improved systems of farming. Lord Cloncurry helped in founding the Kildare Farming Society in 1814, and warmly advocated and supported the reclamation of bogs and wastes. He was created an English peer in 1831, and in 1849 published his *Recollections*.

8. Mr. Benjamin Lee Guinness was born in 1798, and on his father's death became sole partner in the firm of A. Guinness, Son & co. He possessed great powers of organisation, and quickly developed a splendid export trade. Mr. Guinness was elected first Lord Mayor of Dublin under the reformed corporation, and nobly upheld the ancient traditions of the Mansion House. He was elected member of Parliament for the city of Dublin, and between the years 1860 and 1865 restored the venerable cathedral of St. Patrick at a cost of about £150,000. In 1867 Mr. Guinness was created a baronet, and had a special grant of supporters to his arms. Sir Benjamin Lee Guinness died in 1868, and a bronze statue by Foley, erected to his memory, stands on the south side of the exterior of the cathedral.

CHAPTER XV

GENERAL HISTORY OF THE SOCIETY (*continued*)
(1815-1836)

FOR some years prior to the Society's removal to Leinster House, the printed *Proceedings* were much fuller than formerly, and a greater volume of business seems to have been transacted at the meetings. The members began to take fresh interest in agriculture, the Society's chief original object, which they had more or less neglected since the foundation of the Farming Society. Numerous other subjects had attracted attention during the Hawkins street régime, but now when it was found that the Farming Society's operations were not as satisfactory as had been hoped, and its financial position and membership not flourishing, the subject of husbandry was again taken up. Possibly the Society's hand was forced, as extreme depression in that industry prevailed. Early in 1816, it was referred to a special committee to enquire into the embarrassed situation of the agricultural interest of Ireland, so as to enable the Society to submit to the Government information which might distinguish causes of continued depression from merely temporary ones. They wished to be able to contrast the demands necessary for the supply of the home market at present with periods anterior to the late war ; also to look into the state of the British market, and the probable operation of the Corn Laws on this country, so as to ascertain, if possible, a proportion between rent and the produce of the soil.

The committee was asked to report on such measures as might seem likely to relieve the distresses of the agricultural interest of Ireland.   The committee found that since the Corn Act had diverted foreign grain from the home market, continental nations made great efforts to supply the United Kingdom with dairy produce, which then experienced alarming depression. The dairy produce of not less than half a million acres had been imported into the United Kingdom during the previous year, and the home market would soon be glutted with the cheese and butter of foreign nations, unless prohibited by Parliament.   Fresh dried, salted provisions from abroad were recommended to be excluded, unless admitted, as live stock was in times of scarcity, by the King's proclamation.   They considered the restriction of imports of provisions and dairy produce from abroad necessary for Great Britain and Ireland.   It was recommended that prizes should be offered for the best essays on the subjects of the enquiry—100 guineas for the first, 50 for the second, and 20 for the third.

In 1817, Mr. Sadleir the aëronaut, asked leave to ascend from the premises in Kildare street, but his request was refused.   He was, however, allowed the use of the exhibition room in Hawkins street to exhibit his balloon.[1]

In the same year Thomas Archdeacon, esq., presented to the Society a bust of Alexander Pope by Roubiliac.

[1] An ascent had previously been made from the lawn of Leinster House.   On 19th July 1785, the first Irish aëronaut, Richard Crosbie, son of Sir Paul Crosbie, made an ascent.   He was rescued in the channel, and brought to Dunleary, the vessel towing the balloon behind.   Gilbert's *History of Dublin*, iii. 279.

The Right Hon. David La Touche having died, Mr. Peter Digges La Touche was elected a vice-president in his room. Mr. Digges La Touche was a very frequent attendant, serving on committees, and taking his full share in the work of the Society.

Mr. Thomas Pleasants, already alluded to as a benefactor of the Society, by his will, bequeathed to it certain pictures, prints, &c., which were delivered to the Society in April 1818, and deposited in the upper part of Leinster House, when the fine arts committee undertook to distribute them throughout it. Pleasants' will, a very long and remarkable document, is characteristic of this most benevolent but eccentric man. He desired to be buried in the same grave with his wife, expressing a wish " that on my being put into my coffin, her slippers may be laid crossways on my Breast, next my Heart, for I have, since her most sincerely lamented death, constantly had them under my pillow, kissed them, and pressed them to my Heart every night going to bed, and the same in the morning rising." He named, among the pictures bequeathed by him, the " Visitation of the Shepherds," " The Dream," and " Narcissus," " Joseph and Mary," two landscapes by Barret, two grand battle pieces, two smaller battle pieces, " Magdalen in a wilderness," " St. Paul Preaching," Dutch pieces, dead game, fruit pieces, " Holy Family," " Peg Woffington, by Sir Joshua " [1] (print), " Summer " and " Winter " (" two fine Lutherbergs "), " The Oracle," a head of Captain Coram, by Hogarth, and two excellent Garricks; also portraits of Swift, Malone, Sparks, Woodward, Ryder, and Surgeon Daunt ; in crayons, Counsellor Wolfe (a proof given to Pleasants by Wolfe's nephew, Lord Kilwarden), statue of Handel, Rubens, bust of Gay,

---

[1] Reynolds did not paint Peg Woffington.

THOMAS PLEASANTS

(From an oil painting by Solomon Williams)

&c., Ogilby's *History of China*, Ogilby's *Virgil*, and a curious and valuable book, *Relation of a Journey beginning A.D.* 1610, printed in London, 1637. The pictures were bequeathed subject to a proviso that none of them were ever to be lent to the Artists' Gallery, nor was anyone at any time to be allowed to copy them. On this condition being violated they were to be surrendered, sold by auction, and the proceeds added to the residue. The will is undated, and Pleasants made a codicil, dated in 1817 at Booterstown House, his interest in which he left to his brother William. Both were proved on the 16th March 1818, by Joshua Pasley, Abbey street, wine merchant.

Thomas Pleasants, who was born in Carlow in 1728, had an extensive knowledge of classical literature, and was interested in general literature and the fine arts. He was a man of unbounded generosity and philanthropy, as will be seen by gifts of his already noticed. He defrayed the expense of reprinting Dr. Samuel Madden's *Reflections and Resolutions proper for the Gentlemen of Ireland* (1728). Pleasants died on the 1st of March 1818, at his house in Camden street, now the Pleasants asylum for orphan girls, which was founded by him. In 1820, Mr. Solomon Williams presented to the Society his portrait of Pleasants, which now hangs over the mantelpiece in the registrar's office.

The lectures delivered at this time by the professors under the auspices of the Society appear to have been well attended, and the theatre was frequently crowded. The Museum and the Elgin Marbles castrooms were closed during the lectures, so as to enable the porters to attend at the different doors. Not more than 400 tickets were issued for each, and none but members and officers of the Society were admitted to the members' seats. It is amusing to record that on one occasion Lady Rossmore was allowed to choose a seat at the lectures, and the assistant secretary was directed "to convey to her ladyship this resolution."

In 1819, Dr. Anthony Meyler delivered a course of lectures on ventilation, and was invited to deliver another on meteorology, when the committee of chemistry and natural philosophy intervened, alleging that it was not politic to interfere with the Society's professors, who were fully qualified, and should be invited to deliver any special lectures. Dr. Meyler then wrote declining to lecture.

Dr. Dionysius Lardner delivered a course of lectures in 1826 on the steam-engine, which were afterwards published, and a gold medal was voted to him, to mark the Society's appreciation of them. A couple of years later a committee appointed to report on the best means of making the Society's lectures as useful as possible to the working classes, recommended a series of popular courses to be delivered in the evening.

Lardner was born in Dublin in 1793, and in 1827 was elected to the chair of natural philosophy and astronomy in the University of London, when he commenced his *Cabinet Cyclopedia.* He went on a lecturing tour in the United States, by which he realised a very large sum of money, and in 1845 settled in Paris. Lardner wrote on railways, the steam-engine, natural philosophy, heat, optics, &c., and, though not a great original thinker, he was a man of much talent, who made the sciences popular, as no one before him had done.

In 1819, a question arose as to the publication of the *Transactions,* which, having appeared from 1800 to 1810, had been discontinued, and as to the necessity for reviving their appearance. The volumes consisted of papers of minor importance ; extracts from writers in German, Dutch, and French; communications from (as a rule) non-members, and of valuable papers by the Society's professors.   The contents included treatises on cider making, brewing, road making, embankments, planting and draining, on wheat, flax, the rearing of sheep, &c.   The library committee, which was asked to report, gave the following reasons for thinking that the publication of the *Transactions* had become unnecessary.   The literary institutions of the city had now placed within the reach of all works from which extracts were made in the *Transactions*.   Foreign languages were more studied in Ireland, and most of the valuable works of recent foreign writers were translated and published in periodical journals.   Authors of original papers on agriculture and the practical arts preferred weekly and monthly journals, so that the Society had received a lesser supply of scientific communications.   The Royal Irish Academy at this time found some difficulty in procuring materials for half a volume yearly, and even papers in the *Transactions* of the Royal Society of London had not increased in number.   Since the discontinuance of the *Transactions*, many essays and larger treatises had been communicated to the Society which were recorded either in the weekly minutes, or published separately, under the Society's sanction.   As instances, might be mentioned Mr. Higgins on the *Atomic Theory ;* Dr. Wade on *Oaks, Salices, and Grasses ;* Griffith on the *Leinster Coal District*, &c. The publication, too, of the surveys of Irish counties, in utility and extent, well supplied the want of them.

The office of registrar becoming vacant, Captain Theodore Wilson, who had held the post of housekeeper since 1808, was appointed to fill the united offices, at a salary of £200 a year.   Mr. John Litton was elected law agent.

In December 1819, a report was made on the general state of the Society, which will be found in *Proceedings* (vol. lvi. p. 58). A short résumé of it may be useful here, as giving a summary of the Society's activities from its foundation :—

It is found difficult to collect the annual subscriptions. Life subscriptions, which had been increased from ten to thirty guineas, were lately raised to fifty guineas. When the Society first started, attention was devoted to agriculture, first by the publication of papers and tracts, then by premiums for planting, the introduction of proper implements, and importation of cattle; next by manufacturing implements at a cheaper rate; and lastly by improved methods of horticulture and the cultivation of trees, plants, and grasses. After this, trial was made of gratuitous information supplied by lectures and schools. Six professors were appointed, and a theatre capable of accommodating 500 persons was equipped. The botanic garden, the drawing schools, library, and museum were all in full working order. The Act 19 and 20 George III imposed on the Society the superintendence of the silk manufacture, and the regulation of the operative silk weavers' wages, which imposed a great deal of work on the Society. An exhibition room for works of art was also opened. On the whole, the affairs of the Society might be said to have been conducted with as much skill, propriety, and economy as the nature of the institution would admit. From 1801, the parliamentary grant amounted to £10,000. The labours imposed on the Society by numerous Acts of the Irish legislature caused its original designs to be extended from husbandry and the useful arts to literature, sciences, fine arts, manufactures, horticulture, trade and commerce. The expenses of the six professors and their apparatus, the four fine art schools, the Botanic Garden, the purchase of Leinster House, the exhibition room, museum, library, laboratories, the cabinet of mineralogy, and the various bounties and premiums, were all defrayed out of the members' subscriptions and the yearly grant of £10,000. This report was transmitted to the Right Hon. William Grant, Secretary for Ireland, with a special letter from the secretaries of the Society.

In 1820, the Right Hon. George Knox was elected a vice-president, and on the 3rd of February in that year the regular meeting was not held, in consequence of the death of King George the Third. In June, when conveying the new monarch's acknowledgment of the address on his accession, Lord Sidmouth intimated that His Majesty would be pleased to become Patron of the Society, and, on the 29th of June 1820, it assumed the title of the Royal Dublin Society.

The Society nominated a permanent committee of twenty-one members, to enquire into the expense and practicability of reclaiming the bogs and waste lands of Ireland, which reported that every description of bog was capable of reclamation, and of being converted into profitable land, which would repay outlay.

King George the Fourth visited Ireland in August 1821, and on the 24th of that month he went to Leinster House, where a *fête champêtre* and déjeuner were given in his honour on the lawn, on which had been erected a large marquee, fitted up with great taste. Within the tent, under a scarlet canopy, was a richly decorated table, above which were " G. R. IV " and the royal arms. For the entertainment of the company invited to meet His Majesty were provided about fifty tents, ranged round in semicircular form, and in double rows. Three harpers in the garb of

Q

ancient minstrels were close to the King's tent, and a platform for dancers stood near. The crowds that flocked to the ground all wore a blue ribbon, with " R. D. S." in gold letters.

The King arrived at 12.30 P.M., and was received in the courtyard with military honours, 150 members of the Society forming line. The Lord Lieutenant met His Majesty, while near at hand were Lord Oriel, Lord Meath, Lord Frankfort, Sir R. Shaw, Mr. Leslie Foster, Right Hon. George Knox, Serjeant Joy, and others. In attendance on the King were the Duke of Montrose, the Marquis of Graham, and Sir R. Bloomfield. His Majesty inspected with great interest the various noble apartments of Leinster House, the library, model room, and museum, expressing much admiration at all he saw. He then moved to the lawn, where he was received with unbounded enthusiasm, afterwards retiring to the marquee, where he conversed with Lord and Lady Manners, and others. It was remarked that on this occasion the dresses worn were chiefly of Irish manufacture.

A large surplus resulted from this entertainment, and it was resolved to expend it in procuring a statue of the King, which Behnes offered to execute *gratis*, if the Society provided the marble. This was done at a cost of £400, and, strange to say, the statue, which was never quite finished by the sculptor, remained in his studio in London, under one pretence or another, for a period of twenty-four years, until his affairs were being administered in bankruptcy. The Society obtained it from the assignees in May 1845, and an arrangement was made with Mr. Panormo to complete the work for a sum of £100. In October, the completed statue was placed in the hall of Leinster House, where it still remains. There is another statue of

the King, elsewhere noticed, in close proximity to it
(p. 126).

In March 1822, a special committee reported on
the *Statistical Surveys*, and on Mr. Fraser's book on
Fisheries. The committee was of opinion that great
results would accrue from the action of the Board of
Fisheries in undertaking surveys, plans, and estimates
of harbours at fishing stations round the coast. A
statistical survey of the coast, with harbour charts,
was very necessary, and Mr. Fraser should be asked
to undertake it, so as to point out to the Government
the best means of improving the coast. It further
reported that there was a great deficiency of harbours,
which was injurious both to fishermen and trade.

In the year 1822—a very troubled one in Ireland—
considerable distress existed in the south and west,
which the Society was most anxious to relieve, and it
was in contemplation to appropriate the admission fees
during the year to this object. An amendment, however, was carried, that premiums up to £500 should
be offered to those who within three months afforded
most extensive employment to the poor in the southern
and western counties, which was subsequently negatived.
The mining engineer was appointed by the Lord
Lieutenant to lay out roads in the coal districts, so as
to give employment in the distress then prevalent.

As a means of affording permanent employment,
the Society turned its attention to the culture of
hemp. Home-grown hemp was recommended as
helping for sails, cordage, and netting, and it was said
that there would be a never-failing home market for
fish. It was calculated that every vessel of 30 tons
would require on board 10,000 square yards of netting,
made from hemp.

Then the subject of timber was taken up, and the

necessity for a home-grown supply was insisted on, so as to furnish employment, and render the country independent of foreign supplies. In Ireland were to be found 1,255,000 acres of shallow mountain bog, suited for the plantation of forest trees. The want of a supply of naval timber was felt during the wars of Bonaparte. In Sweden, Finland, Norway, and Russia, the forests were gradually destroyed in the manufacture of tar, in iron and copper works, &c., and the American forests were also being devastated.

The committee of agriculture submitted other means of employment and subsistence. The cultivation of the soil by alternate operations of the plough and spade, as in Flanders, was recommended. In that country one-seventh of the arable land was trenched every year, and this winter work effected the renovation of the whole surface under tillage every seven years. The labouring classes would thus be compelled to give up the use of potatoes, and substitute corn.

The manufacture of window glass claimed attention, and it was believed that a properly conducted establishment would be successful. The price of coal alone was thought to militate against it, as very large quantities would be necessary. The saving in freight from England, which in so bulky a material amounted to a good deal, would, however, it was expected, compensate.

In 1824, the Rev. Joseph Cotter, obtained the Society's silver medal for his royal patent basso-hibernicon, or hibernian bass horn, and tenor horn : Kramer, master of the King's private band, members of some cavalry bands, and some distinguished musical professors, bore testimony to the ingenuity of the invention, which it was thought would form a great addition to bands of music.

Surgeon John Hart reported on a specimen of the *Cervus giganteus*, or fossil elk, the bones of which had been found on the property of the Ven. William R. Maunsell, archdeacon of Limerick, which had been presented to the Society, and brought up to Dublin by canal boat. This specimen is still preserved in the natural history portion of the museum.

On the 12th of May 1825, the Society learned that Mr. George Le Touche had bequeathed to it his collection of Etruscan vases; this collection, with some water-colour drawings, formed the nucleus of the art collections now in the National Museum.

In 1826, Dr. Higgins having died, Edmond Davy,[1] who had been attached to the Royal Cork Institution, was elected professor of chemistry, and Dr. Samuel Litton, professor of botany, in the room of Dr. Wade.

Mr. Thomas Walker, in April 1826, presented to the Society three letters in the handwriting of Dean Swift. These are not now in the Society's keeping, nor are they in the National Library. Sir Walter Scott, in his *Life of Swift*, p. 72, prints a fragment of a letter with a lampoon on the Rev. William Tisdall (his rival in the case of Stella). Scott's *Life* was published in 1814, and it states that the original fragment was then preserved in the museum of the Dublin Society, Hawkins street. (See also Dr. F. E. Ball's *Correspondence of Swift*, iv. 479.)

Colonel Stannus, c.b., who had served in Persia, presented several casts from the ruins of Persepolis, which he had visited; also a stone with an ancient Persian inscription, the key to which had been discovered by M. Sylvester de Lacy, a French Orientalist.

[1] A picture of Davy, enlarged by photography, is in the reception-room, Leinster House.

A list of the casts is supplied in appendix to *Proceedings*, 1828.

On the 4th of December 1828, Mr. Isaac Weld was elected honorary secretary to the Society. He was born in Dublin in 1774, and received the name of Isaac after his grandfather. The latter was so named from Isaac Newton, who was a friend of the Rev. Nathaniel Weld, his father. Having travelled in the United States and Canada, Weld, in 1795–97, published his *Travels*. He became a member of the Society in 1800, and in 1849 was elected one of its vice-presidents. He undertook the *Statistical Survey of Roscommon*, and in 1807, published illustrations of the *Scenery of Killarney*. Being keenly interested in Irish industries, Weld was the first to suggest the triennial exhibitions of manufactures, afterwards conducted under the auspices of the Society. In later life Weld travelled a good deal in Italy, and became a friend of Canova. He died at Bray in 1856, and in the following year the members of the Royal Dublin Society erected a monument to his memory in Mount Jerome cemetery.

For two or three years previously the attendance at the meetings was small, and the minutes of the proceedings are very brief.

Government now directed special attention to the estimates, and a committee of the House of Commons made a report, which included certain recommendations. The committee thought the private funds of the Society should be increased. The lectures ought not to be gratuitous, and £200 a year, at least, ought to be produced from those on chemistry, mineralogy, and natural philosophy; otherwise the estimate for each must necessarily be reduced. Only absolutely suitable books should, they said, be purchased for the library. Admission by ballot to a Society mainly sup-

ISAAC WELD

(*From an oil painting by Martin Cregan, P.R.H.A.*)

ported by the public purse was considered objectionable. In addition to the sum fixed, an annual subscription, they thought, might be arranged. On this, the Society communicated with the Government, stating that the suggestions of the committee conveyed to them would be adopted as far as practicable. In answering some of the points, the Society showed that the lectures were principally attended by young people and students, who could not afford to pay. As a matter of fact, the experiment of charging for admission to the lectures had been tried, but, being a total failure, they were again made gratuitous. According to the charter, in cases of admission, the Society was bound to proceed by election. In thirty years only four persons had been rejected, and since 1800, 739 had been admitted. It was very difficult to collect annual subscriptions, and other societies were falling into decay from the same cause. A theatre to seat 500 persons had before that time been erected, the drawing schools were most successful, and the museum, which was in reality the National Museum of Ireland, was visited by 30,000 persons during the year.

Lord Downshire wrote to the Society on the 9th of March 1830, recalling the fact that, in the year 1800, the agricultural department had been handed over to the newly established Farming Society, which had undertaken the duties until 1828, when its Parliamentary grant was withdrawn and that Society came to an end. He pointed out how seriously the want of an efficient society for the improvement of agriculture was felt in the province of Leinster, and thought it would be well worthy of consideration whether the Society might not again take up this subject, especially as Leinster House and the premises around afforded every accommodation. As a result of Lord Downshire's appeal, the chief agricultural work of the Society took its present form. A new special committee, named the "Committee of Agriculture and Planting," was formed, and circulars were addressed to the secretaries of agricultural societies in Ireland, inviting co-operation. It was decided to hold a show of live stock in the yard, Kildare street, which was held on the 26th and 27th of April, as well as one for horses, which was held on the 28th of April 1830. Prizes of only £5 were offered for horses, and £3 for draught stallions of any breed, and similar amounts for Spanish asses. The show was said to have been most creditable in point of number and excellence of the cattle exhibited. The prizes amounted to £100; expenses were under £50, and receipts for admission totalled £41, so that the actual outlay on the undertaking was only £110. The spring cattle show has been continued yearly, and is now one of the leading cattle shows of the United Kingdom.

On the 4th of November 1830, the Society passed a vote of condolence with King William the Fourth, on the death of his predecessor, and of congratulation on his own accession to the throne.

It was decided to erect a bust, by Sievier, of the Marquis of Anglesey, who had just resigned the office of Lord Lieutenant. This bust now stands in the reception-room, and portion of the inscription, on a small marble tablet placed over it, runs as follows:

PAUCIBUS E MILLIBUS HIBERNIS
ADMIRANTIBUS HANC
EFFIGIEM MARMOREAM
IN TESTIMONIUM GRATI ANIMI
PONENDAM CURAVERUNT.

His successor, the Duke of Northumberland, and

the Duchess, were elected honorary members, and his Grace was asked to sit for his bust in London, to an Irish artist, who had been educated in the schools. A farewell address was presented to them, on the termination of the Duke's term of office, for their patronage and attention in sometimes visiting the establishment.

The death of Dr. John Beatty, one of the secretaries, was announced on the 30th of June 1831.

At the end of the year a special committee reported that under existing circumstances some modification of the mode of admission of members had become necessary, and early in 1832 Mr. Isaac Weld, secretary, was entrusted with a special mission to the Treasury, as to the general affairs and financial condition of the Society, when he was asked to take with him a copy of his *Observations on the Royal Dublin Society, and its existing Institutions* (1831); of which 500 copies had been printed.[1]

In 1836 a letter was received, asking the Society to appoint a deputation to confer with the Chief Secretary, Lord Morpeth, as to certain modifications in its constitution, in the transaction of its business, and in the apportionment of its income. By order of the Lord Lieutenant, propositions were laid before the Society, which will be found at large in *Proceedings*, vol. xxii. p. 108. Shortly, the chief points were as follows :—1, Admission to the Society to be by a majority of the members, the mode of voting to be left to that body. 2, A composition sum of £20 to be paid on entrance, and £3 annual subscription. 3, Annual subscribers to be admitted as then, under by-law No. 12, with an annual payment of £2, instead of three guineas. 4, The governing body to be a Council of twenty-three, chosen yearly from among

[1] Haliday Collection, 1831, mdxi. 13.

the members. 5, Five to be vice-presidents, chosen yearly. Ten members of the Council to retire yearly, and not to be re-eligible for a year. 7, Lists of the committees to be prepared by the Council, and submitted to the members at a general meeting. 8, Officers to be proposed by the Council, and nominated by the Society. 9, The accounts to be audited and published yearly. 11, Committees to make annual reports. 15, Purchases of books, &c., to be limited to publications suited to a literary and scientific institution; no newspapers to be taken in the house. The above named points included all that was then in issue between the Government and the Society, which finally led up to the Special Commission of 1836, and the enquiries made under it. Great jealousy prevailed among the members at any interference by the Government with the private regulations, which they conceived the Society had full power to make under its charter.

In connection with these propositions, the *Dublin Evening Mail* of the 24th of February 1836, contained an attack on the Lord Lieutenant, in the shape of a letter from Dr. Anthony Meyler, which attempted to involve the Society—an attempt which it altogether disavowed. In its reply, the Society said that His Excellency's propositions had only been considered, and amendments had been merely proposed. The Society agreed that election was to be by ballot, and fees were to remain as at present. A Council as a governing body it could not agree to, and accordingly propositions Nos. 5, 6, 7, 8, 12, and part of 3, could not be entertained. In reply, His Excellency regretted that the Society had given him so little help, and said that the Government would now find it necessary to take into consideration the question of the renewal of the annual grant. On this the Society felt called on to explain that in their negotiation they were not influenced by political feelings. "This accusation had been made against them in consequence of the Most Rev. Dr. Murray, Roman Catholic Archbishop of Dublin, having been rejected as a candidate for admission. He was proposed by John R. Corballis, LL.D., and seconded by the Rev. Dr. Sandes, S.F.T.C.D., and there was a very large attendance on the occasion, when it was evident that, for purely political reasons, an organised opposition to the Archbishop's election had been set on foot. A short time before, His Grace had written a public political letter, on which a threat of excluding him from the Society having been made, some members connected with the Castle party, which was then opposed to the Society's regulations, openly stated that if this took place the Government grant would be withheld. This effort to prevent a number of independent men from exercising their discretion created a great deal of feeling, and undoubtedly contributed largely to Dr. Murray's rejection, which created a very great sensation in Dublin, His Grace being personally popular with all classes. Dr. Murray wrote the Society a very dignified letter, which was ordered to be entered on the minutes.

Mr. Naper, V.P., and Mr. Hamilton were believed to have conducted private and confidential communications with the Lord Lieutenant, and, through want of experience, and ignorance of the constitution of the Society, both being very new members, they were thought to have influenced His Excellency unfavourably. They acted without authority from the Society, and, while acquitting them of anything but the best motives, a great majority of the members thought that the hostile attitude of the Government was due in a great measure to their ill-timed interference. Mr.

Naper made a special statement to the committee, and contradicted the utterances of some of the witnesses. These circumstances precipitated the outcome of the differences between Government and the Society, for on the 31st of March 1836, a Select Committee of the House of Commons to enquire into its management was appointed.

Before closing this chapter, and entering on the history of the Society under the new conditions which resulted from the report of the committee, there are a few matters of interest which must not be omitted.

In 1832, John D'Alton, author of the *History of the County of Dublin*, made a communication as to Irish manuscripts supposed to be preserved in Copenhagen. He stated that no original documents from the time of the Danes or Ostmen who invaded this country, were to be found anywhere in Denmark. Many interesting comments on Ireland and its inhabitants, relating to migrations of the Irish in the ninth century to Iceland, where they introduced Christianity, were, however, to be found dispersed in old Scandinavian works. Professor Magnussen, keeper of the records, had offered to collect all such passages and to supply Latin translations. He reported that there were old manuscripts at Copenhagen, dealing with the cycle of King Arthur, and giving accounts of his court; and said that the King of Denmark in Queen Elizabeth's reign was believed to have written informing her of the existence of Irish manuscripts in his library, and offering facilities for copying them.

About this period, the committee of agriculture and planting offered premiums for—1, The best essay on the consolidation of farms, and maintaining in Ireland the mixed system of plough and spade industry.

2, For the best account of the state of husbandry in Connaught, in the districts afflicted with famine in 1831, and for suggestions as to practical means of improvement. 3, For best proposal for laying down ground to permanent pasture. 4, For schemes for allotting to the greatest number of cottages a quantity of land not less than one acre, Irish. 6, For the best account of actual experience of the quantity of land required to support a labourer's family with vegetables and potatoes, and to enable him to keep a pig and cow all the year. 7, For best method of fattening cattle. 8, For rearing poultry; and 9, converting peat into fuel. The Society's gold medal for erection of the greatest number of cottages and allocation of land to them was won by Lieutenant-Colonel Close, of Drumbanagher; and a prize essay by Mr. W. Blacker on the management of landed property in Ireland is printed as an appendix to *Proceedings*, vol. lxx.

In 1833 a committee was appointed to report on a proposed establishment, under the Society's auspices, of a yearly exhibition of specimens of the manufactures and products of Ireland, and it was also proposed to form a General Agricultural Association of Ireland.

The committee of agriculture, in 1835, reported that since the Royal Dublin Society had shown an inclination to resume her part in agriculture and husbandry, five times as many members had been enrolled. They now particularly wished to collect information as to the mode of agriculture pursued by the peasantry and the best means of improving it, to urge local societies to communicate with them, to establish museums of seeds, models, and machinery, and to elect a professor of agriculture to deliver lectures.

In 1836, premiums were offered for plans and estimates for farmhouses and cottages, when fifteen guineas were awarded to W. D. Butler, architect, 73 St. Stephen's Green, and ten guineas to Ninian Niven, curator, Botanic Garden.

A committee was appointed to invite the British Association to meet in 1835 in Dublin. The invitation was accepted, and the Association met here on the 10th of August in that year, under the presidency of Dr. Bartholomew Lloyd, provost of Trinity College, the retiring president being Sir Thomas Brisbane. Trinity College was the meeting place of the Association, and Captain Sir John Ross and Sir John Franklin, Arctic explorers, attended this meeting. During its session the geological and geographical sections occupied the theatre and secretaries' office, in Leinster House, while those of zoology and botany were accommodated in the board and conversation rooms. The Royal Dublin Society gave a déjeuner at the Botanic Garden, which was attended by 1300 guests. Sir Thomas Brisbane expressed the opinion that the Association's meeting in Dublin was by far the most brilliant of any as yet held, and the city was highly complimented on all the arrangements made for its reception.

From about this period, the principal scientific work of the Society began to take its present form. Evening meetings for the advancement of science and diffusion of useful knowledge by discussion began to be held monthly, in which members of the Royal Irish Academy, the Zoological, Geological, Arboricultural and Horticultural Societies were invited to take part. The first meeting was held on the 26th of January 1836, Baron Foster occupying the chair; Professor Davy lectured, and Dr. Coulter exhibited the cone of the *Pinus Coulteri* and *Pinus Lambertii*. Mr.

Clibborn exhibited a table of electricity on the bifurcate mode, and Dr. Kane spoke on the interference of sonorous waves.   Dr. (afterwards Sir) Robert J. Kane had been elected professor of natural philosophy in 1834, a post which he held until 1847.   He was born in Dublin in 1809, and became a physician, founding in 1832 the *Dublin Journal of Medical Science*.   Kane published, in 1841, *Elements of Chemistry, theoretical and practical*.   He also edited the *Philosophical Magazine*, and was elected a Fellow of the Royal Society in 1849, in which year he was appointed President of Queen's College, Cork.   Kane paid great attention to Irish industries, and wrote on the industrial resources of the country.   When the Museum of Irish Industry was founded in St. Stephen's Green, he became its director.   Sir Robert Kane obtained the gold medal of the Royal Irish Academy for his researches in chemistry, and in 1877 he was elected its president. A portrait of him hangs in the Academy House.

During the last few years had been elected as honorary members, Sir Robert Seppings, bart., commissioner of the navy, for his great scientific improvements in building ships of war and other vessels ; Sir Martin Archer Shee, who, in his reply to the communication announcing his election, stated that, having been a student of the schools, he would ever revere the names of Morgan Crofton, Thomas Braughall (1), and Burton Conyngham, who exerted themselves with zeal and patriotism in the cause of art; William Rowan Hamilton (2), professor of astronomy, and Sir Frederick Madden, librarian of the British Museum, were also elected honorary members.   Among the ordinary members admitted occur the names of Charles Haliday (3), and the Rev. James Henthorn Todd, F.T.C.D (4).

1. In the reception-room, Leinster House, is a small portrait of Thomas Braughall, by Comerford, the label on which states that he was an active member of the Society for many years, and an honorary secretary from 1792 to 1798. Among the Haliday Pamphlets (1803), mcccxxxviii. 3, is an elegy inscribed to the memory of Thomas Braughall.

2. Sir William Rowan Hamilton was born in Dublin in 1805, and in 1827 became Royal Astronomer for Ireland. He was not only a great mathematician and metaphysician, but also a poet. Hamilton twice obtained the gold medal of the Royal Society—on the first occasion for his great optical discovery as to systems of rays, which disclosed a new science of optics, involving as it did the discovery of two laws of light ; on the second occasion for his theory of a general method of dynamics. His very important work, *Lectures on Quaternions* appeared in 1853. In 1837 Hamilton was elected President of the Royal Irish Academy. From early youth he was distinguished as a linguist, and he wrote many poems and sonnets. Wordsworth, Coleridge, and Southey were numbered among his personal friends. Sir William died in 1865, and the Rev. Robert P. Graves published a memoir of him, in two volumes.

3. Charles Haliday, merchant, born in Dublin in 1789, was a member of the corporation for improving the harbour of Dublin, and superintending the lighthouses on the Irish coast. Haliday published a number of pamphlets on social questions. He was a deeply-read antiquarian, and, after his death, Mr. J. P. Prendergast edited his *Scandinavian Kingdom of Dublin*, which was the substance of two learned communications made by Haliday to the Royal Irish Academy. He died in 1866, and after his death Mrs. Haliday presented to the Academy her husband's splendid collection of pamphlets and tracts relating to Ireland, together with his portrait. The tracts extend from the year 1578 to 1859, and the pamphlets from 1682 to 1859, the former being comprised in 543 boxes, and the latter in 2209 volumes.

4. James Henthorn Todd, senior fellow of Trinity College, and regius professor of Hebrew in the University of Dublin, was born in 1805. His life was devoted to the improvement of the condition of the Irish Church, and the promotion of learning among its clergy, and he founded St. Columba's College, Rathfarnham. As librarian of Trinity College, Dr. Todd arranged its rich collection of Irish manuscripts, and brought the library to a high state of efficiency. He founded the *Irish Archæological Society*, for which he edited the Irish version of the *Historia Britonum* of Nennius, and (in conjunction with Dr. Reeves) the *Martyrology of Donegal;* also the *Liber Hymnorum*, or book of hymns of the ancient Irish Church. His edition of *Wars of the Gaedhil with the Gaill,* in the Rolls Series, appeared in 1867. Dr. Todd was elected President of the Royal Irish Academy in 1856, and his portrait is in the Academy's collection. After his death in 1869, a " Todd Lectureship," to be attached to the Academy, was founded in his memory, a post which has been held by several distinguished Irish scholars.

CHAPTER XVI

SELECT COMMITTEE ON THE SOCIETY, ITS REPORT, AND THE NEW CONSTITUTION (1836–1838)

IT was ordered by the House of Commons on the 23rd of March 1836, that a select committee be appointed to enquire into the administration of the Royal Dublin Society, with a view to a wider extension of the advantages of the annual parliamentary grant to that Institution, when the following members were appointed on it :

Mr. William Smith O'Brien (who took the chair).	Mr. More O'Ferrall.
Lord Viscount Acheson.	Mr. Anthony Lefroy.
Lord Francis Egerton.	Mr. George Evans.
Mr. Sharman Crawford.	Mr. Vesey.
Mr. Dunbar.	Mr. Bellew.
Mr. Wyse.	Mr. William Stuart.
Mr. Jephson.	Lord Viscount Sandon.
	Mr. Robert Stewart.

Lord Acheson, Lord Sandon, and Mr. Bellew were discharged from attendance, and Captain Jones, Mr. Dillwyn, and Mr. Serjeant Jackson were added to the committee. It sat from the 20th of April to the 10th of June 1836, and the following witnesses were examined : Isaac Weld, honorary secretary, Robert Hutton, Charles William Hamilton, Richard Griffith, William Harty, M.D., Samuel Litton, M.D., professor of botany, and Captain Joseph E. Portlock.

THE ROYAL DUBLIN SOCIETY

Mr. Weld described the origin, objects, and constitution of the Society, detailed the history of the
premium system, and the Society's dealings with manufacturers, and with persons engaged in agriculture;
also its dealings with regard to employment of the
poor, reclamation of bogs, planting, fisheries, the fine
arts, the Leskean museum, and the Botanic Garden.
His evidence also dealt with the library, the statistical surveys of counties, and the *Transactions* of the
Society, and he reviewed the lectures and scientific
meetings.

Mr. Hutton was particularly examined as to the
working of the committees, and as to membership, and
the exclusion of the Most Rev. Dr. Murray, which he
conceived to have been brought about by party combination, and as an expression of political feeling; also
as to the parliamentary grant, the officers of the Society,
and the lectures.

Mr. C. W. Hamilton gave evidence as to the agricultural side of the Society. He also spoke of the
violence of party feeling in it at the time, and explained
that such umbrage was taken at the interference of
Government, that a majority of the members would
certainly oppose the changes indicated.

Mr. Griffith was examined as to the management
of the Society, committees, &c., and specially as to
the value of the lectures. He said that men like Sir
Humphry Davy were invited to lecture on the ground
that they might explain their own discoveries.

Dr. Harty gave evidence as to the special objects
of the Society from its foundation, and as to the
high standing of large numbers of the members; also
as to its various professors, and he added some interesting remarks on Arthur Young, and his visit to Ireland
in 1776–7.

Dr. Litton spoke as to the Botanic Garden, the lectures, &c.; and Captain Portlock, who had been connected with the Geological Survey of Ireland, gave his views as to the museum.

Each witness gave general evidence on the special points which the committee tried to elucidate, and much of it is of extreme interest. Finally a report was agreed to, which was ordered to be printed on the 14th July 1836. The following resolutions were also come to:

1. That this committee is not in a situation to pronounce any opinion upon the legal question, how far the property of the Royal Dublin Society, partly acquired by former parliamentary grants, and partly out of the funds arising from private subscriptions, be of the nature of public property, but they are of opinion that it is expedient that, in reference to future parliamentary grants, it should be fully understood that the members composing that Society are to be considered as trustees, administering a public fund, and not as entitled to an absolute right of proprietorship in the property acquired by means of such parliamentary grants; and, in reference to the existing property, that a clear and distinct guarantee should be given by the Society that the public should be entitled to the full and entire use of that property as at present enjoyed.

2. That it is expedient that the admission of all respectable individuals to a participation in the advantages arising from the parliamentary grant to the Royal Dublin Society is most desirable, and in order to guard against the capricious exercise of the power of rejection, it is advisable that its by-laws should be reconsidered, and "that hereafter no individual be excluded, notwithstanding one-third of the members present may have voted for his rejection unless at least

forty members shall have voted against his admission ";
and as regards the admission fee, that it be left optional
whether the candidate shall pay a life composition of
twenty guineas, or a fee of five guineas and two guineas
annual subscription, and that persons admitted on
these terms shall cease to be members, if at any time
their annual subscriptions shall be one year in arrear,
unless the party so in arrear shall make a declaration
in writing to the Council that he has been absent from
the kingdom during the period for which the arrear
has been incurred.

That associate subscribers should be admitted to
the Society for the term of one year, upon the recommendation of two members of the Council, or payment
of two guineas, which payment must be made at the
time of admission.

3. That the management of the ordinary business
of the Society should be confided to a Council, but
that it may be competent for thirty members to call a
general meeting of the Society, when any subject of
importance requires consideration, upon giving a notice
by advertisement at least fourteen days previous to the
day of meeting, of the time at which it will be held,
and of the subjects to be entertained.

That no such meeting shall be called between the
1st of August and the 1st of November, and that
there shall be no adjournment of such meeting without
a new notice.

That the Council should be formed by the union
of the following committees, each of which should
consist of three members, elected by the Society; one
member of each committee to go out annually; and
that the Council should be empowered to associate
with each committee not more than three members of
the Council :—

1. Committee of Fine Arts.
2. Committee of Natural Philosophy and its application to the Useful Arts.
3. Committee of Chemistry and its application to the Useful Arts.
4. Committee of Mineralogy and Geology, and its application to the Useful Arts.
5. Committee of Botany and Natural History.
6. Committee of Agriculture.
7. Committee of Statistics.
8. Committee of Accounts and Domestic Arrangements.

That at an early period in each year an estimate should be presented for sanction to a general meeting of the Society, of the expenditure which will be required in each department of the Society's operations, and that no deviation from that estimate should take place to an extent greater than £50, in the province of any one committee, without the sanction of the Society at large, except upon any extraordinary occasion, when the consent of the Treasury shall be required.

That it should be the duty of each committee to report to the Council upon all matters relating to the department over which it presides; and that all recommendations emanating from the committees should be subject to the final sanction of the whole Council.

4. That the Dublin Society should be considered as the great central association for the diffusion throughout Ireland of a knowledge of practical science, and of all improvements in agriculture, horticulture, and the arts; and that it should place itself in communication with all local societies, founded with a view to similar objects, affording to them assistance, encouragement, and information, and receiving from them in return periodical reports of their proceedings.

5. That the Dublin Society should be enabled, upon application, to send down qualified persons to give lectures in the provincial towns, whenever the travelling expenses of the lecturer, and a reasonable proportion of his remuneration shall be locally subscribed by the parties making the application.

6. That the Botanic Garden should be made as much as possible a school for young gardeners seeking instruction in horticulture.

7. That the museum, the Botanic Garden, and the Lawn should be open to the public for study or enjoyment, under regulations to be framed by the Council.

8. That books should not be lent out of the library, and that, for the convenience of persons desirous to consult the books in the library, a reading-room should be appointed, to which persons not belonging to the Society should have access by special permission of the Council.

9. That the public should be gratuitously admitted to at least one of the courses of lectures, given by each professor, during the year; and that such gratuitous course should be given in the evening, in order to encourage the attendance of persons engaged during the day in industrious occupation.

10. That each committee should periodically publish reports of its proceedings, and that the Council should, by selection from the papers read at the evening scientific meetings, or by the compilation of such other interesting and useful information as they may think it desirable to communicate to the public, cause to be printed, from time to time, publications which should be accessible to the public by purchase.

11. That newspapers and political periodicals should no longer be taken into the Society's rooms, whether

procured by special private subscription, or paid for out of the general funds of the Society.

12. That measures should be taken for securing increased activity and efficiency in the management of all the schools, and that they should be made instrumental rather in giving instruction in the useful and the mechanical departments of the arts, than in those which are purely ornamental.

13. That in order to form a National Museum adequate to the public wants, it is necessary to provide larger accommodation for the exhibition of objects than the present rooms of the Dublin Society are capable of affording, and that such increased accommodation can with advantage be provided by an extension of the buildings of the Society's present house.

On the 3rd of November 1846, the special committee of the Society reported on the foregoing resolutions, and, as to the first, submitted that it ought not to surrender its property, but should abide by the charter. With respect to the annual grant, the committee stated that it was administered as stated in the estimate, approved by the Treasury, and absorbed in the expenditure of the year.

As to No. 2, it agreed that the by-laws should be altered, so as to give effect to the recommendations.

As to No. 3, the Society was willing to adopt it, so far as to confide the ordinary business of the Society to a Council, provided the powers of such Council were strictly defined and limited, so as not to exclude the direct control over its proceedings on the part of the Society at large. Committees of management should be appointed under the following heads :—

1. Botany and Horticulture.
2. Chemistry, with its application to the useful arts.

3. Natural Philosophy and Mechanics.
4. Natural History, Geology, Mineralogy, and charge of the Museum.
5. Fine Arts.
6. Library.
7. Agriculture and Husbandry.
8. Manufactures.
9. Statistics.

The committees should be chosen annually by ballot; each committee to choose its own chairman, who, with one other member fit to be elected by each committee respectively, should be members of the Council. The Council to consist of the seven vice-presidents, the two honorary secretaries, the chairman, and one other member of each committee, and of nine members to be elected by ballot, by and from the Society at large. Monthly meetings to be held in addition to the stated general meetings directed by the charter, for special purposes.

No. 4. The Society wished to act most fully on this recommendation.

No. 5. This suggestion was recommended whenever local institutions took the necessary steps.

No. 6. This should be fully adopted ; and in part it had been anticipated by the Society.

No. 7. The museum and Botanic Garden have been open to the public, subject to regulations. It should be left to the Council to adopt further rules.

No. 8. Lending out scientific books to members should not be continued, except as the library committee deem proper. It would not be expedient to discontinue it in all cases, and the Society should procure such a reading-room as is described in the resolution.

No. 9. It has always been the practice to admit the public to the lectures gratuitously, and the evening courses should be again tried, in deference to the committee's wish.

No. 10. This resolution was recommended.

No. 11. The committee thought that the exclusion of newspapers would hardly be reconcilable with the desire for information as to every branch of science, arts, manufactures, and agriculture. The reduction of the stamp duties encouraged the reading of papers, and it would seem inconsistent to deprive members of this advantage. The committee found that it could not recommend a discontinuance of the practice, but thought that perhaps newspapers should not be purchased out of public money.

No. 12. This resolution was recommended.

No. 13. The Society would gladly co-operate in attaining the objects mentioned in this recommendation, but, in order to carry them out, a considerable extension of its pecuniary means would be necessary.

The entire of this report of the committee was adopted by the Society, and copies were sent to the Treasury and the Chief Secretary. A special committee to prepare by-laws in accordance with the new situation was also appointed. A Treasury minute required a specific admission from the Society with regard to the right of ownership mentioned in the first resolution, and in reply, the Society declared that it did not claim the right of disposing of its property for the advantage of members, or for objects foreign to those for which it was incorporated. The Society admitted that the property was held as a public trust, for the public benefit, with a view to the objects for which the charter had been obtained.

In volume lxxiv. of the *Proceedings*, appendix ii., pp. 9–36, will be found by-laws of the Society, as they stood, on the confirmation of those agreed to on the 9th, 16th, and 23rd of November 1837, at the stated General Meeting in March 1838.

Under them the management of the business of the Society was to be confided to a Council, the powers of such Council to be strictly, as hereafter, limited and defined, and subject to the direct control over the proceedings upon the part of the Society at large.   It was to consist of the seven vice-presidents, two honorary secretaries, the chairman and one other member of each committee, and nine members who were to be elected by ballot.   This Council was to meet weekly, and to keep minutes of its proceedings.   Under a by-law of November 1838, its meetings were to be open to members of the Society, but they were to be without power of speaking or voting.

The following were the first members who were elected on the 26th of April 1838 by the committees, to serve on the Council :

Agriculture and Husbandry . .	George Tuthill, *Chairman.* James Corballis.
Botany and Horticulture . . .	Isaac M. D'Olier, *Chairman.* Simon Foot.
Chemistry	Dr. Meyler, *Chairman.* William Willans.
Fine Arts	George Cash, *Chairman.* Daniel McKay.
Library	E. R. P. Colles, *Chairman.* Richard Hemphill.
Manufactures	Sir Edward Stanley, *Chairman.* B. B. Johnston.
Natural History and Museum	Dr. W. Beatty, *Chairman.* Dr. Hart.
Natural Philosophy and Mechanics.	Henry Adair, *Chairman.* Edward Clibborn.
Statistics	Sir William Betham, *Chairman.* William Smith.

The following nine members were elected by ballot
to serve on the Council :

Henry Carey.	John Hughes.
William Smith.	Edward Tierney.
R. M. Peile.	Villiers B. Fowler.
J. H. Orpen, M.D.	Ambrose Smith.
Wm. Harty, M.D.	

The Council presented its first report to the Society
on the 8th of November 1838, which stated that the
Council was engaged in carrying into effect the object
of the Treasury communication as to delivery of
lectures in provincial towns by the professors. Professor Davy lectured in Portarlington and Wicklow,
and Dr. Kane in Galway, the former on chemistry,
and the latter on natural philosophy. The Council
had the satisfaction of reporting to the Society that
its establishment was in a vigorous and active state.

CHAPTER XVII

GENERAL HISTORY OF THE SOCIETY (*continued*)
(1836–1877)

THE evening scientific meetings continued to be held, and at the first of the series in November 1836, Baron Foster occupying the chair, Dr. Scouler exhibited specimens of lignites and silicified woods from the neighbourhood of Lough Neagh, on which he made observations. Dr. Kane exhibited a modification of Faraday's electro-magnetic apparatus, invented by Professor Callan of Maynooth. At the meeting in May 1837, Mr. Clibborn read a long paper on the theory and practical results of the banking system in America, which is printed in full in the *Proceedings*, vol. lxxiii. appendix viii. In December 1837, Dr. Kane presented specimens of books printed in raised letters, for the use of the blind, and explained the merits of each system; and in 1838, Mr. Grubb read a paper on the comparative and defining powers of different telescopes, and the disappearance of stars, when great magnifying power is used. Dr. Kane explained the electro-magnetic telegraph used in Munich, and Mr. Colles read a paper on street architecture. Later, Dr. Scouler discoursed on the dolomites, or beds of magnesian limestone, found in some parts of Ireland, and Mr. Rigby read a paper on the rifling of gun barrels. In January 1839, when the Lord Lieutenant was present, Professor Davy gave an account of two new gaseous

compounds of carbon and hydrogen; while Sir
William Betham addressed the audience on the advantages to be derived from the study of antiquities,
and Dr. Wilde made some observations on fisheries.
These meetings were the precursors of the scientific
meetings which have since become so important a
feature in the Society.

In 1838, Philip Crampton (1), surgeon-general, in
recognition of the talent displayed in his lectures on the
importance of the study of zoology, and Isaac Butt (2),
professor of political economy in Trinity College, for
his lecture on the importance of the study of zoology
in connection with civilisation, were elected honorary
members.

1. Philip Crampton was born in Dublin in 1777, and in
1798 became Surgeon to the Meath Hospital, where he established a great reputation as a skilful operator, ready and full
of resource. He was appointed surgeon-general to the Forces
in Ireland, and at a later period, surgeon in ordinary to the
Queen, and in 1839 a baronetcy was conferred on him.
Crampton was much interested in zoology, and may be considered one of the founders of the Zoological Gardens in
Dublin. A paper of his on the " Eyes of Birds being accommodated to different distances," obtained his election to
fellowship of the Royal Society. Sir Philip Crampton died
in 1858.

2. Isaac Butt was born in the county Donegal in 1813.
Having been called to the Bar, he founded the *Dublin University Magazine*, of which he was editor, 1834–1841. Butt held
the post of professor of political economy in the University
of Dublin from 1836–1841, and always took a prominent
part in politics, being the recognised champion of the Conservative party. He defended Smith O'Brien in the State
trials of 1848, and in 1852 became M.P. for Harwich, afterwards representing Youghal from 1852–1865, both in the
Conservative interest. The Fenian prisoners were defended

by him, and, soon after, Butt changed his politics, being elected M.P. for Limerick in 1871, as a Home Ruler. He published works on the Irish Corporation Bill, on Zoology and Civilisation, Transfer of Land, National Education, Deep Sea Fisheries, and Irish Federation. Butt died in 1879.

On the 7th of June 1838, the Society adjourned as a mark of respect to the memory of the Right Hon. Henry Joy, chief baron of the Exchequer, a vice-president, whose death was that day announced. Miss Joy, the chief baron's sister, presented to the Society his collection of minerals, which had been arranged by Sir Charles Giesecke, and was very valuable.

The Spring cattle show, held in April 1838, was the most successful hitherto held—"all the space the extensive cattle yard afforded being fully occupied," and the quality of the stock being the universal theme of admiration.

The exhibition of manufactures held in May also showed a great improvement in many branches, the number of visitors amounting to 20,000, and much greater space having to be allotted to exhibitors than was the case at the exhibition of 1835. The committee of the exhibition resolved to grant but one gold medal, which was awarded to Mr. Grubb, for his transit instrument, the first of the kind ever manufactured in Ireland. On each day that the exhibition remained open, Dr. Kane lectured to a crowded auditory in the theatre, on some branch of art or manufacture.

Great injury was done to the stable offices at Leinster House by the great storm of January 1839, and a considerable part of the boundary wall of the Botanic Garden, between the entrance gate and Glasnevin bridge, was blown down.

Henry Cotton, dean of Lismore and archdeacon of Cashel, was admitted a member of the Society. Cotton was born in Buckinghamshire in 1789, and for a time held the post of sub-librarian of the Bodleian library. In 1823, he came to Ireland as chaplain to his father-in-law, Dr. Lawrence, archbishop of Cashel. His *Fasti Ecclesiae Hiberniae*, in five volumes, which appeared between 1848 and 1860, is a most valuable compilation, that must have cost him much labour. That work did for Ireland what Le Neve's had done for England, and Cotton's short memoirs of the various dignitaries of the church have proved very useful. Cotton also published a *List of Editions of the Bible printed between 1505 and 1820*, and *Obsolete Words in our Version of the Bible*. Archdeacon Cotton died in 1879.

The Council reported in May, that additional buildings for the departments of agriculture, manufactures, and natural history had become absolutely necessary. It was proposed to alter the long range of buildings in the cattle yard by raising the walls, and lighting them from the roof, which would give a suite of rooms 220 feet in length. A number of additional sheds for cattle were also contemplated. Considering all the alterations that were peremptorily demanded, the Council agreed that £4000 would be necessary, and that sum was voted. Steps were also taken for planting the lawn, screening off the statue gallery, and concealing the stables by a plantation. The parapet wall was also removed, and the unsightly ditch next Merrion square filled up. The balustrade and entrance from Merrion square were supplied at that time.

In July 1841, R. Butler Bryan died, and Mr. Lundy E. Foot, barrister, was elected as secretary in his room.

The first six months of the year 1841 formed a very anxious time for the Society, for, having settled down under its new conditions, and having, as was supposed, complied with most, if not quite all, of the recommendations of the Select Committee of the House of Commons, the members were suddenly confronted with a letter from the Chief Secretary, dated the 17th of December 1840, conveying the Lord Lieutenant's opinion that the recommendations had been but imperfectly carried out. A long correspondence ensued, and the points to which special attention was called were the continuance of the newsroom, and the principle of an annual subscription not having been adopted. Certain propositions were enclosed, the adoption of which would prevent future collision between the Executive and the Society. The Society was to consist of two sections, having the house, library, theatre, museums, &c., in common, the one to promote chemistry, geology, mineralogy, &c., and the other section agriculture, botany, arts, and manufactures. The members of each section were to be elected as hitherto, but, instead of £21 payment, the admission fee was to be £1, with an annual subscription of £1, or a life composition of £10. A number of other propositions were submitted, but the above named, and one, that no newspaper or newsroom was to be permitted, were the principal. There was an implied threat that the parliamentary grant might be withdrawn, should the Society not see its way to compliance. As a matter of fact, the Society never considered these two recommendations of the Select Committee as of such paramount importance, and never thought the report so mandatory as to exclude all exercise of judgment on its part in matters of detail. The Government had not offered any opinion on the changes of the system, save by a Treasury letter for issue of the balance of the grant then due. No objections having been since raised, and the grants being continued, the Society naturally inferred that the Government acquiesced in the newspapers being retained. The Lord Lieutenant admitted that he had been mistaken as to the admission of annual subscribers, as the Society had adopted the principle in the precise terms recommended by the committee. He considered it essential that the newsroom should not be continued, and that an annual subscription equivalent to the life composition should be fixed.

With regard to the new proposals, the Society thought that the existence of two societies, separately elected, and holding property in common, was anomalous and contained elements of discord, and a number of arguments were urged against them. His Excellency, finding his scheme rejected, regretted that he could no longer recommend the continuance of the Society's grant. The next step was the issue, on the 29th of March 1841, of a commission to the Duke of Leinster, Lord Rosse, Lord Adare, and Messrs. J. F. Burgoyne, W. R. Hamilton, Humphrey Lloyd, Thomas A. Larcom, and J. McCullagh, empowering them to enquire and report in what form, and under what regulations, the parliamentary grant of £5300, voted to the Dublin Society, might be most effectually used for the advancement of science and diffusion of useful knowledge, for the benefit of the Irish nation ; particularly, whether it would be desirable to form an entirely new Institution, or to assist any societies now established in Dublin for the furtherance of science and art. The commissioners reported that the grant should be for the support of one Society only, and as His Excellency had abandoned his intention of having the Society's grant withdrawn, if proper arrangements were made, they suggested points for consideration, which were generally as follows :

That there should be a court of Visitors, consisting of the Lord Chancellor, the Lord Chief Justice, and the Provost.

That the Society should embrace sections for—1, Physical Science ; 2, Geology and Mineralogy ; 3, Botany and Horticulture ; 4, Zoology ; 5, Agriculture. That the General Council should consist of thirty-one members, namely, the president, seven vice-presidents, the two secretaries, and six others, elected by the Society, as well as fifteen members of the Society deputed from the sectional councils. That members of the Society should pay an admission fee of two guineas, and an annual subscription of two guineas ; composition fee to be twenty guineas. That a member of one section should pay half these sums. That the school of mechanical drawing should be continued under the Society, and that the schools of fine arts should be transferred to the Royal Hibernian Academy.

Though, on the whole, these propositions were favourably received by the Society, certain modifications were asked for ; and, on the 16th of June 1841, His Excellency stated that he found with pleasure that the Society appeared disposed to accede to them. They formed, with the original condition as to the abolition of the newsroom, the extent of what the Government desired to see carried out.

On the 11th of November 1841, the Council submitted to the members resolutions embodying the principles on which the Society might meet the expressed wishes of the Irish Government, which provided for discontinuance of the newsroom and newspapers. The Society was to embrace the following sections :

1, Husbandry and Agriculture; 2, Chemistry; 3, Natural Philosophy and Mechanics; 4, Botany and Horticulture; 5, Natural History (Zoology, Geology, and Mineralogy); 6, Fine Arts; 7, Manufactures, &c.; election of associate members of sections, without ballot, as associate members were then admitted, with certain regulations as to the sections; and a General Council consisting of thirty-three members, namely—the president, seven vice-presidents, the two secretaries, nine members elected from the Society, and fourteen deputed from the sections. On the 26th of May 1842, amended by-laws as to associate members of sections were passed.

The Rev. Thomas Romney Robinson, D.D., professor of astronomy at Armagh, was elected an honorary member. This great astronomer and mathematical physicist was born in Dublin in 1792, the son of Thomas Robinson, portrait painter. He became a fellow of Trinity College in 1814, and in 1823 was appointed to the College living of Enniskillen. From the time of his election to the post of astronomer at Armagh Observatory, Robinson resided there, when he published his *Armagh Observations* and his great work, *Places of 5345 Stars observed at Armagh*, which appeared between 1828 and 1854. The medal of the Royal Society was awarded to Dr. Robinson, and he was well known as inventor of the cup-anemometer, which he first described at the British Association Meeting of 1846. Robinson contributed many papers and articles to the *Transactions* and *Proceedings* of the Royal Irish Academy. He died in 1882, and there is a portrait of him in the Academy House.

At the end of vol. lxxviii. *Proceedings*, appeared, for the first time, minutes of the Council, commencing on the 19th of August 1841, which continued to be regularly printed in the succeeding volumes of the *Proceedings*.

In March 1843, a large silver medal, with certificate, was presented to Mr. James Fagan, for his exertions in establishing a dockyard at Kingstown, and building a new ship, the *Duchess of Leinster*, as it was so important to Dublin and the country generally to encourage shipbuilding.

During the cattle show in April 1843, the eminent agriculturist, Mr. Smith of Deanston, lectured on draining land, and on subsoil ploughing, and the committee of agriculture offered premiums for essays on subsoil ploughing, on thorough draining, and on the effects of altitude on vegetation, &c. The first show of farm produce was held in 1844, in connection with the reopening of the agricultural museum, which had been largely improved.

Albert, the Prince Consort, became a Vice-Patron of the Society in 1845, and showed great interest in the exhibition of stock.

In the winter of that year, potato disease occupied the attention of the Council, and Professor Davy was authorised to suspend his lectures, and devote all his energies to conducting experiments with a view to the preservation of that crop. A gold medal and £20 were offered for the best essay on the disease.

The lectures in provincial towns were by this time well established, and Dr. Kane, Professor Davy, and Mr. Oldham delivered lectures on natural philosophy, chemistry, and geology, in Clonmel, Coleraine, Killarney, Galway, and Waterford, Ballinasloe, Newry, Limerick, Armagh, Mallow, Dungannon, &c. £40 were assigned to each town out of the sum voted by Parliament for that service.

In 1846, some friends of Alexander Nimmo,

government engineer for the western district of
Ireland, subscribed for a bust, in memory of him ;
this was offered to the Society, and it now stands in
the reception-room.   The bust was executed by John
Jones, at one time a student in the schools.

Sir Robert Kane resigned the professorship of
Natural Philosophy in November 1847, and Dr. William
Barker was elected in his room.   Dr. W. H. Harvey
became professor of Botany in place of Dr. Litton,
and Dr. Charles Croker King became honorary professor of Anatomy in connection with the fine arts,
in the room of Dr. Woodroofe.

Owing to troubles connected with Smith O'Brien's
rising in 1848, troops were quartered for several
months on the Society's premises.   From the 3rd of
April, cavalry and infantry occupied the cattle yard,
the buildings in it, and other portions of the premises,
while the officers used the conversation and board
rooms.

In 1849, William Stokes, m.d. (1), George Petrie,
ll.d. (see p. 119), and Charles Bianconi (2) were elected
members, and on the 7th of November 1850, the latter
was elected an honorary member.

1. William Stokes, son of Whitley Stokes, regius professor
of Medicine in the University of Dublin, was born in 1804.
In 1825, he published a work on the *Use of the Stethoscope*,
which was the earliest treatise on that subject that appeared
in these countries.   He also wrote on the curability of
phthisis, and in 1834 became editor of the *Dublin Journal of
Medical Science*.   Dr. Stokes was afterwards elected a Fellow
of the Royal Society, and he became regius professor of
Medicine in the University, and physician to the Queen in
Ireland.   He was regarded as one of the greatest physicians
of his time, and his works have been translated into French,
German, and Italian.   Stokes was a warm friend of George
Petrie, and published a memoir of him in 1866.   A portrait

of Stokes by Sir Frederick Burton has been engraved, and a statue by Foley stands in the hall of the College of Physicians. He died in 1878, and is buried at St. Fintan's, Howth.

2. Charles Bianconi was born near Como, in Lombardy, in 1786, and at the age of sixteen came to Dublin as a vendor of prints. From thence he went to Carrick-on-Suir, where he engaged in business as a carver and gilder, finally settling in Clonmel. Here he commenced his system of Irish cars, and in 1815 ran a two-wheeled car to Cahir. So successful were Bianconi's cars that, at the end of thirty years, he was working 3266 miles of road. Bianconi was a great friend of O'Connell, whose nephew, Morgan J. O'Connell, married Bianconi's daughter. Mrs. M. J. O'Connell wrote a biography of her father, who realised a large fortune, which was principally invested in land, including the estate of Longfield, near Clonmel, which Bianconi, who died in 1875, made his home.

In August 1849, Her Majesty Queen Victoria and the Prince Consort, accompanied by some of their children, visited Ireland for the first time. On the 6th of that month, the Queen and Prince visited the Botanic Garden, the former, with Lady Clarendon, arriving in a carriage, while Prince Albert and Lord Clarendon rode. This early visit, the first to any public institution, had not been expected, and there was not time for much preparation. The Duke of Leinster, Mr. Lundy Foot and Dr. Harrison, the secretaries, Sir Thomas Staples, Mr. H. Wybrants, Mr. F. Darley, architect of the new conservatories, Dr. Collins, and some other members met the Royal party, when Mr. Moore, the curator, was introduced to the Queen by the Duke of Leinster. These gentlemen accompanied the Royal party round the grounds, in which a large number of ladies and gentlemen had assembled to greet Her Majesty.

An address from the Society was presented to the

Queen at the levee, by Lords Kildare and Clancarty, and Mr. Isaac Weld. Prince Albert visited Leinster House on the 9th of August, when an address was presented to him in the board-room, which was read by Mr. Foot.

An exhibition of stock and farming produce was being held at the time, and, after the presentation of the Society's address, the Prince paid the show a visit. The Duke of Leinster, the Marquis of Kildare, the Earl of Clancarty, Lord Massereene, Sir William Betham, Lord Hawarden, and Dr. Harrison were in attendance.

On the occasion of the Queen's visit to Dublin, the gate entrance to Leinster House was splendidly illuminated, the Society being the first of all the public institutions to do honour to Her Majesty in this form.

The number of visitors attending the Spring and Winter cattle shows during the year 1849, was 16,748; the museum of natural history, 42,197; the Botanic Garden, 30,324.

During the summer of 1850, the seventh triennial exhibition of manufactures was held. This was formerly confined to Irish products, but now competitors from Great Britain were admitted. The exhibition—the first at which machinery in motion was exhibited—was most successful, and was visited by 30,000 persons, the receipts amounting to £1234, 16s. 2d.

On the 13th of November 1851, Commander Francis Leopold McClintock, R.N. (1), was elected an honorary member, and Mr. William Dargan (2), a life member.

1. Sir F. L. McClintock was born at Dundalk in 1819, entering the navy in 1831. In 1848, he served in the *Enterprise* under Captain Sir James C. Ross, during a voyage to the Arctic regions; and in 1850 he served on a similar voyage of discovery, on board the *Assistance*. McClintock acquired a great reputation as an Arctic

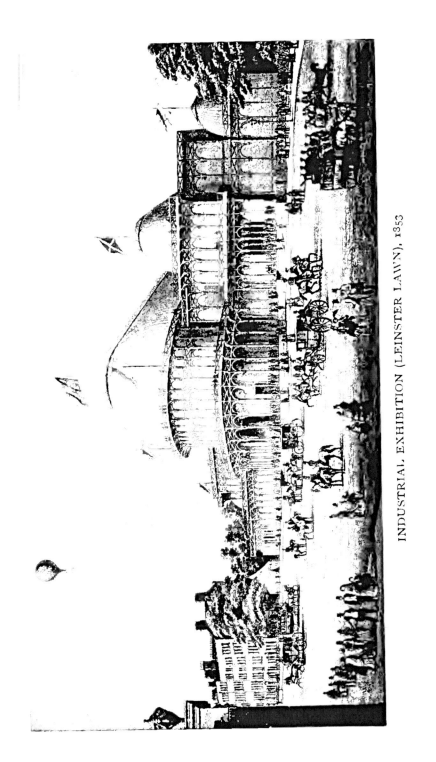

INDUSTRIAL EXHIBITION (LEINSTER LAWN), 1853

explorer, and he commanded the *Intrepid* when a large expedition set out in 1852 for the Polar regions, where he made many remarkable sledge journeys into the interior. Lady Franklin, not feeling certainty as to the fate of her distinguished husband, Sir John Franklin, purchased the yacht *Fox*, and gave McClintock command, with a commission to search for him or any trace of his expedition, when he found absolute proof of Sir John's death, and of the fate of the party. In 1859, he published an account of the search expedition in his *Voyage of the Fox in the Arctic Seas*. McClintock was promoted to the rank of Admiral, and saw further service in the Danish war of 1864, and in the Mediterranean ; in 1879 he was appointed Commander-in-Chief on the North American and West Indian Stations. He lived to 1907, and a bust of him has a place in the reception-room of Leinster House.

2. William Dargan, the great Irish railway projector, was born in Carlow in 1799. He was first employed in a surveyor's office, and subsequently worked under Telford in 1820, when the Holyhead railroad was being constructed. In 1834, the Dublin and Kingstown line (the first in Ireland), which was made by him, was opened. The Ulster Canal, said to be a " triumph of constructive ability," the Dublin and Drogheda, the Great Southern and Western, and the Midland Great Western, railways were all constructed by him. Dargan planned and carried out the great Dublin Exhibition of 1853, his advances on behalf of which are believed to have amounted to £100,000, and by which he lost fully £20,000. When Queen Victoria came to visit it, she honoured Mr. and Mrs. Dargan by calling on them at Mount Anville, when she offered to bestow a baronetcy on him, which he declined. Dargan died in 1867. A bronze statue of him was erected on Leinster lawn, close to the National Gallery.

On the 24th of June 1852, the Council received a letter from Mr. Dargan, who, understanding that the triennial exhibition of manufactures would be held in 1853, wished to give it a character of more than usual prominence. He proposed to place a sum of £20,000 in the hands of an executive committee, on condition that a suitable building should be erected on the lawn, the exhibition to be opened not later than June 1853. Mr. Dargan was to nominate the chairman, deputy chairman, and secretary of the committee, and when the exhibition was closed, the building was to become his property. There were also certain conditions with regard to contingent profits, &c., and, on full consideration, the Society accepted the proposals made by him.

The undertaking was to be known as " The Great Industrial Exhibition, 1853, in connection with the Royal Dublin Society," and the Society nominated Mr. L. E. Foot, secretary, Mr. Walter Sweetman, and Mr. Charles G. Fairfield, to act with Sir W. McDonnell, Mr. George Roe, and the Hon. George Handcock, nominated by Mr. Dargan, who were to be the executive committee. It may be remarked that following the Great Exhibition of 1851, held in Hyde Park, a similar one had been held in Cork in 1852, which may have stimulated Mr. Dargan in his desire to inaugurate a like undertaking in Dublin. He advanced various other sums amounting in all, it is said, to £100,000.

The exhibition was opened on Thursday, the 12th May 1853, in a splendid structure of iron and glass, which had been erected on Leinster lawn, from a design of Sir John Benson. The Lord Lieutenant performed the opening ceremony, at which addresses were presented by the chairman, and by the Lord Mayor and Corporation. A great banquet was held at the Mansion House in the evening, in celebration of the event.

Her Majesty the Queen, accompanied by the Prince Consort, the Prince of Wales, and Prince Alfred,

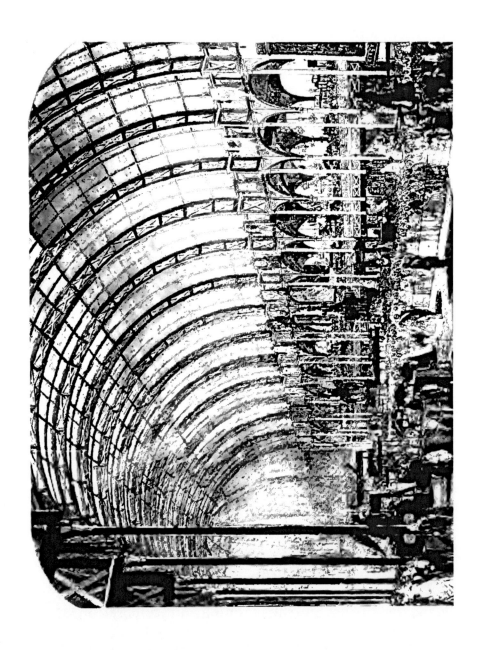

visited the exhibition on Tuesday, the 30th of August, when she sat in a state chair used at her coronation, which had been lent by Lord Conyngham. The Right Hon. Robert H. Kinahan, lord mayor, Mr. Dargan, Mr. George Roe, and Sir Edward McDonnell received the Royal party, who were accompanied by the Earl of St. Germains, the lord lieutenant, and the Countess of St. Germains. In the afternoon Her Majesty drove out to Mount Anville, Dundrum, to pay Mr. and Mrs. Dargan a visit. The Queen also paid visits to the exhibition on the 31st of August and the 1st and 2nd of September, examining different departments on each occasion. During her third visit, Mr. Richard Griffith gave Her Majesty an account of the Irish granites and marbles exhibited by the Royal Dublin Society.

In 1852, Dr. W. E. Steele was appointed assistant secretary. On the 27th of October 1853, the sudden death of Sir William Betham, vice-president, was announced, and in November of the same year, Mr. Henry Conner White was elected registrar, in the room of P. T. Wilson, who had been in the Society's service in that capacity for a great number of years.

When the estimates for 1854 were under consideration, a Committee of the Privy Council, being anxious to extend to Ireland the full benefits of industrial instruction, proposed that the museum should be devoted only to objects that might be necessary for natural history, and for a museum of agriculture. The Society was to be relieved of the educational staff in order that its members might be available for the museum of Irish industry, and for lectures in provincial towns, which would place them under the Science and Art Department, and save the Society a sum of £1772 yearly. The general vote was still to stand at £6000, independent of supplementary votes for building purposes, which would have left a sum of about £1500 for exhibitions, &c.

The Society remonstrated against the proposal to deprive it of the superintendence of the educational staff, the apparent object of which was to support the museum of Irish industry out of public funds, at the expense and to the injury of the Royal Dublin Society. It was thought that the appointment by the Board of Trade of professors with divided duties, would render neutral the benefits experienced from professors attached to the Society. A deputation went to London, which learned that the Government would not, on two points, recede from the position which it had taken up—viz. 1, the maintenance of the museum of Irish industry as a separate Government institution; 2, the determination not to support a double staff of teachers. Eventually the Society agreed to accept the proposals, as they were explained in a report of the department. and in a letter of Mr. G. A. Hamilton. The greater number of their functions was not to be disturbed, namely such as concerned:—1, Accounts; 2, Manufactures; 3, Agriculture; 4, Fine Arts; 5, Botanic Garden; 6, Library; 7, Agricultural Chemistry; 8, Natural History. The museum was to be largely increased, and the educational staff, though under the Board of Trade, was still to pertain to the Society. About £1000 a year additional was to be available, and the Zoological Garden was to be brought into connection with it, while the School of Art would be entirely under its control.

In August 1854, the Government nominated the Chief Secretary for Ireland (or in his absence the Under Secretary), the Right Hon. Maziere Brady, lord chancellor, Mr. Richard Griffith, and Sir Robert

DR. GEORGE JOHNSTONE STONEY, F.R.S., VICE-PRESIDENT, 1881–1911
(*From photograph by W. Whiteley, Ltd., London*)

Kane ; and the Society named Lord Talbot de Malahide, the Right Hon. Francis Blackburne, Mr. F. J. Sidney, and Mr. William Fry, as a joint committee for management of the museum of Irish industry, the Society's lectures, and the lectures in provincial towns, which marked an important change in the functions and ancient practice of the Society. This system continued until the year 1865.

Alterations were made in the by-laws, and annual members henceforth might become life members on payment of fifteen guineas. In 1856, the by-laws were further amended, and the Council was in future to consist of the seven vice-presidents, the two secretaries, the chairman, and one other member of each standing committee, and of nine members to be elected from the Society.

John Francis Waller, LL.D., was elected secretary in 1855, in the room of Dr. Harrison, and Mr. E. R. P. Colles, librarian, in place of Mr. Patten, resigned. In 1856, Mr. Weld, vice-president, who had been a member of the Society for fifty-five years, and in 1857, Mr. Henry Kemmis, another vice-president, died. Mr. Foot was elected a vice-president, and in this year Mr. George Johnstone Stoney became a member of the Society.

Dr. Stoney's is one of the greatest names connected with the Society, for which, during the period that he held office in it, he laboured with unwearying devotion. He conducted with the Government negotiations of a most intricate character, prior to the museum, the Botanic Garden, the library and art schools being taken over ; and the charter and statutes of 1881 were his work. Stoney was born in the King's county in 1826, and in 1848 was appointed astronomical assistant to Lord Rosse at Parsonstown, where he made many observations, and communicated with learned societies, one of his notable papers being on " Shadow Bands in

Eclipses." Stoney held the post of professor of natural philosophy in Queen's College, Galway, and was secretary to the Queen's University in Ireland from 1857 to its dissolution in 1882. He paid much attention to physical optics, to molecular physics, and the kinetic theory of gases, and wrote works on the *Physical Constitution of Sun and Stars*, and on the *Atmosphere of Planets and Satellites*. For twenty years, during a period when its affairs demanded close and unremitting attention, Dr. Stoney acted as secretary to the Society, becoming a vice-president in 1893, and he contributed largely to the *Transactions*. He won the first Boyle Medal in 1899. Owing to his connection with the Society, Government frequently consulted him on questions affecting agriculture, fisheries, railways, &c. He was a consistent advocate of the higher education of women, and inaugurated the recitals of chamber music, now so marked a feature in the Society's yearly programme. Dr. Stoney was elected a fellow of the Royal Society in 1861, becoming a vice-president in 1898. He died in 1911, and his portrait by Sir Thomas A. Jones, presented to the Society by old students of the Queen's University, hangs in the reception-room, Leinster House.

The first stone of the Natural History building was laid on the 7th of April 1856, by the Earl of Carlisle, lord lieutenant.

The British Association again met in Dublin in 1857, when the meetings of its council and of the general committee of the Association were held in the board-room, Leinster House, while the new museum and the Botanic Garden were devoted to other purposes in connection with the meeting. The opening meeting was held in the round room of the Rotunda, on the 26th of August. On Dr. Daubeny resigning the chair to Dr. Lloyd on the evening of the 27th, the Royal Dublin Society gave a conversazione, at which over 1500 guests were present, and the new museum building formed a prominent point of attraction. On the

The Right Hon. Arthur, Lord Ardilaun
President 1897–1915

29th of August a great fête was given in the Botanic Garden, at which 4000 persons were present. During the meeting Mr. Markham, in the geographical section, read an account of the search for Sir John Franklin, by McClintock's expedition; and on the evening of the 31st of August, Dr. Livingstone, the African traveller, lectured on Africa in the new museum.

During the previous year, on the 13th of November 1856, the Council, with the sanction of the Society, issued for the first time the *Quarterly Journal of the Royal Dublin Society*. In 1861 this undertaking was found to be too expensive, and the *Journal* ceased to be published.

Steps were then being taken for appropriating portion of the lawn as a site for a National Art Gallery, and early in 1858, the designs for it were approved. At this time it was proposed to make it also a place of deposit for the contents of Archbishop Marsh's library.

In February 1858, the Society resolved to institute annual examinations in the elementary branches of education, with a view to granting certificates of merit to deserving candidates for appointments in banks, commercial, and manufacturing establishments, &c. The Rev. Joseph Carson, F.T.C.D., Dr. Ingram, F.T.C.D., Messrs. Foot, Steele, and Neilson Hancock were appointed a board of examiners, and in each volume of the *Proceedings* after this date will be found copies of the examination papers, and lists of successful candidates.

On the 4th of January 1860, Mr. Arthur Edward Guinness and his brother, Mr. Benjamin Lee Guinness, jun., were elected members of the Society. The former, now Lord Ardilaun, was president of the Society for sixteen years, succeeding Lord Powerscourt on the 2nd of December 1897, and retiring on the

13th of November 1913. Lord Ardilaun, who is a graduate of Dublin University, always evinced the deepest interest in the work and objects of the Society, and, while one of the representatives in Parliament of the city of Dublin, frequently accompanied deputations of the Society to ministers, urging their claims. To Lord Ardilaun the Society is indebted for a splendid silver mace, which was first laid on the table on the 12th of November 1903, when a cordial vote of thanks was tendered to him for his generous gift. The mace was manufactured by Messrs. West and son, of Dublin, after the design of one presented in 1746 by the then Earl of Kildare to the corporation of Athy. On the dissolution of that corporation in 1841, the mace was presented to John Butler, who had been sovereign of the borough in 1833 and 1841, and it was purchased from his son by the Duke of Leinster. The associations connecting the Society with that family made it fitting that a copy of the mace should be used in Leinster House. A detailed description of the original, which was regarded as one of the finest specimens of Irish work of the period, will be found in *Maces, Swords, and other Insignia of Office of Irish Corporations*, by Mr. J. Ribton Garstin, D.L., reprinted from the *Journal* of the Arts and Crafts Society of Ireland, volume i. no. 2.

In 1861, a Fine Arts Exhibition was held, which was open for 136 days and 66 nights; 190,000 visitors (including the Prince Consort and the Prince of Wales) attended it, and the profit resulting from the undertaking amounted to £1400. The purpose of the exhibition was to bring together the best works, with a view of illustrating the history of modern art, and showing its progress in the country. In carrying out the enterprise, the Royal Dublin Society and the

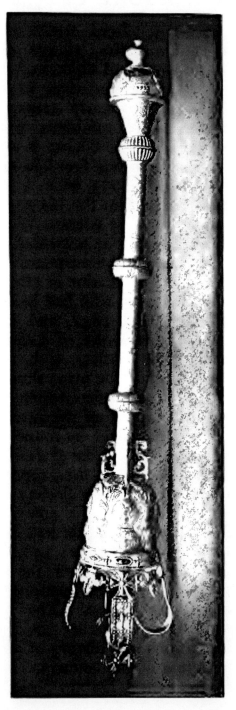

MACE OF THE ROYAL DUBLIN SOCIETY

(Presented by Lord Ardilaun, 1903)

committee of management did the country a great service.

A deputation went to London in this year, to confer with the Science and Art Department as to the terms of a supplementary charter. It was agreed that the Council was to consist of thirty-three members—the president, the seven vice-presidents, the two honorary secretaries, fifteen councillors, and one representative of not more than eight standing committees. The fifteen councillors were to hold office for three years, and the secretaries for two years, five councillors and one secretary going out of office each year. The Council was to have the general management of the Society, with power to enact by-laws.

The new charter was issued on the 27th of December 1865, and among other things, the Society was privileged by it to have a mace. Its principal object was to confer on the Society authority to elect a Council and standing committees, a power which it did not previously possess; also to grant that the general management and control over the affairs of the Society, and over its paid officers and servants, including the power of appointing and dismissing them, as well as that of regulating their duties and emoluments, should be vested exclusively in the Council. Under this charter there were to be standing committees for the purposes of :—1, Agriculture and the Museum ; 2, the Library; 3, Fine Arts; 4, Botany and the Botanic Garden ; 5, Natural History, and the Museum ; 6, Manufactures and Practical Science. Each committee was to consist of eleven members, save that of Agriculture, which was to number twenty-one. There were also special regulations as to members who were to represent the

T

Society on the first Council, which was to consist of thirty-three members.

By his will, which was proved on the 16th of August 1864, Mr. William Smith O'Brien bequeathed to the Irish nation two pictures, one the "Limerick Piper," by Haverty, and the other a remarkable head in oils. He desired them to be exhibited in the exhibition gallery of the Royal Dublin Society, "to which body I make this bequest." In the next year Mr. Joseph Burke, J.P., of 17 Fitzwilliam Place, Dublin, bequeathed to the Society his collection of Incumbered Estates and Landed Estates Court Rentals, in number between 3000 and 4000, arranged in dictionary order, which the testator valued at £1000. The Society was to have the collection bound.

The first horse show under the auspices of the Society was held on the 29th of July 1868. Shows had been held in 1864 and 1866 in the Society's premises, but they were under the auspices of the Royal Agricultural Society. The show held in 1868 was a great success, the Agricultural and Shelbourne halls, and even the Clare lane premises being fitted up with stalls for the animals, which numbered 380. The courtyard was transformed into a huge circus ring, for the jumping, while a raised gallery around accommodated the spectators. Lord St. Lawrence, Mr. R. C. Wade, and Captain C. Colthurst Vesey acted as stewards, with Mr. Andrew Corrigan as superintendent.

The Prince Consort's statue on the lawn was unveiled by the Duke of Edinburgh on the 6th of June 1872.

On Lord Spencer's retirement from the viceroyalty in 1874, the Council suggested that it would be more in accordance with the terms of the charter if, in future, the Lord Lieutenant held the office of vice-patron, and that the presidents should be chosen from among the members. The Society acquiesced in the Council's views, and, on the 5th of March 1874, the Duke of Abercorn, lord lieutenant, was elected to the former office, and the Marquis of Kildare, afterwards Duke of Leinster, became president.

On the 8th of April 1875, Mr. Richard Jackson Moss, F.C.S., was appointed keeper of the minerals and analyst, in the room of Dr. J. Emerson Reynolds, elected professor of Chemistry in the University of Dublin. On the 7th March 1878, Mr. Moss was promoted to be registrar of the Society in the room of Dr. Steele, appointed general director of the Science and Art Museum.

From the year 1872, and indeed still earlier, negotiations had been going on in reference to the establishment of a Science and Art Museum, and the grouping together in a convenient locality, of it, of a national library, a museum of natural history, one of Irish antiquities, a national gallery, and a school of art. It was also proposed to transfer the Royal Irish Academy to the central site. In the meantime, the Society had acquired by purchase from Captain Archdall, for the sum of £1000, No. 1 Kildare place, and the Shelbourne yard.

In 1876 a letter was received from Lord Sandon, then Vice-President of the Committee of the Council on Education, intimating that the Government had formed a scheme for the purpose of augmenting and extending the facilities for Science and Art Instruction in Ireland, and inviting the co-operation of the Royal Dublin Society. The scheme, based mainly upon the recommendations of the Commission of 1868, contemplated

the transfer to the State of most of the Society's lands
and collections, and the surrender by the Society of
control over its Science and Art institutions and library.
The Government proposed to introduce in Parliament
a bill to effect the necessary changes.

A deputation consisting of J. F. Waller, LL.D., vice-
president, Sir Arthur Guinness, bart., M.P., Samuel
Frederick Adair and Charles Uniacke Townshend, proceeded to London and had interviews with Lord
Sandon and other members of the Government with
the view of arranging details. The interchange of
views which took place was followed by correspondence
and further deputations to London, and eventually a
" Memorandum of Provisions supplementary to those
contained in Lord Sandon's letter " was agreed to on
March the 5th, 1877.

This document may be summarised as follows :—

1. The Society was to have sufficient accommodation in Leinster House for its functions in science and
agriculture.

2. A sum of £10,000 was granted as compensation
for rights, &c., and this sum was to be invested.

3. The librarian of the British Museum was to
be asked to give his opinion as to any books not
necessary for the National Library, and such were
to be re-transferred to the Society.

4. The Society was to provide its own staff and
printing.

5. The lecture hall, laboratory, &c., were to be
reserved to the Society.

6. The passage through Leinster lawn and the
courtyard was to be reserved to members.

7. The collections in the Botanic Garden and
Natural History Museum were to be available for the
illustration of papers.

8. Members elected before the 1st of January 1878, were to have the privilege of borrowing books from the National Library.

9. The Government was to permit agricultural shows to be held in Kildare street, or to provide for their transfer to some other convenient place.

10. Should such transfer take place, account should be taken of any loss sustained by reason of the removal of the shows from the city to the suburbs.

11. Vested interests of officers paid from public funds were to be preserved.

12. The Society was to be relieved from all expense connected with the School of Art.

13. The library and collections of the Society, which were to be conveyed to Government, were to be placed in the National Library and Museum, and retained in Ireland.

14. The Society undertook to concur in any bill vesting the library and collections in the Government.

15. The Government would be prepared to recommend the grant of a new charter, if necessary.

The Dublin Science and Art Museum Act, entitled: "An Act to authorise the Commissioners of Public Works in Ireland to acquire from the Royal Dublin Society and others lands for the erection of a Science and Art Museum in Dublin, and to establish a National Library in Dublin ; and for other purposes"—received the Royal assent on August the 14th, 1877. It was contemplated that the Agreement of March the 5th, 1877, should be ratified as soon as possible after the Act had passed, under a clause which had been included in the Act for this purpose. The negotiations which took place before this ratification was accomplished are referred to in the next chapter. They involved delay which at a critical period proved most embarrassing to the Society. In the course of these negotiations another agreement was entered into with the Government in 1879, the terms of which were shortly as follows:

1. In consideration of a sum of £25,000, the Government was to be discharged from all claims under clauses 9 and 10 of the agreement of the 5th of March 1877.

2. The Royal Dublin Society was to retain the right to office accommodation for its functions in agriculture, provided that if amalgamated with any other society, such amalgamation was not to entitle the other society to any right of occupation in Leinster House.

3. The rooms indicated on a certain plan to be those appropriated to the Society.

4. The Society to have the use, but not the exclusive use, of the entrance hall and passages.

5. Appropriation of the rooms was to be liable to revision by the Committee of the Council on Education, when the new Science and Art Museum was built.

6. The agricultural shows were to be removed from Kildare street, within a year from the payment of the first instalment of £10,000.

7. All strictly scientific *Proceedings* and *Transactions* of the Society were to be printed in as good a style as those of the Royal Society, and 1000 copies were to be furnished to the Society free of expense.

CHAPTER XVIII

GENERAL HISTORY OF THE SOCIETY, 1878
TO THE PRESENT

(*Contributed by* Mr. R. J. Moss, *Registrar*)

THE ACT OF 1877 AND AGREEMENT—THE ROYAL AGRI-
CULTURAL SOCIETY OF IRELAND AND AMALGAMATION—
ACCOMMODATION IN LEINSTER HOUSE.

WHEN the Dublin Science and Art Museum Act,
1877, received the Royal assent, the old order passed
away and a new era in the Society's history opened.

In March 1877, some months before the Act
passed, the terms upon which the Society was willing
to assent to the measure were agreed to (see p. 292).
The first of those related to the future accommodation
of the Society in Leinster House; it was to be such as
in the judgment of the Government would be sufficient
for the functions in Science and in Agriculture still remaining to the Society.   The Society was to be free of
rent and taxes, and the conditions of occupation were to
be the same as those accorded to the learned societies in
Burlington House.   The sum of £10,000 was to be
paid to the Society for its proprietary rights in the
property to be transferred, and this sum was to be
invested with the approval of the Government, and
made subject to the trusts of the Society's charters or
any alteration of them.   The agricultural shows were
to be allowed to continue in Kildare street, or a site
was to be provided elsewhere by grant or by providing

land and buildings.   There were other important considerations which need not be referred to here.

When the draft bill was submitted to the Society, it was found that provisions to which the Society attached great importance were not included in it, notably those relating to accommodation in Leinster House, and to the shows.   The Government was asked to rectify the omission, but this it declined to do, pointing out that the better plan would be to leave these details to be dealt with under the clause in the bill that enabled the Society and the Government to enter into agreements, which would have the same force as if they had been included in the bill.   The Society consented to this course, on receiving an assurance that these considerations would be embodied in agreements to be entered into as soon as possible after the bill had become law.

In the forecast of the intentions of the Government conveyed in Lord Sandon's letter of February the 9th, 1876, it was proposed that the Royal Irish Academy should be transferred to Leinster House, " where ample space may be found for both the Royal Dublin Society and the Royal Irish Academy, with well adapted and dignified rooms for their meetings, and for the library of the latter Society."

Shortly after this letter was written, the Science and Art Department suggested that many difficulties would be removed if an amalgamation could be effected between the Royal Dublin Society and the Royal Irish Academy.   At the same time it was indicated that if the Royal Dublin Society could effect an amalgamation with the Royal Agricultural Society of Ireland, the Government would provide for the agricultural shows in the Phœnix Park.

The creation of a body analogous to the Royal

Societies of London and Edinburgh was desired by many of the scientific men of Dublin,[1] most of whom were members of both the Royal Dublin Society and the Royal Irish Academy, and the moment for a decisive step seemed opportune, but the Royal Irish Academy at once declined to entertain the project. The Royal Agricultural Society, on the other hand, was quite ready to agree to the proposed amalgamation, as matters had, in fact, reached a stage when it seemed no longer possible to carry on its work on the old lines.   In October 1877, a joint committee of the two societies reported in favour of amalgamation and the formation of a new body to be called the Royal Agricultural Association of Ireland.

The Royal Agricultural Society of Ireland was originally established in the year 1841 under the title of the " Agricultural Improvement Society."   From the very first it received the support and assistance of the Royal Dublin Society, for at a meeting of the latter Society held on March the 25th, 1841, it was resolved—" That this Society is ready and willing to give such aid and co-operation as its means and premises afford to the new Agricultural Improvement Society, should the same be required."

The objects of the new Society were (1) To hold a show each year in one of the provinces, taking them if possible in rotation ; (2) to promote the formation of local or district agricultural societies, and assist them in advancing farming and cattle-breeding ; (3) to establish an agricultural museum ; (4) to disseminate practical and useful knowledge connected with agriculture by means of publications, and establish an agricultural library in Dublin ; (5) to establish an

---

[1] Report on the scientific prospects of the Royal Dublin Society, *Proceedings*, cxiii. p. 44.

agricultural college for the education of the farming
classes. Improvement in the dwellings and domestic
conditions of the farming and labouring classes was
undertaken at a later stage.

The Society was incorporated by Royal Charter,
under the title of the Royal Agricultural Society of
Ireland, on June the 28th, 1860. The early publications of the Society contain detached reports of drainage
and reclamation schemes carried out by successful
competitors for the Society's gold medals. Schemes
for improving the dwellings of the people, with plans
for farm homesteads and labourers' cottages, and
estimates of the cost of erecting them, also occupy
a considerable space. The reports of local farming
societies show that the efforts of the Society in establishing and assisting these bodies were not unsuccessful.
In the year 1877 there were on the list twenty-one
local societies, which received grants varying from
£3 to £39, amounting in all to £296, in addition to
which certain medals were offered for local competition.
Though the financial support given to the farming
societies was small, it had the desired effect of stimu-
lating interest and encouraging local effort.

It is, however, by its provincial shows that the
Royal Agricultural Society of Ireland will be best
remembered. These were modelled after the shows
of the Royal Agricultural Society of England and the
Highland and Agricultural Society of Scotland, of
which two societies shows are still the leading features.
The provincial shows were on the whole an undoubted
success, and they had a marked effect in improving
the breeds of stock, and introducing new agricultural
methods. These shows were held without intermission from 1842 to 1866, when rinderpest prevented
the holding of a cattle show ; instead of it, a horse

show was held, by permission of the Royal Dublin Society, in the Kildare street premises.   Next year a general agricultural show was held in St. Stephen's Green, Dublin; this was followed by another un-broken series of provincial shows up to the year 1880. In the year 1881, and in the two succeeding years the disturbed state of the country prevented the Society from holding shows in the provinces.   A show was held in Kilkenny in 1884, and one at Londonderry in 1885.   An attempt was made to organise a show for the year 1886, when Armagh was the only town that could be induced to entertain the proposal; but as it was found impracticable to raise the necessary local guarantee fund of £500, the project was abandoned.

One of the modes in which the Royal Agricultural Society of Ireland aided agriculture in the provinces was by granting subsidies to local societies to assist them in holding their shows.   This work was con-tinued by the Royal Dublin Society, and gradually expanded, until the expenditure, which in the year 1888 amounted to £16, 10s. for one society, ten years later reached the aggregate of £491, in grants to twenty-five societies of sums varying from £10 to £40.   The system was continued until 1900, when the Council, in its report, pointed out that the Agricultural and Technical Instruction (Ireland) Act enabled local farming societies to obtain aid from the funds of the newly established Department, and from local rates, far in excess of the grants which the Society had been giving from its private resources. The grants were accordingly discontinued.

Nine years had elapsed since the terms of amalga-mation had been drawn up.   The original idea was to form a new association devoted to agriculture ex-clusively; the members of the two societies were to coalesce, and half the annual subscription of members of the Royal Dublin Society was to go to the new agricultural body. The first Council of fifty members was to be elected, half by the one society and half by the other. The capital of the Royal Agricultural Society and that of the Agricultural Department of the Royal Dublin Society were to form the capital of the new body. These provisions were dependent upon Government undertaking to extend to the new Royal Agricultural Association all the advantages to agriculture contained in Lord Sandon's letter of the 9th of February 1876, and the agreement of the Government with the Royal Dublin Society of the 5th of March 1877.

The Government withheld its assent to this condition, and after six months' delay proposed to hand the Society £20,000 (subsequently increased to £25,000), in discharge of the undertaking to provide for the removal of the shows from Kildare street, and for office accommodation for agriculture in Leinster House.

The Society declined to relinquish its right to office accommodation for agriculture in Leinster House, but agreed to accept the sum offered for the removal of the shows, provided the site already selected at Ballsbridge for future shows were also given by the Government, rent and taxes free.

It would be tedious to follow the correspondence and negotiations which ensued. The Science and Art Department desired to remove all agricultural work from Leinster House; while the Society desired to maintain the continuity of its future operations in agriculture with the historical associations of the past.

The scheme of amalgamation with the Royal

Agricultural Society of Ireland, already referred to, contemplated the formation of a new body which would be quite distinct from the Royal Dublin Society; and very naturally the Government declined to regard this new body as entitled to accommodation in Leinster House. To remove this difficulty the proposed bifurcation of the Royal Dublin Society was abandoned, and it was agreed that the Society should admit the members of the Royal Agricultural Society, and take over its property. This change in policy was facilitated by the fact that since amalgamation had been originally proposed, the agricultural work of the Royal Dublin Society had rapidly developed, while the prospects of the Royal Agricultural Society had gone from bad to worse.

While the negotiations were proceeding, it became evident that there was a wide diversity of opinion as to what accommodation the Society would require in Leinster House for its future work. This and the friction that arose on other points induced the Society to press for an immediate ratification of the agreement with the Government of March the 5th, 1877, under the provisions of the Dublin Science and Art Museum Act, which enabled the Society and the Government to make agreements in furtherance of the Act, that would have the same effect as if the agreements had been embodied in it.

The formal agreement under the Act was not signed until March the 1st, 1881, though the main points at issue had been settled in an interview with some members of the Government at the Privy Council Office, Westminster, in May 1879.

A report of the settlement was laid before the Society on June the 5th, 1879, in which the Council said :

"Through the kind intervention of Sir Arthur Guinness, to whom the Council feel that the Society is under a deep obligation, an interview was brought about between My Lords of the Committee of Council on Education, and a deputation from the Council of this Society, at which Sir Michael Hicks Beach and Mr. Smith, two of the members of the Government who had contracted the original agreement, were fortunately present. At this interview the deputation were able to satisfy the Government that the statement of the original agreement made by the delegates in their report to the Council of the 8th of May 1879 was correct, and that the Society had throughout only sought a fulfilment of the agreement entered into in 1877. This resulted in the Government consenting to limit their offer of £25,000 to clauses 9 and 10, with such an explanation of clause 1 as removed a difficulty felt by the Government, without in effect limiting the rights of the Society under that clause."

The report concludes by quoting the terms of the agreement drawn up and signed by Lord George Hamilton on the part of the Government, and by Dr. G. Johnstone Stoney on the part of the Royal Dublin Society.

The Council considered that by this agreement the Society gained what it had claimed from the first, and that a position had been secured which would leave the Society "independent of all Government control, and in a state of efficiency for the discharge of all its functions."

Though the Royal Agricultural Society of Ireland and the Royal Dublin Society had agreed to amalgamate in October 1877, it was not until March 22nd, 1880, that the formal articles of agreement were executed. The Royal Dublin Society had already invested £35,000 in its agricultural premises at Ballsbridge; the shows there had been established on a secure basis, and the most hopeful views were entertained as to the future.

It was under these circumstances that the Royal Agricultural Society decided to surrender its charter under the provisions of the Dublin Science and Art Museum Act, 1877, and to transfer its members and its property to the Royal Dublin Society. The property consisted of Government stock valued at £7,094, 13s. 6d.; cash amounting to £247, 2s. 2d.; and five challenge cups valued at £280.

In 1888, the new library building was approaching completion, and the Society asked the Government to reconsider the allotment of rooms in Leinster House. After a long delay Government made a proposal which the Society considered wholly inadequate. Repeated efforts to arrive at a settlement with the officers of the Science and Art Department proved abortive. The Society determined to ignore them, and to appeal directly to the Government. Personal interviews took place with the lord lieutenant, the Earl of Zetland; the president of the council, Lord Cranbrook; the chief secretary, Mr. A. J. Balfour; and the vice-president of the council, Sir William Hart-Dyke. Finding that there was a risk of the decision of the Government being deferred until Parliament rose, a memorial signed by 1216 members was forwarded to the prime minister, Lord Salisbury. A full statement of the whole case was prepared, and the Society was about to forward it to every member of both houses of Parliament when a proposal was received from the Government. This was in the form of a Treasury minute dated July the 30th, 1890, and, as it conceded nearly everything the Society had claimed, it was at once accepted.

Thus ended a controversy which had lasted with little intermission for twenty-three years. It was a bitter conflict at times, and personal friendships of long standing were strained to the breaking point.

The Society's final triumph was due to the justice of its cause and the dogged determination of one man— George Johnstone Stoney.

The Second Supplemental Charter and Statutes

Under the original charter of April the 2nd, in the 23rd year of Geo. II (1750), the general management of the business of the Society was vested in the corporation, any seven of whom constituted a quorum.

In 1836 a select committee of the House of Commons recommended, among other things, "That the management of the ordinary business of the Society should be confided to a Council." The Society assented, and the following by-law was adopted : " The management of the business of the Society shall be confided to a Council, whose powers are strictly, as hereafter, defined and limited, and subject to direct control over its proceedings, upon the part of the Society at large."

Some years later the authority of this Council was disputed, when an officer of the Society maintained that the Council had not the power to dismiss him, and other difficulties of a similar kind arose. In 1862, a Commission appointed by the Treasury expressed the opinion that full powers ought to be vested in an Executive Council acting on behalf of the Society. The Commission held that the Government could not properly entrust the administration of public funds to the existing Council, whose decisions were liable to be reversed by a popular vote.

The principles to be embodied in a supplemental charter, in furtherance of the views of the Commission, were agreed to at a conference in South Kensington in

1863, but in deference to the wishes of some Irish members of Parliament further action was postponed. When the consideration of the draft charter was resumed two years later, the attention of the Council was called to the fact that the draft contained a paragraph excluding the privileges of members from the control of the Council. The Council urged the Society to forego this exemption, but by 33 votes to 21 a general meeting carried an amendment declining to do so. The Science and Art Department thereupon refused to recommend the Treasury to sanction certain increased grants which the Society had applied for, until the paragraph in question was omitted. A special meeting was held, at which the Lord Justice of Appeal presided, and 148 other members were present, and it was agreed to omit the provision exempting the privileges of members from the control of the Council. With this difficulty removed, the terms of the supplemental charter were soon agreed to, and it was enrolled on the 14th of June 1866.

This charter directs that the general management and control over the affairs of the Society (excepting so far as might affect the constitution of the Society) should be vested in and exercised by the Council exclusively. This important change was effected for the purpose of increasing the Society's efficiency in the administration of public funds. The Science and Art Museum Act of 1877 relieved the Society of this work, but left the Council with its power unaltered, and in possession of unrestricted authority such as few representative bodies of a similar kind enjoy.

In the negotiation which preceded the passing of the Act of 1877 it became evident that a new charter adapted to the altered circumstances of the Society would be necessary. At the request of the Society,

U

provision was made in the Act for the surrender of the existing charter, and the granting of a new one.

The intention of the Society to apply for a charter which would place it in a position to promote science, and to carry on the other branches of its work with greater efficiency, had been openly expressed. The Royal Irish Academy took alarm, and in a letter to the secretary of the Treasury, dated May the 22nd 1877, protested against the Society embarking in the cultivation of abstract science, contending that the existing charters restricted the Society to science in relation to its industrial or economic application. The Society drew up a "Statement of Facts," in which it was shown that of 200 printed papers in the previous twenty years, 98 dealt with pure science, 70 with applied science, and 32 with non-scientific subjects. The Society held that the severance of applied from pure science, which the Academy advocated, had long ceased to be practicable, and had not been observed by the Academy itself. To emphasise this point, the recent address of Dr. Andrews as President of the British Association was quoted. He said : "It is with the greater confidence, therefore, that I have ventured to suggest that no partition wall should anywhere be raised between pure and applied science." The Lords of the Committee of Council on Education expressed their belief that the strictures contained in the letter of the Academy were fully met by the Society's reply, "and therefore that it could not be said that the former Society had any claim to a monopoly as against the Royal Dublin Society in the cultivation of abstract science."

It was not until January the 18th, 1883, that the Council was in a position to submit the draft of the second supplemental charter to the Society for approval. A division was taken at the meeting held on that day, and 103 votes were recorded in favour of the draft, 82 being cast against it. The Act required a majority of three-fifths of those voting, and as the majority was eight votes short of that number, the motion was accordingly declared lost. The Council made some amendments to meet objections which had been raised, and issued an appeal to the Society with the notice convening another meeting for April the 5th. On this occasion the draft was adopted by 326 to 54 votes, a majority considerably exceeding that required by statute.

In May 1883 the Royal Irish Academy forwarded a memorial to the Lord Lieutenant, in which the conviction was expressed that "the grant of a charter extending the functions of the Royal Dublin Society to the field of science generally, as the draft in question purports to do, ought not to be recommended by Your Excellency to Her Most Gracious Majesty." In support of this opinion the Academy stated that "the number of investigators in abstract science in Ireland is not sufficient for the support of more than one body chartered for science generally." It was anticipated that scientific men in Ireland, rather than disoblige either Society by favouring its rival, would probably send their papers to neutral societies out of Ireland. The memorialists added that "although they have not been invited by the Royal Dublin Society to concur in any of the provisions of the draft in question, they would be well pleased to see the Society placed in a position legally to fulfil here such functions as are performed by the Society of Arts in London, or the Royal Scottish Society of Arts in Edinburgh."

The Society, in a lengthy reply dated July the 9th, 1883, stated that the draft charter "simply provides for the continuance, under improved conditions, of the work which the Society is at present carrying on under its existing charters." It was pointed out that "the functions performed by the Society of Arts of London, and the Royal Scottish Society of Arts of Edinburgh, to which the Council of the Academy wish the Royal Dublin Society to be reduced, represent only a small part of the work in which the Royal Dublin Society has been hitherto engaged."

The draft recited the fact that the Society was also known as the Royal Society of Dublin, and it contained a clause empowering the Society to confer the title of Fellow. The Lord Lieutenant expressed his unwillingness to recommend a charter including this recital and provision. The negotiations which followed occupied two years. In January 1886, the Royal Agricultural Society of Ireland decided to "become merged in the Royal Dublin Society." This step necessitated the addition of certain clauses to the draft charter, and it was decided at the same time to omit the portions to which the Lord Lieutenant had taken exception. The second supplemental charter in its amended form was granted, and it was enrolled on May the 20th, 1888.

The second supplemental charter confirms the amalgamation agreement with the Royal Agricultural Society of Ireland and dissolves that body. It directs that the Royal Dublin Society shall continue to be incorporated "for the advancement of agriculture and other branches of industry, and for the advancement of Science and Art"; thus leaving the Society an unrestricted field in all branches of its work. Details relating to meetings of the corporation, the honorary officers, the constitution and mode of election of the council and of the committees, are embodied in statutes appended to the charter. Those statutes, which may be repealed or altered by royal warrant on petition of the Society (a procedure much simpler than the alteration of a royal charter), confer great elasticity upon the Society's arrangements, enabling it to regulate by by-law many details which were rigidly prescribed in the earlier charters.

The Dublin Society was in its eighteenth year when it was first incorporated by royal charter. At that time the total number of members was only thirty-one, and the management of the Society's business, then comparatively limited, was naturally entrusted to the members at large. When the number of members grew larger, a central governing body was found to be necessary; there were 1146 members at the time of the first supplemental charter, and the number had increased to 1486 when the second supplemental charter was granted. Thus, as the number of members increased, the control over the Society's affairs became centralised. The one thing needful at the time of the second supplemental charter was to ensure that the management of the various branches of the Society's work, so widely different in character, should be entrusted to persons possessing the necessary qualifications, and that those persons should be left a fairly free hand within their own sphere. This the second supplemental charter did, and at the same time it greatly increased the power of the Society to adapt itself to its ever altering environment.

This charter was practically the work of two members—Geo. Johnstone Stoney, F.R.S., then a vice-president, and Geo. Francis FitzGerald, F.T.C.D., who was then an honorary secretary.

The charter rendered it necessary to revise the by-laws completely, and on February the 6th, 1889, the

Council submitted the proposed new by-laws to the Society for approval. They included provision for the election of a class of honorary officers to be called Fellows, and provided that the first Fellows should be those already Fellows of the Royal Society. This proposal was not favourably received, and the Council was obliged to withdraw it. Professor FitzGerald thereupon resigned the office of honorary secretary. In his letter of resignation he described the rejected by-laws as "the only serious attempt that has been proposed to encourage scientific members to work for the Society." A few weeks later a code of by-laws, with the provision relating to Fellows omitted, was submitted to the Society and approved. In recent years a few amendments have been made from time to time, as experience suggested.

In 1892, on petition of the Society, the statutes were amended by royal warrant. In their original form the statutes provided that the number of the whole Council, exclusive of the president, should not exceed forty-five. The amendment limited the number of elected members to a maximum of thirty-six, and did not place any limit to the number of the whole Council. The other members of the Council are the honorary officers as *ex officio* members. The Society has the power by by-law to include any number of *ex officio* members in the Council, and to determine their titles, tenure, duties and mode of election.

While the protracted negotiations concerning the issue of the new charter were in progress, some changes of far-reaching importance were made in the by-laws. On the 30th of June, 1887, the Society decided that members might be either men or women, and that "he" in the by-laws should be interpreted as either

" he " or " she." It was also decided to admit ladies as Associates, with limited privileges; this has proved a great boon, and in a few years more than twelve hundred names have been enrolled.

BALLSBRIDGE PREMISES

When the negotiations that preceded the passing of the Science and Art Museum Act, 1877, were in progress, the Government informed the Society that it would be prepared to provide for the removal of the agricultural shows from Kildare street to the Phœnix Park; this suggestion, was, however, never seriously entertained. In 1871 the Royal Agricultural Society of Ireland held a show on grounds at Ballsbridge, which the Earl of Pembroke kindly lent for the occasion. The Prince of Wales, then President of the Royal Agricultural Society of Ireland, was present, and the Council of the Society, in reporting upon the show, stated that it was " by far the most important and successful" the Society had held since its formation. Again in 1878 the same Society held a show on the same site. This show the Council regarded as " second only in excellence to the show of 1871." It was natural that a site with such a favourable record should be considered suitable as a permanent home for the shows of the Royal Dublin Society. Accordingly in 1879 the Society leased from the Earl of Pembroke fifteen acres of land for a term of 500 years, at a yearly rent of £180. Plans for the new agricultural halls, prepared by Mr. George Wilkinson, were adopted, and the work of erection and laying out the grounds was at once commenced. In the report laid before the Society on June the 3rd, 1880, the Council stated that a contract for the erection of what is now known as the central hall and offices for the sum of £11,690 had been concluded. A much larger building had been suggested, but it was decided "not to include anything that the lengthened experience of the Committee of Agriculture had not shown to be requisite," so as to keep within the limits of the sum of £25,000 received from the Government as compensation for the removal of the shows from Kildare street. Later in the year a further contract was concluded for the removal of the agricultural hall from Kildare street, and its re-erection at Ballsbridge, at a cost of £3259. This is the building now known as the south hall. It was originally erected in Kildare street at a cost of about £5000, most of which was subscribed by the members and by the public, His Royal Highness the Prince Consort subscribing £50. The hall was used for the first time at the spring cattle show held in 1858. The gallery which formed part of the hall in Kildare street is now the gallery of the central hall, Ballsbridge.

The first show held in the new premises at Balls-bridge was the spring show of April 19–22, 1881. The receipts of this show amounted to £1705, as compared with £1132 at the last show in Kildare street. A horse show followed in the autumn of the same year, it being held on August 30th and 31st and September 1st and 2nd. At this show the entries numbered 589. There was an attendance of 15,736 persons, and the receipts exceeded the expenditure by £816. The corresponding figures at the last show in Kildare street were—entries, 600; credit balance, £500. The attendance, unfortunately, is not on record; that for a three-day show held in 1879 was 9698; there was no show in 1878. The last four-day horse show in Kildare street at which the attendance is recorded was in 1877, when the total number of visitors was 10,844.

It had already become evident that more ground would be required, and it was decided to take the remainder of the triangular area enclosed by Merrion, Simmonscourt, and Anglesea roads. The additional twelve acres Lord Pembroke very liberally granted on lease at the same rate as the first holding. The Society subsequently purchased the fee simple of the entire holding on very favourable terms. Building now proceeded rapidly, and every available interval between the shows was utilised to add a new hall, or to carry out the improvements which experience suggested. It is interesting to examine the plans published in the catalogues of successive shows of this period, and to observe the progressive growth of the buildings. In a report of December 1891, the Council pointed out that there was room in the permanent buildings for the stabling of 1350 horses.

The construction of what is known as the loop line, which connected the Kingstown railway with the other railways having termini in Dublin, afforded the Society the opportunity of placing the show grounds in immediate communication by rail with the Irish railway system generally. With this view the Society purchased from Lord Pembroke eleven acres of ground lying between Merrion road and the railway, and constructed the branch line and sidings which have proved such a convenience to exhibitors and to the public. The Society bore the entire cost of this work, including an expenditure of £500 on the property of the railway company, in making the necessary connections. The first train passed over the line on April the 7th, 1893.

On the morning of August the 19th, 1905, when preparations for the horse show, which was to have opened in three days, were being completed, a fire broke out in the building known as the Paddock Hall. In less than one hour from the time the fire was detected, the three halls adjoining the veterinary paddock were completely gutted, and a great deal of woodwork which had been erected in the paddock was destroyed. While the fire was in progress, steps were taken to provide horse-boxes and stalls for the coming show in other parts of the premises, and the show was held without any serious inconvenience to exhibitors or the public. Most of the damage was covered by insurance, and new buildings of an improved type were at once erected on the site of the old ones.

The Society learned a valuable lesson from this disaster. For many years it had been the practice to erect temporary timber stalls for each horse show. These had many advantages, and when they were cleared away the floor space was left unobstructed. They were, however, extremely combustible, especially when furnished with straw bedding. By way of experiment, concrete stalls were erected in the Anglesea and Simmonscourt halls in the year 1906, and the result was deemed so satisfactory that shortly afterwards stalls of this type were erected wherever practicable.

It would be tedious to follow the development of the premises in recent years: suffice it to say that at the close of the year 1913, the total expenditure on the land and buildings, charged to capital, was £96,477. This expenditure is not represented by the premises as they now appear; part of the money was spent on structures which have long since disappeared,

Laurence Earl of Rosse,
President 1887–1892

and have been replaced by more substantial and more commodious structures, better adapted to the Society's present requirements.

HORSE AND CATTLE BREEDING—THE PROBATE DUTIES GRANT

Early in 1887, the Government was asked to give the Society financial assistance in promoting improvement in the breeding of cattle and horses. Mr. Arthur J. Balfour, then chief secretary, induced the House of Commons to vote the sum of £5000 in aid of the scheme. Subsequently this sum became payable annually to the Society under the Probate Duties (Scotland and Ireland) Act, 1888. This grant enabled the Society to offer premiums of £10 to £15, to aid farmers in the purchase of pure-bred bulls selected by competent judges. Premiums of £200 each were also offered for thoroughbred stallions. These premiums and those in aid of the purchase of bulls were subject to certain conditions of service. Both schemes were subject to the approval of the Lord Lieutenant. The arrangement placed the Society in a unique position, as it became the only body in the United Kingdom administering Government funds for improving horse and cattle breeding. The first allotment of bull premiums took place at the spring cattle show of 1888, when 28 bulls were allotted to Leinster, 21 to Ulster, 9 to Munster, and 4 to Connaught. The Committee of Agriculture, in its report of the show, specially noted the fact that while the Ulster farmers competed keenly to secure premium bulls, farmers of the south and west of Ireland displayed comparatively little activity. After a few years the farmers of Munster and Connaught realised the advantages of the scheme, and the premium bulls were more evenly distributed. To aid in administering the horse-breeding scheme, committees were formed in Strabane, Antrim, Portadown, Lisnaskea, Ballymote, Ballinrobe, Longford, Kells, Edenderry, Banagher, Loughrea, Templemore, Tullow, Rathkeale, Cappoquin and Dunmanway. Subsequently the horse-breeding scheme was changed, and, instead of giving premiums to stallions, a register of stallions was established, and the sum of £3200 was allotted to the counties, in sums varying from £80 to £140 each, to be distributed amongst the owners of approved mares in the form of nominations to thoroughbred stallions on the Society's register. To carry out this scheme a committee was appointed in each county. With slight variation, this system continued in force until the establishment, in 1899, of the department of Agriculture and Technical Instruction for Ireland. The new department was entrusted with the administration of all public funds devoted to the advancement of agriculture in Ireland, with the sole exception of the Royal Dublin Society's grant of £5000 a year. One of the first acts of the department was to adopt schemes for improving horse and cattle breeding practically identical with those which the Society had been carrying out for the preceding thirteen years. Early in the year 1902, a committee, which the Council had appointed to consider the new position that had arisen, recommended that the Society should be relieved of the administration of the fund on the grounds that: (1) It involved a great deal of work the cost of which was borne by the Society's private funds; (2) that friction with the department was inevitable so long as both bodies continued to work on nearly identical lines; (3) and finally, that the Society was not independent so long as it continued to administer public funds. This latter consideration had influenced the Society from the beginning, for it was not without serious apprehension on the part of some of the members, who had fought so hard to secure complete freedom from Government control, that the administration of the grant was originally undertaken.   Acting on this recommendation, the Council arranged with the Government for a transfer of the administration to the department.   This was effected by the Agriculture and Technical Instruction (Ireland) (No. 2) Act of 1902.   As a consideration for the transfer, the Society asked for a grant in aid of providing a suitable hall at Ballsbridge for the Art Industries Exhibition held annually in conjunction with the horse show, and in compliance with this request the sum of £5000 was paid to the Society.

EXHIBITIONS OF MANUFACTURES

Reference has been made at pp. 253 and 271 to the exhibitions of manufactures first projected in the year 1833.   Exhibitions were held in 1834 and 1835, and after the latter year, these exhibitions became triennial. They were at first confined to Irish manufactures, but in 1850 the products of other countries were admitted ; the exhibition of that year was in fact the first step in the United Kingdom in the direction of international exhibitions which afterwards assumed such large proportions. The series culminated in the International Exhibition of 1853 ; the exhibitions which followed this great effort were on a much smaller scale.   In 1858, advantage was taken of the newly-erected Natural History Museum to hold an Art Exhibition.   Stimulated by the success of this new departure, a larger exhibition of fine arts and art manufactures was held in 1861, in the Agricultural Hall which had just been erected in Kildare street.

In 1864 the exhibition was exclusively Irish so far as manufactures were concerned, but it included a section for home and foreign machinery. This was the last of the series of triennial exhibitions. The Dublin Exhibition Palace and Winter Garden Company erected the buildings at Earlsfort terrace in which an international exhibition was held in 1865, but the venture proved disappointing as a financial speculation. For various reasons the Society made no attempt to revive the exhibitions, one being the fact that the horse show had come into existence, and that it occupied the premises at an inconvenient time.

A committee appointed by the Council on May the 7th, 1885, to consider the advisability of holding an international exhibition on the Society's premises at Ballsbridge, reported in favour of the project, and recommended that the exhibition should be held in the year 1887. It was proposed to open a guarantee fund and subscription list, the control and management of the exhibition to remain in the hands of the Council, in accordance with the charter. Six months later, the Registrar reported the results of his visit to exhibitions in London and Antwerp, and the committee, on reconsideration, decided " that the present state of the country is not such as to warrant the Society in embarking in an enterprise of such magnitude and importance." Acting on this opinion, the idea was abandoned.

It was then proposed to see what could be done to assist Irish industries by holding an exhibition in London, and it was suggested that the building then occupied by the Indo-Colonial Exhibition might be obtained. Enquiries were made, and it was soon found that the Society would have to undertake financial responsibilities so large that they seemed out of proportion to the results that might be achieved.   Attention was next directed to making more use of the spring cattle shows for the promotion of local industries, and this proposal was under discussion when it was suggested that the Centenary Exhibition about to be held in Manchester would afford a good opportunity for bringing Irish manufactures under public notice. This suggestion was warmly supported, and the Manchester committee at once fell in with the idea.   A guarantee fund was started, the Society heading the list with a contribution of £500.   Deputations were sent to Belfast and Cork, and the co-operation of the respective Chambers of Commerce was secured.   On the recommendation of the Cork committee, it was decided to offer space to exhibitors free of charge. Applications were received for 40,000 superficial feet, the space available being barely 27,000 feet.   This made the difficulty of allotment very great.   It is not surprising that the executive committee, of which Mr. Thomas Pim, jun., acted as chairman, reported that they had held forty-three meetings in thirteen weeks. The exhibition was a decided success.   The executive committee, in its final report, said that it "was pleased to be able to state that the objects aimed at by the Society in inaugurating an Irish exhibition in England have to a large extent been attained.   A substantial benefit has been conferred upon our home manufactures, and upon a number of small industries which were much in need of encouragement and support."

The business transacted in the section by some of the Irish exhibitors was large, and in some cases they were induced to open branch establishments in England, or to appoint local agents to develop the connection which the Irish section was the means of procuring for them.   These results are most encouraging, and it is hoped that Irish manufacturers will remember that the markets of England are open to them, and that a British and foreign trade is better worth cultivating than one depending upon the very limited demands of our own small population.

The Society had organised an exhibit of the industries of Dublin at the Paris Exhibition of 1855, but the Irish section at the Manchester Exhibition was the first general display of the products of the industries of Ireland ever shown as a distinct section at any exhibition held out of Ireland.

The Art Industries Exhibition

In the year 1888, the Council approved a scheme for holding an exhibition of lace during the annual horse show, and voted a sum of £50 to be awarded in prizes. Next year the amount was increased to £75, when seventy exhibits, value £376, were submitted for competition.

In 1890 the scope of the exhibition was enlarged, sections for embroidery and for designs were added, and for the first time wood carving was included. The exhibition continued to progress until the space allotted to it became inconveniently overcrowded, and it became evident that increased space must be provided. The present art industries hall was erected in 1903–4 at a cost of £7000, part of which was provided by the grant paid to the Society by the Government on the surrender of the administration of the probate duties grant.

On August the 23rd, 1904, the seventeenth art industries exhibition was formally opened in the new hall by the Earl of Dudley, then lord lieutenant, when an address was presented to His Excellency by Lord Ardilaun, president of the Society.

At the exhibitions held in recent years, the number of entries is usually about 1000, and the amount offered in prizes is generally about £300. The exhibition no longer enjoys the monopoly of former years; its success has induced others to promote similar exhibitions, and in some cases exhibitors, finding that the horse show offers a unique opportunity for the sale of work, now take stalls each year on their own account. As a means of promoting some important branches of applied art, and as a stimulus to home industries, the exhibition continues to fulfil a most useful function.

IMPROVEMENT IN TILLAGE IN SMALL HOLDINGS: SWINFORD DISTRICT

During the autumn of the year 1890, it became evident that the failure of the potato crop would lead to widespread distress throughout the poorer districts in the west of Ireland. At the first meeting of the Council in the session which commenced in November 1890, Mr. Thomas Pim, junior, called attention to the fact that the Royal Dublin Society was now practically the Agricultural Society of Ireland, and suggested the appointment of a committee of the Council to act in conjunction with the committee of agriculture, to consider what might be done "to improve the nature and quality of the potato plant in the west of Ireland in places where the root has repeatedly failed." The proposal was agreed to, and the sum of £400 was voted to defray the expenses of the first year's operations. A committee was appointed, and its labours led to important results. It was soon

realised that improvement in potato culture could be
dealt with only as part of the larger question of
farming generally. It was decided to offer induce-
ments to farmers in a selected district to adopt better
methods of cultivation. For this purpose it was resolved to secure the services of a practical agriculturist,
known to be versed in the best methods of tillage
farming—"a man acquainted with the circumstances
and habits of the small farmers, and who would be
likely to command their confidence and respect." It
was arranged that this instructor should lay down a
plan upon which a certain number of example holdings
were to be cropped, that he should see that his instructions were carried out, and, by visiting neighbouring
farmers, endeavour to stimulate their interest in the
work, and enforce upon their attention such lessons
as might be conveyed by ocular demonstration on the
example holdings. Mr. D. O'Dowd, formerly National
School teacher at Dooncastle, co. Mayo, was appointed
to the office of practical instructor. The district of
Swinford, co. Mayo, was selected for the Society's
operations, and an advisory committee consisting of
influential persons resident in the district was appointed.
As an inducement to farmers to take an interest in
the scheme, prizes were offered for the best worked
holdings. At the first competition, the report states,
"no fewer than 134 small farmers entered for these
prizes. Considerable rivalry was aroused, and unusual
efforts were made by some to keep down weeds and
promote the growth of crops."

The descriptions of prize holdings which are
appended to reports of the Council for the years 1891
to 1894 are interesting records of the condition of
farming in the district at the time, and show the
results of the first systematic efforts at improvement.

In August 1891, the Act for the improvement of the congested districts in Ireland received the royal assent, and large sums of public money became available for carrying out such work as the Society had initiated, and carried on at its own expense. The few years during which the Society's scheme was in operation sufficed to show the utility of the method adopted, and the possibility of effecting a vast improvement with comparatively little expenditure.

POTATO CULTURE

While the effort was being made to improve agriculture in the Swinford district by means of itinerant instruction and example holdings, experiments were carried on in Ireland generally with the view of improving the potato crop. In the years 1891–2–3, experiments on different varieties of potato were tried in nearly every county in Ireland, and the results were published in detail. The general conclusion was that, in addition to the Champion, other main crop varieties were well suited for cultivation in Ireland.

In 1893, the experiments were mainly directed to testing the efficiency of spraying with copper preparations. It was in June 1891 that the Society first decided to put spraying to practical test in the Swinford district. The first report which refers to the use of copper sulphate preparation in the form of powder was discouraging, as it states that no " beneficial influence could be traced to the powder." Experiments carried out on the Society's own ground at Ballsbridge proved abortive, as no disease appeared. The experiments conducted in 1893 showed conclusively the value of spraying, the increased profit being estimated at from 22s. to 48s. per acre. In 1894, experiments in spraying were extended, and spraying machines were sent to thirty-four farmers, who subsequently sent interesting reports on the results obtained. The value of the treatment was becoming widely recognised. In 1895, the Society distributed 202 spraying machines, and over five tons of copper sulphate. Eighty-five per cent. of the reports received were favourable to the treatment. It was no longer necessary for the Society to continue the work; the great value of spraying as a means of combating the attack of *phytophthora infestans*, and of prolonging the period of growth of the potato plant, had been fully established.

FARM PRIZES

In 1890, prizes were offered for the best cultivated farms in the province of Leinster, and twelve farms were entered for competition. In 1892, prizes were offered for farms in the province of Munster, but only five farmers entered. In 1893, the province of Ulster was selected, and fourteen farmers entered their farms for competition. In 1894, a competition was again held in the province of Leinster, and twelve farmers entered. In 1895, Connaught was selected, but only four farmers submitted their farms for examination. In 1896, a second competition in Munster took place, ten farms being entered. In 1897, Ulster was again selected ; the number of farms entered was twelve, but only three out of the nine prizes offered were awarded by the judges. The disappointing results of the past three years induced the committee of agriculture to discontinue the competitions. The reports on these competitions, which were published each year, are interesting records of the state of farming during the transition period that followed the early Irish Land Acts.

Mervyn Viscount Powerscourt.
President 1892—1897

THE LECTURE THEATRE

Clause five of the " Memorandum of Provisions" agreed to by the Government and the Society in March 1877, as a preliminary to the passing of the Science and Art Museum Act, provided that :—" The Lecture Hall, Laboratory, and the necessary offices were to be reserved to the Society, or an equivalent provided."

The old buildings referred to were of humble origin. In May 1815, a few weeks before the Society moved from Hawkins street to Leinster House, a committee reported "that the outbuilding called the kitchen (at Leinster House) could be appropriated, with the necessary alterations, to the purposes of a laboratory and theatre, with the apartments for the professors' apparatus." The alterations were completed shortly afterwards, and for 78 years the transformed kitchen served the purposes of a laboratory and lecture theatre. In 1836, Mr. Isaac Weld, in giving evidence before a select committee of the House of Commons, said, in answer to a question about the theatre and laboratory :—" There is a small range of furnaces and sand baths in the theatre for the purpose of exhibiting some chemical processes ; there is adjoining to it a large laboratory besides ; and also another room for the finer apparatus, and for nicer experiments which Mr. Davy may be particularly engaged in himself, secluded and kept apart for himself, that he may not be interrupted." He also said that the laboratory was a good one, "the chemical apparatus extensive, some of it fine. The galvanic battery is of a very superior description."

The lapse of half a century brought about great changes ; ideas about the requirements of a theatre had totally altered, and the public had become more exacting in their demands. In a memorandum submitted to the Lord Lieutenant in January 1892, it is stated that as regards facilities for entrance and exit, and arrangements for heating and ventilation, "the Society's theatre is singularly deficient, and the building is now in a dilapidated state." It was with some difficulty that the Society induced the Government to recognise the necessity for providing new buildings. Deputations waited upon the Lord Lieutenant and the Chief Secretary in Dublin, and upon the Financial Secretary to the Treasury in London, and at length they succeeded in getting something done. Plans were prepared by the firm of Sir Thomas Deane & Son, and it was found that the cost of the theatre and laboratory, &c., would be at least £10,000. The Government asked the Society to pay half the cost. Recognising that the new buildings would be more than the equivalent which the Government was under an obligation to provide, the Society agreed to pay a fixed sum of £5000. The old buildings were handed over to the contractor, and in the autumn of 1893 the work of demolition was commenced.

Before the new building had proceeded very far, and fortunately before it was too late, it was found that due consideration had not been given to the question of ventilation. The subject was discussed at scientific meetings held on December the 19th, 1894, and January the 16th, 1895, and, though no formal resolutions were adopted, it was agreed that the fresh air should enter the upper part of the theatre, and that the foul air should be removed from the lower part. The volume of air required for an audience of 600 persons was estimated at 600,000 cubic feet per hour. The velocity of the air at the inlets was not to exceed 2 feet per second, at a distance of 6 feet from any person, or 5 feet per second at any other place. A temperature of 60° F. should be guaranteed, the outer air being at 32° F., and provision should be made for moistening the air when necessary. These requirements necessitated the construction of a number of air shafts in the walls of the building, and proper openings for the fans to be used for propelling the air.

The new theatre was opened by a conversazione on March the 10th, 1897. In addition to the sum of £5000 paid to the Board of Works towards the cost of the building, the Society spent £2430, mainly on the equipment for heating, lighting and ventilation. The theatre seats 700 persons, but on several occasions room has been found for an audience of 1000. Fresh air is taken in at an opening 35 feet above the ground, and forced into the building by an electrically driven fan 5 feet in diameter. The air enters the theatre at twenty-seven openings in the ceiling and walls; these openings have an effective area of 92 square feet. The air is removed through openings of about the same area, chiefly under the seats, and is expelled from the building by another electrically driven fan. It has been found by actual measurement that the fans are capable of sending 800,000 cubic feet of air, about 27 tons weight, through the theatre in one hour. It is rarely necessary to use more than half this quantity of air. By means of steam-heated pipes, the air, before it enters the theatre, can be warmed when necessary. Daylight can be excluded by means of a false ceiling which descends below the level of the windows of the lantern in the roof. The Society is indebted to Sir Howard Grubb, f.r.s., for the design for this device. The screen for lantern projections, which has an area of 340 square feet, is capable of being raised, disclosing a stage room, communicating directly with a roadway, so that large or heavy objects can be brought straight into the theatre without trouble. The floor between this room and the lecturer's table can be raised to the level of the table, thus providing a raised platform, which is used for musical recitals. Mr. Samuel Geoghegan, C.E., was good enough to furnish plans for the platform and screen.

Electrical energy for lighting, and for driving the ventilating fans, is supplied from an installation in the basement, including a 30 h.p. steam-engine. The waste steam is used for heating.

The organ with which the theatre is furnished was constructed by Messrs. Henry Willis & Sons, London. It contains four complete manuals from CC to A—58 notes, and two octaves and a half of concave and radiating pedals—30 notes. There are thirty-four speaking stops, with 1946 pipes and eight accessories. The first public performance took place on April the 20th, 1899, when Mr. R. G. Sinclair, organist of Hereford Cathedral, gave a recital.

The chemical laboratory adjoins the theatre, and consists of a principal room equipped with working benches, and extensive fume chambers, which admit of all kinds of operations being carried on without any risk of the air of the room being overheated or contaminated. There is a second room furnished with various types of air pumps, which is used mainly for work involving the handling of gases. A third room is furnished with balances, microscopes, spectroscopes, and other optical apparatus. On the story above these are a large glass-roofed room and a dark room for photographic work.

An installation for the liquefaction of air and of

hydrogen was presented to the Society by Mr. William Purser Geoghegan and Mr. Samuel Geoghegan; it is a valuable acquisition for the purposes of research, as well as for lecture illustration.

A recent addition to the laboratory is an outfit for dealing with radium emanation under the supervision of the Radium Institute referred to at p. 377. This includes provision for the storage of the radium, mercury air pumps for removing the emanation, apparatus for purifying the gas with the aid of liquid air, and apparatus for sealing it in minute capillary tubes for therapeutic purposes.

MUSICAL RECITALS

In a report laid before the Society on March the 4th, 1886, the Council reported that " Since the transfer to the Government of the Art School, which the Royal Dublin Society maintained for upwards of 130 years, the Council have had under their consideration to what other work, for the promotion of Art, the Society could most usefully apply itself. After much consideration the Council have directed, as a tentative measure, that weekly recitals from the works of some of the best composers of instrumental music shall be performed in the Society's theatre during the rest of the present season : such as, if continued in future years, will enable music as an art to be systematically brought before the public as effectually as painting and sculpture now are in our public galleries. In taking this step, the Council have had the advice of musicians, both professional and amateur, who have expressed their opinion that, by undertaking this work, the Royal Dublin Society will do important service to the cause of Art."

Three months later, the Chamber Music Committee

submitted its first report, in which it is said that "the extraordinary success which has attended the Society's first efforts in this direction is most encouraging, and an augury of the important service to Art which continued efforts in this direction are likely to effect." Chamber music was selected as the class of composition in which the great composers embodied many of their best thoughts, and as few performers were required, it seemed the most promising field for the Society's efforts. The co-operation of the Instrumental Music Club was sought, and arrangements were made to direct the attention of the audience to points of special interest in each composition. At the course of recitals which began in October 1886, analytical notes on the music performed, prepared by Sir Robert Stewart, were given gratuitously to the holders of tickets. Two years later this plan was given up, and those attending the recitals were offered facilities for obtaining scores of the pieces performed in a cheap and convenient form. In 1898, the analytical notes were resumed; they were prepared by Professor Ebenezer Prout and sold at a nominal price. Next year the notes were continued by Mr. J. S. Shedlock. In recent years these educational features have been allowed to lapse, largely because the recitals have had the effect they were intended to produce, and Dublin audiences are no longer unacquainted with the masterpieces of the great composers of chamber music. With this change has come a more critical taste, and instead of relying solely, as at first, upon local talent, the services of the most distinguished artists in this country and abroad are now drawn upon to ensure the best results in the promotion of this branch of art.

The organ with which the lecture theatre is provided is described at p. 328.

BUTTER-MAKING

During the closing years of the Royal Agricultural Society of Ireland, a complete revolution took place in the system of land tenure in this country. While this change was being effected, an important branch of agricultural industry underwent a total transformation all over the world. German fiscal policy had obliged the farmers of neighbouring states to seek a new outlet for their produce, and the open British market was an easy prey. The farmers of the United Kingdom soon discovered that the superior technical education of their neighbours in Denmark and other countries had made them formidable rivals, with serious consequences to the British butter-making industry.

In 1876, the first of a series of dairy shows was held in London, and on that occasion Professor J. P. Sheldon proposed the formation of the British Dairy Farmers Association. Two years later the Royal Agricultural Society of Ireland deputed the Rev. Canon Bagot and Mr. James Robertson to visit several of the northern states of Europe and inspect the various systems of dairy farming carried out in those countries. They were accompanied by the secretary, Mr. Dawson Milward, whose very interesting and instructive report was published by the Society.[1]

The Royal Dublin Society joined the Royal Agricultural Society in an effort to improve Irish dairy industries. A joint dairy show was held in 1879, at which continental systems of butter-making were shown at work. Similar shows were subsequently held by the Royal Dublin Society alone. The Royal Agricultural Society instituted a travelling educational dairy which

[1] *Report on the Butter Manufacture of Denmark and other Countries*, 1879.

toured the provinces and brought instruction to the farmers' doors. A description of this dairy is to be found in the Spring show catalogue, 1881.

In 1883, the Royal Dublin Society induced the Commissioners of National Education to establish a dairy school at the Albert Farm, Glasnevin, and voted a sum of £50 to be offered in prizes. The railway companies were also induced to co-operate by granting free passes to pupils. The Royal Dublin Society subsequently raised the vote to £100, and voted £50 to the Munster Dairy School, Cork. These votes were continued for many years. In 1885, Mr. J. C. Lovell, the well-known London butter merchant, who had acted as a judge at one of the Society's dairy shows, recognising the importance of the work which it was doing, gave a donation of £100 in aid of dairy industries.

Meantime a momentous change in dairy methods was in progress. For some years attempts had been made to devise a machine that would separate cream from milk by centrifugal force. The problem was at last solved by Lafeldt, a German civil engineer, in Schöningen, Brunswick. Mr. Milward, in the report above referred to, mentions a visit to the works of the Centrifuge Company at Hamburg, where he saw the Lafeldt separator at work, and recognised the importance of the invention for butter-making in factories. At the same works he saw the Laval separator, and remarks that if it is to work at 6000 revolutions a minute, he would rather not place it in the hands of his dairymaid. The centrifugal cream separator underwent rapid development, and revolutionised butter-making in the same way that the Arkwright spinning frame and Cartwright power loom had revolutionised the textile industries in the latter part of the eighteenth

Thomas Kane, Lord Rathdonnell
President 1915

century. Recognising the value of this important invention, the Society offered space, free of charge, at the Spring cattle show of 1888 for the exhibition of hand separators in operation.

The fact that milk production is widely distributed, the dairy cattle being owned by numerous farmers who could not individually undertake butter-making on a large scale, rendered some system of combination necessary. The conditions were peculiarly favourable to the co-operative system, which was soon taken up extensively in Denmark. In Ireland, Mr. (afterwards Sir Horace) Plunket, and his colleagues of the Agricultural Organisation Society, laboured assiduously, and with marked success, in introducing co-operation in butter-making, and in agriculture generally. The Royal Dublin Society was approached on the subject in 1891, but the committee of agriculture recommended that the Society should not advocate one system of trading over another, while they fully recognised the importance of the movement, and advised that the Society should rather devote attention to promoting technical instruction in dairying.

The new methods of butter-making, once introduced, needed no artificial stimulus. The market demanded a uniform and cleanly-made article, of high quality; and this the mechanical method alone could supply on a large scale. The method in the ordinary course of trade competition soon captured the market.

FISHERIES—MARINE LABORATORY

From the first year of its existence, the Society had made efforts to promote the fishing industry, and the subject was often discussed at the evening meetings of a comparatively recent period, but it was not until our own time that an attempt was made to deal with the fisheries on scientific lines.

At the opening meeting of the session, 1883-4, the attention of the Council was called to the important work being done in other countries at stations established for the investigation of marine zoology, and the beneficial effect of the knowledge thus acquired on the fisheries of the country. A committee was appointed to consider whether the Society could not usefully employ itself in this direction. The committee, learning that the Rev. William Spotswood Green, of Carrigaline, co. Cork, had made a special study of fishery problems on the south-west coast of Ireland, asked his advice. A report from him was submitted to the Society on June the 2nd, 1887. Mr. Green was asked to extend his enquiries, and he submitted a second report, which was laid before the Society on March the 1st, 1888. This report dealt with the more important fish, and their relative abundance on the south coast; the local and distant markets, the fluctuation of prices, with the question of transport; and suggestions were made as to the best means of improving the industry. It was pointed out that there is a large consumption of cured fish in Ireland, practically all of which comes from Norway, Scotland, and Newfoundland. If proper steps were taken, avoiding the errors of the past, this industry might be developed in Ireland. Next year Mr. Green visited America, and at the request of the committee he furnished a report on American Fisheries, which was submitted to the Society on March the 7th, 1889.

In November 1889, a correspondence took place with Mr. J. H. Tuke, of Bancroft, Hitchin, in which he suggested that a complete survey of the fishing grounds from the coast of Kerry to Donegal should be made, and that Government assistance should be sought, as the expense would be considerable. It was ascertained that the work would cost about £1200 per annum, and would probably occupy two years. Mr. Arthur J. Balfour, then chief secretary, was approached; he evinced deep interest in the work, and urged the importance of directing attention to the distribution of the fish supply on the west coast, and as to how far the fisheries could be relied upon for the support of a large fishing population. Finding that Mr. Balfour was prepared to recommend the Government to pay half the cost of the work, the Council voted the sum of £600 for the current year, and the survey was at once commenced. For the purposes of the survey the *Fingal*, a steam yacht of 158 tons, was chartered and suitably equipped.

Before the plans for the survey were completed, a vacancy occurred in the inspectorship of Irish fisheries, through the death of Major Hayes, and Mr. Green was appointed to the office. Mr. Green was still willing to act for the Society, and to this arrangement the Government readily consented. Professor A. C. Haddon, who had just returned from Torres Straits, acted as naturalist, and Mr. T. H. Poole undertook topographical work. Mr. Green's very interesting report, with a narrative of the cruise of the *Fingal*, is included in the report of the Council laid before the Society on June the 4th, 1891.

The steam yacht *Fingal* was not available for the season of 1891, but a suitable substitute was found in the s.s. *Harlequin*, a ship of 139 tons tonnage, which was accordingly engaged. Mr. Green again took command of the survey, Mr. Ernest W. L. Holt acted as zoologist; Mr. G. Beamish took charge of physical observations, and Mr. D. H. Lane acted as general assistant. Mr. Green's report on the work accomplished forms an appendix to the report of the Council laid before the Society on December the 5th, 1891. This valuable contribution to the subject of west coast fisheries extends to 307 pages, the greater part of which is occupied by Mr. Holt's report on the results of the fishing operations of the cruise. Full particulars are given of the fish captured, their size and weight, their condition as to maturity, and the contents of their stomachs. There is a list of stations, with soundings, temperature, and specific gravity records. The report concludes with a discussion of the scientific results and their bearing on economic questions. The results were also published in a series of papers by Mr. Holt, which appeared in vols. iv. and v. of the *Transactions*, and vol. vii. of the *Scientific Proceedings* of the Royal Dublin Society. The value of this piece of work has been widely recognised, and it has been extensively quoted in almost every recent work on marine food fishes, both British and foreign.

The creation of the Congested Districts Board in 1891 transferred the responsibility for work of this character to the shoulders of a Government department. Mr. Green was a member of the board, which renewed the charter with the *Fingal*, and continued the work which the Society had initiated, at least in its more economic bearings.

In 1897 the Council was asked to consider the advisability of undertaking a further investigation of the life-history of food fishes. The economic importance of the scientific work of the surveys of 1890 and 1891 was beginning to be realised, and there was every hope of further scientific work producing similar results. The Government again promised assistance,

and the sum of £1400 was placed at the Society's
service, on the understanding that in the course of five
years, at least an equal sum should be provided from
the Society's own funds.   Steps were immediately taken
to equip a laboratory, and for this purpose the *Saturn*,
a brigantine of about 220 tons, was purchased and
properly fitted.   Mr. E. W. L. Holt was appointed
marine naturalist to the Society, Mr. Charles Green
and Mr. A. F. Townshend consenting to act as
assistants.   Subsequently fishing boats were purchased
and provided with nets, to enable the staff to conduct
operations at sea.

Brief reports of the work carried out appeared in
the annual reports of the Council for the years 1898,
1899, and 1900.   Before the expiration of the five
years, a new Government department had been created
by the passing of the Agriculture and Technical Instruction Act, 1899.   There were now two Government departments engaged in dealing with different
aspects of the fisheries question, and it seemed unnecessary for the Society to devote any part of its private
funds to doing work provided for by the State.   An
arrangement was made with the Department of Agriculture and Technical Instruction for the joint management of the marine laboratory for the unexpired term
of the five years, and subsequently the Department
became solely responsible for the work.

THE VETERINARY COLLEGE

None of the many projects in which the Society
has engaged took so long to mature as the establishment of a veterinary college.   The greater part of the
nineteenth century passed in abortive efforts before
success was attained.

The first attempt to raise veterinary medicine to

the position of a science was made in France in 1761, when a veterinary college was established at Lyons. Thirty years later the London College was founded, and Mr. St. Bel, who had studied at Lyons, was the first professor. In 1793, Mr. Coleman, who had already acquired a reputation as a surgeon, succeeded him.

In the year 1800, the attention of the Dublin Society was called to the progress that other countries, especially France, were making in veterinary science. It was decided that the books on the subject in foreign languages which belonged to the Society should be translated into English ; that the transactions of foreign academies should be searched for articles on veterinary subjects, and extracts made from English books on farming and husbandry, all the information to be condensed into one work, and properly indexed. This decision was only partially carried out. Articles which appeared in the *Transactions* about this time were no doubt published in furtherance of this decision.

The Society was empowered by Act of Parliament to acquire ground for a veterinary establishment, and the houses numbered nine to fourteen in Townshend street were taken for the purpose. Acting on the recommendation of Mr. Coleman, Mr. Thomas Peall was appointed in November 1800, " professor and lecturer," and Mr. Watts " assistant professor and practitioner." The general character and scope of the lectures which Mr. Peall was to deliver are set out in the minutes. In addition to dealing with " the constitution, nourishment, diseases, cures and treatment of horses, cattle, and other animals," the various breeds now in repute in Great Britain, particularly " of sheep and neat cattle," were to be " accurately described and compared, their several excellences pointed out, their shapes marked, and the nature of the soil or food

most advantageous for each."   Dr. Wade, professor of
botany, was also to lecture "on the nature of the
several grasses and native plants of Ireland so far as
they ought to be the object of the farmers' attention
or knowledge, in respect of each species of animal, and
in what degree they are calculated to give him strength,
or fat, or value, or otherwise."   The scope of the
lectures therefore embraced rural economy as well as
veterinary science, such as it was understood a century
ago.   The fees to be paid by pupils, and the fees to
be paid to professors for professional services, were
published in *Transactions*, vol. ii. part 1, p. 39.   The
sum of £100, 7*s*. was paid to Dr. John Percival of
London for "a veterinary museum for the use of the
Society's veterinary lectures."

Mr. Peall seems to have occupied a rather independent position.   In 1807, he informed the Society
that he had been appointed veterinary surgeon to the
Royal Artillery, and expressed his intention to deliver
his annual course of lectures at the Society's Repository.
About this time an effort was made by Government
to reduce expenditure in every possible way, and the
veterinary establishment was one of the victims of this
wave of economy.   There was a feeling that Mr. Peall
had been badly treated, and that the expectations he
had been led to entertain had not been realised.   No
doubt it was for this reason that we find the Society, in
1813, voting the sum of twenty-five guineas for a copy
of Mr. Peall's book, *Practical Observations on the Diseases
of the Horse*.   He continued to deliver brief courses of
lectures annually until a short time before his death,
which took place in May, 1825.   In June of the same
year a committee submitted a scheme for a Veterinary
Institution "differing in several essential respects from
that which had been agreed to by the Society in 1800."

Mr. Coleman wrote to Lord Oriel, then senior vice-president, giving his opinion as to what should be done. Incidentally he observes that "Dublin has now (1825) three veterinary practitioners." The regulations of the London Veterinary College which accompanied Mr. Coleman's letter, were printed in *Proceedings* vol. 61, pp. 210-16. These proposals were not, however, carried out.

Six years later (1831), the "Committee of Agriculture and of the House" recommended that a Veterinary Professor be appointed at a salary of £200 a year, on condition that he should deliver certain class lectures, as well as public lectures, and maintain at his own cost, and for his own profit, a hospital for invalid horses and other live stock. The committee desired to impress on the Society "the importance of great caution in the election of a professor." The Society adopted this report, and resolved "that the Society are of opinion that the veterinary professorship should be revived in connection with a Veterinary School." Again, no definite action was taken, and two years later it was proposed that the Society's veterinary anatomical preparations should be offered in exchange to the College of Surgeons. This suggestion was not adopted, and eventually a place was found for the specimens, which probably formed part of the collection subsequently known as the "Agricultural Museum." This museum was part of the property transferred to the Crown by the Science and Art Museum Act, 1877. In 1886, specimens relating to veterinary science were, with the Society's concurrence, transferred on loan to the Albert Institution, Glasnevin.

When the question of appointing a successor to Dr. Davy was under consideration in 1858, it was proposed that part of the anticipated savings should be appropriated to the salary of a professor of veterinary surgery; this, however, was not done.

In 1864, the attention of the Board of National Education was called to the recommendations of the select committee of the House of Commons on scientific institutions in Dublin, relative to the establishment of an Agricultural and Veterinary School in connection with the Society. The reply of the Commissioners was referred to a special committee, which reported to the Council early in 1865. The report briefly sketches the work of the Society early in the century, mentions the veterinary museum as " in good order and available," suggests that it is useless to communicate with the Commissioners, and expresses the belief that the Council will willingly undertake any duties in this connection that Parliament may see fit to throw upon the Society.

In 1866, an influential committee was asked to consider the possibility of founding a veterinary school. The next year this committee submitted an important report, which was the first attempt made to deal with the question exhaustively and in a business-like manner. A curriculum was drawn up, and it was estimated that the annual cost of the staff of the institution would be £600, but the committee pointed out that the Society had no funds for this purpose. The committee was asked to furnish an estimate of other expenses. In 1868, a memorial to the Treasury in favour of the establishment of a veterinary school was ordered to lie for signature during the Horse Show of that year, but the minutes do not show whether this memorial was ever forwarded. About this time the formation of an Association of Veterinary Surgeons in Dublin was projected, and the Society lent offices for the meetings of the promoters.

The next move was not made until 1883, when, in conformity with a resolution of the Society, a committee was appointed to report to the Council as to the most effectual means of founding an Irish college or school of veterinary surgery and medicine, with independent powers of examining and of conferring diplomas. The committee proceeded on the lines of its predecessor of 1866, by preparing a curriculum, and estimating the probable income and expenditure. They showed that a deficit of about £800 a year might be expected, while at least £5000 would have to be spent on buildings. It was shown that the Royal Veterinary College of London possessed by charter the sole power of granting veterinary diplomas in the United Kingdom, and that to attain the desired object a body with independent power would have to be incorporated in Ireland. The committee expressed the opinion that a veterinary establishment, managed as a perfectly independent body on a commercial basis, like the Scottish institutions, would pay its way and be self supporting. This would mean competition with veterinary surgeons in Dublin, which of course the Society could not undertake. The committee concluded that the best thing the Society could do was to assist a veterinary college (if one were started) by grants in aid, such as were given to the veterinary colleges of England and Scotland by the leading agricultural society of each country. The report of the committee was adopted by the Society in February 1884, and, though nothing further was done at the time, the report formed the basis of the final step taken ten years later. In 1894, the project was again revived; to get over the financial difficulty a committee of the Council recommended that a guarantee fund should be raised, and that the Society should, in addition, contribute £200 a year for five years. A Parliamentary grant of £15,000 was promised, and on the strength of this promise an appeal was made to the public. The guarantee fund, including donations (which some contributors preferred to give), eventually reached the sum of £2253. A charter of incorporation was applied for, and, after negotiations in relation to some details, the charter was granted, and it was enrolled on May the 29th, 1895. Under this charter the governing body of the Royal Veterinary College of Ireland consisted of twelve persons nominated by the Crown, twelve persons nominated by the Council of the Royal Dublin Society, four persons nominated by the Commissioners of National Education in Ireland, and four persons to be elected by subscribers.

In 1906, this charter was annulled, and a new charter issued, increasing the number of the Society's nominees to fifteen, and giving to the Department of Agriculture and Technical Instruction for Ireland, which had been created since the first charter was issued, the power to nominate thirteen persons. The power of the Crown to nominate twelve persons was retained, but the Commissioners of National Education ceased to have the power of nomination.

In 1913, the Board of Governors decided to surrender their charter, and to transfer the government of the college to the Department of Agriculture and Technical Instruction for Ireland. Under the proposed new charter the functions of the former Board of Governors will become advisory in character. The Council of the Royal Dublin Society concurred in the proposed change, believing that it would be greatly to the advantage of the country.

AGRICULTURAL SHOWS AND THE HORSE SHOW

The last spring cattle show held in Kildare street in April 1880 was the fiftieth of a series of shows held annually without intermission, beginning in the year 1831. There were still earlier cattle shows, but they were not held on the Society's premises, nor were they under the direct management of the Society; they were held by the Farming Society, a body founded in 1800, which carried on its operations "under the patronage of the Dublin Society"; it received a subsidy of £200 a year from the Society's funds, and held its meetings on the Society's premises. The shows were held at Smithfield, Dublin, in the months of April and November, and at Ballinasloe in the month of October. A report on one of these shows held on November the 20th, 1800, which shows the extraordinary care that was taken in awarding the prizes, is published in the *Transactions* of the Dublin Society, vol. ii. pp. 353–364. In some classes, the animals were weighed, and after slaughter, detailed weighings and measurements of the various cuts were made. In the case of two three-year-old wethers, there are eleven measurements and seven weighings given, and in the case of two heifers there are the weighings of ten different parts of each animal. So completely did the Farming Society withdraw agricultural interests from the parent body, that we find it stated in evidence before the Parliamentary Commission of 1836, that the Society had "lost its original character, and become more an institution for the encouragement of Arts and Sciences."

The spring cattle show of 1831 was the Society's response to the appeal that had been made by the Marquis of Downshire, who had urged the Society to resume its agricultural work. The show opened on Tuesday, April the 26th, 1831. The first two days

CHARLES UNIACKE TOWNSHEND, VICE-PRESIDENT, 1893-1907

(From an oil painting by William Orpen)

were devoted to cattle, and the third day to horses. The breeds included in the classes for cattle (bulls, cows, heifers and oxen) were Durham, Holderness, Ayrshire, Devon, and any other breed. There were only two breeds of sheep recognised—Leicestershire and South Down. The only class of horse in the list is " draught stallion." There was also a class for Spanish asses as sires. The prizes varied from a silver medal, or £5 to £3, and no entry fee was charged. One of the rules was that " The oxen must not have been fed on distillery wash or grains, and when all other circumstances admit of it a preference must be given to the lot which has been fattened upon the most wholesome and least expensive food." The show was a great success. The number and excellence of the cattle far exceeded the expectations of the committee, who expressed themselves as "sanguine enough to think" that the exhibition " has laid the foundation of much useful improvement."

In the prize list for 1832, the classes for cattle embrace the longhorned breed, the shorthorned breed, Herefords, and any other breed, and a section was introduced " for promoting the breed of poultry in favour of the cottager." No money prizes were offered except for poultry. A new section also appears for "implements of husbandry." Lectures on agricultural chemistry and botany were to form a feature of the show.

In 1834 there was a sweepstake of two sovereigns in each fat cattle class, the names of the subscribers to which were—J. L. W. Naper, Robert Holmes, Robert La Touche, and George Garnett. This arrangement was not repeated at subsequent shows.

In 1837 the committee suggested that, " under existing circumstances, and the extraordinary scarcity and high prices of provender," no show should be held ;

but a few weeks later this recommendation was withdrawn, and the show was held.

In 1838 there was a great increase in the number of cattle, and a great improvement in their quality. On September the 18th, an autumn show of breeding stock and a public sale by auction were held.

In 1839 money prizes were resumed. In the following year, through lack of funds, it was decided to abandon the autumn show, and to concentrate attention upon one good show, with money prizes.

Owing to the epidemic among cattle in the year 1841, the abandonment of the spring show was contemplated, but finally the show was held, and it turned out a very successful exhibition.

At the show of 1844, Professor Dick of Edinburgh lectured on the diseases of cattle, and Professor (afterwards Sir Robert) Kane, on the relation of science to agriculture.

In 1845, in addition to the spring show held in April, there was an exhibition of farm produce in November; and from this date a winter show in some form or other was held for many years.

In reporting on the spring show of 1848, the judges said that the shorthorns were particularly good, and they anticipated that English breeders would soon be purchasers in Ireland. " Irish breeders have fully earned this mark of distinction by a steady perseverance in supplying themselves with stock from the most distinguished herds in Great Britain, irrespective of cost."

The show in 1850 was visited by a great storm, and all the cattle sheds in Leinster Lawn were blown down.

Following the example of the Industrial Exhibition of 1851, a book for members to sign at the entrance was instituted for the first time; this practice continues to the present day.

At the show of 1852 an entry fee of 2*s*. 6*d*. was charged on each head of cattle entered by a non-member; this was done with the view of "excluding cattle of an inferior class."

In the report of the show of 1855, it is pointed out that there were 290 shorthorns, whereas the number at the Lincoln show of the Royal Agricultural Society of England was 111, and at the Berwick-on-Tweed show of the Highland and Agricultural Society the number was 223.

Mr. Henry Smith of Dease Abbey, Yorkshire, in reporting on the show of 1856, says:—"The county of Durham has been called the land of shorthorns; Ireland is that country now. I say, as an Englishman, and an English shorthorn breeder, that Englishmen must look to themselves, for, unless they improve in a very short time, Ireland will beat them. . . . The progress that has been made in the country in the breeding of shorthorns is something most extra-ordinary." Other reports of this period are even more laudatory, but enough has been said to afford some idea of the stimulus that was given to cattle breeding by the Spring show, in the first quarter of the century.

The erection of the Agricultural Hall (now the south hall at Ballsbridge) in Kildare street in 1858, was the first important step in the direction of permanent buildings for the shows. It was a necessity at the time, because the erection of the Natural History Museum and the National Gallery had greatly encroached upon the space available for agricultural exhibitions. In 1862, it was ordered that the Lawn should no longer be used for shows, and space had to be found elsewhere on the site now occupied by the Science and Art Museum.

During the last twenty years of the Kildare street

spring shows there was no great change in the number
of cattle entered each year, and the shows seem to
have reached their full development.   So far as premises were concerned, there was no room for further
extension.   Nevertheless, we find the Council reporting in 1876, when the removal of the shows to another
site was contemplated, that " the success of the annual
shows depends greatly upon their being held within
the city.   Should they be removed to the suburbs, it is
apprehended that they would be less numerously attended, and the receipts suffer serious diminution."
This apprehension was not unfounded ; the earlier spring
shows at Ballsbridge were not well attended, but a way
of making them more attractive was soon discovered, and
the last show held there (1913) was attended by 24,358
persons, more than twice the best Kildare street record,
which was in 1875, when 12,034 persons attended.

It is, however, in the entries of breeding stock that
the progress of the Ballsbridge shows has been most
marked.   The best record in Kildare street was 308
animals in 1872.   Three shows were held at Ballsbridge before this number was exceeded, and then
rapid progress was made ; the Kildare street record
was more than doubled at the Ballsbridge show of
1896, and more than trebled six years later.   At the
Ballsbridge show of 1908, the entries of breeding
stock reached the record number of 1051.

In 1908, after an interval of seventy years, the
auction sales were revived.   The number of animals
entered for sale was 463, and of these 173 were sold.
Five years later, the number entered for sale had increased to 654, and the number sold to 549.

In 1904, to meet the demand for an early market,
a show and sale of pure-bred bulls was instituted,
and February the 10th was fixed upon as the date of

the show.   The number of entries at this show was
183, and at the corresponding shows held in the succeeding nine years the average number has been 164.

Since the year 1896, Winter shows have been held
at Ballsbridge in the month of December.   These shows
had their origin in the exhibition of farm produce
which commenced in 1845, and they were held in the
Agricultural Museum, Kildare street.   In 1858 the
Agricultural Hall, then newly erected in Kildare street,
enabled the committee to add sections for fat stock
and poultry.   In this form the shows continued up to
1879, with the exception of the year 1871, when the
cattle sections were omitted in consequence of foot
and mouth disease.   The winter shows were not resumed at Ballsbridge until 1890.   The attendance at
the show was discouraging; in 1891 the expenditure
exceeded the receipts by £533, and the shows were
discontinued for several years.   Since the shows were
resumed in 1896, the expenditure on them has exceeded
the receipts by £7418, an annual loss of £412, which,
however, the Society considers justified mainly in the
interests of the fat stock and poultry industries.

The Society is indebted to a number of gentlemen
interested in promoting improvement in malting barley,
and known as the Barley Committee, who, for some
years contributed annually two or three hundred
pounds to be awarded in prizes varying from £2 to
£5, which were allocated to counties according to a fixed
scheme.   At the show of 1913, there were 288 entries
for these prizes.

No enterprise in which the Society ever engaged
has attracted so much public notice as the annual event
now known all over the world as the Dublin Horse
Show, which opens at Ballsbridge with unerring regularity on the Tuesday preceding the last Friday in the

month of August in each year.[1] As a show of horses, especially hunters, the exhibition is unrivalled, and in the society world the horse show has acquired an assured position among the leading social events of the United Kingdom. The first Dublin Horse Show was organised by a committee appointed by the Royal Agricultural Society of Ireland, on the suggestion of the late Lord Howth, then Lord St. Lawrence. It was held on April the 15th, 1864, on the Kildare street premises of the Royal Dublin Society, which were lent for the occasion. There were 370 entries, and the animals were judged in an enclosure in the courtyard of Leinster House. The second show was held in September 1866, under somewhat similar conditions, the Kildare street premises being again lent to the horse show committee by the Royal Dublin Society. The number of entries at this show was 303.

In August 1867, the committee of agriculture of the Royal Dublin Society recommended the Council to hold an annual horse show, and a special committee was appointed to carry out the recommendation. A subscription list was opened, and contributions to the amount of £793 were received, including £100 from the Royal Dublin Society. The show was held in the Kildare street premises on July 28th, 1868, and two following days. The number of horses entered was 366, and the number of persons who visited the show was 6029. The following resolution appears in the minutes of the horse show committee of June the 25th, 1868 :—

Proposed by Lord St. Lawrence, and seconded by R. C. Wade—"That this committee, judging from

---

[1] The war with Germany (1914) interrupted this regularity. It was not possible to hold the show, as the military authorities occupied the premises at Ballsbridge for remount purposes.

BALLSBRIDGE PREMISES, JUMPING ENCLOSURE

the precedent afforded by the interest created at the
Islington horse show, of seeing hunters exhibit their
fencing powers, have come to the conclusion that it
would prove expedient to offer prizes for jumping,
especially as such a course will be attended with little
or no pecuniary risk, and will add considerably to the
attraction of the horse show." This was the beginning
of the jumping competitions, and the first of the series
took place on the afternoon of June the 28th in the
Kildare street courtyard. A correspondent in the
Irish Farmers' Gazette, referring to the stone wall
jump, says—"the wall was five feet ten inches, in
cold blood, off wet sawdust, in a crowded courtyard."

The general arrangements of the show of 1868
differed very little from those of recent shows. The
entries closed about a month before the show opened,
and, in addition to the entrance fee, exhibitors were
required to lodge a deposit of £2 on each horse. At
the adjudication there was a preliminary selection of
horses to be examined by veterinary surgeons before
the prizes were finally awarded. The horses were
classified very much as they are at present.

The difficulty of conducting the business of the
show in the limited area available was very great,
especially in the earlier shows, when the members
claimed the right to enter the judging ring. At a
meeting of the Society in 1873, specially convened
for the purpose, this practice was ordered to be
stopped ; a resolution was passed empowering the
horse show committee "to clear and keep the ring and
jumping and exercising grounds free of all persons
whomsoever, whether members of the Society or
others," whenever the committee thought fit.

The financial results of the first show were considered
quite satisfactory, when a balance of £162 remained

out of the £793 which had been subscribed. The subscriptions in aid of the second show also amounted to £793, but the attendance rose to 10,529 persons, and the show closed with a credit balance of £923; from this time no further appeal was made to the public for funds. In 1873, the horse show funds were regarded as quite distinct from the other funds of the Society, and were transferred to trustees consisting of two members of the committee, with the registrar and treasurer. A year later we find the horse show committee in a position to vote £300 to the general funds of the Society in aid of the purchase of premises. In 1879, the balance of £1488, standing to the credit of the horse shows, was transferred to the general funds of the Society.

The entries at the Kildare street shows reached the maximum in 1874, when they numbered 636, and the attendance rose to its highest point in 1875, when 21,857 persons passed the turnstiles during the four days of the show.

There were two breaks in the series of horse shows held by the Society in Kildare street—one in 1871 and the other in 1878, when shows of the Royal Agricultural Society were held at Ballsbridge; on each of these occasions the Society's horse show was not held.

The entries at the first show held in the Society's new premises at Ballsbridge in 1881 were 589, and there were 15,736 visitors. These numbers had been surpassed many times at Kildare street, and they reflect the opinion, then widely entertained, that the people of Dublin would find Ballsbridge too much out of the way in comparison with the very accessible Kildare street site. By 1884 this feeling had passed away; the entries then numbered 806, and the attendance reached 26,558. The Duke of Edinburgh was present at this

show; for the first time seats on the grand stand were reserved, and were eagerly booked. Next year the stand was greatly enlarged and placed in a better position. The next record in entries and attendances was on the occasion of the visit of the Duke and Duchess of York in 1897, when the entries numbered 1431 and the visitors 66,167.

At the show of 1899, a sale of horses by auction was held on the Society's premises to the north of Merrion road; and similar sales have taken place annually since that date. At first, these sales were limited to horses regularly entered for competition at the horse show, but afterwards they included horses not entered for the show. In 1907, for example, there were 499 horses offered by auction, and of these only 56 were entered for the show. The sales are every year increasing in importance, and already they have acquired a high reputation among the breeders and buyers of thoroughbred horses.

THE LIBRARY

Under the Science and Art Museum Act of 1877 the greater part of the library was transferred to the Crown, and became the National Library of Ireland. The agreement entered into between the Government and the Society placed the National Library under the superintendence of a Council of twelve trustees, eight of whom are appointed by the Society and four by the Government. The officers of the Library are appointed by the Council of trustees, and the Society has the power by by-law to determine the mode of election and tenure of office of its representatives on the Council of trustees. Under the existing by-laws the Society's eight members retire annually, and are eligible

z

for re-election.   The Society thus retains a substantial voice in the management of this important institution. The National Library remained in Leinster House until 1891,when it was transferred to the handsome new building it now occupies, in close proximity to its old quarters.

The part of the library which remained in the Society's possession after the Act of 1877 consisted of scientific serials, the transactions and publications of other learned societies, and certain early editions, and duplicates of modern works.   Many of these books had been presented to the Society in exchange for its own publications, a system which is still continued on an extended scale.   By agreement with the Government the Society has undertaken to afford full and free access to the public at all reasonable times to the scientific serials and publications of learned societies reserved to the Society by the Act.

The books retained by the Society formed the nucleus of the present library, which now occupies nearly as much room in Leinster House as the National Library did when it was transferred to the Crown.   The difficulty of finding room for this library is one of the problems which the Society must face in the near future.   In the past twenty years the Society has spent £7253 in purchasing books, which is at the rate of £362 per annum, and the number of volumes purchased annually is about 600.   In addition to this, several hundred volumes are received in exchange.   A general catalogue of the library up to June 1895 was published in a single volume in 1896, and additional volumes have since been published at intervals of five years.   A card catalogue which is kept posted up to date is accessible to the members and associates, to whom lists of accessions are sent from time to time during each session.

CHAPTER XIX

SURVEY OF THE SCIENTIFIC WORK OF THE SOCIETY

(*Contributed by* Mr. R. J. Moss, *Registrar*)

THE ground acquired in 1733 was intended "to be employed by the Society as a nursery for raising several sorts of trees, plants, roots, &c., which do not at present grow in this kingdom, but are imported from abroad, and when raised in such nursery may be dispersed to be propagated in this country." At that time botany as a science was only beginning to take form ; Linnæus had not yet published his *Systema Naturæ*. It was not until 1790 that the Society took steps to establish a regular Botanic Garden, and in 1796 it commenced its educational work in science by appointing Dr. Wade "professor and lecturer in Botany." The foundation of the Natural History Museum was laid in 1792 by the purchase of the Leskean collection of minerals. In 1795 Mr. William Higgins was placed in charge of this collection, and it was ordered : "that from Mr. Higgins' extensive skill in chymistry, he be directed from time to time to make such experiments on dyeing materials and other articles, wherein chymistry may assist the arts, as may occur ; and that, for that purpose, a small chymical apparatus should be procured and erected in the

repository, under the direction of Mr. Higgins."
Thus was established the Society's chemical laboratory, probably the first of the kind in the United
Kingdom. That practical instruction in chemistry
was given in the laboratory is evident from advertisements which appear in *Saunders's News Letter*, and
in the *Hibernian Journal* of 1797 and later years.
Systematic courses of lectures in chemistry and natural
philosophy were instituted in the year 1800, and
soon became an important feature in the Society's
work in Dublin, and in the provinces, to which
they ultimately extended. For many years these
lectures, delivered by the Society's professional staff
and others appointed to assist them, were the only
means open to the Irish public of obtaining instruction
in science.

In 1845 the Government decided to create in
Ireland an institution similar to the Museum of
Practical Geology, London ; the institution eventually
took the form of the " Museum of Irish Industry
and Government School of Science applied to Mining
and the Arts," with premises in St. Stephen's Green.
To avoid duplication of professorships, some of the
lectures were delivered in the Society's theatre, Kildare
street, and some in the Museum of Irish Industry,
St. Stephen's Green ; while the regular class lectures
were delivered at the latter institution only. Eventually the scope of the Museum of Irish Industry was
enlarged, and it became the Royal College of Science
for Ireland. Thus the systematic teaching of science
gradually passed out of the Society's hands, though its
lectures still survive in a popular form in the courses
of afternoon lectures and in the Christmas lectures for
juveniles which are delivered every session.

The services of the scientific staff had not been

confined to lecturing. In 1802 the Commissioners of His Majesty's Revenue requested that Mr. Higgins, professor of chemistry, should be sent to London " as a person of skill and ability to assist in ascertaining an hydrometer which shall hereafter be made use of to judge the strength of spirits subject to excise or import duty." Occasionally questions arose on which expert information was required, and the members of the scientific staff were often asked to report on such points. At the request of the Society, Mr. Higgins reported on the ashes of different weeds and of potato tops. Mr , afterwards Sir Richard, Griffith, who held the office of mining engineer to the Society, gave his detailed opinion as to the utility of chemical analysis of rocks and soils.

In 1822 a committee was appointed to enquire into " the possibility of introducing potato starch as a substitute for the root in substance." This led to an extensive experimental investigation which was carried out in the chemical laboratory under the supervision of the scientific staff. The reports are interesting in connection with the efforts made at this time to find some way of relieving the distress which arose from failures in the potato crop. The committee finally concluded that " it would be illusive to hold out potato starch as a practical relief upon the present emergency."

The Botanic Garden staff was frequently asked for advice, and experiments were made there on the cultivation of various grasses and fodder crops. The Society obtained 10 lbs. of Swede turnip seed in the year 1801 for the use of the committee of agriculture ; half a pound was sown in the Botanic Garden, and the seed was saved for further use ; thus this important fodder crop was introduced into Ireland. Dr. Walter Wade and his successors in the professorship of botany frequently brought before the Society the results of experimental work carried out in the garden, and these reports were laid before the ordinary business meetings of the Society.

Sir Charles Giesecke was constantly engaged in mineralogical excursions, and his reports are of frequent occurrence in the minutes.   Mr. Griffith submitted a great many interesting reports in his quest for coal and other minerals of industrial value.   Edmund Davy, who succeeded Higgins as professor of chemistry in 1826, brought many reports and other communications on work done in the Society's laboratory before these meetings.   The first of these, " On a species of tallow recently found in a bog near Ballinasloe," was the earliest attempt at a scientific examination of the substance so frequently found in Ireland in peat bogs, and known as bog butter.   This paper appears as an appendix to the minutes of the meeting of December the 14th, 1826 ; but as it is not indexed, it has completely escaped notice.   Another report by Davy of permanent interest is his " Account of some experiments made on different varieties of bituminous coal imported into Dublin, with a view to ascertain their comparative value for domestic and other uses."   This appears as an appendix to the minutes of June the 12th, 1828, but there is no reference to it in the index to the volume for that year.   In 1833 the Corporation of Tallow Chandlers and Soap Boilers of Dublin sought Davy's assistance in " investigating the causes of the present ruinous state of the Irish soap manufacture." In his report Davy pointed out that the mode of levying the duty on soap by measurement instead of by weight caused the Irish article to be at a disadvantage. This report was ordered to be forwarded to the Treasury.   Next year the Commissioners of Public

Works sought Davy's assistance in devising some method of preventing the rusting of iron in the sea water of Kingstown Harbour.

The *Transactions* of the Dublin Society published from the year 1800 to 1810 contain very little of permanent value. Most of the articles relate to agriculture and veterinary subjects; potato cultivation is frequently dealt with, and there are papers on dyeing, bleaching, tanning, malting, kelp-making, peat, inland and sea fisheries. A few papers contain original matter of scientific interest, such as Higgins on the use of sulphuret of lime as a substitute for potash in bleaching; Kirwan on a method of estimating the richness of milk and the strength of alcoholic liquids. The method is based on the rate of evaporation compared with water under similar conditions, and on specific gravity. Kirwan also outlined a plan for the management of the mines of Ireland. His paper entitled "What are the manures most advantageously applicable to the various sorts of soils, and what are the causes of their beneficial effect in each particular instance," is of great interest in the history of agricultural chemistry. The paper was published in 1802, before Sir Humphry Davy had begun to lecture on agricultural chemistry, two years before De Saussure's work was published, and more than thirty years before Liebig's time. There are several papers by Wade on the rare plants of Ireland, on *Buddlea globosa*, *Holco odorata*, and other botanical subjects. Among papers of historical interest are those on the Wicklow gold mines.

Several of the volumes contain returns of meteorological observations taken at the Botanic Garden, Glasnevin; there are also catalogues of plants in the garden, programmes of lectures, lists of premiums, and other particulars of the Society's work. When the *Transac-*

tions ceased to appear there was no medium of publication for some years except the minutes of the business meetings, which were regularly printed.

In 1836 an important innovation took place, and for the first time, instead of bringing scientific papers before the ordinary meetings, special meetings for reading and discussing such communications were held ; these meetings were called the "Evening Scientific Meetings." At the first meeting, held on the 26th of January, Professor Davy gave an account of an apparently new gas, produced by the action of water on a substance obtained by heating tartrate of potash in a retort, and exhibited some experiments with the gas. This was the gas now known as acetylene, the discovery of which was one of considerable scientific importance ; the gas is now extensively employed, and it is prepared by a method very similar to that which Davy used in the Society's laboratory, except that calcium carbide is used instead of potassium carbide. The manufacture of calcium carbide for the preparation of acetylene has become an important industry. Exactly eighteen months later, Davy submitted to the Royal Irish Academy a paper on this discovery, which was published in vol. xviii. of the *Transactions* of the Academy. He determined the composition of the gas and called it bicarburet of hydrogen. In 1859, the gas was rediscovered by the French chemist Berthelot, and, curiously enough, it is to Berthelot that the credit of the discovery is commonly attributed in chemical text-books, notwithstanding Davy's twenty-three years of priority. It is alleged that Davy did not establish the actual composition of the gas, but anyone who takes the trouble to read his paper will see that this is a mistake. The minutes of the evening meetings appear regularly in the *Proceedings* down to 1839.

The chief contributors during that period were Davy on chemical subjects ; Scouler, on raised beaches, on the dolomites, on lignites and the silicified woods of Lough Neagh ; Grubb on improvements in optical instruments ; Kane on physical subjects. The only papers printed *in extenso* were not on scientific subjects, such as Mr. Clibborn's on Banking, and Mr. Coulter's reply to it. The evening meetings continued to be held, but they gradually became less scientific in character. In 1843, by-laws were adopted which enabled persons to join a section of the Society, with restricted privileges ; and meetings called " Sectional Evening Meetings " were held. The manuscript minutes of those meetings, which are very full and contain a good deal of information of historical interest, have fortunately been preserved. Some of the papers were printed *in extenso* and appear as appendices in the Society's *Proceedings*. For example, Mr Antisell's "Analysis of the important soils of Ireland "—the earliest record of work of this kind in the country—appears in vol. lxxx. (1843-4) ; Mr. McCalla's paper on Irish algæ appears in vol. lxxxii. (1845-6). In the same volume will be found a paper by Mr. William K. Sullivan, in which the " Wasteful management of manure heaps " is scientifically treated. In vol. lxxxiii. (1846-7) the following papers appear :—" The effects of meteorological conditions on potato disease," by Edward J. Cooper ; " The Irish fisheries as an industrial resource," by J. C. Deane ; " Irish flora and fauna," by Mr. McCalla. In the same volume are printed two scientific papers which were read at agricultural evening meetings, viz. Dr. John Aldridge " On the comparative nutritive and pecuniary values of various kinds of cooked food," and Sir Robert Kane " On the composition and characters of certain soils and waters belonging to the flax districts of Belgium, and on the chemical composition of the ashes of the flax plant." In vol. lxxxiv. appears a paper by William Hogan, entitled, "A report of the result of experiments made in 1847 on M. Zander's method of propagating potatoes from seed." The reports of the proceedings at the meetings held from November the 28th, 1848, to June the 7th, 1855, are printed in a volume entitled *Reports of Scientific Meetings*, published in 1855. This is a rare volume; very few copies seem to have been issued, and there is only one in the Society's possession. A short notice of the contents, so far as they seem to be of permanent interest, will not be out of place. Irish Fisheries and allied industries are dealt with by Professor Allman, Mr. William Andrews, Mr. J. Knight Boswell, and Dr. William Barker. The manufacture of beet sugar in Ireland formed the subject of communications by Mr. Samuel Copland and Mr. John Sproule. Mr. Copland also read a paper "On the history and cultivation of tobacco with reference to the question of its profitable cultivation in Ireland." Professor Edmund Davy contributed papers on the manufacture of sulphuric acid, on some applications of peat and peat charcoal, on cabbage as food for the horse, and on the detection and preparation of salts of manganese. Dr. E. W. Davy read papers on new explosive powders and gun-cotton, on native phosphate of lime, on a new test for nitric acid, on a new method for producing nitro-prussiates, on ozone, on a new test for strychnine, on the quantitative analysis of urea, on the determination of nitrogen in guano, and on the decomposition of calp.

Dr. William Barker's communications dealt with black rain, the preparation of charcoal for electrical purposes, and portable fuel for Arctic voyages. Professor M. H. Harvey read papers on recently discovered plants new to Ireland, and on various substances used in the manufacture of paper.   There are communications on Arctic fossils by Professor Scouler, Mr. Jukes and Professor Samuel Haughton ; and botanical notes by Mr. David Moore and Mr. Isaac Weld.   The registering barometer described by Mr. George Yeates in 1851 was evidently the precursor of the automatic mercurial barograph constructed by Messrs. Yeates & Son, which has been in the hall of Leinster House for many years.   Mr. W. K. Sullivan read a paper on the amount of sugar in Irish-grown roots.   This is now of interest, as it shows that sixty-four years ago the fact was established (to use the author's words)—" that the climate of Ireland is remarkably adapted for the growth of bulbous roots of a superior quality, whether for the manufacture of sugar or for feeding purposes."

There is another paper by Mr. Sullivan and M. Alphonse Gages on the comparative value of large and small roots, one of the conclusions arrived at being— " that the system of encouraging the growth of monster roots which has hitherto prevailed, and of which we have such examples at the Society's Show, is erroneous." Notwithstanding this exposure, and the fact that no farmer would dream of growing such roots for profit, the system still survives.   In 1849, Mr. Henry Hutchins read a paper " On aërial travelling," and exhibited to the meeting drawings of the method proposed by him for giving direction to aërial locomotive machines.   Unfortunately this paper was not printed, and there is nothing to show what Mr. Hutchins' proposal was.   At that time, Henson's flying machine was six years old, but the first attempt to make a dirigible balloon is attributable to Henri Giffard, of injector fame. There are in the volume some papers of purely social or economic interest, such as the Earl of Devon's paper "On the social condition of the people of Ireland," which is printed in full ; Mr. Cheyne Brady's paper " On the practicability of improving the dwellings of the labouring classes," given in abstract ; and Dr. George Ellis's, " On emigration as affecting the West of Ireland," printed in full.

The necessity for wider and more systematic publication of the Society's work was now fully recognised. In the annual report to the President of the Board of Trade, dated December the 31st, 1856, the Council said, that "within the past session the Council, with the sanction of the Society, issued for the first time the *Journal* of the Royal Dublin Society, three numbers of which have now been published. The Council consider the publication of this periodical to be of great importance to the institution, inasmuch as in its pages will be found a public record of its proceeding, as regards the advancement of those arts and sciences for the promotion of which the Society was incorporated. As the record of the scientific and educational departments, it will be found to awaken a degree of interest therein which cannot fail to aid their extension, while from its being the medium of publication of those communications on the natural and applied sciences made to the Society from time to time, the reputation of the institution will be enhanced. The Council, impressed with these convictions, have urged upon the Society the advisability of its working out this project with energy, especially sanctioning a liberal use of illustrations, by lithography and other means, of the papers that may from time to time be published in its pages."

The *Journal* continued to appear until the year 1876, when it was replaced by the publications devoted solely to the Society's scientific work. The *Journal* was more widely distributed, and it was sent in exchange to some of the leading scientific societies. Seven volumes were published; the principal papers in vol. i. are McClintock's "Reminiscences of Arctic Ice-Travel in search of Sir John Franklin," with illustrations of the fossils found in the course of the expedition; Edmund Davy, on a simple electrochemical method of detecting arsenic; Mr. Carte, on the climate and zoology of the Crimea; Dr. J. R. Kinahan on the habits and distribution of marine crustacea on the eastern shores of Port Philip, Australia, with descriptions of undescribed species and genera. The same author contributed a paper on *Crustacea* collected in Peru, the high seas, and South Australia, and described some new species. The Rev. Dr. Samuel Haughton contributed an important paper on the tides and tidal currents of the Irish Sea and English Channel, considered with reference to the safe navigation of those seas by outward and homeward bound ships. The volume also includes an appreciative memoir of Edmund Davy, who succeeded Mr. Higgins as professor of chemistry to the Royal Dublin Society in 1826, and held that office until his death in 1857. There is also a memoir of Mr. Isaac Weld, a vice-president of the Society, by Mr. L. E. Foot. Mr. Weld for many years exercised a controlling influence over the Society's work, and the writer claims that it was Mr. Weld who suggested the Society's triennial exhibitions of manufactures which culminated in the great International Exhibition of 1853.

Vol. ii. contains a paper by Mr. Patrick Buchan on the iron ores of the Connaught coalfield, and notes by the Rev. Professor Haughton on a mineralogical excursion from Cairo into Arabia Petræa. The same author contributed a mineralogical description of rocks from Nagpur, Central India, and described some new *Orthocerata* from Cork and Clonmel, and *Cyclostigma*, a new genus of fossil plants, from Kiltorcan, co. Kilkenny. Mr. Edward Brenan gave an account of the discovery of mammoth and other fossil remains at Shandon, co. Waterford, and Dr. Robert McDonnell contributed a paper on the habits and anatomy of *Lepidosiren annectens*.

The principal papers in vol. iii. are those by Professor E. W. Davy on ferrocyanide of potassium as an analytical agent ; further contributions by Dr. Haughton on the tidal currents of the Irish Sea, and a paper on the fossils brought from the Arctic regions by Captain McClintock. Dr. David Walker contributed notes on the zoology of the Arctic expedition under McClintock. Mr. Thomas Grubb described a new table microscope, and Mr. John Dowling wrote on the comparative value of the different feeding-stuffs for horses. Dr. Henry Lawson suggested the formation of a new class of Annuloida, to include *Trematoda*, *Planariæ*, and *Hirudinei*, and Mr. William Andrews wrote on the cod and ling fisheries of Ireland. The volume includes a catalogue of the minerals collected by Sir Charles Giesecke between Cape Farewell and Baffin's Bay in the Arctic regions. Mr. Charles W. Hamilton's paper on the condition of the Irish agricultural labourer in 1859 is historically interesting ; the tabulated abstracts of the answers to the Society's agricultural queries, and the lists of labourers' families which accompany the paper contain much curious information.

The following papers in vol. iv. are of permanent interest :—A. Leith Adams on the fossiliferous caves of Malta ; Dr. Henry Lawson on the anatomy,

histology, and physiology of *Limax maximus*; Mr.
Andrews on the salmon fisheries of Ireland, and on
the sea fisheries and trawling; Mr. Scott on the
mineral localities of Donegal; Mr. Carte and Mr.
Baily on a new species of Plesiosaurus, which they
named *P. Cramptoni*—the specimen described is still one
of the treasures of the Natural History Museum;
on the chemistry of the feeding of animals for the
production of meat and manure, by Mr. afterwards
Sir John Burnet Lawes, bart.; Mr. H. O'Hara on
the Irish coalfields and peat; Dr. Edmund W. Davy
on "Flax, the practicability of extending its cultivation
in Ireland, and the proper management of the crop."
Dr. Evory Kennedy's paper on the "Neglect of sanitary
arrangements in the homes and houses of the rich and
poor in town and country" makes one wonder how
our immediate predecessors managed to survive in
such unhealthy surroundings. Dr. Emerson Reynolds
contributed to this and succeeding volumes several
papers on chemical subjects, and on spectroscopy.

Vol. v. contains a paper by Mr. Hoare, and several
by W. Andrews, on Irish fisheries; the latter author
also contributed papers on deep-sea soundings, the
ichthyology of the south and west coasts of Ireland,
and on the pines and other timber trees of New
Zealand. An account of a submarine earthquake is
given by Dr. J. M. Barry, and Dr. Oswald Heer
described the miocene flora of North Greenland; the
specimens described formed part of the collection presented to the Society by Captain Colomb and Sir
Leopold McClintock. Dr. Mapother's paper on
"Labourers' dwellings and the efforts made to improve them" is of considerable interest. The oft-
recurring subject of the manufacture of beet sugar
in Ireland is dealt with by Mr. Baruchson. A paper

by Mr. James Hayes, though in no sense scientific, is of great interest from an economic point of view ; it was read in 1870, and is entitled " Suggestions for the organization of co-operative farming associations in Ireland." The author points out the necessity for a better division of labour, especially in the manufacture of butter and other dairy products ; shows how well fitted these and other agricultural industries are for the application of co-operative methods ; and suggests a scheme for developing the principle. The contribution is entitled to a prominent place in the history of the co-operative movement in Ireland.

In vols. vi. and vii. there are very few scientific papers, containing actual contributions to knowledge, which have not been published elsewhere. It had become more and more the practice of authors to send contributions to scientific societies in London, or to the *Philosophical Magazine*, and thus to secure wider publicity in the scientific world. The principal papers of industrial and economic interest were contributed by Mr. J. R. Wigham, who wrote on the application of gas to lighthouse illumination ; by Mr. Hardman on coal-mining in the county of Tyrone, and by Mr. Andrews on the sea-coast fisheries of Ireland. The concluding volume of the series consists mainly of abstracts of lectures on public health, a subject of perennial interest. The *Journal* contains many very interesting reports and memoirs by Mr. David Moore, the curator of the Botanic Garden, by Dr. William Carte, the curator of the Natural History Museum, and by Mr. A. G. More and Mr. William F. Kerby, his assistants. Each of the volumes contains, in addition to the original communications above referred to, reports on various branches of the Society's work, and especially of the School of Art. There is appended to each volume a meteorological journal, which includes the barometric and thermometric readings, the rainfall and other meteorological records taken at the Society's Botanic Garden, Glasnevin, every day from January the 1st, 1856, to December the 31st, 1876. The Science and Art Museum Act of 1877 profoundly influenced the Society's scientific work.

It was fortunate that at this time the Council included men who had themselves been actively engaged in research, and who quite realised the manner in which the interests of science might best be promoted by such a complex body as the Royal Dublin Society. The new charter placed the Society in a better position for promoting science than it had previously occupied. For a few years after the passing of the Act the scientific work was carried on in two sections, one for physical and experimental science, and one for natural science. The second supplemental charter of 1888 gave each of the three branches of the Society's work, science, art, and agriculture, equal representation on the governing body, and the by-laws under this charter provided for three corresponding standing committees. There was thus a single committee dealing with science in all its branches.

In accordance with the agreement made with the Government, the cost of printing the Society's scientific publications was defrayed by the Government for five years from the date of the passing of the Act. Since that time the cost of printing has been borne by the Society's private funds, and the income arising out of the sum of £10,000, the first payment to the Society under the Act, has always been regarded as specially allocated to this branch of work.

The new series of scientific publications commenced in 1877, and consisted of *Scientific Transactions*, in *quarto*

2 A

form, and *Scientific Proceedings,* in *octavo.* In 1909 it was
decided to adopt an intermediate size of page as more
convenient, and since that date the Society has issued
but one scientific publication entitled the *Scientific
Proceedings of the Royal Dublin Society.* This is sent in
exchange to all the important scientific societies in the
world ; the number on the exchange list at present is
474, so that wide publicity is ensured for every paper
printed in the *Proceedings.* Papers of a purely economic
character are still published in *octavo* form in the *Economic
Proceedings of the Royal Dublin Society,* which is also
widely distributed in exchange for the publications of
other societies. These recent scientific publications
are easily accessible to those who desire to consult
them, so that it will be unnecessary to summarise
their contents here.

Votes in Aid of Research

Votes in aid of scientific research are of comparatively recent origin, though it had been the practice
for a long time to afford aid in experimental investigations, especially by providing apparatus for use in
the Society's own laboratories.

Since 1890 the following grants in aid of research
have been made by the Science Committee with the
sanction of the Council:—Dr. John Joly, on the
constant of gravitation, £20 ; Mr. H. H. Dixon, the
locomotion of anthropoda, £10 ; Mr. Calderwood,
investigation of fishes obtained in the survey of 1894,
£50 ; Professor Sollas, the bog slide in Kerry, £30 ;
and apparatus for anthropological investigations in
Borneo, £50 ; Professor Preston, research in the
magnetic field, £50 ; Professor C. J. Joly, solar
eclipse expedition, £170 ; Dr. Adeney, measurement
of spark spectra, £20 ; and on the streaming pheno-

mena of dissolved gases in water, £50; Mr. C. S. Wright, the radio-activity of Antarctic water, £15; the Clare Island Survey, under the auspices of the Royal Irish Academy, £100; Professor T. Johnson, the Kiltorcan fossils, £6, 15s.

In addition to the above, the Society granted a sum of £10 per annum for three years in aid of the publication of annual tables of constants and numerical data, chemical, physical, and technological, under the commission appointed by the seventh International Congress of Applied Chemistry.

SCIENCE TRAINING IN SCHOOLS

In 1899 the Committee of Science and its industrial applications submitted a report to the Council, in which they reviewed the condition of science teaching in the Irish Intermediate Schools, and pointed out that the position indicated a complete abandonment of science teaching in the near future. The report contains statistics, showing the total number of boys presented for examination in all subjects, contrasted with the number presented in science subjects. In 1887, for example, the total in all subjects was 4613, and of those 4113 presented themselves for examination in natural philosophy and chemistry. Ten years later the total number presenting themselves for examination had risen to 6661, while only 905 out of that number entered for examination in the science subjects referred to. It was pointed out that this great falling off took place, notwithstanding the fact that in the same period the amount paid to the owners of schools in the form of result fees had risen from £10,000 to upwards of £50,000 per annum. Owing to the almost complete absence of any attempt to teach science practically in the Dublin schools, the Society in 1890 introduced short systematic courses of lectures on science subjects, suitable for boys and girls. The lectures were still continued when the report was drawn up. The committee emphasised the necessity for practical work in science teaching, and it was stated that more especially to promote this kind of study, the Department of Science and Art gave grants in aid to schools which fulfilled the requirements of their inspectors. The report shows that the amount of these grants was diminishing at an alarming rate. In fact, it did not pay to teach science, and the committee urged that science should be made to rank equally with literary subjects in its power of earning result fees for the schools, and exhibitions and prizes for the pupils.

The Council sent the report to the Lord Lieutenant with a covering letter urging that " education, to be efficient and to fit the future men and women of the country for the discharge of their duties, must be practical, and deal more with things and less with words than it has done in the past. Science is the basis of such teaching, and it is certainly a singular fact that whilst science is every day receiving more attention in other countries, it is rapidly passing out of the curriculum of Irish intermediate schools."

The Society subsequently learned that shortly after the Science Committee had adopted their report, the Lord Lieutenant had appointed a commission " to inquire into the system of Intermediate Education in Ireland under the Act of 1878, its practical working, as to the desirability of reforms, and as to the necessity of further legislation." The Act of 1899, creating the Department of Agriculture and Technical Instruction, placed science teaching in Ireland in a much more favourable position than it had previously occupied, and the teaching of science and other practical subjects in Irish schools is no longer neglected.

Prior to the Act of 1899 there were only six secondary schools in Ireland with laboratories for the teaching of experimental science. In the financial year 1901–2, 154 schools possessed the necessary equipment ; these schools were giving practical instruction in science to 6615 pupils, and receiving grants in aid amounting to £7577. The latest return (1912–13) shows that the practical teaching of science was being carried on in 274 schools, with 12,772 pupils, receiving grants in aid amounting to £21,129.

THE BOYLE MEDAL

In June 1895 the Committee of Science and its industrial applications, on the suggestion of Professor D. J. Cunningham, F.R.S. (then one of the honorary secretaries), recommended the Council to institute two gold medals, " to be awarded from time to time with a view of encouraging worth in the different branches of science." The proposal eventually took the form of a single medal, to which the name of Robert Boyle was attached. The reasons which influenced the Society in selecting the name of Boyle cannot be better expressed than in the words of Professor John Joly, F.R.S., who had succeeded Professor Cunningham as secretary when the medal was first awarded. Speaking at the evening scientific meeting of March the 22nd, 1899, Professor Joly said :

" In former years it is on record that the Royal Dublin Society occasionally presented medals to men distinguished in science. But the Society never at any time possessed a medal specially instituted for the purpose—a medal dedicated to the memory of a great

Irishman and destined to mark the Society's appreciation of the scientific work of those happily still living
amongst us.   The awarding of such a medal is a recent
addition to the functions of this Society.   The value
of such an institution is unquestionable ; it is to the
Society a power of speech, a means of expressing her
measured opinion that the work of the recipient is
worthy of the highest honour.

"But not only is this old Society thus enabled to
speak her thoughts and to place them upon record,
but as the roll of the Boyle medallists lengthens with
the passage of time, will not this roll be an honourable
record for her ?   The greatest Irishmen will, as we
hope, have their names inscribed upon it, and be
numbered among those who have honoured her by
accepting her honours.

"It was not without due consideration that the
life-work of the Hon. Robert Boyle was chosen as
that which might be most fitly commemorated by this
medal.   That Boyle did more for science than any
other of the great Irishmen who have passed away is
not too much to maintain.   His name is not indeed
associated with any profound discovery ; the celebrated
law by which it is known to every educated man might
have been achieved by a lesser mind.   Boyle stands
before the world as the great pioneer in the application of the experimental method.   By its aid he shed
light on many dark places in science.   Many valuable
methods and facts have their origin in Boyle's labours.
His wide intellect made its influence felt over the
entire range of the science of the seventeenth century.

.   .   .   .   .   .

"Boyle first distinguished between a mixture and a
chemical compound.   He defined the elements, in
a manner strangely prophetic of the most modern

speculations of our own times, as all compounds of one universal matter, to the various modes of movement and grouping of which the constitution of the entire visible part of the universe was to be ascribed. He showed more clearly than his predecessors that air was necessary to combustion and respiration. He prepared phosphorus and hydrogen, although he failed to recognise the independent nature of the last. He first used vegetable colour tests for alkalinity and acidity, and introduced the use of chemical reagents into investigation. He believed heat to be a brisk molecular motion and not a material substance, thus forestalling in part ideas which only assumed full sway in this present century. He first suggested the freezing and boiling points of water as fixed points on the thermometer.

"Boyle also studied light (which he endeavoured to weigh), as well as sound (the propagation of which by the atmosphere he is said to have first demonstrated); also electricity, magnetism, and hydrostatics. He invented what is practically the modern air-pump, and by its aid made many new experiments. His discovery of the elastic law of gases in 1662, fourteen years before Mariotte confirmed it, is known to all, and doubtless inspired Hook to make his celebrated investigation into the elastic law of metals." . . . .

"The fitness of attaching Boyle's name to our medal resides not alone in his universality, but in the fact that he it was who chiefly introduced the scientific society into our civilisation. Lastly he was an Irishman. The Oxford Junior Scientific Club has celebrated him by founding Boyle Lectures. To these the greatest living thinkers have already contributed. If the Royal Society has omitted to commemorate him with a medal, it is fitting that we should make good the omission, and claim what is our own.

The medal was executed by Mr. Alan Wyon, the well-known medallist, and bears on the obverse a profile of Boyle taken from the bust in the possession of Trinity College, Dublin, with the following inscription, which the late Professor Tyrrell was good enough to supply :—*In Honorem Roberti Boyle et Augmentum Scientiarum. Felix qui potuit rerum cognoscere causas.* On the reverse is a modification of the figure of Minerva which was adopted as the seal of the Society, with the inscription :—*Regalis Societas Dublinensis condita, A.S. MDCCXXXI.*

The medal has been awarded four times, and on each occasion the report of the committee, setting forth the grounds upon which the award was made, was published in the Society's *Scientific Proceedings.*

Dr. George Johnstone Stoney, F.R.S., was selected in 1899 as the first recipient of the medal, in recognition of his many important contributions to science, especially in molecular physics and the kinetic theory of gases, and of his great personal influence on scientific advance in Ireland.

A year later the medal was awarded to Professor Thomas Preston, F.R.S., chiefly for the important advances he had made in our knowledge of the phenomena of radiation in a magnetic field, and the publication of his well-known text-books, *The Theory of Light, The Theory of Heat,* and *Spherical Trigonometry.*

In 1911, Professor John Joly, F.R.S., was selected as the third recipient of the medal. In their report recommending the award, the committee "direct attention to the wide range of subjects covered by Dr. Joly's researches, as well as the general excellence of his work. His researches deal with various branches of physics, geology, mineralogy, botany, and biological theory ; and in several of these widely different subjects

THE BOYLE MEDAL

(*Designed by Alan Wyon*)

he has enriched our laboratories with accurate instruments of research." The list of Dr. Joly's contributions to science appended to the report extends, between 1883 and 1910, to eighty-one publications, many of which appeared in the Society's *Transactions* and *Proceedings*.

The most recent occasion on which the medal was awarded was in 1912, when it was conferred on Sir Howard Grubb, F.R.S. His contributions to the scientific publications of the Society covered a period of forty-two years. Most of these took the form of communications on improvements in the construction and mounting of telescopes and other optical instruments. It was, however, more especially for the skill and ingenuity exercised in the actual construction of the instruments that Sir Howard Grubb's name was selected. His achievements include the great Melbourne telescope, the first large reflector mounted equatorially ; the Vienna refractor, then the largest refractor in existence ; the Greenwich refractor, and many other optical instruments, including a new form of gun-sight, and the submarine periscope.

RADIUM INSTITUTE

At the suggestion of Professor John Joly, F.R.S., in February, 1914, the Science Committee recommended the Council to establish a Radium Institute, and to contribute a sum of £1000 towards a fund for the purchase of radium, in addition to the sixty milligrammes of radium bromide which the Society had purchased ten years ago. This the Council agreed to do. To carry out the object in view, a large sum of money was required, and Lord Iveagh at once undertook to contribute £1000, Sir John Purser

Griffith very generously subscribing another £1000. Other subscriptions were received in response to an appeal made to the members, and in a short time the Radium Committee was in a position to conclude a contract for 200 milligrammes of radium bromide, which has since been delivered to the Society. In the meantime the small quantity in the Society's possession has been in constant use. The emanation it produces is pumped off at certain intervals, in the Society's laboratory, purified by means of liquid air, and transferred to minute glass tubes which are handed over to the surgeon for therapeutic use. Already new methods in the manipulation and application of the emanation have been devised, and the results obtained in its therapeutic application are most encouraging. Though the quantity of radium in the Society's possession is still very small, it will admit of a more extended use of this remarkable substance, which has proved to be one of the most potent agents that science has placed in the hands of man for the relief of human suffering.

APPENDIX I

THE SOCIETY'S OFFICIALS
1731–1914

Presidents

Lionel, Duke of Dorset	1731–1737
William, Duke of Devonshire	1737–1745
Philip, Earl of Chesterfield	1745–1746
William, Earl of Harrington . . . ·	1746–1751
Lionel, Duke of Dorset	1751–1755
William, Marquis of Hartington, afterwards Duke of Devonshire	1755–1757
John, Duke of Bedford	1757–1761
George, Earl of Halifax	1761–1763
Hugh, Earl of Northumberland . . .	1763–1765
Francis, Earl of Hertford	1765–1766
George William, Earl of Bristol . . .	1766–1767
George, Viscount Townshend	1767–1772
Simon, Earl Harcourt	1772–1777
John, Earl of Buckinghamshire . . .	1777–1780
Frederick, Earl of Carlisle	1780–1782
George, Earl Temple	1782–1783
Robert, Earl of Northington	1783–1784
Charles, Duke of Rutland	1784–1787
George, Marquis of Buckingham . · .	1787–1789
John, Earl of Westmoreland	1790–1795
John, Earl Camden	1795–1798
Charles, Marquis Cornwallis	1798–1801
Philip, Earl of Hardwicke	1801–1806
John, Duke of Bedford	1806–1807
Charles, Duke of Richmond	1807–1813
Charles, Viscount, afterwards Earl Whitworth .	1813–1817
Charles, Earl Talbot	1817–1821

Richard, Marquis Wellesley	1822–1828
Henry William, Marquis of Anglesey . .	1828–1829
Hugh, Duke of Northumberland . . .	1829–1830
Henry William, Marquis of Anglesey . .	1831–1833
Richard, Marquis Wellesley	1833–1835
Constantine, Earl of Mulgrave, afterwards Marquis of Normanby	1835–1839
Hugh, Viscount Ebrington	1839–1841
Thomas P., Earl de Grey.	1841–1844
William, Lord Heytesbury	1844–1846
John, Earl of Bessborough	1846–1847
George, Earl of Clarendon	1847–1852
Archibald William, Earl of Eglinton and Winton (February–December)	1852
Edward, Earl of St. Germans	1853–1855
George W. F., Earl of Carlisle	1855–1858
Archibald William, Earl of Eglinton and Winton	1858–1859
George W. F., Earl of Carlisle. . . .	1859–1864
John, Lord Wodehouse, afterwards Earl of Kimberley	1864–1866
James, Marquis, afterwards Duke of Abercorn .	1866–1868
John Poyntz, Earl Spencer	1868–1874
Charles William, Duke of Leinster . . .	1874–1887
Laurence, Earl of Rosse	1887–1892
Mervyn, Viscount Powerscourt . . .	1892–1897
Arthur Edward, Baron Ardilaun . . .	1897–1913
Thomas Kane, Baron Rathdonnell . . .	1913

Vice-Presidents.

Hugh Boulter, Primate	1731–1742
John Hoadley, Primate	1742–1747
George Stone, Primate	1747–1765
Charles Cobbe, Archbishop of Dublin . .	*1750–1765
James, Earl of Kildare, afterwards Duke of Leinster	*1750–1773
John, Earl of Grandison	*1750–1766
Humphrey, Viscount Lanesborough . . .	*1750–1768
Sir Arthur Gore, afterwards Earl of Arran .	*1750–1773
Sir Thomas Taylor, Bart., M.P. . . .	*1750–1757

* Probably elected before 1750, but the minutes between 1746–1750 are not now extant.

Robert Clayton, Bishop of Clogher . . . 1757–1758
Redmond Morres, M.P. 1758–1776
William Bury 1758–1772
Rt. Hon. John Ponsonby, Speaker H.C. . . 1764–1787
Sir Robert Deane, Bart. 1764–1770
Isaac Mann, Archdeacon of Dublin . . . 1764–1767
Richard Robinson, afterwards Baron Rokeby,
    Primate 1765–1794
Thomas Le Hunte 1765–1773
Theophilus Brocas, Dean of Killala . . . 1767–1770
John Leigh 1770–1803
Sydenham Singleton 1772–1783
Richard Woodward, Dean of Clogher . . 1773–1782
William, Duke of Leinster 1774–1804
Anthony, Earl of Meath 1774–1775
Rt. Hon. John Foster, Speaker H.C., afterwards
    Lord Oriel 1775–1828
Lodge Morres, afterwards Viscount Frankfort de
    Montmorency 1776–1822
Morgan Crofton 1783–1801
John Wallis 1783–1792
Edmond Sexten Pery, afterwards Viscount Pery 1785–1799
Thomas Burgh 1792–1810
General Charles Vallancey 1799–1812
Rt. Hon. David La Touche 1801–1817
Charles William, Earl of Charleville . . . 1803–1822
Charles Agar, Archbishop of Dublin, afterwards
    Earl of Normanton 1804–1809
Rev. Dr. George Hall, provost of T.C.D., after-
    wards Bishop of Dromore 1809–1811
Rev. Dr. Thomas Smyth 1810–1813
John Chambré, Earl of Meath 1812–1836
Robert Shaw, afterwards Sir Robert Shaw, Bart. 1812–1849
John Leslie Foster, M.P., Baron of the Exchequer 1813–1842
Peter Digges La Touche 1816–1820
Rt. Hon. George Knox 1820–1827
The Rev. the Hon. John Pomeroy, afterwards
    Viscount Harberton 1822–1833
Henry Joy, Chief Baron of the Exchequer . 1822–1838
John Henry North, M.P. 1827–1831

John Boyd 1828–
Arthur, Marquis of Downshire 1831–
James L. Naper, D.L. 1833–
Jos. D. Jackson, serjeant at law, afterwards Justice
   of the Common Pleas 1836–
Henry Kemmis, Q.C., Assistant Barrister . . 1836–
Sir William Betham, Ulster King of Arms . 1838–
William Thomas, Earl of Clancarty . . . 1842–
John, Marquis of Ormonde, K.P. . . . 1843–
Charles William, Marquis of Kildare, afterwards
   Duke of Leinster 1845–
George A. Hamilton, M.P. 1847–
Isaac Weld 1849–
James, Lord Talbot de Malahide . . . 1853–
Rt. Hon. Francis Blackburne, lord chancellor . 1856–
Lundy Edward Foot 1857–
Rev. Humphrey Lloyd, D.D., provost T.C.D. . 1868–
Hon. George Handcock 1863–
Sir Richard Griffith, Bart. 1868–
Robert, Lord Clonbrock 1868–
George Woods Maunsell, D.L. 1871–
Sir George Hodson, Bart. 1872–
John Francis Waller, LL.D. 1874–
Laurence, Earl of Rosse, K.P., F.R.S. . . . 1878–
George Johnstone Stoney, D.SC. F.R.S., . . 1881–
Mervyn, Viscount Powerscourt . . . 1883–
George A. Rochfort Boyd, D.L. . . . 188
Arthur Edward, Baron Ardilaun, D.L. . . 1887–
George Stephens, Viscount Gough, D.L. . . 1887–
James L. Naper, D.L. 1887–
Charles Kelly, Q.C. (County Court Judge) . . 1887–
Charles Uniacke Townshend 1893–
Sir Howard Grubb, F.R.S. 189
James, Duke of Abercorn, K.G. . . . 1893–
Rt. Hon. William H. Ford Cogan, D.L. . . 1891–
Samuel Ussher Roberts 1894–
Sir Thomas Pierce Butler, Bart. . . . 1894–
Charles Stewart, Marquis of Londonderry, K.G. . 189
Professor D. J. Cunningham, F.R.S. . . . 1897–
John E. H., Baron de Robeck, D.L. . . . 1898–

Hon. Mr. Justice Walter Boyd . . .	1900
Thomas Kane, Baron Rathdonnell . . .	1902–1913
Charles Owen, The O'Conor Don, H.M.L. .	1904–1906
Edward Cecil, Viscount Iveagh, K.P. .	1905
Sir James Creed Meredith, LL.D. . .	1906–1912
Sir Charles A. Cameron, C.B., M.D. . . .	1906
Rt. Hon. Frederick Wrench	1907
Captain J. Lewis Riall, D.L.	1909
Professor John Joly, D.SC., F.R.S. . . .	1912
Anthony Ashley, Earl of Shaftesbury . .	1913
Charles Mervyn Doyne, D.L.	1914

Honorary Secretaries

William Stephens, M.D.	1731–1736
Thomas Prior	1731–1751
Rev. Dr. Whitcombe	1732–1733
Rev. Gabriel Maturin	1736–
Rev. Dr. John Wynne	1750–1758
William Maple	1751–1762
John FitzPatrick	1764–1765
Colombine Lee Carré	1764–1771
Thomas St. George	1765–1771
Holt Waring	1771–1785
Michael Dally	1772–1784
Abraham Wilkinson	1783–1803
Richard Vincent	1784–1789
Thomas Burgh	1788–1792
Thomas Braughall	1792–1798
Arthur McGwire	1798–1808
Rev. Thomas Smyth	1803–1810
John Leslie Foster	1808–1813
Jeremiah D'Olier	1810–1817
Henry Joy	1813–1822
John Boyd	1817–1828
John Beatty, M.D.	1822–1831
Isaac Weld	1828–1849
C. Stewart Hawthorne	1831–1834
Robert Butler Bryan	1834–1841
Lundy Edward Foot	1841–1857
Robert Harrison, M.D.	1849–1858

John Francis Waller, LL.D.	1855–1861
Hon. George Handcock	1858–1861
Richard, Lord Dunlo, afterwards Earl of Clancarty	1861–1866
George Woods Maunsell, D.L.	1861–1871
Laurence Waldron, D.L.	1867–1875
George Johnstone Stoney, F.R.S.	1871–1881
Charles Kelly, Q.C. (County Court Judge)	1875–1887
George F. FitzGerald, F.T.C.D.	1881–1889
Charles Uniacke Townshend	1887–1893
Sir Howard Grubb, F.R.S.	1889–1893
Hon. Mr. Justice Walter Boyd	1893–1900
Professor Daniel J. Cunningham, F.R.S.	1894–1897
Professor John Joly, D.SC., F.R.S.	1897–1909
Robert Romney Kane (County Court Judge)	1900–1901
Thomas Cooke Trench	1901–1903
Captain J. Lewis Riall, D.L.	1903–1909
Richard G. Carden, D.L.	1909
Sir Joseph McGrath	1909

Assistant Secretaries

Rev. Dr. Peter Chaigneau	1762–1774
Rev. Dr. Thomas Lyster	1774–1808
Bucknall McCarthy	1808–1829
Edward Hardman	1829–1850
William Vicars Griffith	1850–1852
William Edward Steele, M.B.	1852–1877

(In 1878, Dr. Steele was transferred to the Science and Art Department.)

Registrars

William Maple	1731–1762
Patrick Brien	1765–1798
Rev. Dr. Peter Chaigneau,	1798–1808
Thomas Lysaght	1808–1819
Captain P. Theodore Wilson	1819–1853
Henry Connor White	1853–1877

(In 1878, Mr. White was transferred to the Science and Art Department.)

Registrar of the Royal Dublin Society

Richard Jackson Moss, F.I.C., F.C.S.	1878

Treasurers

Anthony Sheppard, jun., M.P.	1731–1737
Robert Ross	1737–1743
Robert Downes	1743–1754
John Putland	1754–1772
Thomas St. George	1772–1785
Sir William Gleadowe Newcomen, bart. . .	1785–1807
Sir Thomas Gleadowe Newcomen, bart. . .	1807–1814

(From 1814, the Bank of Ireland has acted as
Treasurer to the Society.)

APPENDIX II

(See p. 68-9.)

PREMIUMS OFFERED BY THE DUBLIN SOCIETY IN THE YEAR 1766

THE following premiums were published in the Society's last list of premiums, and are now repeated as they are hereafter to be adjudged.

Bog	£	s.	d.	To be adjudged
For effectually reclaiming the greatest quantity of bog (not less than 60 acres) so that in the year 1766 it shall be under tillage, a gold medal		...		1767 Jan. 15th
To the renter of land who shall reclaim effectually the greatest quantity of bog (not less than 30 acres) so that in the year 1766 it shall be under tillage	50	0	0	„ 15th
For the next greatest quantity, not less than 25 acres	35	0	0	„ 15th
For the next greatest quantity, not less than 20 acres	25	0	0	„ 15th
For the next greatest quantity, not less than 15 acres	18	0	0	„ 15th
For the next greatest quantity, not less than 10 acres	12	0	0	„ 15th

Every claimant is to lay before the Society the nature of the bottom of his bog, and the several methods he shall have taken to reclaim it.

MOUNTAIN

To the renter of land who shall bring in, improve and effectually manure, to

	£	s.	d.	To be adjudged
the satisfaction of the Society, the greatest quantity (not less than 15 acres) of dry mountain, so that in the year 1766 it shall be under tillage .	22	10	0	1767 Jan. 15th
For the next quantity, not less than 10 acres	15	0	0	,, 15th
For the next quantity, not less than 5 acres	7	10	0	,, 15th

The above premiums for reclaiming dry mountain are offered for each of the provinces respectively.

WHEAT

To the person who shall sow the greatest quantity of land (not less than 10 acres) with wheat in the year 1766, and before the 12th of October, the seed to be covered with the harrow .	20	0	0	1766 Oct. 23rd
To the person who shall in the year 1767 reap the greatest quantity of wheat by the acre from no less than 10 acres of land, and from the smallest quantity of seed	20	0	0	1768 May 5th

The above premiums for the encouragement of the culture of wheat are offered for each of the provinces respectively.

To the renter of land who shall sow the greatest quantity of land (not less than 10 acres) with wheat in the year 1766, and before the first day of October	50	0	0	1766 Oct. 23rd

Every claimant must give the Society an account of the nature of his soil, the number of ploughings given, and the manner of manuring and sowing.

PARSNIPS

To the renter of land who shall sow the greatest quantity of land (not less than two acres) with parsnips, to be made use of only in feeding cattle,

	£	s.	d.	To be adjudged 1766
giving an account of the soil, culture, produce, and their effect on cattle fed with them	10	o	o	Oct. 30th
For the second quantity, not less than one acre	5	o	o	,, 30th

TURNIPS

To the renter of land, not already encouraged, who shall in the year 1766, sow the greatest quantity of land (not less than five acres) with turnips	10	o	o	,, 30th
For the second quantity, not less than four acres	7	o	o	,, 30th
For sowing the greatest quantity of land (not less than two acres) with turnips in drills, horse-hoeing the intervals	6	o	o	,, 30th
For the next quantity, not less than one acre	3	o	o	,, 30th

These premiums to encourage the culture of turnips are offered for each of the provinces respectively.

BURNET

For sowing or planting the greatest quantity of land (not less than three acres) with burnet, giving an account of the soil, culture, produce, and its effect on cattle fed with it . . .	12	o	o	Nov. 20th
For the next quantity, not less than two acres	8	o	o	,, 20th
For the next quantity, not less than one acre	4	o	o	,, 20th

LUCERN

For sowing or planting the greatest quantity of land (not less than one acre) with Lucern, giving an account of the soil, culture, produce, and its effect on cattle fed with it . . .	5	o	o	1766 Nov. 20th

CLOVER SEED

To the person not already encouraged who shall in the year 1766 save the greatest quantity (not less than 12 cwt.) of clean and sound clover seed, the growth of land of his own holding . . . . . . 15 0 0 Jan. 29th

For the next quantity, not less than 8 cwt. . . . . 7 0 0 ,, 29th

For the next quantity, not less than 4 cwt. . . . . . . 5 0 0 ,, 29th

£ s. d. To be adjudged 1767

WHITE CLOVER SEED

To the person not already encouraged who shall in the year 1766, save the greatest quantity (not less than 2 cwt.) of clean and sound white or Dutch clover seed, the growth of land of his own holding . . . 10 0 0 ,, 29th

For the next quantity, not less than 1 cwt. . . . . . . 5 0 0 ,, 29th

TREFOYLE SEED

To the person not already encouraged who shall in the year 1766, save the greatest quantity (not less than 10 cwt.) of clean and sound Trefoyle seed, cleared of the hull, and the growth of land of his own holding. 10 0 0 Feb. 5th

For the next quantity not less than 5 cwt. . . . . . . 5 0 0 ,, 5th

ST. FOIN SEED

To the person who shall save in the year 1766, the greatest quantity (not less than three barrels) of clean and sound St. Foin seed, the growth of land of his own holding . . . 10 0 0 ,, 5th

HOPS

For producing in the year 1767, the greatest quantity (not less than 8 cwt.) of good merchantable Hops of the growth of that year, a sample of 1 cwt. to be produced to the Society . 50 0 0 Nov. 12th

LIQUORICE

		£	s.	d.	To be adjudged
For raising in the year 1766, the greatest quantity (not less than 12 cwt.) of Liquorice		12	0	0	1761 Feb. 5th
For the next quantity, not less than 8 cwt.		8	0	0	,, 5th
For the next quantity, not less than 4 cwt.		5	0	0	,, 5th

MUSTARD

To the person who shall produce the best and greatest quantity (not less than 10 barrels) of Red Mustard seed		8	0	0	1766 Nov. 27th
For the second quantity, not less than 4 barrels		4	0	0	,, 27th

MILLET

To the person who shall raise the greatest quantity (not less than 1 cwt.) of Millet		10	0	0	,, 27th

RAPE SEED

For raising and saving the greatest quantity of Rape seed from boggy, rushy, or mountainous ground, not less than 20 acres cultivated for this purpose, shall entitle any claimant to the first premium of		34	2	6	[1767] Jan. 22nd
For the second quantity, not less than 15 acres		22	15	0	,, 22nd
For the next quantity, not less than 10 acres		17	1	3	,, 22nd

An account of the methods taken to cultivate the ground and to raise the Rape to be laid before the Society.

WELD

To the person not already encouraged, who shall cultivate and save the greatest quantity of weld or bonymoore, not less than 10 cwt. . .		6	0	0	1766 Nov. 20th
For the next quantity, not less than 5 cwt.		4	0	0	,, 20th

WOAD

	£	s.	d.	To be adjudged
To the renter of land, not already encouraged, who shall grow and prepare for the dyer, the greatest quantity of woad, not less than 1 cwt. . .	6	0	0	1766 Nov. 20th
For the next quantity, not less than 70 lbs. weight	4	0	0	,, 20th

HONEY AND WAX

	£	s.	d.	
To the person who shall have the greatest quantity of honey and wax, not less than 6 cwt., including the hive and bees	30	0	0	Oct. 9th
For the next quantity, not less than 5 cwt.	25	0	0	,, 9th
For the next quantity, not less than 4 cwt.	20	0	0	,, 9th
For the next quantity, not less than 3 cwt.	15	0	0	,, 9th
For the next quantity, not less than 2 cwt.	10	0	0	,, 9th

The hives are to be weighed in the gross, the bees being alive (which is known by experience not in the least to prejudice them) in the presence of the minister or curate of the parish, or any Justice of Peace in the neighbourhood, or any other person of a reputable character, known to a member of the Society, and by a person appointed by the proprietor of the bees.

A certificate of such weight and the number of hives must be signed by such minister, or curate, or Justice of Peace, or reputable person.

The person weighing the hives is to make an affidavit of their number and gross weight, that they are of the usual size and thickness, and that to the best of his knowledge, no fraud has been practised to increase their weight.

The proprietor of the bees is also

to make an affidavit that the number
of old hives, so weighed, attested, and
certified, have been all his property
for six months before, that all the new
hives so weighed, attested, and certified, are swarms from the old hives,
and that to the best of his knowledge,
none of those hives were above six
Irish miles from his dwelling-house
when weighed and certified, or for six
months before.

These certificates and affidavits are
to be produced by the claimants of
the premiums, as the condition upon
which only they can receive them.

N.B.—The weighing of bees is by
no means difficult; it is to be done
after sunset, in the following manner:
a linen cloth is slipped between the
hive and the stool, and knotted at the
top of the hive, which is then lifted
up by the knot, and put into the scale;
after weighing the hive is again put on
the stool, and the cloth slipped from
under it.

It is found by experience that bees
will thrive at least as well in boxes as
in hives, and it is recommended that
they be as well made use of as hives.

Whereas the usual method of obtaining honey from stocks of bees, is
by destroying the bees; and whereas,
it is found by experience that the honey
may be obtained, and the bees preserved at the same time, by which large
quantities of both honey and wax are
collected, the Society will therefore
give—

To the person who shall collect the
greatest quantity of honey or wax from
stocks of bees of his own property
within the year 1766, without destroy-

	£	s.	d.	To be adjudged 1766
ing the bees, and shall leave a sufficient quantity of honey for their winter sustenance	10	0	0	Oct. 9th
For the next quantity . . .	7	0	0	,, 9th

FOOD FOR BEES

    To the person who shall invent the best and cheapest food for bees in the winter season, without sugar or honey   5   0   0   ,, 9th

BEE HIVES

    To the person who shall make the best and greatest number of bee hives, not less than 80   3   0   0   ,, 9th

    For the second number, not less than 40   2   0   0   ,, 9th

    The premiums for bee hives are promised for each of the provinces respectively.

EMPLOYING CHILDREN

    To the person (not already encouraged by any other Society) who shall have employed from the first day of September 1765 to the first day of September 1766, in any manufacture, the greatest number of children (not less than 40, and not exceeding the age of 13 years) with a particular account of their work, upon the affidavit of the person employing them, and the certificate of two neighbouring Justices of the Peace, and the minister or curate of the parish, if in the country; and in towns, of the clergyman and principal residing magistrate . .   12   0   0   ,, 9th

    For employing the next greatest number, not less than 30 . . .   8   0   0   ,, 9th

TANNING

    The sum of £100 will be given in premiums, at the rate of five shillings for every Irish hide or skin which shall

	£	s.	d.	To be adjudged
be completely tanned with bog myrtle only, provided the number of hides or skins so tanned shall not exceed 400, and if it should, then the said sum of £100 shall be distributed in proportion to the number of such hides or skins	100	0	0	1766 Nov. 6th
The sum of £50 will be given in premiums at the rate of five shillings for every Irish hide or skin which shall be completely tanned with oak dust only, provided the number of hides or skins so tanned shall not exceed 200, and if it should, then the sum of £50 shall be distributed in proportion to the number of such hides or skins	50	0	0	1766 Nov. 6th
SALTPETRE				
To the person who shall produce the greatest quantity (not less than 10 lbs.) of saltpetre made and prepared in this kingdom . . .	10	0	0	1767 Jan. 22nd
For the second quantity, not less than 5 lbs.	5	0	0	,, 22nd
TURBOT FISHERY				
To the person who shall promote and establish a Turbot fishery on any of the coasts of this kingdom, so that there shall be sold from said fishery in the year 1766, 2000 at the least of well-cured merchantable turbot . .	30	0	0	Mar. 12th
STOCK FISHERY				
To the person who shall promote and establish a Stock fishery on any of the coasts of this kingdom, so that there be sold from said fishery, in the year 1766, 10 cwt. at least of well-cured merchantable stock fish . .	20	0	0	,, 12th
FLOUNDER FISHERY				
To the person who shall promote and establish a Flounder fishery on				

any of the coasts of this kingdom, so
as there shall be sold from said fishery
in the year 1766 5 cwt. at least of
well-cured merchantable flounders   .   11   7   6   Mar. 12th

Note.—That the curing of flounders
must be after the Dutch method, by
very little salt, and the fish dried in
the air in the summer.

£ *s.*   *d.* To be adjudged

1767

COD AND HEAK FISHERY

To the person who shall promote
and establish a Cod and Heak fishery
on any of the coasts of this kingdom,
so as there shall be sold from said
fishery in the year 1766 10 cwt., at
the least, of well-cured merchantable
cod or heak   .   .   .   .   .   22 15 0   ,,   12th

LING OR HADDOCK FISHERY

To the person who shall promote
and establish a Ling or Haddock
fishery, on any of the coasts of this
kingdom, so as there shall be sold from
said fishery in the year 1766 10 cwt.,
at least, of well-cured merchantable
ling or haddock   .   .   .   .   22 15 0   ,,   12th

HERRINGS

To the owner of any fishing-boat
or wherry, not less than 26 feet in the
keel, who shall in the year 1766, between the 1st day of May and the
1st day of September, on the east
coast of this kingdom, between the
Lough of Carlingford and the Hill of
Howth, with such boat in any one
night, first take any quantity of herrings not less than three mease, which
shall be sold fresh and sound in
Dublin market   11   7   6   Oct. 16th

[1766]

To the owner of any fishing-boat
or wherry not less than 26 feet in the
keel, who shall in the year 1766,

	£	s.	d.	To be adjudged

between the first day of May and the first day of September, on the east coast of this kingdom, between the Hill of Howth and the Head of Wicklow, with such boat, in any one night, first take any quantity of herrings, not less than three mease, which shall be sold fresh and sound in Dublin market . . . . 11 7 6 — 1766 Oct. 16th

To the owner of any fishing-boat or wherry to be built hereafter not less than 26 feet in the keel, who shall in the year 1766, between the first day of May and the 1st of September, on the east coast of this kingdom, between the Lough of Carlingford and the Hill of Howth, with such boat in any one night, first take any quantity of herrings not less than three mease, which shall be sold fresh and sound in Dublin market . . . . . . 11 7 6 „ 16th

To the owner of any fishing-boat or wherry to be built hereafter, not less than 26 feet in the keel, who shall in the year 1766, between the 1st day of May and the 1st day of September, on the east coast of this kingdom, between the Hill of Howth and the Head of Wicklow, with such boat, in any one night, first take any quantity of herrings not less than three mease, to be sold fresh and sound in Dublin market 11 7 6 „ 16th

NATURAL HISTORY

To the person who shall, any time within five years, produce a Natural History (such as will be approved of by the Society) of any County in this kingdom ; for each of the provinces respectively 50 0 0

WRITING ON HUSBANDRY

To any practising farmer who shall write a farmer's monthly Kalendar,

after the manner of Miller's Gardener's Kalendar, setting forth what is to be done each month in relating to tillage, pasture, and meadow grounds . .	£	s.	d. To be adjudged 1766
	22	15	o Oct. 23rd

August 7th, 1766

PREMIUMS OFFERED THIS YEAR FOR AGRICULTURE, PLANTING, &c.

BOG

For effectually reclaiming the greatest quantity of Bog (not less than 30 acres), so that in the year 1767 it shall be in tillage or meadow .   .   .   . 50 0 0 Jan. 14th

For the next quantity, not less than 25 acres .   .   .   .   .   . 35 0 0 ,, 14th

For the next quantity, not less than 20 acres .   .   .   .   .   . 25 0 0 ,, 14th

For the next quantity, not less than 15 acres .   .   .   .   .   . 18 0 0 ,, 14th

For the next quantity, not less than 10 acres .   .   .   .   .   . 12 0 0 ,, 14th

Every claimant is to lay before the Society the quality of the bog before reclaiming, the several methods he shall have taken to reclaim the same, and the depth and breadth of the drains he shall have made. No person shall be entitled to any of the above premiums, unless the depth of the bog before reclaiming shall have been at least four feet from the surface to the bottom of the bog, nor shall any person receive more than one premium for the same ground ; everything else alike, renters of land shall have the pre-ference.

The above premiums for reclaiming bog were first published in July 1765, and it was then notified that they would be continued for five years from ·

that time, so that they will be given for reclaimed bog which shall be in tillage or meadow in the year 1768, 1769, or 1770.

For every renter of land, not holding above 20 acres, who shall effectually reclaim one acre of red unprofitable bog, so that in the year 1769 it shall be under tillage or meadow, the Society will give a premium of Fifty shillings. The sum of Fifty pounds will be appropriated in these premiums to each province, and if more than 20 claimants, entitled to the said premium, should appear for any one province, then the sum of £50 will be divided among such claimants   .   .   . 200 0 0

£   *s.*   *d.* To be adjudged

1769
Dec. 7th

The like premiums will be continued for bog which shall be brought into meadow or tillage in the year 1770.

For making the greatest number of perches in drains through unprofitable bog (not less than 4000 perches), to be at least 5 ft. wide and 3 ft. deep   . 16 0 0 Nov. 19th

1767

For the next number, not less than 3000   .   .   .   .   .   . 12 ·0 0   ,,   19th

For the next number, not less than 2000   .   .   .   .   .   . 8 0 0   ,,   19th

For the next number, not less than 1000   .   .   .   .   .   . 4 0 0   ,,   19th

The like premiums for cutting such drains through unprofitable bog, will be continued for another year, and adjudged in November 1768.

MOUNTAIN

To the person or persons who shall bring in, improve, and effectually manure, to the satisfaction of the Society, the greatest quantity of dry mountain (not less than 15 acres), so that in the year 1768 it shall be in tillage   .   .   .   .   .   . 22 10 0 Jan. 14th

1768

For the next quantity, not less than 10 acres . . . . . . £15 0 0 To be adjudged Jan. 14th

For the next quantity, not less than 5 acres . . . . . . 7 10 0 „ 14th

Every claimant must lay before the Society the nature of his mountain land before reclaiming, and the several methods he shall have taken to reclaim it.

The like premiums will be continued for mountain land which shall be effectually reclaimed and in tillage in the year 1769 or 1770.

WHEAT

To the person who shall, in the year 1767, reap the greatest quantity of wheat by the acre, and from no less than 10 acres of ground, to be sown before the 1st of November 1766, with no more than 12 stone of seed to the acre, half of the seed to be sown and covered with the plough, and then the other half to be sown on the same ground and covered with the harrow 15 0 0 April 7th

To the person who shall, in the year 1767, reap the greatest quantity of wheat by the acre, and from no less than 5 acres of ground, to be sown before the first of November 1766, with no more than 12 stone of seed to the acre, half of the seed to be sown and covered with the plough, and then the other half to be sown on the same ground and covered with the harrow. 7 10 0 „ 7th

To the person who shall, in the year 1767, reap the greatest quantity of wheat by the acre, from no less than 10 acres of ground sown with 10 stone of seed, and no more, to the acre, and which shall be covered only with the harrow . . . . . . 15 0 0 „ 7th

To the person who shall reap the

greatest quantity of wheat from the same ground for three years successively, beginning in the year 1767, the ground to be sown in drills, horsehoeing the intervals, and no less than one acre 30 0 0

£ s. d.   To be adjudged

1769
Dec. 14th

No person shall be entitled to any of the above premiums for the culture of wheat, who shall not, on or before the first day of January 1767, by letter to the Society's Assistant Secretary to inform him that he intends to be a claimant of one or more of the premiums offered, and also of the manner in which he shall have prepared his ground.

To the renter of land who in the year 1767 shall sow the greatest quantity of land with wheat (not less than 10 acres) and before the 1st of October 5 0 0   Oct. 22nd

For the next quantity, not less than 8 acres . . . . . . 4 0 0   ,, 22nd

For the next quantity, not less than 6 acres . . . . . . 3 0 0   ,, 22nd

TURNIPS

For sowing in the year 1767 the greatest quantity of land (not less than two acres) with turnips in drills, horsehoeing the intervals . . . . 6 0 0   ,, 29th

For the next quantity, not less than one acre . . . . . . 3 0 0   ,, 29th

An account of the soil and produce to be laid before the Society.

PARSNIPS

For sowing in the year 1767 the greatest quantity of land (not less than two acres) with parsnips, to be made use of only in feeding cattle or swine, giving an account of the soil, culture, produce, and their effect on cattle fed with them 10 0 0

1768
Feb. 25th

For the next quantity, not less than one acre . . . . . . £ 5 s. 0 d. 0 — To be adjudged Feb. 25th

It has been found by experience that swine will thrive remarkably well by being fed upon parsnips.

CARROTS

For sowing in the year 1767 the greatest quantity of land (not less than two acres) with carrots, to be made use of only in feeding cattle, giving an account of the soil, culture, produce, and their effect on cattle fed with them 10 0 0 ,, 25th

For the next quantity, not less than one acre . . . . . . 5 0 0 ,, 25th

See a pamphlet lately published by the Society in London on the culture of carrots and their use in feeding cattle.

BURNET

For sowing or planting in the year 1767 the greatest quantity of land (not less than 3 acres) with Burnet, giving an account of the soil, culture, produce, and its effect on cattle fed with it 15 0 0 ,, 25th

For the next quantity, not less than two acres . . . . . . 10 0 0 ,, 25th

For the next quantity, not less than one acre . . . . . . 5 0 0 ,, 25th

LUCERNE

For sowing or planting in the year 1767 the greatest quantity of land (not less than one acre) with Lucerne, giving an account of the soil, culture, produce, and its effects on cattle fed with it . . . . . . 5 0 0 — 1767 Nov. 5th

The like premium will be given for sowing parsnips, carrots, burnet and lucerne in the year 1768.

CLOVER SEED

To the person not already encouraged who shall in the year 1767 save

2 C

the greatest quantity (not less than 12 cwt.) of clean and sound clover seed, the growth of land of his own holding

For the next quantity, not less than 8 cwt.

For the next quantity, not less than 4 cwt.

	£	s.	d.	To be adjudged 1768
the growth of land of his own holding	15	0	0	Feb. 18th
8 cwt.	7	0	0	,, 18th
4 cwt.	5	0	0	,, 18th

WHITE CLOVER SEED

To the person, not already encouraged, who shall in the year 1767, save the greatest quantity (not less than 2 cwt.) of clean and sound white or Dutch clover seed, the growth of land of his own holding . . . . 10 0 0 ,, 18th

For the next quantity, not less than 1 cwt. . . . . . . 5 0 0 ,, 18th

TREFOYL SEED

To the person, not already encouraged, who shall in the year 1767, save the greatest quantity (not less than 10 cwt.) of clean and sound Trefoyle seed, the growth of land of his own holding 10 0 0 ,, 18th

For the next quantity, not less than 5 cwt. . . . . . . 5 0 0 ,, 18th

The samples of Trefoyle seed produced must be cleared of the hull.

The like premiums will be given for saving the aforesaid grass seeds in the year 1768.

HOPS

For producing in the year 1768 the greatest quantity (not less than 8 cwt.) of good merchantable hops, of the growth of that year, a sample of 1 cwt. to be produced to the Society . . 50 0 0 Nov. 3rd

This encouragement for hops was first published in the year 1765, and it was then notified that it would be continued for five years from 1767; the like premiums will therefore be given for hops produced in the year 1769, 1770, 1771 and 1772.

Hop Poles

To the person possessed of hop yards, who shall plant out with any kind of timber trees any piece of enclosed ground, for the purpose of raising hop poles, no less than a rood being allowed for each acre of hop yard, the sum of £60 will be given in premiums, at the rate of £3 for each rood so planted, no one person being to receive a higher premium than £12   60 o o

1767
April 16th

To be continued for five years from 1767.

No person can be entitled to any premium who shall not give security for preserving his plantation for seven years.

Planting and Cutting Sallows

To the person who shall in the year 1770 cut the greatest quantity of sallows fit for basket-makers use from not less than 1 acre of land to be planted before the 25th March 1767, leaving not less than 2000 standing for hoops, hop poles, and timber   .   . 10 o o

To the person who shall cut the second greatest quantity   .   .   . 6 o o

To the person who shall cut the third greatest quantity   .   .   . 4 o o

To the person who shall cut the greatest quantity of hoops in the year 1772 from those sallows which were left standing after the former cutting, leaving not less than 500 standing on an acre   .   .   .   .   .   . 10 o o

To the person who shall cut the second greatest quantity   .   .   . 6 o o

To the person who shall cut the third greatest quantity   .   .   . 4 o o

To the person who shall in the year 1775 cut the greatest quantity of hop poles or hoops from those sallows left

	£	s.	d.	To be adjudged

after the two former cuttings, leaving
what he shall think proper for timber £10 0 0 To be adjudged April 16th

To the person who shall cut the second greatest quantity . . . 6 0 0

To the person who shall cut the third greatest quantity . . . 4 0 0

No person shall be entitled to any of the aforesaid premiums for sallows who shall not send an account of his plantation to the Society's Assistant Secretary before the first day of April 1767, specifying the land on which, and the county, barony, and parish in which such plantation is made, and the person for whom it is made ; and whoever shall be proprietor of such plantation at the respective times of cutting shall be entitled to be a claimant of the premiums offered, tho' he did not make the plantation himself, but is possessed by descent, purchase, or otherwise : such proprietor shall be entitled to be a claimant of the premiums for the second or third cutting, tho' he shall not have obtained one for the first.

PLANTING WEYMOUTH PINES

To the person who shall plant the greatest number of Weymouth pines (not less than 500) under five years old, between the 1st September 1766 and the 1st April 1767, not nearer to each other than 15 feet, a gold medal ...   ,, 16th

LARIX

To the person who shall plant the greatest number of Larix (not less than 1000) under five years old, between 1st September 1766 and 1st April 1767, not nearer to each other than 15 feet, a gold medal . . . .   ,, 16th

Oaks

£ s. d. To be adjudged

To the person who shall plant between the 1st of October 1766 and the 1st of April 1767 the greatest number of oaks (not less than 1000) under five years old, not nearer to each other than 15 feet, and shall engage to cut them down close to the ground within 12 months after planting, a gold medal . . . . April 16th

Scotch Fir

To the person who shall plant between the 1st of September 1766 and the 1st of April 1767, the greatest number of Scotch firs (not less than 5000) under five years old, and not nearer to each other than 10 feet, in coarse mountain land, a gold medal . ... ,, 23rd

Beech

To the person who shall plant the greatest number of Beech (not less than 2000) under five years old, between the 1st of October 1766 and the 1st of April 1767, not nearer to each other than 15 feet, a gold medal ... ,, 23rd

Sycamore or Ash

To the person who shall plant the greatest number (not less than 5000) of Sycamore, Ash, or Norway Maple, under five years old, between the 1st of October 1766 and the 1st of April 1767, not nearer to each other than 10 feet, and shall engage to cut them down close to the ground within 12 months after planting, a gold medal . ... ,, 23rd

Planting Bog with Sallows

To the person who shall plant the greatest quantity of bog (not less than

five acres) with apple, black timber, or
chesnut sallow sets, not nearer to each
other than 10 inches, a gold medal .

£   s.   d.   To be adjudged

...   April 23rd

All the above plantations must be
well fenced in, and secured from
cattle.

The above premiums for planting,
are offered for each of the provinces
respectively.

NURSERIES

That improvers in all parts of the
kingdom may be the better and more
conveniently supplied with trees, the
Society will pay for every person in
each of the several counties of Ireland
who shall first keep a well enclosed
nursery of forest trees (the trees in
each nursery being of two years growth)
a yearly rent of thirty shillings per acre
for three years, for the ground so
occupied in a Nursery; the whole of
the yearly rent promised for any
Nursery not exceeding £7, 10s. 0d. . 240 0 0

N.B.—Five of the Grand Jury of
the Spring Assizes where this encouragement shall be claimed are to
certify concerning the condition of the
Nursery, and the quantity of ground
occupied therein.

The Society will pay the above rent
on the conditions mentioned, the first
Thursday in every month of May.

DITCHING

For making the greatest number of
perches in ditching (not less than 200
perches) between the 1st day of
October 1766 and the 1st day of
April 1767, six feet wide and five feet
deep perpendicular, to be as narrow as
possible at bottom, and well quicked
with White Thorn or Crab Quicks,

with English Elms planted quickways   £   s.   d.   To be adjudged
on the same bed with the Quicks, or a
little above it, in the face of the ditch,
and distant from each other not more
than two perches, with one or two
forest trees of any kind, except Ash
between the Elms, a gold medal   .   ...   April 9th
　　For the second number of perches,
a silver medal .   .   .   .   „   9th
　　For the third number of perches,
a silver medal .   .   .   .   „   9th
　　To the lessee paying rent, who shall
make the greatest number of perches
in ditching as above, not less than 200   12   0   0   „   9th
　　To the second number, not less than
150   6   0   0   „   9th
　　To the third number, not less than
100   4   0   0   „   9th
　　The above premiums for ditching,
are promised for each of the provinces
respectively.

LIQUORICE

　　For raising in the year 1767 the
greatest quantity (not less than 12
cwt.) of good sound liquorice .   .   12   0   0   Nov. 26th
　　For the next quantity, not less than
8 cwt.   ·   8   0   0   „   26th
　　For the next quantity, not less than
4 cwt.   5   0   0   „   26th
　　This encouragement for liquorice
was first published in the year 1764,
and it was then notified that it would
be given for liquorice raised in 1766,
1767 and 1768.

RAPE SEED

　　For raising and saving in the year
1768 the greatest quantity of Rape
seed, from boggy, rushy, or mountain-
ous ground, not less than 20 acres   1769
being cultivated for this purpose   .   34   2   6   Jan. 19th

For the second quantity, not less than 15 acres . . . . . £ 22 s. 15 d. 0 To be adjudged Jan. 19th

For the third quantity, not less than 10 acres . . . . . . 17 1 3 ,, 19th

An account of the soil and culture to be laid before the Society.

WELD

To the person not already encouraged who shall cultivate and save the greatest quantity of weld or bonymoore, not less than 10 cwt. . . 6 0 0 1767 Jan. 3rd

For the next quantity, not less than 5 cwt. . . . . 4 0 0 ,, 3rd

WOAD

To the person not already encouraged who shall cultivate and prepare for the dyer the greatest quantity of woad, not less than 1 cwt. . . 6 0 0 Dec. 3rd

For the next quantity, not less than 70 lb. weight . . . . . 4 0 0 ,, 3rd

ACORNS

For sowing and well securing in the year 1766, 1767, or 1768 the greatest quantity of land (not less than one acre) with acorns, a gold medal . ... 1769 Jan. 19th

To the person who shall have the greatest number (not less than 160 on every acre) of oaks in a thriving condition on land, for the sowing of which with acorns he has claimed the above premium, and in the 7th year after the premium has been claimed . . 20 0 0

For the next number as above . 15 0 0

For the next number . . . 10 0 0

SAFFRON

For raising and saving in the year 1767 the greatest quantity (not less than 2 lb. weight) of good merchantable saffron . , 12 0 0 1767 Dec. 10th

For the second quantity, not less than 1 lb. weight . . . . £6 0 0 To be adjudged Dec. 10th

HONEY AND WAX

To the person who shall have the greatest quantity of honey and wax, not less than 6 cwt. including the hive and bees . . . . . . 30 0 0 Oct. 15th
For the next quantity, not less than 5 cwt. . . . . . . 25 0 0 ,, 15th
For the next quantity, not less than 4 cwt. . . . . . . 20 0 0 ,, 15th
For the next quantity, not less than 3 cwt. . . . . . . 15 0 0 ,, 15th
For the next quantity, not less than 2 cwt. . . . . . . 10 0 0 ,, 15th

The hives are to be weighed in the gross, the bees being alive, (which is known by experience not in the least to prejudice them) in the presence of the minister or curate of the parish, or any Justice of Peace in the neighbourhood, or any other person of a reputable character, known to a member of the Society, and by a person appointed by the proprietor of the bees.

A certificate of such weight, and the number of hives, must be signed by such minister or curate or Justice of Peace, or reputable person.

The person weighing the hives is to make an affidavit of their number and gross weight, that they are of the usual size and thickness, and that to the best of his knowledge no fraud has been practised to increase their weight.

The proprietor of the bees is also to make an affidavit that the number of old hives so weighed, attested, and certified, have been all his property for six months before, that all the new hives so weighed, attested, and certified, are swarms from the old hives, and that to the best of his knowledge, none of those hives were above six Irish miles from his dwelling house when weighed and certified, or for six months before.

These certificates and affidavits are to be produced by the claimants of the premiums, as the condition upon which alone they can receive them.

Whereas the usual method of obtaining the honey from stocks of bees is by destroying the bees; and whereas it is found by experience that the honey may be obtained and the bees preserved at the same time, by which larger quantities of both honey and wax are collected: The Society will therefore give

To the person who shall collect the greatest quantity of honey and wax from stocks of bees of his own property, within the year 1767, without destroying the bees, and shall leave a sufficient quantity of honey for their winter sustenance

	£	s.	d.	To be adjudged
sustenance	10	0	0	Oct. 15th
For the next quantity . . .	7	0	0	,, 15th

BEE HIVES

To the person who shall make the best and greatest number of bee hives, not less than 80

not less than 80	3	0	0	,, 15th
For the second number, not less than 40	2	0	0	,, 15th

The premiums for bee hives are promised for each of the provinces respectively.

DISCHARGED SOLDIERS

The sum of £200 will be given in premiums of £5 to every discharged soldier or sailor not already encouraged, who hath served His Majesty

out of Great Britain or Ireland, and £ *s.* *d.* To be adjudged
who between the 1st of November
1766, and the 1st of November 1767,
shall take a lease of lives, of not less
than five, or more than twenty acres,
in the province of Leinster, Munster,
or Connaught, producing his discharge,
together with a certificate of his parish
minister, or two neighbouring Justices
of the Peace, of his having been in
possession of his said farm one year,
and also of his industry and the prob-
ability of his continuing on his said
farm; provided the number of such
soldiers or sailors shall not exceed
forty, and if it should, then the sum
of £200 shall be divided according
to the number of such soldiers or
sailors   .   .   .   .   .   . 200 0 0   Nov. 19th

BREEDING MARES
    To the person or persons who shall
first import into this kingdom, before
the 1st day of February 1767, strong
able mares, from 4 to 6 years old, and
from 14½ to 15 hands high, fit for the
plough and other country work, and
in foal, a premium of five pounds will
be given for every such mare, the
number not exceeding twenty   .   . 100 0 0   Feb. 12th

MANUFACTURES

IRON MADE WITH COAK
    For making the greatest quantity
(not less than two tons) of tough bar
iron, with coak only or Irish coal
charred, the iron being equal in good-   1767
ness to that made with wood charcoal 50 0 0 Oct. 22nd
    A sample of at least 1 cwt. must be
produced to the Society, and satisfactory proof will be required of the
quantity manufactured.

STEEL REEDS

In making silk weavers' steel reeds, as good and perfectly made as any imported, a premium of twenty shillings will be given for every such reed, provided the number shall not exceed 60, and if it should, then the sum of £60 will be divided proportionably to the number of reeds made by each claimant 60   0   0   Oct. 8th

The sum of £40 will be given in like manner for silk weavers' steel reeds which shall be made as above, between the 1st of October 1767, and the 1st of October 1768 .   .   . 40   0   0   ,,   6th

No person shall be entitled to any premium for making steel reeds, who shall not engage to the Society to take an apprentice, and also that he will continue to carry on in this kingdom the making of steel reeds for silk weavers for seven years.

And for ascertaining the number and goodness of steel reeds, for which the above premiums will be given, the Corporation of Weavers of the city of Dublin, or such committee as they shall appoint, shall examine the same, and certify to the Society the number of them, and that they are of equal goodness with those imported.

STEEL WOOL COMBS

For making three pitched steel wool-combs of equal goodness with those imported, a premium of twenty shillings will be given for each pair, provided the number of pairs shall not exceed 30, and if it should, then the sum of £30 will be divided in proportion to the number of pairs made by each claimant 30   0   0   ,,   8th

STOCKINGS $£$ $s.$ $d.$ To be adjudged

For manufacturing knitted ribbed stockings, such as are now imported, and sold from 4s. 6d. to 6s. per pair, to weigh 5 lbs. per dozen, to measure 24 inches from the heel to the top of the leg, and 10 inches from the toe to the heel, and to be made of soft worsted of 3 threads, spun on the small wheel, one shilling will be given as a premium for every pair of such stockings, provided the number of pairs shall not exceed 300, and if it should, then the sum of $£15$ will be divided proportionably to the number of pairs so manufactured by each claimant . . . . . . 15 0 0 March 19

SILKEN GLOVES

For manufacturing the greatest number of pairs (not less than 100 pairs) of silken gloves or mitts . . 10 0 0 ,, 26
For the next number of pairs, not less than 50 . . . . . 5 0 0 ,, 26

BONE LACE

For the encouragement of the manufacture of bone lace by children in the work-house of the city of Dublin, 30 guineas will be given to the most deserving, in such proportions and in such manner as the Rt. Honble Lady Arabella Denny shall judge will most conduce to the improvement of that manufacture in the said work-house . 34 2 6 April 30
To any manufacturers of bone lace, except of the city work-house, a sum not exceeding 30 guineas will be given, as the Society shall judge the claimant's merit, and in proportion to the value of bone lace which each shall have manufactured . . . . 34 2 6 ,, 30

THREAD LACE KNIT WITH NEEDLES   £   s.   d. To be adjudged

For manufacturing thread lace, to
be knit with needles, the sum of 15
guineas will be given in proportion to
the respective merit of the claimants,
no less than 4 yards of such lace in
length, and 2½ inches in breadth, shall
entitle any person to a premium : regard will be had to the fineness and
clearness of the work, and the beauty
of the pattern 17   1   3   April 30

FELT HATS

For manufacturing the best Felt
hats of lambs' wool only, new claim-   1768
ants to produce at least 200, and old
claimants to produce 400 .   .   . 15   0   0   Jan. 21

PEARL BARLEY

To the person not already encouraged, who shall make the greatest
quantity (not less than 5 cwt.) of   1767
French or Pearl barley   .   .   . 10   0   0   Feb. 19

EMPLOYING CHILDREN

To the person not already encouraged by this or any other Society,
who from the 1st day of December
1766 to the 1st day of December 1767,
shall employ in any manufacture, the
greatest number of children, (not less
than 40, and not exceeding the age of
13 years) upon the affidavit of the
person employing them, setting forth
their number and the work they shall
have done, together with a certificate
to the same purpose, of two neighbouring Justices of the Peace, and the
minister or curate of the parish, if in
the country ; and in towns, of the
clergyman   and   principal   residing
magistrate   12   0   0   Dec. 10

For employing the next greatest number, not less than 30 . . . £ 8 s. 0 d. 0 To be adjudged Dec. 10

SMALT

To the person who shall produce the greatest quantity (not less than 1 cwt.) of Smalt, made in Ireland, and of Irish materials, equal in goodness to any imported, and giving security to continue the work . . . . 50 0 0 ,, 17

SALT PETRE

To the person who shall produce the greatest quantity (not less than 10 lbs.) of salt petre, made and prepared in this kingdom . . . 10 0 0 ,, 17
For the second quantity, not less than 5 lbs. . . . . . 5 0 0 ,, 17

FINE ARTS AND MECHANICS

PAINTING

For the best original landscape painted in oil colours, on a canvas of 4 feet 2 inches in length, by 3 feet 4 inches in height . . . . 11 7 6 1767 May 7
For the best original full length portrait painted as large as the life . 11 7 6 ,, 7

PATTERN DRAWING

For the best invention in pattern drawing, either in foliage or flowers, by boys or girls under the age of 18 years, each claimant to produce six full patterns proper for paper hangings, carpets, damasks, or some other article in one of the several manufactures . . . . . . 4 0 0 ,, 14
For the next best . . . . 3 0 0 ,, 14
For the next best . . . . 2 0 0 ,, 14
For the next best . . . . 1 0 0 ,, 14

		£	s.	d.	To be adjudged

FIGURE DRAWING

For the best drawings of human
figures and heads by boys under the
age of 18 years, each claimant to pro-
duce 2 full figures and 2 heads .   .   6   0   0   May 21
For the next best   4   0   0   ,,   21
For the next best   3   0   0   ,,   21
For the next best   2   0   0   ,,   21
For the best drawings of human
figures or heads by girls under the age
of 18 years, each claimant to produce
two full figures and two heads .   .   4   0   0   ,,   21
For the next best   3   0   0   ,,   21
For the next best   2   0   0   ,,   21
For the next best   1   0   0   ,,   21
All boys or girls who have received
the first premium for drawing are ex-
cluded from any for the future

ARCHITECT DRAWING

For the best drawing of the plans,
elevations and section of an house in
the Corinthian Order, and not less
than 120 feet in front, by boys under
the age of 18 years   6   16   6   ,,   28
For the next best   4   11   0   ,,   28
For the next best   3   8   3   ,,   28
For the best drawing of an arched
door in the Doric Order, and also of
a window in the Corinthian Order,
with whole and half pilasters fluted .   2   5   6   ,,   28
For the next best   1   14 $1\frac{1}{2}$,,   28
For the next best   1   2   9   ,,   28

MODELS

For the best model in wood of an
house of no less than 50 feet in front
with first and second stories, to be
made by a scale of not more than
five-eights of an inch to a foot .   .   11   7   6   ,,   28
For the second best   .   .   .   5   13   9   ,,   28

MEDAL   £   s.   d. To be adjudged

For a Copper Medal of the size of
an English Crown piece, which shall
be best executed in point of workman-
ship and boldness of relief, the subject
to be King William passing the Boyne ;
the medal and dye to become the pro-
perty of the Society .   .   .   .   22 15   0   May 21

PRINT

For the best engraved print or
Metzontinto from an original design .   5 13   9   „   21

MACHINE FOR DRAINING LAND

For a plough or machine of the
simplest construction, which shall with
the least force, cut a new drain of at
least one foot in depth perpendicular,
one foot eight inches wide at the top,
and ten inches wide at the bottom,
both sides of the drain to be equally
sloping, and the earth to be equally
thrown out on both sides .   .   .   28   8   9   Oct. 22

Certificates of the machine having
performed the work in the manner
aforesaid, must be delivered in, together with a model of the machine,
which model is to become the property
of the Society.

WHEEL CARRIAGE

For the best wheel carriage, for the
use of the farmer or manufacturer,
which shall be adjudged by a committee to be appointed by the Society,
as most effectually constructed, and
on the simplest principles, for removing
the greatest weight with the smallest
power and in the shortest time, from
any one given point to another on a
hilly road   11   7   6   Feb. 26

A model to be produced and to be-

2 D

come the property of the Society, if   £   *s.*   *d.* To be adjudged
the contrivance shall have sufficient
merit to obtain the premium.

FISHERIES

TURBOT

For curing Turbots on any of the
coasts of this kingdom, so as there
shall be sold in the year 1767, 2000
at the least of well-cured merchantable
Turbot 50   0   0   Mar. 10

		£	s.	d.	
at the least of well-cured merchantable Turbot	1768	50	0	0	Mar. 10
For the next quantity, not less than 1000		30	0	0	,, 10

WHITEINGS

For curing Whiteings on any of the
coasts of this kingdom, after the manner practised at Tinmouth in Devonshire, £20 per cent. will be given on
the value of Whiteings so cured and
sold, provided the same shall not exceed £500, and if it should, then the
sum of £100 will be divided in proportion to the value of Whiteings so
cured and sold by each claimant . 100   0   0   ,, 10

The method of curing Whiteings at
Tinmouth is by slitting open and
washing them with sea water, then
drying them in the sun, and now and
then sprinkling them with sea water
whilst they are drying.

HERRING FISHERY

To the owner of any Fishing Boat or
Wherry, not less than 26 feet in the keel,
who shall in the year 1767, between
the 1st day of May and the 1st day of
August, on the east coast of this kingdom, between the Lough of Carlingford and the Hill of Howth, with such
boat in any one night, first take any

quantity of herrings, not less than three mease, which shall be sold fresh and sound in Dublin market . . . £ s. d. 11 7 6 To be adjudged 1767 Oct. 29th

To the owner of any Fishing Boat or Wherry, not less than 26 feet in the keel, who shall in the year 1767, between the 1st day of May and the 1st day of August, on the east coast of this kingdom, between the Hill of Howth and the Head of Wicklow, with such boat in any one night, first take any quantity of herrings, not less than 3 mease, which shall be sold fresh and sound in Dublin market . . 11 7 6 ,, 29th

To the owner of any Fishing Boat or Wherry to be built hereafter, not less than 26 feet in the keel, who shall in the year 1767, between the 1st day of May and the 1st day of August, on the east coast of this kingdom, between the Lough of Carlingford and the Hill of Howth, with such boat in any one night, first take any quantity of herrings, not less than three mease, which shall be sold fresh and sound in Dublin market . . . . 11 7 6 ,, 29th

To the owner of any Fishing Boat or Wherry to be built hereafter, not less than 26 feet in the keel, who shall in the year 1767, between the 1st day of May and the 1st day of August, on the east coast of this kingdom, between the Hill of Howth and the Head of Wicklow, with such boat, in any one night, first take any quantity of herrings, not less than three mease to be sold fresh and sound in Dublin market . . . . . . 11 7 6 ,, 29th

DISCOVERIES

BLACK LEAD

To the person who shall discover a

	£	s.	d.	To be adjudged 1766
mine of blacklead, and produce a sample of at least 10 lbs. . . .	40	0	0	Dec. 4th

FIRE CLAY

To the person who shall discover within 20 miles of a seaport or navigable river, a fire clay such as the Stourbridge clay, and fit for the use of glass houses, producing a sample of a ton weight, and giving security to supply glass houses and all other works with a sufficient quantity . . 50 0 0 ,, 11th

FULLER'S EARTH

To the person who shall produce the best Fuller's earth (not less than 5 cwt.) discovered in this kingdom . 10 0 0 ,, 18th

All matters for which the Society offer premiums must be begun after the publication of such premiums, unless there be a particular exception in the publication.

The Society reserve to themselves a power of giving in all cases such part only of any premium as the performmance shall be adjudged to deserve, or in case of want of merit, no part.

A candidate for a premium or a person applying for a bounty, being detected in any disingenuous methods to impose upon the Society, shall forfeit all such premium or bounty, and be incapable of obtaining any for the future.

The Society being desirous of avoiding as much as possible the multiplication of oaths in the disposal of their premiums, request that the nobility, magistrates, gentry and clergy in their several districts will give their attention, when applied to for certificates of the merit of any candidate for a premium, to examine the pretensions of such person, that the Society may not be under the necessity of tendering an affidavit to him, which they apprehend has sometimes occasioned the misapplication of their fund, and the guilt of perjury.

All claimants of premiums are requested to send in their claims at latest on the day before such premiums are to be adjudged, directed to the Rev. Mr. Peter Chaigneau, at the Society's House, in Shaw's Court, Dame Street.

By order of the Society.

APPENDIX III

LIST OF WORKS OF ART IN LEINSTER HOUSE

PORTRAITS IN OILS

Thomas Braughall . . .	*John Comerford.*
Right Hon. John Foster (Lord Oriel), last Speaker of the Irish House of Commons . . .	*Sir William Beechey.*
Richard Kirwan, F.R.S. . .	*Hugh D. Hamilton.*
Sir Charles Giesecke . . .	*Sir Henry Raeburn.*
General Vallancey . . .	*Solomon Williams.*
Thomas Pleasants . . .	*Solomon Williams.*
Isaac Weld	*Martin Cregan, P.R.H.A.*
Jasper R. Joly, LL.D. . . .	*S. Catterson Smith, R.H.A.*
Mervyn, Viscount Powerscourt .	*Sarah Purser.*
George Johnstone Stoney, F.R.S. .	*Sir T. A. Jones, P.R.H.A.*
Charles Uniacke Townshend .	*William Orpen, R.H.A.*

John, Lord Bowes, lord chancellor (*coloured crayons*) . . .	*Alexander Pope.*
George Daunt, surgeon (*coloured crayons*)	*Alexander Pope.*

Beggar Woman and Child . .	*George Gratton.*
Two Landscapes	*William Ashford, P.R.H.A.*
A Seaport	*Van Bredall.*
Two Landscapes	*George Barret, R.A.*
Two Landscapes	*Unknown.*
Fruit Piece	{ *Michelangelo Pace* (called *Di Campid glio*).

Wolf caught in a Trap . . .	*M. F. Quadal.*
Landscape	{ *Jan Frans Van Bloemen* (called *Orizonte*).
Cymbeline	*James Barry*, R.A.
Lady Lyster	*James Northcote*, R.A.
St. Paul Preaching . . .	*Nicholas Poussin.*
St. Paul released from Prison .	*J. G. Cuyp.*
Departure of King George IV from Kingstown	*T. C. Thompson*, R.H.A.
Polyphemus	*Poussin.*
Narcissus	*François Boucher.*
Two Battle Scenes . .	{ *Jacques Courtois* (*le Bourguinon*).
Dead Game	*William Gow Ferguson.*
Dead Game (*three pictures*) .	*Unknown.*
Boors (*two pictures*) . . .	*Egbert Van Heemskerk.*
Magdalene in the Wilderness .	*P. Francesco Mola.*
Holy Family	*Hendrik Van Balen.*
Holy Family	*Unknown.*
Peg Woffington (*unsigned*) . .	*John Lewis.*

(Copy or replica of a portrait of 1753, now in England. It differs from the original in colour of hat and mantle This portrait has been ascribed to Reynolds and Latham. See Strickland's *Dictionary of Irish Artists.*)

Miss O'Brien	*Unknown.*
Portrait of a Lady, time of James I	*Unknown.*
Portrait of a Gentleman, time of James I (*two pictures*) . .	*Unknown.*
Portrait of a Lady . . .	*Sir Peter Lely.*
Portrait of Mr. Bowdon . .	*William Cuming*, R.H.A.
A Lady reading (*portrait of Miss Vigne, the artist's sister-in-law*) .	*George Chinnery.*
St. Mark	*Salomon Koninck.*
Jacob's Dream	*Jakob Jordaens.*
Two Battle Pieces . . .	*Jan Van Hughtenburgh.*
Adoration of the Shepherds . .	{ *Erasmus Quellin* or *Quellinus.*
Science and Agriculture (Ceres and Triptolemus) *monochrome* (see p. 92)	*Peter de Gree.*
A painted table top (*design for ceiling of St. Patrick's Hall, Dublin Castle.*)	*Vincent Waldré.*

Two engravings (by *Vivares*) of the Giant's Causeway from drawings by Susanna Drury, for which she was awarded £25 prize in 1740 (see p. 57).

Twelve Engravings of Irish scenery (six of Killarney and six of Carlingford Lough) . . . } *Jonathan Fisher*, 1772.

(see p. 57)

King George the Fourth (marble statue). . . . . } *William Behnes* (completed by *C. Panormo*).

King George the Fourth (marble statue) . . . . . } *Thomas Kirk*.

Erected by the Linen Merchants of Ireland to commemorate His Majesty's visit to the Linen Hall, Dublin, 23 August, 1821. Afterwards presented to the Society.

BUSTS IN MARBLE

Thomas Prior	*John Van Nost.*
Samuel Madden, D.D. . .	*John Van Nost.*
William Maple . .	*Patrick Cunningham.*
Philip, Earl of Chesterfield .	*John Van Nost.*
Professor Gregory Von Feinagle .	*Thomas Kirk.*
Henry, Marquis of Anglesey, lord lieutenant . . . . }	*R. W. Sievier.*
Thomas Philip, Earl de Grey, lord lieutenant . . . . }	*Terence Farrell*, R.H.A.
Alexander Nimmo, C.E. . .	*John Ed. Jones.*
Sir Richard Griffith, Bart. . .	*Sir Thomas Farrell*, P.R.H.A.
Sir F. Leopold McClintock, admiral	*Joseph R. Kirk*, R.H.A.
Right Hon. Francis Blackburne, lord chancellor . . . }	*Shakspere Wood.*

Discobolus (marble) . . . *M. Kessels* (Rome, 1820).

(Bequeathed by Mrs. Anne Putland, 1856)

Bust—Flora (marble) . . . Attributed to *J. Gallagher.*

Bust—Mercury (marble) . .

Cave Scene. Drunken Banditti, ⎱ *Thomas Kirk.*
(bas relief in marble). . .⎰

Venus and Cupid (bas relief in ⎱ *Thomas Kirk.*
marble) . . . . .⎰

Amazon (bronze) . . . . After *Kiss.*

Girl playing at Tali (bronze after the antique at Berlin).

Figure of Hibernia . . . *Edward Smyth.*

BUSTS IN PLASTER

Daniel O'Connell
William, Duke of Cumberland
Frederick, Duke of York
Edmund Burke
Henry Grattan
Dean Swift (two busts)
Lord Byron (two busts)
Sir Walter Scott
Humphrey Lloyd, D.D.
Arch. Hamilton Rowan . . *C. Panormo.*
Cardinal Manning . . . *M'Donald.*
John Hanning Speke
Earl of Clarendon, lord lieutenant
George Tierney . . . . *William Behnes.*
Oliver Goldsmith
Lord Plunket, lord chancellor . *Chr. Moore.*
George Canning
Hon. Robert Boyle
Archbishop Ussher
Earl of Eglinton, lord lieutenant
John Philpot Curran
George, Prince of Wales
Duke of Wellington
Sir Edward Stanley . . . *C. Panormo.*
Bust (*unknown*) . . . .
Edmund Burke (statuette) . . *John H. Foley.*
Oliver Goldsmith (statuette) . *John H. Foley.*
Two Statuettes (*unknown*) . . .

CORRIGENDA

Page 245, line 9, *for* 'Le Touche' *read* 'La Touche.'

,,   248, line 10, and page 344, line 5 from end, *for* '1830' *read* '1831.'

,,   363, line 1, *for* 'M. H. Harvey' *read* 'W. H. Harvey.'

INDEX

Brereton, Wm., brewer, premium for using Irish hops, 61

Brett, Richard, 202

Brewery, in Ulster, premium awarded for a, 72

Brewing, articles on, 37; premiums for, 61, 62, 64

Bride, Patrick, 187

Brien, John, collector, &c., 93

Brinkley, Bishop, statue of, 128

Brinkley, Dr., 221

Brisbane, Sir Thomas, 254

British Association, meetings in Dublin, 254, 286

British Dairy Farmers' Association, 331

British Museum Library, 181

Broad cloth, premiums for, 63-4

Brocas, Henry, Master of the Ornament School, 118, 132

Brocas, Theophilus, Dean of Killala, 199 *and n.*, 381

Brooke, Henry, 28; the *Interest of Ireland* by, 84

Brooke, Robert, premiums for cotton, velvets, &c., 72, 153

Brophy, Peter, 229

Browne, William, 126. *See* Mossop

Browne, William, premium for cottons, &c., 72

Bryan, Robert B., Hon. Sec., 177, 272, 383

Buchan, Patrick, paper on the iron ores of the Connaught coalfield, 365

Buckingham, Marquis of, 154, 379

Buckles, premiums for, 57

Building. *See* Gaol, Houses

Bulbous roots: on the growth of, in Ireland, 363; comparative value of large and small roots, 363

Bulls, &c., premiums for, 63

Burgh, Captain Thomas, Hon. Sec. and Vice-President, 115, 219, 381, 383

Burgh (or Bourgh), Thomas, 25, 28

Burke, Edmund, 121

Burke, Joseph, bequest to the Society, 290

Burlington and Cork, Lord, 27

Burnet, premiums for cultivation of, 388, 401

Burton, Sir Frederick, 279

Burton, Samuel, 122

Burton, Colonel William (afterwards the Right Hon. Wm. Conyngham), 115, 146, 221-2

Burton, Right Hon. Francis, 221

Busts in marble and plaster, in Leinster House, 424, 425

Busts, purchase of, by the Society, 42

Butler, John, 288

Butler, John Thomas, discovers *lapis calaminaris* in Sligo, 84

Butler, W. D., premium for plans, 254

Butt, Isaac, 270

Butter-making, 331; serious consequences of foreign rivalry, 331; cooperation in, 332

Buttons: premiums for, 57

By-laws of the Society, 1766 . . . 140-1, 285, 310; 1837 . . . 267; as to subscriptions and arrears, 146, 152, 214; as to committees, 215, 216; to enable persons to join a section of the Society, 276, 361. *See also* Fellows

Byrne, Thomas, premium for ale, 62

Byron, *English Bards and Scotch Reviewers*, quoted, 116

CABBAGE as food for the horse, 362

Cake-basket in silver, presented for reclaiming bog, 145-6

Calamine stone, an award for producing, 84 *and n.*1

Caldbeck, Mr., 150

Calderwood, Mr., 370

Calderwood, Robert, gold thread manufacturer, 69

Caldwell, Andrew, 115, 187

Callage, Rev. Andrew, 221

Callan, Professor, 269

Calves, on a method of feeding, 51

Cam, John, engaged as itinerant adviser in husbandry, 50

Campbell, Rev. Mr., awarded a silver medal for an *Essay on Perfecting the Fine Arts*, &c., 114

Canning, Rt. Hon. George: honorary member, 230

Carbampton, Lord. *See* Luttrell, Simon

Carlisle, George W. F., Earl of, 286, 380

Carpet: premium awarded for a, 59

Carrots: cultivation of, premium offered for, 401

Carson, Rev. Joseph, 287

Carte, Dr. William: papers contributed to the *Journal* by, 365, 367, 368

Carteret, Lord, 188

Carve, Thomas, his scarce works (*cir.* 1640-6) in the Joly collection, 179

Carver, Mr., (artist), 113

Casey, Anne, premium for lace, 61

Casey, Laurence, premium for ale, 62

Casey, Mary, premium for edging, 62

Cash, John C. (a former pupil), and his plans of public buildings in Dublin, 152

2 E

Von Feinagle, Professor Gregor, lectures on Mnemonics, &c., 229

Von Haller, Albrecht, x; *Bibliotheca Botanica* of, 173

Von Rumford. *See* Rumford

WADE, John (chemist), 144

Wade, R. C., 290, 350

Wade, Dr. Walter, professor and lecturer in botany, 160, 187, 194, 355; lectures in rural economy by, 339; the *Flora Dublinensis* of, 189; papers by, in the Society's *Transactions*, 359; mentioned, 187, 224, 228, 245, 357

Waldron, William, 118

Walker, Alderman, 60

Walker, Dr. David, notes on the zoology of McClintock's Expedition, 366

Walker, Thomas, 245

Wallace, Thomas, 177

" Wallace," a lion in a Dublin menagerie, model for pupils of drawing school, 129

Waller, John Francis, Hon. Sec. and V.-P., 285, 292, 382, 384

Wallis, John, Vice-President, 115, 219, 381

Walsh, Andrew, premium for planting old Danish forts, 74

Walsh, Edward, premium for velvet and silk, 68

Wand of the hall porter, the, 224

Warburton, Richard, premium for planting old Danish forts, 74

Warburton, cited, 142

Ward, Michael, 6, 7

Ward, Philip, 24

Ware, [Harris'], cited, 20

Ware, James, 46

Waring, Henry, premium for osiers and willows, 68

Waring, Major, 115, 383

Warner, Rev. Ferdinando, his works, &c., 172 *and n.*

Watchplates, premium for, 65

Waterford, glass manufacture in, 74

Waterford county, mineralogical survey in, 154

Watkins, Bartholomew, premium for landscapes, 126 *and n.*

Watkins, B. Colles, artist, 126 *n.*

Watson, William, presents to the Society King's Warrant for the charter, 76 *n.*

Watson's Almanac, 1741-2 . . . 58

Watts, Mr., assistant professor in the veterinary establishment, 160, 338

Weaver, Thomas, mineralogist, 157, 163

Weavers, corporation of, petition to Parliament, 198

Weavers, silk, 198, 202; petition the Society for aid against unemployment, 199

Webster, Joseph, 202

Weekly Observations, Dublin Society's, 34 *et seq. ;* 37 *and n.*

Weld, Rev. Dr. Isaac [son], 44–5, 246

Weld, Isaac [great grandson], Hon. Sec., appreciation of, 246; survey of county of *Roscommon* by, 183, 184; mission to the Treasury, 249; evidence before House of Commons Select Committee, 259, 325. *Observations on the Royal Dublin Society, and its existing Institutions* (1831), by, 249; otherwise mentioned, 132, 149, 165, 176, 177, 258, 280, 285, 363, 382, 383; memoir of, contributed to the *Journal,* 365

Weld, Rev. Nathaniel [father], 46, 246

Weld, Dr. Richard, 85

Weld cultivation, premiums for, 390,408

Wellington trophy, 97 *and n.*[2]

Werner, [A. J.], cited, 156, 163

West, Francis R. [son], 120 *n.*[2]

West, Robert [father], (master of figure drawing), 109; drawing academy of, in George's Lane, taken over by the Dublin Society, 109; mentioned, 110, 111, 116, 117, 118, 120 *n.*[2], 131, 132

West, Robert L. [grandson], 120 *and n.*[2], 122, 130

West, Mr. (of Clontarf), 163

Westropp, Dudley, cited, 146

Wexford county, mineralogical survey, 154

Wheat, special competitions for, 58; premiums for, 59, 60, *and n.,* 387, 399

White, Annie C., Taylor prize, 135

White, Henry Conner, Registrar of the Society, 283, 384

White House, Washington, stated to have been modelled on Leinster House, 103

White, John, Glasnevin, 191

White, Luke, 229

White, Major-General Sir Henry, bequest, 128 *and n.*

Whitecombe-Whetcombe, Rev. Dr. John, 6, 8, 21, 383

Whitefoord, Caleb, 120

Whiteings, premiums offered for curing, 418

Whitelaw and Walsh, *History of Dublin* cited, 96, 194

Whitton, Benj., premium for scythes, &c., 57

Wicklow, county, gold mines, 359

Printed by BALLANTYNE, HANSON & CO.
at Paul's Work, Edinburgh

ImTheStory.com

Personalized Classic Books in many genre's

Unique gift for kids, partners, friends, colleagues

Customize:

- Character Names
- Upload your own front/back cover images (optional)
- Inscribe a personal message/dedication on the
  inside page (optional)

Customize many titles Including
- Alice in Wonderland
- Romeo and Juliet
- The Wizard of Oz
- A Christmas Carol
- Dracula
- Dr. Jekyll & Mr. Hyde
- And more...

CPSIA information can be obtained at www.ICGtesting.com
Printed in the USA
BVOW03s0835021213

337891BV00019B/863/P